L. A. LORE

Stephen Brook is the author of numerous travel books, including *New York Days, New York Nights, Honkytonk Gelato, The Double Eagle, Winner Takes All,* and *Claws of the Crab: Georgia and Armenia in Crisis.* He also wrote the bestselling *The Club: The Jews of Modern Britain.* In addition he writes regularly about wine for *Vogue* and other publications.

Other books by Stephen Brook

New York Days, New York Nights
Honkytonk Gelato
The Double Eagle
Winner Takes All
Claws of the Crab: Georgia and Armenia in Crisis

L.A. LORE

STEPHEN BROOK

PICADOR

First published in Great Britain 1992 by Sinclair-Stevenson Limited

This Picador edition published with a new Afterword 1993
by Pan Books Limited
a division of Pan Macmillan Publishers Limited
Cavaye Place London SW10 9PG
and Basingstoke

Associated companies throughout the world

ISBN 0 330 33159 0

: 3 5 7 9 8 6 4 2

A CIP catalogue record for this book is available from
the British Library

Typeset by Cambridge Composing (UK) Limited, Cambridge
Printed by Cox & Wyman Ltd, Reading, Berkshire

FOR
ZACH AND ALICE

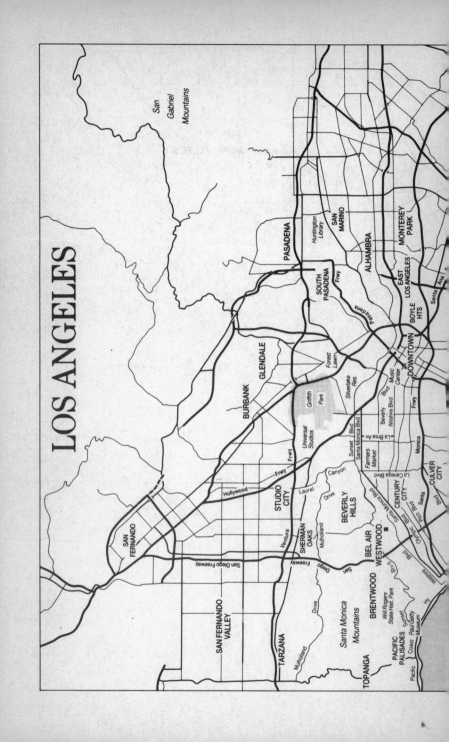

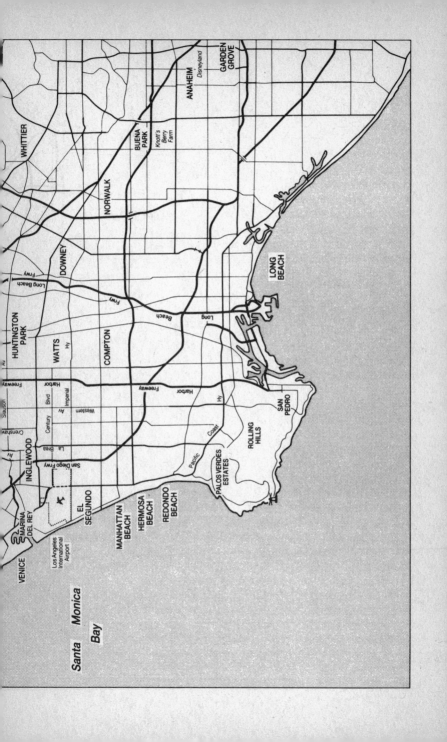

CONTENTS

Acknowledgments   xi

1   Sunset On-Ramp   1
2   No Furs in Rustic Canyon   10
3   Migrants Old and Young   20
4   Suffer the Little Gerbils   34
5   Trashitecture   44
6   Pigs with Wigs   56
7   Rodney King Drives Too Fast   66
8   Hammer Horror   74
9   Armed Guards Are Watching Our Plants   86
10 Old Rope   101
11 Tawnya's Helping Hand   111
12 The Sony Side of the Street   124
13 Indian Cucina   134
14 No Hablo Inglés   144
15 The Karen Salkin Story   156
16 Skip Eats an Olive   168
17 Development Sluts   179
18 Hubba Hubba   192
19 Lives of Leisure   202
20 An Encyclopedia of Life   213
21 Chapter with Orange Slice   224
22 Termites in the Valley   234
23 Dead Fish Pluckers Wanted   243
24 In the Hood   255
25 Hour of Power   265

26	Watts Happening	273
27	Eternal Life in One Convenient Package	283
28	Whiplash and Ding Dong	295
29	Tofu in Topanga	309
30	Slaughtergate	322
31	Nip and Tuck	333
32	Mellow and Out	343
	Afterword	357
	Index	364

ACKNOWLEDGMENTS

I was fortunate enough to enjoy the help, cooperation and generosity of countless Angelenos, and particularly wish to thank the following: Skip Arnold, Severin Ashkenazy, Robert del Bartelo of the Beverly Hills Gun Club, the Bel Air Hotel, Al Braunmuller, Michelle Bolton, Terrill Burnett and Jason Wallace, Jane Dietrich, Richard Dimitri and Rosanna Noriega, Shel Erlich, Howard Fox, Dan Freund, Rick Galin, Michael B. Gonzalez of Beverly Hot Springs, Ralph Grierson, Professor David Hayes-Bautista, Professor Leroy Hood, Scott and Fredda Johnson, Hal Kimbell, Korean Federation of Los Angeles, Matt Kramer, Roz Leader, Zoe Leader and Jay Heit, Professor Carver Mead, Mickey McKee, Dr Timothy A. Miller, Jack Moscowitz, Louise Nicholson, Mike Nolan, Ronan O'Casey and Carol Tavris, Pat Polinger, Toribio Prado, Janna Roth of the LA Convention and Visitors Bureau, Judy Rothman, Karen Salkin, Stephen Silverman, Patrick Stansfield, Leonard Stein and Heidi Lesemann of the Arnold Schoenberg Institute, Dr Edward Stone, Erik Tarloff, Frank and Lee Tarloff, Ella Taylor, Juliette Thompson, Ed Turley, Monica and William Webb, and the Santa Monica Convention & Visitors Bureau.

Really sincere winsome Hollywood-style acknowledgments now follow:

For those who helped me struggle towards the completion of a remarkable book, some thanks:

To Maria, my wife, for walking through the valleys and the mountains with me.

To Nina, princess of rap.

To my cat Phylloxera, and the ghost of my previous cat Lola, for showing respect.

To Fifi LaVerne, my friend, my assistant, you poor fuck . . .

To Woody Schwarz, my psychiatric nurse, who kept my nails clean.

To Klyt Ward, friend, grammarian, nobody better than whom to split an infinitive with.

To Tweety, Milk, Bobo, and Marty, role models.

To Lu and Lou, both of whom kept saying, you can do it, don't give up now.

To Anand, for the mantra.

To Dannii, Lorayne, SherLee, Wong Foo, Mimi, Roxann, Amber, and all the other cheerleaders too numerous to mention. I love what you do to me.

To Robert, for fiddling the books and keeping the tax man off my ass.

To the Randolph Clinic, for the pills, the jabs, the tabs.

To Philip, for the haircuts, and to Mel the Snip, for the other haircuts.

To Viv, who closed the deal, and to Penny, who wrote the cheque.

To Saul Bellow, for sharing his gift with me.

To all the guys at Burger King, Moti Mahal, and Le Gavroche, who kept the dishes coming and never called the cops.

To Toshiba, for persuading me to get rid of the pen, the ink, the mind.

To God, for making me such an incredible person.

To Julia Phillips, who inspired me to write the above.

Love ya.

1

SUNSET ON-RAMP

The door was flung open. There was an eruption of swirl and billow as the hot steam was invaded by the cool of the evening air and by the striding form of an intent woman. What I took for maracas turned out to be a bottle she was shaking over the stove. Retreating, she insisted that we would enjoy ourselves all the more when half asphyxiated by the potent fumes of brandy. Heady volatile aromas sprang up from the stove and infused the steam. We breathed deep.

Minutes later Francesca rose from the wooden bench, flicked open the door. Gently giddy from the heat and the fumes, we followed her as she ran towards the pool and dived in.

The shock of the water cleared my head. Hauling myself out of the pool, I strode to the edge of the garden. Spread before me like a galaxy suddenly transposed from the heavens to the earth were the lights of the city, distant, glittering, busy, subservient.

I was eighteen, the censer with the cognac was named Zsa Zsa Gabor, the house was her mansion in Bel Air, and the city was Los Angeles.

A series of chance encounters was giving me and a handful of other English students access to mansions where the garages alone outnumbered the bedrooms in my own home. Knowing it couldn't last, I revelled in the explosion of unforeseen luxury. Zsa Zsa chauffered us in her Rolls-Royce, her Filipino houseboy brought us trays of food, and she called me 'dullink', just as she was supposed to. Francesca, her daughter, ferried us back and forth from Bel Air to Malibu in her red Pontiac convertible, Bob

Dylan's 'Like a Rolling Stone' blaring from the radio. Rationed by my student traveller's budget to just a few dollars a day, I relished the unreality of it all, and wrung every last drop of hedonistic enjoyment from my time in the city.

In twenty-five years Los Angeles has changed, opening its doors to the world, filling its valleys with crisp houses and heated pools. Yet for me its secret interior presence is unaltered. Los Angeles remains a city of dreams, of fantasies, of preposterous yet satisfying excess. Those who think they know me well marvel at my preference for Los Angeles over San Francisco. They can't understand that if I want quaint, if I want Victorian, if I want men commuting to the office in three-piece suits, if I want shellfish and symphonies, bridges and fogs rolling back grudgingly to unveil the sun, I can stay in Europe and have them all. Los Angeles gives me guilt-free motoring, open necks, the loyal attendance of a perfect climate, the nodding rapport of ocean and mountain snow, an absence of expectation, the dismissal of history, the thong bikini, and space to stretch.

At the airport I am restless in the queue. I am always restless in queues, but today, fresh off the plane with its plastic spoons, sanitised paper pillows, and trays too small to accommodate a meal and a book, I am especially impatient to claim my car.

Richard – the man behind the counter tells me his name is Richard, not that I care, but he has to tell me because he is proud to be serving me, punching the keyboard with numbers of credit cards, codes of licences, acceptances and refusals of multiple insurances – Richard eventually drops into my palm the keys of something called a Geo. He has offered me a larger car, as though four seats were insufficient for a man on his own. When I lay eyes on the Geo I see what he means. Nobody with any self-regard in Los Angeles would want to be seen behind the wheel of a Geo. Nobody in this city *is* seen behind the wheel of a Geo unless he has rented it. It is as though the manufacturers had expressly designed it to match the lowliest economy compact stratum of the car rental menu. The Geo is not merely small, it is insignificant. In a city where cars are fashion statements, the Geo is mute.

I slide up the ramp onto the San Diego Freeway, remembering to counter my instincts by increasing my speed as I rise to the level of the other lanes. It comes easily, a reflection of my confidence in the engineering, my eagerness to join in the glide and sidle, the gradual leftward shift from ramp to lane. Confidence too that other motorists will allow for my entrance, just as I will permit their exits. Hogging the road on the freeways is a self-defeating exercise. I waft into the middle lane, which keeps me clear of the comings and goings to my right, and of the faster, more ruthless traffic to my left.

With one hand on the wheel, I use the other to roll up my sleeves. I lower the window so my bare arm can rest above the glass, taking care not to let my elbow jut, since the freeways are full of jetsam that whirring tyres can flick up with the force of missiles that can tear the flesh. My other hand, finger erect, jabs at the radio buttons until the popular trash of the moment blares out. I have now achieved stable freeway mode. There is nothing for me to do except keep the wheels straight and keep an eye out for the Santa Monica Boulevard exit, which will take me east to my temporary home. Beyond the immediate haze of a balmy afternoon, the barren, murkily green slopes of the Santa Monica Mountains mark the boundary of serious Los Angeles. Beyond the mountains lies the San Fernando Valley which, for the time being, can safely be stowed in a lower drawer of consciousness.

I feel perfectly comfortable dozing along, but there are many drivers, even native Angelenos, who are terrified of the freeways. For the timid, help is at hand from the likes of Sy Cohn, who will sell you tapes – 'Introduction to Stress-free Driving' – to play while you shudder behind the wheel. Another of his tapes, 'Audible Affirmation', gives you 'positive audible affirmations to repeat verbally while driving'. He also offers individual or group counselling, in which he employs music, hypnosis and astral projection to help you up the on-ramp.

A tow truck comes roaring past on my left, straining to increase its already excessive speed. This was my first glimpse of a bird-dogger, a native species of entrepreneur who thrives in a city beribboned with freeways. When a traffic accident occurs, and there are almost two hundred a day in Los Angeles, the police department dispatches to the scene its tow trucks which will remove your wreckage for a fixed charge. Bird-doggers operate unlicensed tow trucks equipped with police scanners. On first reports of an accident they race towards the scene. Sometimes the police are there first. If not, or if the official tow trucks are tardy, the bird-doggers will drag the crippled vehicle to the bodyshop of their choice, from which they receive generous kickbacks. The dozens of bird-doggers are all in competition with each other, which explains the great speed at which they travel on their missions of rescue and profit. Bird-doggers also participate in insurance scams, setting up bogus accidents; uninjured victims collude with crooked lawyers and doctors, the insurance companies pay out, and all the conspirators take a slice of the profits.

This is part of the culture of the freeway. You may have thought the freeway was simply a means of getting from A to B. Not in Los Angeles. An entire large-format paperback maps the best short cuts when the freeways are jammed and you want an alternative route. You also have to learn a whole new language. Bird-dogger for a start. And SigAlert. Radio bulletins announcing SigAlerts usually mean serious trouble, such as a pile-up or a blocked freeway. They are named after Loyd Sigmon, a traffic reporter who chronicled snarls and wrecks in the 1950s; his skill in intercepting police dispatches allowed him to alert the public rapidly to potential trouble spots.

I come to Santa Monica Boulevard, and swing east, past the featureless towers of Century City, across Wilshire, keeping the shopping district of Beverly Hills on my right and the pastoral five-servant domesticity of the Beverly flats on my left. I fork right onto Beverly Boulevard. Across Doheny, with the neoclassical hut of Chasen's restaurant on the left. Over Robertson, and then the boulevard curves past the Cedars-Sinai Hospital and the Beverly Center. A few streets on, and I turn right and park outside the small Spanish Colonial Revival house and its former garage, now surrounded by patio, that is to be my home from home.

Those who deride Los Angeles for its lack of beauty are not only wrong, they are missing the point. The city is not about beauty, nor about the picturesque conjunction of landscape and dwelling; it is about location. Between the mountains and ridges and the ocean lie the plains and foothills, formerly treeless expanses that cried out for habitation. The city floor, flat and featureless, renders the city invisible. It can be seen only from the fashionable mountainside heights and the canyon ridges, or from the leg-up of the freeways, from which it is at least possible to make out a few landmarks: the mound of the Palos Verdes peninsula, the newly thrusting downtown towers, the Hollywood sign set fifty-foot-high letters against the slopes of Beachwood Canyon.

Los Angeles is a horizontal city, an urban omelette, an epic concrete smear, and the energies of its inhabitants are directed at traversing its expanses. In the early years of this century rail networks carved out routes that today are supplanted by the mighty rivers of the freeways. The Pasadena Freeway was the first to be constructed in 1939, and the entire system was more or less complete by the early 1960s. These routes define the city. Phone a restaurant for directions, and the instruction 'Drive four blocks east off the 405 on Wilshire' tells you all you need to know. Except in the rush hours, the length of journeys can be calculated to within a five-minute margin of error. Nobody discounts the problems generated by the freeways – the snarl-ups, the accidents, the pollution – but they are also remarkably efficient. Their accessibility – even the very name 'freeway' has libertarian overtones – means that the city is within reach of all. Almost all. Dereliction, where it exists, seems not unrelated to the absence of nearby freeways, as in Watts, ghettoised by its location along a neglected rail line and by the three-mile journey from the nearest freeway. The freeways have opened up the city and permitted its ceaseless expansion, but they have also hemmed in certain districts and thrown them into the shadow of oblivion.

The problem with equal accessibility is that it makes nonsense of the notion of a city centre. Downtown is a district much like any other in the city, not a hub in the centre of a radiating wheel and certainly not the major social or cultural centre of Los Angeles, despite recent efforts to endow it with concert halls and smart restaurants.

In a city where the aesthetic impulse, moviemaking apart, has usually been restricted to the construction of domestic architecture, the freeways offer an accidental aesthetic that is as exhilarating as any modern urban landscape. Close to downtown a number of freeways converge with balletic and mathematical sophistication to resemble a manual of knots. Some freeways have been used as a blank canvas, their tall concrete walls along sunken stretches now painted over with murals depicting the human parades so absent from the freeways themselves.

To get the measure of Los Angeles I needed to rise above it, so one afternoon I headed north to Mount Wilson. I drove by numbers. East along Santa Monica to the 101, and north through

Hollywood to the 134, the Ventura Freeway that traverses the San Fernando Valley. East on 134 to the 2, and north to the 210, which links some of the new communities in the foothills of the Verdugo mountains. East on 210 to Route 2 (not to be confused with Freeway 2), a well-engineered road that climbs high into the San Gabriel Mountains. The junction of Route 2 with 134, the point where the ramp sweeps over the freeway and heads northwards, is one of the most breathtaking in a city of a thousand interchanges, and the roadway soars and descends like a great sigh.

One of the false promises of Los Angeles is that land is cheap and plentiful. It may have been so sixty years ago, but the watered plains near the ocean are now filled with houses, and lots large enough to have been subdivided long ago suffered that fate and spawned yet more houses. Out here in the hills there is land, to be sure, but the topography is ungenerous. So alongside Route 2 at the Greenridge estate, a 'community' no different from countless others in the outer suburbs, immense houses occupy small lots, their pretension and architectural fussiness providing a weak compensation for their crowded setting. Soon the road left suburb behind and entered the National Forest, rising into the wooded mountains and climbing with some rapidity to 4000 feet before a branch road pulled off in the direction of Mount Wilson. As the winter afternoon drew on, sinister shadows crept down the sides of the ridges around me. From 5000 feet up on the mountain, the shadows were beneath me, and from the observatory, I saw the great city splayed out in the distance.

It had been a bright sunny day when I left Los Angeles. Up at Mount Wilson there was snow, still glistening in the fading sunlight. Yet the city below panted beneath a vast sea of brown dragon's breath, a cloak that never lifted from its shoulders even on a crisp winter afternoon, when the smog monitors were barely registering and the air-quality graphs in the morning newspaper crawled sleepily along the base line. It was an ugly sight, and I decided I didn't want to see the like again. From now on I would stay at ground level, well beneath the dome of chemical and effluent, particle and discharge, happier in the fiction that the sky above really was as blue and uninterrupted as it looked.

My resolution wavered only once. Riding the freeways, I was seeing only the bare outlines, the mountains and the ocean, palms as slender as young asparagus, the sun flashing off the mirrored skin of downtown skyscrapers. Where, among all this, was Glendale? Or Alhambra? Or Crenshaw? Where was the lake of Silver Lake? Where were the hills of Rolling Hills, the heights of Boyle Heights?

I stood inside the terminal of Martin Aviation at Burbank airport, gazing at the Cessnas and Lear jets parked outside. A few businessmen and families sat about flicking through magazines while their planes were being refuelled or serviced. Flying appeared as inconsequential to them as taking a taxi. Then a small plane taxied up towards the terminal and I recognised the numbers on the fuselage as those of KFI radio station. This was my ride. Mike Nolan kept the engine churning as he waved me over, and I made an inelegant leap onto the wing and from there into the cockpit. Once my safety straps and headphones were in place, Nolan headed out to the runway, fretting at a delay in takeoff, since he had to file his next traffic report just a few minutes later.

While we waited he simultaneously monitored the Highway Patrol scanner for reports of accidents on the freeways, communicated with air-traffic control, and complained about poor reception to the producers of the two radio stations to which he contributes his bulletins. Once we were in the air, heading over the Hollywood hills, Nolan collated all his information to give an authoritative report on the afternoon traffic, even though we were still twenty miles away from most of it. He sing-songed his signature – 'This is Mike Nolan, KFI in the Sky' – then he found time to shake hands and say hello.

Nolan is lean, slender, tanned, a copybook native Californian. For twelve years he has been flying the skies to monitor the failures of the roads to deliver the traffic. Other radio stations in Los Angeles have pilots and reporters in the sky, but Nolan is the only one who flies and talks at the same time. There are only a few days each year when he can't get airborne. Sometimes in summer the smog lies horizontally over the city, and he can only see directly downwards while more distant areas, usually visible, remain obscured. Very occasionally, the cloud cover is so low and dense that not only is the ground invisible but so is other air traffic, and on those days he either stays on the ground or rents a helicopter, which is permitted to fly at lower altitudes than planes. Even on relatively clear days he lands in the evening to find a flesh layer of grime on the fuselage, skimmed over three hours from the brown froth atop Los Angeles.

Residential Hollywood came into view, with a strict grid system clearly visible south of Sunset Boulevard. The vagaries of habitation – house paint, parked cars, architectural quirks, trees and shrubs – ensure that the streets of Los Angeles with their single-family houses are far less monotonous than, say, a row of terraced houses in Britain, yet from above the geometric precision was overwhelming since all the detail and fine tuning of the myriad acts of residence couldn't be detected. Even the grass fringes between pavement and kerb were unwavering and regular. We kept flying south towards downtown, and looking down onto the towers made a welcome change from the usual standpoint of looking up at them. Heading east I saw below the immense industrial and warehousing districts, where the grid system collapsed as arteries of dried water channels, old rail lines and curving freeways broke the blocks into irregular shapes.

Flying over the city I could see how thoroughly it had been built up. The only green spaces in Hollywood and Silver Lake seemed to be cemeteries and a very few playing fields. In the richer suburbs to the west there are golf courses, but not here. The slight haze had the effect of robbing the city of its colour. On the ground Los Angeles is bright and brassy, with strident blues and pinks and greens that keep their depth of colour even in the strongest sunshine. But from above everything looked grey, with the only strong colour the azure of the backyard pools.

Further east and south we came to the fringes of Orange County. Los Angeles County merges into Orange imperceptibly, yet the psychological perception the residents of one have of the other could hardly be more marked. If Los Angeles seemed undernourished in terms of landmarks, Orange County seemed even more so, and from this height I had to ask Nolan to point out the Matterhorn at Disneyland; even the legendary theme park seemed a mere dab on the palette stretching for dozens of miles around us. Towards Riverside County to the east there were some new tract developments, some of them little more than brown swirls where earthmovers were still preparing the ground. Nolan perked up here, as we spotted a fender-bender applying to a tourniquet to Route 91. As we circled above, we could see the middle lane slowly come to a halt and back up.

We flew west, towards the ocean, following the Santa Monica Freeway, where the cars were moving at little more than a fast jogger's pace. We curved north at Century City, keeping well above its towers, and headed up towards Bel Air and the fashionable end of Beverly Hills. In the late afternoon the canyon floors were already deep in shadow while up on the slopes the mansions, their pools and tennis courts, were drenched in warm buttery sunshine. From below, the dramatic houses on the canyon ridges, some of them cantilevered out in the most breathtaking way, seem disconnected, as though dropped from above. From the sky I could see the lanes that wind between them curving up and along the ridges until they come to some spectacular dead end at gates and electric fences.

Moving east into the Hollywood hills, the lots became smaller, the houses more huddled, and then the mountains subsided through the Arroyo Seco district until the descent into Pasadena, the most verdant and stately of Los Angeles' cities within the city. Behind Pasadena the San Gabriel Mountains, still covered with spring snows, loomed imperiously.

'I'm going to have to take you back about now,' said Mike.

'Whatever you say,' I said, sounding accommodating when I was in fact feeling urgent, since the swoops and curves of the tiny plane were beginning to make an impact on my own equilibrium, and the nervous connections between eye and stomach, throat and ear, were no longer as smooth as they had been an hour earlier. Suppressing the mutinies of the body, I sat tight until the wheels touched down at Burbank. As before, Nolan kept the engine running – 'Remember to jump off the *back* of the wing,' he counselled – as I clambered out and away.

Terra firma. And never more welcome. To inspect Los Angeles from the sky is no more than a scholarly quirk. It runs counter to the grain of the place to defy its horizontality. A few deep breaths of wholesome diesel-tinged Burbank air, and then I headed for the familiar casing of my invisible Geo.

2

NO FURS IN RUSTIC CANYON

Settled into my new quarters, I soon established my routines. Coffee first thing in the morning, and if time permitted, a visit to the nearby Farmers Market on Fairfax to buy fruit and other supplies. The Farmers Market is a local landmark although there are no farmers there and not much of a market. During the Depression there were working farms in the valleys, but today any farmer would need to chug for about three hours in his Chevy pickup to get anywhere near Los Angeles from any place where they actually grow things.

Nonetheless the Farmers Market is immensely popular. Tourist buses park nearby to show bewildered Nipponese that it is still possible to buy loose grapefruit in Los Angeles. Locals come here too, both to shop and to sample the stands where you can buy a dozen oysters, a Cajun gumbo, a pastrami sandwich, papaya juice, a cauldron of chow mein. You fling your food on a tray, and carry it to any of dozens of tables scattered about the half-covered market.

I come here to buy bread. Californians are proud of their sour-dough breads, but I prefer the caraway crunch of good rye. Buying a loaf at the Bread Bin demands patience. It is obligatory to exchange banter with the grouchy lady behind the counter. A little joke about the children (I don't have any), an inquiry about the recent Jewish festivals (I don't celebrate them), an exchange of medical bulletins, and then the plunge: the dithering order of bagels ('Make it five, no give me six') or the choice of loaf. Then the grouchy lady, with infinite pains, gets the order wrong. ('No,

I didn't say sliced.') Addition and subtraction are too distracting when you're also discussing your Seder, so you count your change.

Certain tables and corners are the preserve of movie directors or screenwriters. Tourists spend hours wandering about hoping for a glimpse of a veteran director and his clique munching their Muffelata sandwiches or gumbo-yaya. They are usually disappointed, since those in danger of being recognised retreat to an upstairs area where they can sip and gossip without a lens in their faces. My favourite corner was lunatics' row, where very old but perfectly preserved men and women sit with blank yet urgent eyes and talk to themselves. Fairfax is a heavily Jewish area, but the average age of the community seems to be about ninety, and most of the denizens, at some time during the day, drive – their jaws resting daintily on the steering wheel – down to the market for coffee and conspiracy. They are very tiny, the ladies have tinted hair, and the men read the newspaper and grumble.

Returning one morning with my purchases, I found the answering machine winking at me. The message was reassuring, for Society had beckoned. I'd been invited to a tennis party. Not that I knew what a tennis party was – fifty people in white shorts sipping martinis on a tennis court?

McKee's house lay at the end of a short lane south of Sunset Boulevard in the Pacific Palisades. Her house stood at the top of a small canyon that wound its way down to the ocean. Rustic Canyon was not a belated attempt to bestow rural qualities on a suburb; it truly was rustic, with log cabins and horse paddocks half concealed beneath tall redwoods and oaks.

McKee's acre of land accommodated a tennis court, of course, gardens of various degrees of wildness, and a large sprawling wooden bungalow with interconnecting rooms. This was all that remained of a family estate that once included a number of houses that have now been sold off.

McKee herself was a stocky woman in her early sixties, with a loud drawl that didn't sound especially Californian to me, though she's as Californian as they come. Her talk was often interrupted by loud heedless laughter and she exhibited the casual eccentricities of the carelessly rich, although she was probably far less well off than most of her neighbours. A staunch environmentalist, she drove a battered old Mercedes painted a sickly green. In her bathroom the reading material on offer was a *Handbook to Higher Consciousness*.

This corner of the Palisades had long attracted those who sought quasi-rural living in the heart of West Los Angeles. The English colony had lived nearby – Huxley and Isherwood, among others – and Thomas Mann had lived just north of Sunset, and Arnold Schoenberg had set up house over towards Brentwood on Rockingham Drive. The University of California at Los Angeles (UCLA) owns a splendid photograph showing the immensely tall conductor Otto Klemperer taking a walk through Rustic Canyon with the diminutive Schoenberg. The Viennese composer Hanns Eisler had lived here too. Brecht had given the Palisades a try but couldn't stand it. 'Pacific Palisades doesn't exist', he wrote, 'it's just trees and hills. When someone is sick there is no doctor; when you need a pharmacy, there's nothing to buy. You cannot live so far away from civilisation.' He moved south to Santa Monica.

McKee and her neighbours clearly relish what Brecht regarded as the lack of civilisation. He would not, I imagine, have enjoyed her party very much. The tennis contingent took it in turns on the court, having devised a baroque tournament structure. The non-participants stood or sat in the gardens, drinking McKee's wine – among some rather undistinguished bottles was Trimbach's best cuvée of 1983 Alsace Riesling, which I attempted to monopolise. There was food too, including a gastronomically contradictory vegetarian chilli.

An Englishwoman, Diana Ayres, who was married to the actor Lew Ayres, told me about her progression from London to Los Angeles about thirty years ago. I then asked her about our hostess, since I knew next to nothing about her.

'I have to tell you,' she began, 'that this is not a typical Los Angeles house.'

At which point a peacock left its rooftop perch and flapped onto the lawn. I admired the bird, and McKee came over to tell me how both the peacocks and the chickens (confined to their quarters for the duration of the party) were part of her recycling team. 'I only put out one bag of garbage a month. Isn't that something? The birds eat the rest.'

A large cake was carried out to the garden. There were three clumps of candles ablaze, one for each of the birthdays being celebrated that afternoon. Photographs were taken, candles blown out, and there was great hilarity as McKee presented one of her gifts, a jumbo pack of recycled lavatory paper.

A croquet game evolved and in honour of my nationality I was urged to participate. I didn't want to disappoint the Californians, and agreed to humiliate them. Perhaps it was the Riesling, but I was not at my best and despite some healthily aggressive play I came in fourth. Americans of course are disagreeably competitive, so my quieter, more refined sportsmanship had little chance against New World double-hander ruthlessness.

I phoned McKee a few days later. She sounded breathless and I asked her if I had caught her at a bad moment.

'I'm on the treadmill,' she gasped. She had twelve minutes to go, so I phoned her back later to arrange to join her on a tour of Rustic Canyon. As I drove in, past the hounds and peacocks, I found her waiting for me on the patio, a large black fedora on her head. I leapt from my car into hers, flicking jelly beans off the seat. As we drove along the winding lanes, she explained that the canyon was blessed with a small stream that never dried up.

'It runs past the back of my house, and in back of many other houses too. We pick watercress from it. We're all very conscious of our environment here. We're into recycling, and you'll find that most of the people who live here, they may have lots of money, but they'll also be no-furs people.' The canyon dwellers, she kept telling me, were not glitzy, even though there probably wasn't a house for sale here for under a million dollars. There are no palaces in Rustic Canyon, and none of the self-promoting urge to impress passers-by that is so common in Beverly Hills. 'Nobody around here feels they need to prove their status to the world.'

We drove down Brooktree, a lane flanked by shallow troughs of dark green moss along which rivulets trickled down from the many natural springs. No. 711 was one of the few new houses in the canyon, a smart number with expensive wood veneers and marble floors. I found out about the marble floors because I trailed behind McKee as she strode into the house. A maid and a handyman were on the premises, but their mild Spanish protestations at our invasion made no impression on my guide. This house, she told me, had taken two years to construct, since the springs beneath it required tons of rock to be laid below the foundations to prevent subsidence.

Hightree is a cul-de-sac, from which a small private drive leads to a few houses in a hollow.

'There's a great peace here – it's not like the rest of the city.'

We parked, and McKee led the way to one of the houses, where her friends the Gowlands lived. As we passed the pool in front of the house, she remarked: 'Funny, I remember the pool being out back.' We had come to the wrong house. 'I don't know whose house this is, but isn't it wonderful?' And we peered in the windows, admiring the art on the walls.

There was another house near the end of this drive, so obviously that was the Gowlands' place, and we walked over to it. 'I'm sure you'll like the Gowlands. They're so lively, you'd never think they were about to celebrate their golden wedding.'

I stepped over the tricycles and skateboards blocking the path, and remarked to McKee that the Gowlands must be exceptionally youthful.

'Funny,' said McKee. 'The Gowlands don't have any children.' She continued up the path towards the porch. 'Oh, this must be it! I can see the pool at the back.'

It wasn't it. 'Gee, I think we've made a mistake. This is Randy Newman's old house.'

From the porch we surveyed the hollow. Two other houses were accessible from footbridges across the Rustic stream. One of them *had* to be the Gowlands', and indeed it was. Peter Gowland is a tall thin man of exceptional energy, who greeted us as though he hadn't seen a human being in months, although his charming wife Alice was standing beside him. A photographer, Gowland works exclusively, it seems, with scantily clad young women. His visiting cards reproduce vivid black-and-white nudes on the front and self-promoting essays on the back, from which I quote: 'Peter Gowland has a worldwide reputation as one of the finest photographers of women. Almost every assignment involves a product with a beautiful model. His pictures of models and Hollywood personalities have graced over 1000 magazine covers and appeared in national advertisements . . . Peter has the help of his wife, Alice, who attends to the tedious details.' Oh. 'This Aries couple have collaborated on 21 photography books.'

Like most of the canyon women, Alice did not look as though she had had recourse to the arts of the cosmetic surgeon –

another difference between Rustic Canyon and Beverly Hills. The canyon dwellers also have a weakness for eccentric pets, and the Gowlands had shared their home with a desert turtle that had alarmed various models by making a slow stumble across the floor during shooting sessions. Alice showed me the dressing room used by the models; two drawers were filled to overflowing with bikinis. That appeared to be the complete wardrobe.

The house was ideal as a studio. Like many of the International-style houses in the city – this one dated from 1954 – it minimised the difference between exterior and interior by replacing walls with panels of glass. The interior walls were flexible too, so that spaces could be enlarged or diminished according to the purpose they were being put to. Not far away was the architect's own house, built in three stages as the household grew larger, thus evolving into a series of blue-grey cubes.

The canyon also contains a number of houses by one of the city's greatest living architects, Raymond Kappe, who brings to the International model a particular refinement. Their strong horizontal lines, the runways of base deck and roof, sandwich not only glass walls but sumptuous wooden veneers. A couple who had been to the tennis party lived in one of Kappe's houses, beautifully situated at the top of a steep slope among tall trees and shrubs. They weren't home, but that didn't prevent us from having a good look round. The verdant surroundings protect the house from prying eyes (other than ours), so the rooms, like most in the area, were left uncurtained. We were able to make a thorough inventory of the contents.

We drove down Latimer to the Rustic Canyon park, once a polo field for those who had built cabins in the canyon as weekend retreats, and now equipped with a pool and tennis courts. On nearby Haldeman are log cabins and some fine ranch houses built of roughly hewn stone. Behind McKee's own house and the main estate house next door are smaller houses that had once belonged to her family. One of them, the former children's playhouse but now considerably expanded, was lived in by a very rich rare-metals dealer and his young Polish wife. In some respects theirs was still a children's house, as the dealer has a fondness for whimsical art. Attached to an interior arch are half a dozen illuminated orange piglets, and the main feature of the living room, other than the sculpture collection, was a full-size pool table. The garden, fenced to keep the deer out, was thickly blanketed in a ground cover of nasturtium and ivy, from which apple and kumquat trees rose colourfully.

'Oh, this lemon!' exclaimed McKee, picking the fruit and thrusting it in front of my nose. 'The scent!' And indeed it had a richer scent than any lemon I had previously sniffed. With a touch of complacency McKee added that she hadn't bought a lemon or orange in thirty years – all the gardens were full of them.

The next house we invaded belonged to the Farbsteins, whose garden was one of the loveliest I was to see in a city filled with glorious gardens. A silver-dollar eucalyptus leaned over the driveway, ferns flickered up to the height of trees, and a silk-floss tree, its pods drooping from its upper branches, rose up behind the shrubberies of azalea and camelia. Next to the entrance of the Japanese-style house stood an immense splayed California live oak. Around the house, as well as within it, were countless orchids, many of them exquisitely beautiful. I complimented Olga Farbstein, who greeted us in gardening gloves, but she insisted that they were easy to cultivate and profited from the cool moist breezes that came up the canyon from the ocean.

At a house higher up on the canyon slope, flora gave way to fauna. Cy Carr, an oral surgeon, and his wife Dolly had stuffed their home with fluffy cats and a turtle; behind the house their horses stood about dozily in the paddock. Tennis rackets leant in readiness just inside the door, as in most canyon houses. Dolly told me that her political views, in contrast to McKee's, were liberal, so McKee had teased her by presenting her with a mug decorated with the legend: Pacific Palisades – Reagan Country. The Great Communicator had indeed lived in the Palisades, until, that is, he had been presented with an even more desirable residence in Bel Air. What a marvellously generous and beneficent country this is, where a group of very rich men can rustle up $3 million to buy a mansion for another very rich man who just happened to have been the President of the United States.

Our last call was at a house of greater architectural interest, a sprawling, angular brick design with an additional storey tucked unobtrusively beneath the eaves. It had been designed by Lloyd Wright Jr, son of the great Frank Lloyd Wright. We had been invited for tea by Martha Newman Ragland, but I had to earn my refreshments by hauling fifty-pound bags of dog food from her car into a shed. This attracted the attention of three very large

Alsatians. Martha assured me that they were loving creatures, as do all owners of savage dogs just moments before they drink your blood. On this occasion I was not seriously mauled.

We had arrived late, but Martha was late too. Like others we had visited that afternoon, she had been off to see her accountant. Tax deadlines were looming. She and McKee breathed a joint sigh of relief over the once controversial Proposition 13, which had put a halt to ever-rising property taxes when it was passed in the late 1970s. The Proposition had cut property taxes by 50 per cent and limited future taxation of property to 1 per cent of the assessed valuation. To pay for this relief, there had been cuts in other services provided by the state. Constantly rising property taxes in the 1970s had been a severe burden to those on fixed incomes, especially the retired, who found they could no longer afford to live in their houses. Now the balance was swinging the other way. Like other long-term owners of expensive property, Martha was still paying a third of what she had been paying before Proposition 13 had been passed, since the assessments of her property's worth had remained unaltered. Once you move, a fresh assessment is made, but as long as you stay put the valuation, and hence the taxation, remains fixed.

Martha has more land than most residents of the canyon, and shares it with horses, which she could lead down the Rustic stream, through a tunnel that burrows beneath Sunset, and up into Will Rogers Park, where there are extensive horse trails. Martha, raised in Alabama, retains a certain Southern graciousness, the aura of the practised hostess. She had been a Goldwyn Girl before marrying Alfred Newman, who until his death in 1970 had been one of Hollywood's leading music directors and composers. He composed over 250 scores and had carried off nine Oscars, which are now distributed among their children, who are also musically gifted. So was her nephew, who turned out to be the great songwriter Randy Newman, whose former house we had been inspecting earlier in the day. Could she, by any chance, engineer an introduction to her nephew? She thought it unlikely.

Martha was well into her sixties – 'she hasn't had a thing done to her face,' McKee told me admiringly – and had lived here since 1948. The canyon hadn't changed much in forty years, as deed restrictions discouraged the building of new houses. There had been reminders that despite its paradisaical air, Southern

California can exhibit a sub-tropical violence at times. In 1969 torrential rain had caused the stream to break its banks, and many trees had been destroyed by the lingering flood waters. Nine years later fire had raged across the Palisades, but to the relief of canyon dwellers Sunset Boulevard had acted as a firebreak.

She had known the original inhabitants of the large house next door to McKee's. With the help of a banker's salary the owner had built a pool in the shape of the state of California. He would relax by the pool in his favourite rocking chair fiddling with the special controls which enabled him to change the colours of the spotlights that illuminated the waterfall he had constructed in the garden. There had been four colours to choose from. The banker went broke and the house was sold to a family whose days in the canyon were marred by alcoholism and mental illness; in the 1960s it was bought by the Synanon foundation.

'That was an awful time,' added McKee. 'The house was full of strange people, who kept wandering over into my garden. That's when I had to build a fence between the properties. Luckily we were able to get the Synanon people out after a few months.'

The next inhabitant was Dennis Wilson of the Beach Boys. A generous soul, he allowed a guitarist whose gifts he admired to park his trailer in the grounds.

'The guitarist was good with kids,' recalled McKee, 'so all the local children, including mine, loved to go over to the trailer to listen to him strumming away. His name was Charlie Manson, but this was his pre-carnage period. Eventually he moved away, and the murders took place not long after that.'

After Wilson left, the house was bought by Geordie Hormel, another musician, heir to the Hormel meat company fortune and sometime husband to Lesley Caron. He still lives there, and is busy constructing recording studios beneath the house. His long-term affection for mind-enhancing substances is well known.

Much of Los Angeles is volatile and restless, but Rustic Canyon seemed a stable community, tucked away and private. What the residents share, apart from wealth, is not so much eccentricity as a feeling that you can pursue your own interests and recreations without worrying that your neighbours will find it odd or irritating – unless, of course, you're into mass murder. Relations with neighbours are usually cordial, although Martha reported that she had problems with an irascible resident who couldn't abide her horses, which is rather odd, given that horses probably outnumber human beings in the canyon.

'He would become very aggressive on the subject, so one day I casually let it be known that I was thinking of starting up a pig farm on my property. Of course I had no such intention, but it kept him busy. He must have spent at least five hundred dollars checking into the legal position on pig farms in residential areas.'

3

MIGRANTS OLD AND YOUNG

Dawn. Or thereabouts. Awakenings are no easier in Los Angeles than anywhere else. There's the same slow ascent to the surface, the cataloguing of the aches of the night, the dismissal of dreams, the pinning up of the eyes, all before the Californian morning, resplendent, sunny, and full of promise, can shift the day into gear.

While sipping my coffee, I flick on the television, which receives the three major network channels, all of which are aimed at mentally retarded adults, two Spanish-language channels, and a Chinese programme. The networks are in fierce competition with each other to present the most risible morning news programmes. I usually tuned in to NBC, a random choice. First we have to get the news out of the way at the top of the hour. This doesn't take long. The Gulf War is over, so the news mostly consists of film coverage of returning American marines and soldiers. On a good day we might get a snippet of Irving R. Levine, a veteran reporter who only speaks Brooklynese, and, mindful of the average intelligence of the viewer, talks very, very slowly.

Willard Scott is another veteran. His role on the NBC morning show is to wear a funny hat and keep his arm round the shoulder of a hapless child or an old man. They are usually promoting a good cause, and so is Willard. He chatters away in a rich baritone about the 'wonderful folks' he's with, then he congratulates some old biddies – photographs of crones in white shawls flash onto the screen – who are either 105 or 108 today, and then he gabbles through a weather report so continental in its coverage that you have to wait for the local weather report to garner any pertinent information.

After Willard's frolicsome bonhomie, there's a 'station break', a syntactically unanalysable euphemism for a bunch of advertisements and the cue for a refill of coffee cups across the nation. Then back to the armchair for the meat in the televisual sandwich. Bryant or Grant or Buck or Susie or whichever presenter hasn't been fired that week or hasn't left to give birth to an excessively publicised baby launches into news analysis, usually with the help of two or more experts who are allowed to speak for ten seconds each. Since the format of the morning news has withheld any information on which an analysis could be based, this discussion tends to be unenlightening.

Even in my semi-somnolent morning grope towards consciousness there are limits to what I can stand, and Bryant and Dana and Barbara and the rest of them don't pass the test. I resolve to find a radio station that will prove more stimulating.

No time for that now. The coffee is drunk, and I have a long car ride, all the way to the San Fernando Valley. I drive steadily north up the 405, gloating as I watch the commuter traffic making its second-gear crawl over the Santa Monica Mountains. However bad the traffic is, it's almost certain to get worse. There is a shortage of housing near the central parts of the city where most of the jobs are; bloated Los Angeles constructs its new housing on the edges of the city, which thus spreads ever further outwards. The consequence is a growing number of commuters and greater congestion. The average speed on the freeways was about thirty mph by the end of the 1980s, but the report *LA 2000* predicts that, unless remedial measures are taken, by the end of the century that average will brake to about nineteen mph.

I follow a series of freeways up to the northern end of the valley, where the San Fernando Mission of 1797 provides an islet of old Hispanic culture in a suburban ocean. Spanish clerics dotted dozens of these missions across coastal California, and they functioned both as religious and economic centres. The San Gabriel Mission controlled no fewer than 1,500,000 acres. Most of them, including this one, fell into a ruinous condition after California became part of first Mexico and then the United States, but they have been scrupulously restored or, in some instances, reconstructed.

San Fernando was largely rebuilt in the 1940s, and after the 1971 earthquake the church, too badly shaken to be repaired, was replaced by a facsimile. The lovely arcaded building along the roadside, the Convento, dates from 1810; by the end of the last century it was delapidated but still standing. The reconstructed mission now serves as a parish church as well as a museum and destination for tourists. In its heyday the mission supported 1500 local Indians, who were encouraged to learn agricultural skills that would keep the community economically self-sufficient. In 1819 San Fernando Mission had 22,000 livestock as well as extensive orchards and workshops.

The missions are often presented as a benign system within which wise clerics operated a paternalist supervision over obliging Indians. The truth was less rosy. The missions flourished by enclosing the Indians within their domains. These natives were virtually enslaved, losing their economic independence and their tribal culture. Sanitation and diet were of wretched standards. Native women were subject to the usual amorous attentions of visitors and European diseases killed off Indians in their thousands. The mission lands were theoretically held in trust for the Indians, but after secularisation in the 1830s their claims were disregarded as more powerful Californians vied to acquire these riches.

The San Fernando Mission is built on a scale not unlike that of an Oxford college, with grassy courtyards and low buildings ranged around them. In the main courtyard, with the church at the far end, a peacock strolls about and water splashes into a large eight-lobed fountain. The Convento has been turned into a museum, and some of the principal rooms have been restored, such as the prettily painted Sala. The room of the first bishop of California, Garcia Diego, is filled with mostly eighteenth-century Spanish furniture, and the large mission library he assembled has, after many years in storage, been reinstalled.

Travellers were welcome to stay here. Ordinary visitors were lodged in a room filled with crude wooden beds; more honoured guests could frolic in a four-poster. A photograph of the mission, or what was left of it, from the 1880s shows the San Fernando Valley as broad and treeless, a reminder that most of Southern California is a semi-arid region. All the vegetation one thinks of as typically Californian – palm and eucalyptus, and a variety of flowering shrubs – has been imported.

The mountains, of course, separated the San Fernando Mission from the principal settlement of El Pueblo de Nuestra Senora la Reina de Los Angeles de Porciuncula, which was founded close to present-day downtown Los Angeles in 1781. A Spanish expedition had visited the spot, at that time a friendly Indian village called Yangna, twelve years earlier, and recorded its suitability for settlement. For forty years El Pueblo remained a sleepy little hamlet, its houses built of mud and roofed with the tar that bubbled in pits that still survive a few miles west of downtown. Crops were sown, vineyards planted, and a church built. In 1822 California became part of Mexico, but that scarcely affected this small Hispanic community. Under Mexican rule, the missions were secularised, and their lands were redistributed. Eight million acres of mission lands were transformed into immense ranches.

There was a flurry of political activity in the 1840s, during which California asserted its independence, lost it, and then fell contentedly into the arms of the Union in 1850. Los Angeles remained a prosperous ranching community, gradually invaded by migrants from the rural Midwest who were attracted by the plentiful land and the benign climate. The 1870s saw the construction of a Southern Pacific rail link to Northern California and to other parts of the United States, and this was the turning point in the town's fortunes. No longer an isolated agricultural backwater, Los Angeles developed rapidly into a solid little town, with paved streets, a hospital, a college, and an opera house. In ten years its population doubled. Gaslights first flickered in 1867 and seven years later streetcars began to traverse the city.

In 1885 the Santa Fe Railroad came onto the scene, and also came into direct competition with Southern Pacific. A rates war followed, and by March 1887 the fare from Kansas City to Southern California had dropped from a steep $125 to a single dollar. Midwesterners in search of a less stressful life could hardly resist. A tremendous boom developed. A succession of droughts cast doubt on the feasibility of ranching, and many old ranches were sold off to building developers, while irrigation helped small farmers to cultivate citrus and other crops. The city fathers promoted across the breadth of the United States the virtues and attractions of Los Angeles, and innumerable entrepreneurs peddled land and houses to the thousands of migrants who arrived each month. The boom reached ludicrous proportions; townships were founded that never attracted a single resident.

Although the ideology of the frontier exalts the virtues of free enterprise, the first railways in the Los Angeles area were publicly financed, since the city fathers were all too aware of the enormous economic benefits that would accrue from better communications. Lines connected downtown Los Angeles with Santa Monica, San Fernando, Anaheim, and San Bernardino, as well as the port of San Pedro, thus establishing the nuclei of the greater Los Angeles area.

The growth of the city was phenomenal, as the gaps between the nuclei were filled in. The development of the harbour boosted trade, oil was located and pumped, and water was funnelled off the sierras and brought in abundant quantities to the Los Angeles basin. Despite pitfalls and slumps, Los Angeles had the means to deliver on the promises with which its leaders enticed new settlers, who continued to come in droves, especially from the Midwest. By 1920 there were half a million inhabitants in the city of Los Angeles, and almost as many spread out in other parts of Los Angeles County. Ten years later, the population had more than doubled to over two million.

It was not only agriculture and fine weather that brought the migrants in their hundreds of thousands. The movie industry was acting as a magnet not only to hopeful actors and directors, but to technicians and lawyers and publicists. A decade later the Second World War was to provide another layer of economic vitality, with the rapid creation of the aerospace industry. Aircraft had been manufactured in Southern California for some time, and the need for planes and ancillary equipment promoted immense new regional investment. By the time the war ended, the foundations for the modern aerospace industry were in place, and hundreds of thousands of people found employment that remained relatively secure until the late 1980s, when some of the largest companies began to move to states such as Georgia where labour was less expensive.

Patterns of settlement established over a century ago have blurred the distinction between the City and the County of Los Angeles, and between the County and its equally immense neighbouring counties of Orange, San Bernardino and Riverside. In terms of the economy of the region, these boundaries seem increasingly arbitrary. The city occupies 465 square miles, no more than 2 per cent of Southern California but containing about a quarter of its population. Over eighty enclaves within Los Angeles County have declared their independence, setting up their own municipalities and administrations, providing in some instances their own fire, police, and water services. Despite what might seem to be a formula for administrative chaos, the growth of the city, aided by the freeway system, proceeded smoothly enough, with vast new tract developments planned and executed with remarkable speed. Today the population stands at about 14 million.

The old photograph at the San Fernando Mission recorded a moment that now seems inconceivably remote. It shows a place virtually deserted by the human race, and dealt a mediocre hand by nature. The valley floor sashays with swaying grassland and little more. Looking today at the Valley it is impossible to imagine the bustling, densely populated, far-flung, freeway-crossed ulti-mate suburb as an empty steppe. Yet the transformation of the region has been so rapid that you don't have to be immensely old to recall Los Angeles before it became the iconic Los Angeles of the freeways and the tracts. There were no freeways here before 1939; now there are 700 miles of them.

Warren Isham remembers this prelapsarian Los Angeles. Lean-ing on his walking frame, he met me on the porch of his modest house near Melrose and Fairfax. A little jowly with age, he has vivid eyes and a shock of white hair that take a few years off his ninety-three. His stocky figure could still move with considerable speed on its metal supports. Warren was a typical migrant. Born in Detroit, he studied history at the University of Michigan, served in World War I, and came out to Los Angeles in 1920. Before long he had a job at Universal Studios.

'Horse operas, as we called Westerns in those days, that's what I was working on. Of course this was before we had sound and colour in the movies. I worked as a back-of-the-camera electrician, moving from studio to studio. I worked for most of them, and the only one I didn't like was MGM because they used too many night crews. To knock out a Western in those days took three or four weeks. They weren't too interested in perfection. If errors were made, they glossed them over.'

It was hard to stop Warren talking about the stars he had worked with. I suppose any old Angeleno with experience of the movie industry in its infancy is frequently called upon to reminisce, and I was happy enough to listen.

'John Barrymore was a terrible drinker, but perfect on the set. Perfect. Joan Crawford too, in spite of the things people have said about her. Although her contract stipulated she was to have a fresh bottle of Scotch and another of Bourbon every day, she wasn't a heavy drinker, though she did entertain a great deal in her bungalow. She was a hard worker, and I've seen her insist on another take at two in the morning if she thought it was necessary. I also worked at DesiLu. Desi drank too, but Lucille was one of the best. And was she ever crazy about him! I worked with Charles Laughton on *Henry VIII*. He was easy to talk to, friendly.

'But let's to proceed,' he said in his quaint but very precise English, aware that I was more interested in primeval Los Angeles. Once he was established here, he bought the house we were sitting in when it was built in 1924. 'There wasn't a tree anywhere here, and my family was worried that our house would be too far from town. But the lots quickly filled up. At weekends we'd go down to the beach, to Ocean Park or to Venice – they were great places for meeting girls.'

Warren worked until he was seventy-one. 'I only gave up working because I got tired of six a.m. calls. May I give you a word of advice? Never retire.'

I had to excuse myself after an hour because I had also arranged to visit a neighbour of Warren's. Ernie Hobden was waiting for me as he sat on his porch, and although he never left his chair I could tell that he was a large man. His vellum-like skin now fitted loosely over his bones, but his face remained handsome and craggy, though much spotted and gnarled and stubbled. A battered straw hat fitted snugly on his large head. His voice was robust yet quiet, although, like Warren, he is slightly deaf. According to his neighbours Ernie is indestructible. He keeps falling over, yet never breaks any bones and refuses even to contemplate moving out of his own house into easier surroundings.

In his hundredth year when I called on him, Ernie, like Warren, had come out from Detroit. He first came to Los Angeles in 1911. 'After the beautiful winter of 1911, I never wanted to see Detroit again. The climate back there was vicious.' He had trained as a mechanical engineer in the nascent automobile industry, but had difficulty finding work in Detroit. 'I'd never heard of Los Angeles till some friend in the navy told me I should try my luck there. Once I got out here I found work, but it only paid me a dollar a day. I lived at the Y and did all kinds of work. I was even a pall bearer. I found work in the automotive business at a dealer downtown on Olive. In those days Olive was automobile row. Everybody was there, all the dealers, the tyre companies. I could easily have found work as a mechanic, but I was tired of dirty work.'

Here he digressed, and told me something that he had told very few other people. He was not native-born at all but had been born in Kent, and had worked at the Wolseley factory from the age of fourteen. 'I was exceptionally smart, I had a very quick mind.' He had planned to emigrate to Australia but had gone to America instead. It was not clear to me whether this second version of his early life was supposed to precede the first or replace it. Ernie offered to show me documentary evidence to back up his claim to be English-born, but I couldn't work up enormous interest in the whereabouts of the infant Ernie.

The story continued. Ernie was hired by Mr Spalding. As far as I could understand a tale that twisted and turned in the telling, Spalding had married a daughter of a business associate of the oil magnate Edward Doheny. This had brought Mr Spalding a huge amount of money, some of which he spent on a sixty-eight-acre property in Beverly Hills. 'In those days,' he reminded me, 'there were only dirt roads in Beverly Hills. I was hired by Spalding as a mechanic, but before long I was doing everything for him. I was always at his side, and eventually I became manager of his property. As well as the property in Beverly Hills he had 100,000 acres near San Diego and other properties in the north. He was a wealthy man but a bad boy. He chased skirts, all the time.

'After the war, we came back to Los Angeles from San Francisco, where Spalding had been in the army, and I became one of the top persons in Beverly Hills. I was on the election board for twenty-five years and sat on various bank boards. All the gardeners and servants of the Spalding estate reported to me. I shouldn't really be telling you this, but part of my job was to keep Spalding out of trouble, to keep him out of fights that could have led to scandal. We didn't want some of the stories about him to get out.'

Story followed story about Spalding's scandalous behaviour, about Ernie's own closeness to a senior American general, and about his own power and influence in Beverly Hills. Most of these stories led only to digressions, which in turn sprouted fresh anecdotes. There was no way to disentangle truth from fiction. Ernie evidently wanted to impress me for some reason, unaware that his mere existence was impressive enough. Working for Spalding for forty years, it seemed entirely plausible that he had indeed wielded considerable influence as a kind of *consigliere*. When he talked of the 1947 Cadillac he owned, he was not bragging, as I found the car still parked in the garage behind the house. With the passage of the decades, the kind of society that Spalding represented became swamped. The movers and shakers of Los Angeles were no longer property owners and oilmen but movie moguls, lawyers, surgeons, and junk-bond dealers. Ernie was a relic of the time when Los Angeles was still making the transition from frontier town to self-confident city. The past in which his memory had become mired no longer bore much relationship to the vast city in which the old man on his porch – 'you'll find me here 365 days a year' – sat and reminisced.

It wasn't easy to get hold of Karen Salkin. But then Karen, as her visiting card specifies, is a Major Celebrity, and major celebrities tend not to pick up the phone on spec. However, as one artist unable to reject the friendly approaches of another, she agreed to meet me, and proposed a rendezvous for tea. Since it had been a while since Karen herself had taken tea, she insisted on conducting some research, and asked me to phone her back once she had gathered sufficient information to enable us to make a sensible decision. Fancy hotels such as the Westwood Marquis, she subsequently reported, lay on a teatime spread. This didn't appeal to me.

'Or,' she continued, 'we could go this place in Beverly Hills I once went to. It has the couch setting with spaniels. No? Okay, let's talk again on Thursday.'

I phoned on Thursday. She picked up the phone panting, and admitted to being in a frantic state. 'I've misplaced an important business letter among all my fan mail, and I've been searching for it *all* morning. So maddening.'

We decided on a place called Paddington's, English-run and rather charming, Karen vaguely recalled.

'Okay, I'll see you tomorrow, Stephen. It'll be fabulous. Hope you show up.'

I did show up, early, but saw no one that corresponded to Karen's self-description. I took a short stroll along this block of La Cienega, then returned and entered the tearooms, choosing a vacant table. Thirty seconds later a striking dark-haired woman in a full-length scarlet dress strode in. She spotted me at once. She too, she confided, had been early, but had waited for me to enter Paddington's before joining me.

'So what d'you think?' whispered Karen across the table.

'The authentic British red phone kiosk outside is a bit worrying,' I confessed, 'and sitting in this room is rather like being condemned to inhabit a doll's house. But let's not prejudge.'

Paddington's was more than a tearoom. It also sold a bewildering array of British-theme souvenirs, such as Union Jack mugs, Buckingham Palace tea towels, Easter eggs filled with Smarties, Maltesers in packages large enough to feed Himalayan trekking parties, ceramics of quaint cottages and full-skirted milkmaids and Mrs Tiggywinkle, packets of tea and herbal infusions. The land of Canterbury Cathedral, Shakespeare, and Gazza had, in the eyes of its commercial ambassadors, been reduced to knick-knackery and trash. So I wasn't surprised that Paddington's notion of high tea was distinctly eccentric, a porridge of British tradition, American expectation, and old-fashioned gorging.

We began with rusklike toasts served with a pâté and a vinegary egg and dill mush. Then a selection of cold vegetables with a spinach dip – tasty and very Californian, but a dish that would be regarded as an abomination in any Dorset shoppe. After about two hours the next course arrived: soft, bland scones with cream. But Karen said firmly, and correctly, 'This is not my idea of clotted cream.' When I called for the bill, Karen pointed out to the English owner that we had not been offered the final course of the set tea described as 'petite fours'. This consisted of a disgusting biscuit neither of us would even taste, and a small, slushy rum truffle. Magnificent cream-stuffed pastries might have redeemed the establishment after its attempt to bill me for a course we hadn't consumed and wouldn't have known about had it not been for Karen's sharp memory for menus.

Karen is practised at this, as she fills in the time between acting jobs with restaurant reviewing. She came out to Los Angeles from New York as a student and now says she wouldn't, couldn't live anywhere else. Eight years ago, her boyfriend, Mr X, suggested she should make use of public access television. Her boyfriend does have a real name but as a successful television actor, he prefers to keep a few steps away from the glaring spotlight of publicity in which Karen loves to sizzle. Public access television is a fancy way of saying you rent air time and then use the spot in any way you wish. Karen offers the viewer autobiographical monologue loosely structured around restaurant reviews.

She is now a veteran of the genre, having taped well over 200 half-hour shows. She has a following that consists of distant fans as well as a small group of devoted friends who provide a small live audience. Karen is rarely lost for words – let's be frank: never lost for words – so there is hardly any need to edit her outpourings. What the invited audience hears is what the viewers get. There is no script, so Karen lets her imagination wend and swerve. Sometimes she tries to get to a point, but more often than not she'll wander off the subject, never to return. It hardly matters. After eight years Karen has become something of an institution, and has appeared on shows even more illustrious than her own by the likes of Johnny Carson and Merv Griffin.

Her fans speculate incessantly about the identity of Mr X, to whom she coyly refers in her monologues. An acquaintance spotted her lunching with her agent and immediately rushed to the conclusion that this man was none other than Mr X. The conclusion was a false one, but even though I am not really at liberty to do so, I shall now reveal that Mr X is in fact –

'At the end of my show we give out a phone number so that people can contact me. Not my private number of course. This means I have lots of fans, but I have to tell you that people either love my show or they hate it. One woman called all the way from New York to tell me I was a fishwife. A fishwife. Can you believe it?' I couldn't. This graceful, dramatic, bright-eyed young woman with a distinct resemblance to Cher ('Lots of people say I look like Cher') – a fishwife?

I noticed that Karen had long, brightly painted nails. You may think this is a trivial matter, but the nail business in America grosses $3.5. billion annually. I asked whether she knew anything about the subject.

'Everything.'

'Oh good. There are so many nail salons in my neighbourhood and I'm curious about the mysteries. What's acrylic nails?'

'That's when the nail is extended outwards with acrylic using your real nail as a base.'

'And sculpture nails?'

'Similar. I'm not sure. Similar but for shorter nails.'

'And what's a fill?'

'Well. As your nail grows, a gap opens up between the base of the nail and the acrylic overlay. Twice monthly this will have to be filled in, and that's a fill. The problem with acrylics is that it turns you into a slave to the nail salon. You have to maintain them. If you try to remove them, that can wreck your nails for years. But the good thing about them is that they're very tough and never break.'

'Paper wraps? Juliette wraps?'

'That's where a fibre paper is wrapped around the nail and glued over it. This reinforces the nail, and it becomes more thick and full. After a month or so it could soak off and you'll have to repair it. The best wrap is silk, which uses a liquid silk of fibres in a creamy base.'

'Tips?'

'Simple. They're just projecting nails glued onto your existing nail. Quick. Give me your notebook. I have to write down some directions for you.'

I handed it over. What could this be? An assignation? She scribbled away, then, tight-lipped, returned the notebook to me. I read: 'I think this is a famous rock musician to your left. Look later and tell me what you think.' I glanced casually to my left. A man was seated at the next table sipping a cup of tea; he had the conventional number of limbs and ears but his hair was beginning to thin. A short while later, he left. Even superstars like a nice cup of tea.

Karen stared at me intently, blue-green eyes blazing from within their frame of long black hair. 'So what d'you think?'

'It's embarrassing, I know, but the last rock musician I'd be likely to recognise probably hung up his guitar for good in about 1970.'

She shook her head impatiently.

'Colin. That's his name. English group.'

'Er, let me think. Herman's Hermits? Dave Clark Five?'

'No, no, no. I've got it! Men at Work. That's it. Australian.'

'Uh huh.'

'So what were we talking about?'

'Your fans.'

'Oh yes. I was going to tell you, I was in the supermarket one day and this woman came up to me. "Are you the woman who has that TV show?" she asked me. Yes, I am, I told her. She said she didn't recognize me at first because I wasn't on TV.'

'But you are on TV.'

'No, she meant at the supermarket. Isn't that weird? People think that if you're on TV you wander round with your head inside a box.'

While we were talking, while Karen was talking, women kept arriving with large boxes tied with ribbon. They wriggled past our table into the back section of Paddington's, which was separated from the rest of the tea room by a counter filled with Royal Family mugs and boxes of liquorice allsorts, and took their places at a long table laid with cups and plates and dishes. I asked Karen what was going on.

'It's a shower. Either a wedding shower or a baby shower. I think it's a baby shower.'

'How can you tell?'

'I heard one of the women say April. That must be when the baby's due.'

'That could also be the name of one of the women.'

'April the ninth?'

'You're right, an unlikely name.'

'Of course these days you can have a wedding shower and a baby shower combined.'

'A sad reflection on our times.'

'Stephen, I need your notebook again. God, this scone is so mediocre . . .'

She scribbled, handed back the notebook. I read her latest bulletin from the world of stardom: 'I have to check this out further,' she had written, 'but I'm sure that's Diane Keaton.' She jerked her head towards the door.

I could see what she meant: two women were seated at a table near the entrance. One of them had a turned-up nose, a gently wrinkled face, a quiet manner, baggy clothes, a rounded loose-fitting hat . . . The profile was right, but face on I was more doubtful. When we left, Karen took another discreet but careful look and, outside, turned to me. 'You're right. That wasn't Diane

Keaton. What I want to know is why a woman with a strong physical resemblance to Diane Keaton should dress the way Keaton looked in movies made fifteen years ago.'

I agreed that it was a puzzle, for the woman was evidently impersonating Annie Hall. Of course we expect movie stars to look like their roles because few of us ever get to see them first thing in the morning, cigarette in mouth, night-smear in the corners of the eyes, depilatory cream on the chin. And the women probably look even worse.

'I mean, people say I look like Cher, but that wouldn't make me want to go around dressed the way Cher dresses.'

'You'd be arrested, for a start.'

'Would you like to come to the taping of my next show?'

'Karen, I wouldn't miss it for anything.'

'Where's your car? This is mine.'

'Mine's around the corner from those red awnings.'

'I'll drive you.'

'It's only fifty yards. I think I can walk it.'

'It's no trouble. I can drive you.'

But I persisted in my quaint English ways, and put one foot in front of the other. It took me about ten minutes to cover the distance because I decided to jay-walk across La Cienega, and found myself stranded in the centre lane while fifty other drivers swooshed past in both directions. Karen waved as she sped towards Melrose. I could see her receding licence plate: MONOLOG.

4

SUFFER THE LITTLE GERBILS

My journeys downtown could be undertaken swiftly on one of the freeways, but a more enjoyable route took me along Wilshire, a boulevard founded in 1895 and soon to become the city's most famous street. As long ago as 1949 someone called Ralph Hancock wrote a 310-page encomium entitled *Fabulous Boulevard*. Today Wilshire reflects the patchiness of the unplanned city as a whole, but it still contains vestiges of its decades of greatest glory, the 1920s and 1930s. Even then it recognised the primacy of the motor car. At the surviving department stores along Wilshire, the main entrances face the parking lot at the rear. The street facade was a composition to be admired in passing.

From the coast Wilshire passes through nondescript sections of Santa Monica, beneath the anonymous towers of Westwood, through downtown Beverly Hills, and into Los Angeles proper as a thoroughly commercial street. Beyond the County Art Museum, I would come to a handful of surviving Art Deco structures, of which my favourite was the gorgeous Security Pacific Bank Building of 1929, a rich sleek design in black and gold terracotta, a cigarette box of a building filled with money instead of Virginias.

Residential streets cross the boulevard, some of them modest, others sumptuous indeed. Just to the left on Lucerne is a simply vast house in what Americans perversely call the Queen Anne style. The Californian version, loosely modelled on the ideas of the British architect Norman Shaw, is an excuse for turrets, verandahs, conical roofs, and immense sash windows, all assembled with a wilful but pleasing disregard for symmetry. American Queen Anne is a compendium of volumes, sometimes balanced but more usually contrasted, presenting domestic values on a deliberately overblown scale.

Two classy Art Deco blocks follow, the sea-green Wiltern building on the corner of Western and the Bullock's Wilshire department store at the junction with Vermont. From the car park you enter Bullock's beneath a vast porte-cochere, its ceiling painted in 1929 by Herman Sachs with a visual ode to modern transportation. The interior is Art Deco at its most stylish. In the perfume hall, mottled marble panels are laid in diagonal slabs across the walls, and in between the panels bronze-framed Art Deco panels screen fluorescent lighting. The jewellery section has remarkable, vaguely Cubist wall reliefs among luxurious tropical wood veneers. Even the lifts are defiantly monumental, their heavy metal doors embellished with brass inlays and overlays reminiscent of handmade leather bindings.

Such splendours in a commercial building not only advertised the store's munificent exclusivity but also applauded the taste of its patrons. But the rich deserted these streets for the calmer suburbs of the Westside decades ago. Today Koreatown is around the corner, and further east are Latino sections, not all of them wholesome. The Bullock's Wilshire has become a relic, immaculately preserved but no longer part of a coherent commercial strip.

Just after Hoover, Wilshire gives up. Around MacArthur Park the neighbourhood is too poor to aspire to glamour, and beyond the Harbor Freeway, one of the concrete moats around downtown Los Angeles, Wilshire simply grinds to a halt. Yet the environs of MacArthur Park were once a fashionable suburb, and a few splendid houses remain as sporadic survivals in communities that lack the means with which to care for them. Fantastical structures are now divided into flats and warrens for recurrent waves of immigrants. On South Bonny Brae wooden houses from the 1890s sport splendidly carved window frames not enhanced by peeling paint and rickety verandahs. The eclectic Wright-Mooers house is the wildest, with rococo swirls in front of the top balcony and a Cambodian turret all imposed on an essentially Queen Anne design. Only along Alvarado Terrace, a landscaped terrace of seven mansions some blocks south of Wilshire, are older houses properly cared for. Mostly built in 1902, their styles vary from Queen Anne to Mission Revival to English Tudor, often combined within the same design.

Equally close to downtown but further north is the district around Echo Park, probably the loveliest public gardens in a city notoriously short of them. Tall palms and eucalyptus shade the children playing along the edge of a lotus-studded, fountain-freckled lake. Quite close to the Hollywood Freeway the Angeleno Heights district is rich in old wooden houses, some of them in the eclectic Queen Anne style, others showing more Craftsman influences; the most intriguing offer a highly fantastical architectural coloratura of gorgeous oriental-style screens and fanned shingling.

From here it is only a few blocks to downtown Los Angeles, a most perplexing part of the city. About twenty years ago, when other run-down city centres elsewhere in America were being treated to a dose of regeneration, the same process was lavished on Los Angeles. Office skyscrapers and modern hotels rose up, transforming shabby commercial streets into gleaming canyons of glass and metal. The old residential district of Bunker Hill in the northern part of downtown was razed and replaced by concert halls and public buildings. The western parts of downtown are bordered by the Harbor and Hollywood freeways which impose concrete barriers between the downtown banks and the mostly wretched residential areas on the outer side.

The imposition of office complexes on a century-old street pattern has destroyed the grid system and replaced it with a chaos of one-way streets, ramps, and dead ends. To get where you are going you have to know how to get there. The Westin Bonaventure Hotel is one of the most handsome structures in the area, with its rounded towers bulging like cable wire from the central core. But it is placed amid a nightmarish jumble of skyways, multistorey car parks, and ramps. There is no room for pedestrians here, and a stroll down South Flower Street, close to the hotel, is one of the most depressing experiences in Los Angeles.

Moving eastwards from this mostly rebuilt section of downtown, you come to streets such as Broadway that preserve some of the older buildings that once invested the district with a raffish glamour. Broadway has now been appropriated by the Latino community, as have many of the neighbouring streets such as Olympic, where indistinguishable clothes emporia spill onto the pavement. Just off Broadway, making a swift transition from bustle and energy to inertia and stumbling despair, is Los Angeles' Skid Row, mired in a squalor that has no place in a country as rich as the United States. The move, so sudden, from corporate anonymity to the barrio is extraordinary both because of the swiftness with which it is accomplished and because there seems to be an invisible barrier between the two. The two districts are side by side, yet utterly separated. One is lifeless, the other too much alive; one is impenetrable except to those with reserved parking places in subterranean car parks, and the other is best reached by bus or on foot, since the traffic on Broadway is thick and reluctant to budge.

Each new building has to make a statement, and so each parcel of post-modernist architectural flurries is a rival to its neighbours. A downtown tower is designed to stand out from the pack around it, not to blend in. Thus the corporate district is stylistically restless and bludgeoning. Harmony is beside the point, and thus the few old buildings left standing by the developers, such as the California Club and the Public Library, have to fend for themselves as best they can. Their original scale may, in the context of the downtown of the 1920s, have been imposing, but today they are dwarfed by the sheaths of glass and steel that rise on all sides.

You have to work hard to find the original downtown sumptuousness, but some of it does survive. Step inside 811 West 7th Street, and you'll find a Moorish-Romanesque galleried extravaganza decorated with mosaics, geometrical carvings, bronze showcases, cast-iron lanterns, and a flower-filled fountain. Or enter the Oviatt Building of 1928 at 617 South Olive. The lobby, screened from the street by a complex of iron and glass, is a splendidly restored example of Art Deco. There is a wonderful and complex use of mirrors and glass (by none other than Lalique) and marble, yet the effect is not, as one might expect, busy and distracting, but airy and graceful, consciously importing Gallic chic into an avenue of American braggadocio. The Garfield Building at 408 West 8th Street is equally superb, its lobby a cave of purple and dark green marble and gilt friezes.

The stylistic adventurousness and assurance of these interiors was not inherited by the developers and architects who either tore them down or designed new buildings all around them. Next door to 811 West 7th Street is the cream-coloured Home

Savings of America building, a box with recessed surfaces and corner turrets. Its mansard roof, a cliché of pretentious suburban mass design, forms a backdrop to tall gabled windows. Reacting against the faceless masks of the glass boxes of the 1960s and 1970s, the architects have here opted for a mock-decorative style that embroiders and twiddles and makes playful historicist references. The result is frivolous and structurally dishonest.

A few yards away, on Figueroa, the Seventh Street Market Place of 1986 tries to take heed of the criticism that corporate downtown lacks shopping areas for its thousands of office workers – other than the merry but alien mayhem of the Latino markets of Broadway and Olympic. Here developers made amends, devising this hole in the ground that rises through several levels linked by escalators to street level. The Market Place is an open-air mini-mall of no real architectural distinction, yet at least designed on a scale more appropriate for human beings than the grim towers around it. In this dehumanised townscape there is something grimly apposite in forcing shoppers to descend into a crater in search of a bunch of flowers or a Danish pastry.

One would imagine that this competitive, huddled, profoundly enclosed downtown area reflected American corporate capitalism at its most aggressively self-effacing. The joke is that by 1985 three-quarters of the towers were foreign-owned, and the figure has probably grown since then. Billions of dollars of foreign investment, mostly from Japan but also from Canada and Britain, have financed the burgeoning of downtown Los Angeles. The Japanese takeover of many of Southern Californian golf courses is a tangible expression of this Oriental love affair with the west coast of America, but the domination is far more complete in these few blocks that comprise the business centre of California. By 1988 three of the state's largest banks were Japanese-owned, and 600 Japanese firms were operating in Los Angeles alone. Radical observers such as Mike Davis, whose book *City of Quartz* presents a dark and occasionally paranoid vision of Los Angeles, argue that 'control over the Los Angeles economy is being alienated, with incalculable consequences, to power centers six thousand miles away'. Other commentators would presumably hail a new era of cooperation between Japanese and American financial interests, a mutually beneficial hands-across-the-water expression of the indivisibility of the Pacific Rim.

After the yawn-inducing office towers of corporate downtown,

Broadway offers relief in the form of happily conflicting visual delights. The avenue is a festival of eclecticism, borrowing styles from other cultures and then trumping them with absurd extravagance. At 929 Broadway you'll find an unusual example of Spanish Gothic flamboyant, and a block away, at 849, the Eastern Building, the best Art Deco skyscraper in the downtown area. It's wonderfully sleek, with vertical bands of blue-green terracotta giving an elegant sheen to its thrust; its ornament of deep blue and gold is not tacked on to provide aimless visual variety – as in the HSA Building – but is integral to the harmoniousness of the structure.

Buildings that would be laughable in any other context, such as the Churrigueresque (a term named after José de Churriguera, who devised the ornamental style in about 1915) Million-Dollar Theater of 1918 with its extraordinary pendants dropping daringly from the top storeys, make a joyful contribution to a bustling street. Across the street the superlative Bradbury building demonstrates that it wasn't the Hyatt hotel chain that invented the atrium. The Bradbury, designed by George Wyman in 1893, has at its core an immense skylit court, knit together visually with gorgeous ironwork, lifts in open cages, and elegant staircases linking the galleries.

Almost next door to the Million-Dollar is the Grand Central Market, a far cry from the sterilised decorousness of Westside supermarkets such as Ralph's. You enter past a phalanx of shoeshine boys, and can gather strength for the shopping ahead by pausing at stalls where you can wolf down bowls of Chinese noodles or fried rice for under two dollars a portion. In the market hall itself there's a tortilleria and stands selling every known variety of Mexican chilli, mole, tamarind, and other spices. You'll find fruit and vegetable stalls, of course; buckets and sacks of filberts and pecans and seeds, dried pears and figs; slippery wet slabs on which gleaming fish bloodily flop. Only the butchers' brutally hacked steaks and wrinkled chicken parts, and the bakeries' flabby breads in plastic wrappings and bloated muffins and pastries are disappointing, incursions of standardised American foods into an emporium that is otherwise entirely Hispanic, as is the clientele.

One might expect that the Cathedral of St Vibiana, which is just off Main Street on East Second Street, would be an arresting structure, and no doubt the cupola'd tower did make an impression when it was built in the 1870s. But today the 3000-seater vaguely neo-renaissance cathedral is under the thumb of the steep milk-chocolate and Pacific-blue glass skins of the skyscrapers behind it. At Mass one Sunday morning I was surprised to find the place half empty. Although the congregation was mostly Latino the service was conducted in English, presumably to accommodate the handful of Anglos and Asians who also worship here regularly. A verger explained that the church had become marooned in an area now almost wholly commercial, and thus its catchment area had shrunk. Most Catholics preferred to attend neighbourhood churches where services would be conducted in their own language.

I had entered the cathedral from the Second Street car park. But on leaving by a side door I found myself in a small garden, from which I gazed through locked gates onto Main Street. There I saw, spaced out every few yards, the prone or seated bodies of Skid Row residents, mostly black, some beneath blankets, some perched on the kerb. Crutches were propped against the wall; a jacket was slung over a parking meter. One man, in white shirt and dark tie and with a Walkman arched over his head, was incongruously seated between two bums. Everybody was lined up on the west side of the street to catch the morning sunlight, which might dissipate their pallor but not their irredeemable distress. That there had been habitation along the east side adjoining the cathedral was confirmed by my nose, which was being tickled by a cocktail of urine and rotting food. Main Street itself, scarcely travelled, was awash in paper, bottles, cans, as though its torpid residents found comfort among their lingering detritus. Behind me the cathedral garden blazed with scarlet azaleas and magnolias in full waxy bloom, but in front of me, screened by the gates of the inaccessible church, was a line-up of human dereliction. In the sunlight it did not strike me as excessively miserable. There was conviviality among the filth, and the sleepy tranquillity of a Sunday morning converted the sidewalk into a kind of concrete park. This, presumably, was Skid Row putting its best foot forward.

I walked out onto Second Street. There was no sign here of the squalor splayed out on the neighbouring street. From here I could look up towards the elegantly monumental City Hall with its ziggurat roof. For thirty years after it was built in 1928, this was the tallest building in the city, the sole exception to an ordinance outlawing the construction of buildings taller than 150 feet. I walked east a short distance to Little Tokyo, a community founded in 1885, although most of the buildings are recent. Behind the anonymous New Otani Hotel, which caters specifically to a Japanese clientele, are small-scale paved malls such as Japanese Village Plaza and Little Tokyo Mall, packed with restaurants, bookshops, bakeries, boutiques, and Buddhist temples. These malls are irregular in layout, suggesting a village-like enclave within the stern grid of downtown Los Angeles. Within another plaza across the street two large boulders turned out to be a statue by Noguchi. Clambering children clung to its side like inefficient limpets.

The Japanese are not newcomers to Los Angeles. In the 1920s and 1930s they dominated the farming and fishing industries in the region. Because Japanese-Americans are well integrated into the host community, Little Tokyo is less of a tourist spot than Chinatown, instead offering its resources to local and visiting Japanese. The Yaohan Plaza mall debouches into the thoroughly Japanese Yaohan supermarket and video shop, and the Tokai Bank of California has a branch in the plaza. This is the place to come to consult Dr Rocky Lee at his Pain Control Sports Medicine office. Most of the shops are those one might find in any suburban mall, but there is also a Japanese restaurant, a huge Japanese-language bookshop, and a shop selling bridal wear in Nipponese and American styles. The most bizarre hybrid is a bakery that offers advice in illiterate French on its windows: '*S'il vous reste de pain pour le lendemain, vous la mettrez dans un torchon hunmide . . .*' The goods on display weren't recognisably French either and the most prominent items on the racks were square white loaves, sliced and wrapped in plastic.

A few blocks away the Hollywood Freeway forms the northern boundary of downtown. Beyond lie Union Station, the Pueblo Historic District, and then Chinatown. The present-day Chinatown was reconstructed in 1938, a few blocks from its original site. Today only a handful of the Angelenos of Chinese descent live here. There have been Chinese residents of the city since the 1850s, yet their lives were made wretched by discrimination, threats of deportation, and murderous racial riots directed against them. Their descendants have moved to suburbs such as Monterey Park and Alhambra in such numbers that they now account for about half the population.

Union Station is a delightful building, its existence barely justified by the infrequent train service. A cream-coloured structure with rust-toned trimmings, it has the proportions of a large church. The decorative details – pantiled roofs and painted tiles – are Spanish Colonial Revival. The interior is more demonstrative, with cool tile and stone paving, flying-saucer chandeliers, and deep armchairs for waiting passengers, furnishings that would be considered unsuitable for modern termini on the grounds that their comfort could persuade passengers – or, worse, non-passengers – to stay put. The restaurant is in a separate building, linked to the passenger hall by a lofty arcade that crosses pleasant formal gardens complete with hedges and tiled benches.

Across the street lies the Historic District, located close to where the original pueblo of Los Angeles once stood. From its central plaza you enter Olvera Street, which is paved with tiles so as to simulate the supposed style of a Mexican street. The district's claims to authenticity are essentially bogus, for Olvera Street is little more than a theme park, anthologising the more kitschy elements of Latino culture along its hundred yards. In the 1920s the city had intended to raze this slummy alley in a slummy district. But Mrs Christine Sterling, a local worthy, decided to save Olvera Street by transforming it into a Mexican enclave. This undisguised effort to create a tourist attraction has been a resounding success. The lane is filled with stalls selling leather goods to tempt souvenir-thirsty tourists, while the much-restored brick buildings have been remodelled as cafés, clothing shops, and galleries. What little space remains is taken over by mariachi bands and food stalls. The crowds are dense because they have to be, and the atmosphere is raucous but cheerful.

Some of the Olvera Street buildings are not nearly as old as they look. Others are. The Avila Adobe dates from 1818, making it the oldest surviving structure in Los Angeles. The interior has been restored and furnished in an appropriate Spanish Colonial style. Wooden arcades provide shade in the courtyard. Like most of the early houses of Los Angeles, this is an adobe, constructed from mud bricks mixed with straw after they had been left to dry and solidify in the California sun. The oldest brick building in Los Angeles, the Pelanconi house of 1850, stands a little further up the street and is now a café.

In the plaza there's usually a mob around the fruit stand selling freshly chopped melons and pineapples, succulent grapes and egg-sized plums. On the south side of the plaza stands the Italian-Renaissance-style Pico House of 1870, its speckled stucco masquerading as granite. This was the city's first modern hotel, sumptuously decorated, and equipped with speaking tubes that allowed orders to be transmitted from the rooms to the front desk. On Sundays a corner of the plaza is invaded by well-dressed Latino evangelists, a singularly depressing sight. That wintry Protestants should turn to the excitements of high-wire, hot-coal Christianity is comprehensible, just, but that Latinos, with their easy access to image-laden, festival-rich, saint-strewn Catholicism, should turn instead to the haranguings and abasements of evangelism is perplexing indeed. But there they are, holding up their banners while a female preacher, in corporate black suiting, declaims with one eye on the text and the other on her melon-sucking, popcorn-chomping temporary congregation.

Across Main Street stands the church of Nuestra Señora La Reina de Los Angeles, which can accommodate relays of up to 13,000 worshippers on a busy Sunday, and evangelists crumple against this kind of competition. The arcaded courtyard is filled with Mexican food stands, the church gift shop, and a raffle stall, and crowded with christening parties clad in dazzling whites. A grotto of Our Lady of Guadalupe is thrown in for good measure, and ranks of candles in colourfully painted glass jars generate superfluous heat. The buff-coloured church was built in the 1860s, although an earlier church had stood on the same site. Even in the middle of the afternoon it was packed with a congregation that included babies on bottles, teenyboppers with wildly eccentric hairstyles, as well as more sober-looking families.

Tourists do visit the Historic District, but most visitors are Hispanic, who come here as an alternative to driving out to the beach or picnicking in a favourite park. In my experience most middle-class white Angelenos are notionally aware of the existence of this place but have never set foot here. It is at its most weird and singular the Saturday before Easter, during the annual Blessing of the Animals. The Latino faithful bring to Olvera Street their pets – dogs, cats, fish, mice, birds, iguanas and other reptiles, turtles, gerbils – which are individually blessed by water-sprinkling priests. Any small animal on the loose in downtown Los Angeles would soon be minced by traffic, but here for one day they are offered anarchic immunity.

5

TRASHITECTURE

A new dawn, a new day, a new resolution. No more morning TV shows for idiots. There was a radio by my bed, and I was going to find a radio show for idiots. I thirsted for news. The *Los Angeles Times* was delivered to my door daily, but before my cups of coffee, I didn't have the strength to lift it off the mat. The paper is plump with sections – Real Estate, Lifestyle, Business, Sport, Calendar – but thin on news. It covers a single story or part of the world exhaustively – the paper grew tremendously excited about Yugoslav provinces for a week, then they vanished from view to be replaced by Somalians or other unfortunates – but there was no regular sweep across the world.

There was a public radio station on the left of the FM band, but the droning worthiness of its reports sent me back to sleep. No public radio broadcaster ever gets excited. Starving Kurds, the savings and loan scandal, rebellious South African townships, all were treated with the same bland earnestness. A flick away was a lefty news station, quite a rarity in Southern California. But the morning show consisted of chat with a gruff elderly crust called Charles, who would allow each caller about one minute flat to voice an opinion on the latest world outrage, before switching to another call with the catchphrase: 'This is Charles, talk to me.' I couldn't stand it. I made the long journey across the bands to 1051 FM, where constant classical music was interrupted only by frequent ads. I could at least shave to Haydn.

Heading today for the richlands, my Geo bumbled along Santa Monica Boulevard, which splits Beverly Hills in two, with the business district and apartment blocks to the south and mansions along broad streets to the north. I turned north up Crescent, crossed Sunset, and continued to Elden Way, passing a parked Rolls-Royce with a sign in its back window, 'Expensive But Worth It', which made me think there was something to the class war after all. At the foot of the drive that led to the Robinson house – a mansion now open to the public by appointment – a girl with a clipboard inquired: 'What is the name of the party?' I parked, then I walked to the patio, where the guide was waiting. Packs of gift cards depicting the mansion were on sale – or rather, they may be pocketed in exchange for a $5 'donation', that being a new genteelism used by people who want your money but are too nice to ask you for it.

Mr Robinson owned a department store in downtown Los Angeles and bought himself an estate here in 1911, just before Beverly Hills was properly developed. The site was steep and had to be extensively landscaped and the gardens, which are the estate's principal claim to pride, were created from scratch. The grounds are replete with magnolias and camellias, azaleas and rhododendrons. The residence is a sprawling reinforced-concrete ranch house, frenchified with rooftop balustrades. Mrs Robinson lived here into her hundredth year and in 1974 bequeathed the estate to the city of Beverly Hills, which declined the gift, so the house and gardens are now cared for by the Los Angeles Arboretum. Behind the house a lawn carpets the only flat surface on the estate and leads to the pool and its poolhouse. The borders along the lawn are lined with cypresses and splashed with marguerites and stock. On either side of the lawn brick paths and steps wind up and down, linking a series of small patios, some of which have fountains, and the various corners of the gardens. I marvelled at the tree fuchsias and macadamia trees, and tiptoed beneath immensely tall palms and contorted banyan trees. At eye level I moved through a chorus line of ferns, frumpish aspidistras, and kaffir lilies.

The only male on the tour, I found myself in the company of middle-aged women who kept comparing horticultural notes. I was dazzled by their knowledge, setting this Australian king palm off against another specimen in Florida or Brazil. I shared their enthusiasm for the gardens, and envied their scholarship, but was at a loss to understand why they marvelled at the house, which struck me as ordinary. Standardised wood panelling and a portrait of a woman with pearls round her neck seemed to impress them no end, and they tweeted with excitement in the service wing, asking the guide where the dishes were kept, and admiring the size of the laundry room.

Driving back down Elden Way, I could hardly fail to notice a new house of stupendous vulgarity nearing completion. 1017 Crescent is a debased neo-rococo French chateau with a stone fountain in the forecourt. The act of imitation had coarsened the design: a country chateau had been squeezed onto a town lot. The gates were open, and the foreman allowed me to look inside the house. The hall was dominated by an immense double staircase with bronze balustrades that swept up through two storeys. But its fate was to be inhabited by men in yellow golf slacks and women in track suits, rather than Monsieur le Comte in silk coats, breeches and buckled shoes. The house, even though bogus, would always mock its owners.

'That's something, eh?' said the foreman.

'It's big. It's also ugly. This is one of the ugliest houses I've ever seen.'

He looked surprised. 'I think it's beautiful architecture.'

'Architecture?'

'Only I guess it's in the wrong neighbourhood.'

Walking out of the gate I saw opposite me a rambling brick house set above a large sloping lawn. It looked oddly familiar, and I realised that this was the house, 1014 Crescent, where I had stayed during my first visit to Los Angeles. Zsa Zsa Gabor had provided a pool, snacks, an impromptu basement disco, and motoring services, but I hadn't slept at her house. Instead I, and three British companions, had flopped down in a large airy room above the garage of a Beverly Hills mansion. Our hosts had been a film producer, his beautiful delicate wife with platinum-blonde hair, and their six young children, whose idea of good sport had been to raid our quarters early in the morning and jump on us as we slept. I'm not sure I ever knew why this delightful family had offered hospitality to four English students.

Seeing the house again I marvelled at the ease with which we had climbed the American social heights. Then as now, nothing commands such awe as the presence of a star. Thomas Mann, Stravinsky, Schoenberg, and countless other giants of European culture had lived in Los Angeles, but who were they in comparison with an Errol Flynn, a Bette Davis, a Marilyn Monroe? In those pre-Manson times, teenagers were not to be feared. Aged eighteen, I was at liberty to wander round Zsa Zsa's house, peering at her photographs, memorabilia, and gewgaws, raiding her refrigerator, and sunning myself in her garden. I can conceive of no circumstances in which I could do that kind of thing today. Age brings attributes, accomplishments, ambition, and motive, all of which require you to define who you are and what you want.

In Beverly Hills the local hotel was built before the town after which it is named. Early in this century, parts of Los Angeles, notably Pasadena, spawned huge resort hotels that were patron-ised by Easterners in search of winter sunshine. Unlike most of these hotels, the large pink palace of the Beverly Hills Hotel has survived intact. The flower-filled lobby, as pink as the exterior, is quintessentially Californian, with graceful pilasters in the shape of palm trees, and a ubiquitous wallpaper motif of large lazy banana leaves. The main restaurant, offering California-French cuisine, is self-consciously glitzy, listing dishes under the rubric 'Favorites of the Stars', whose tastes fortunately coincide with those of well-heeled guests. The main focus of attention, how-ever, is not the restaurant but the Polo Lounge, where agents and moguls come to make their deals. With its pink and green decor it's a charming room, and its tables flow out onto the patio, where a venerable Brazilian pepper tree provides shade.

Alternatively you can haggle over your contract by the pool, or more surreptitiously in one of the cabanas set back from the water. Fifty-two phone extensions allow you to receive private calls in a public place. There is no point being a celebrity or a power-broker in Los Angeles if you can't occasionally take a bow in public. Exposure to the adoring gaze has of course to be rationed and monitored, and the hotel staff are expert at the arts of table placement and cabana reservation, so that the right balance of awesome presence and protective privacy can be maintained.

Behind the main blocks of the hotel are the luxurious bunga-lows. Set among neat gardens, they are accessible from the street, so your limousine can drop you off at the path and save you from exposing yourself to the vulgar view in the lobby.

Greta Garbo once flitted through these grounds. The hotel, although not even as old as the century, has gathered its lore, its luminaries, its legends, in emulation of the hoarier Ritzes and

Savoys of Europe. Yet in the early years of the century Beverly Hills was no more than a lima bean farm. Back in 1854 the site, then the Rancho Rodeo de la Aguas, changed hands for $500. In 1905 the land was bought up by a syndicate that hoped to find oil beneath its acres. They found enough to sink two wells, which are both still in production, but this wasn't enough to justify the cost of the purchase. To recoup their investment the owners decided to develop the site as a fashionable suburb. Their strategy was ingenious, since they chose to build the hotel first to establish the reputation of the area. They also had the good sense to enlist the distinguished firm of Olmsted to landscape the property. When Ernie Hobden came out to Los Angeles in 1911 the Beverly Hills Hotel was still a building site. Its completion certainly helped the sale of lots around it, but it was not until the end of the decade that Beverly Hills became the residence of choice of the high-fliers of the movie industry.

The estates higher up in the foothills of Beverly Hills were the most prestigious. Sprawling, inaccessible, private, they were lavish without necessarily being ostentatious. The first citizens of Beverly Hills, Douglas Fairbanks and Mary Pickford, bought and named the Pickfair estate in 1919, the fused name of their property reflecting their conjugal stability, itself the perfect association that Hollywood publicists sought between glamour and respectability. They certainly lived in great style but their mansion, while large, was no palace or castle. Others were less reticent. Harold Lloyd's 220-acre Greenacres estate encompassed not only a vast neo-Renaissance villa but immense gardens and a children's house. John Barrymore had his own zoo and aviary. The houses on the flats, between Santa Monica and Sunset, are the most visible and thus the most ostentatious. Later subdivisions, such as the Trousdale Estates along Loma Vista Drive in the hills, are open to the same charge. The Trousdale Estates were built on part of the former estate of the oil-rich Doheny family. Their neo-Tudor mansion, Greystone, is set in a beautiful 18-acre park that is open to visitors. When a later oilman, Armand Hammer, wanted to donate his formidable art collection to the city for display in Greystone, the city fathers, as usual, said no.

Much has been written about the excesses of Beverly Hills architecture, and much fun has been had by pointing to lapses of taste. Heavy wrought-iron gates with quasi-baroque designs open onto a short hook of a driveway and guard a house that is no mansion but a dinky box sprawled over a few thousand square feet. Squat functional gateposts support electrified iron lamps, a Viennese touch in a Mediterranean landscape. There is little sureness of eye or steadiness of hand; instead there has been excessive reliance on the smooth talk of ignorant interior decorators. Yet these absurd touches are usually compensated for, especially on hillside sites, by tumbling gardens of flowering shrubs and clumps of lilies rising above an undulating lake of ground cover. What rankles is when architecture is reduced to no more than a bundle of decorative effects to be employed at random, without outward reference or inward cohesion. At 9707 Yoakun stands a house with steep gables, windows of varying sizes and shapes, brass lamps in profusion, bells, pinnacles, and turrets, each feature simplified and degraded into a self-parody too witless even to recognise itself. Californian theme parks go in for this kind of thing, to provide a lowest common denominator that will evoke a specific atmosphere without suggesting too precisely any one location or period. The same principle extended to domestic architecture is a folly.

In Beverly Hills the need to impress is all too palpable. Size will do it, as will splendour, as will carefully calculated siting. Where imaginative or financial resources are limited, tricks can be employed to add gravitas to plodding design and tacky construction. It is the LA door that has provided some classic examples. It is based on the principle that a door should be the same height as the house. It is best visualised, as the architectural historian Robert Winter has remarked, as an upright paperclip. To provide enough area for it to make a suitable impression, the LA door is invariably a double door, with additional panels, often the same height as the doors themselves, over the bits that open. Its dramatic effect can be enhanced by placing it within a porch or canopy that is larger than the door itself. That other abomination of Beverly Hills trashitecture, the mansard roof, is particularly appropriate here, since the lower horizontal of the mansard can swoop to a level lower than the top of the doorframe. The whole point of the LA door is, of course, to make the house appear larger and grander than it is.

It would be puritanical to dismiss all mogul house design. Beverly Hills would be worse off without some of its more fanciful examples of filmset architecture. On the flats, at 516 North Walden, is the Spadena House, built in 1921. The house is

misshapen, intentionally. With its needlelike gables, precipi-
tously shingled roof, tall chimneys, lead-paned windows, and
confected garden within a quaint picket fence, the house is pure
Hansel and Gretel. Like many of the fantastical houses in Beverly
Hills and Hollywood, it takes its fictional source seriously and
thus gives new life to an imaginary existence. The result may not
be great architecture but it has wonderful integrity and, in this
case, menacing humour too.

The commercial district of Beverly Hills has no redeeming
quirkiness, but the Civic Center, just east of the shopping zone,
is municipal design of remarkable quality. The buildings and
towers seem too large to serve this small community of 30,000,
but as an independent municipality, Beverly Hills has to provide
its own schools, water supply, and policemen. The school system
is its pride and joy, and many families move to Beverly Hills not
only for the prestige of the address, but because children can be
well educated within the public system rather than at expensive
private schools.

The Civic Center was built in 1931, focused around a tall tower
with a tiled cupola, blending 1930s Streamline Moderne with
strongly Hispanic elements. Over the last decade it has been
expanded, and there is a Roman splendour to the newly created
elliptical courtyards. The additions maintain the somewhat
hybrid stylistic individuality of the 1930s structures, but do so in
a modern idiom, which is highly successful. Yet driving through
the Center, I hardly ever saw a human being. It was as empty as
a stage set at dawn. Any expectation that the Civic Center would
perform some social function as a forum for the citizenry has
proved false. The rich and leisured of Beverly Hills do not
congregate in plazas and courtyards close to the firehouse and
police station. Instead they sit by their pools, jog across the flats,
drive about in their cars, do lunch, or go shopping. Standing
about in togas is not their idea of a good time. Angelenos as a
whole find the concept of a public space, other than the beach,
bizarre. It's no different downtown, where the open spaces of
MacArthur Park or Pershing Square are populated almost exclusively by down-and-outs.

The outrageous prices and garish decor of the smart shops of
Rodeo Drive or Beverly Drive have not been an unmixed blessing
for Beverly Hills. Yet, as happens so often in Los Angeles, the
most exclusive of places can also be the most accessible. True,

the armed guards are intimidating, and the lofty staff, who dare you not to wince when you read the $899 price tag on a simple leather handbag, can be even more so. The most exclusive shops won't even admit you without an appointment. But at the same time the city provides free two-hour parking at a number of lots close to the shopping streets. This welcoming attitude will puzzle Europeans, who know that the more exclusive the shopping area, the more determined are the authorities to make it difficult for you to get close to it. Not in Beverly Hills. Of course the motivation is commercial, but the thinking behind it is open-hearted, not snobbishly excluding.

Celebrities are occasionally seen darting out of their limos on their way to a fitting session, and I myself have been stared at and photographed by admiring Japanese tourists. You have to accept these attentions with a certain grace. One morning, when Rodeo was distinctly underpopulated, who do I see walking towards me but Ken Kercheval, better known to millions and his bank manager as Cliff Barnes of the heroic television series *Dallas*. Ken and I don't actually know each other but, aware of the celebrity code, we act as though we do, or at least Ken does, giving me a broad smile as our paths cross. He had a little paper carrier bag containing the tie or sunglasses he had just purchased, and I was on my way to The Sharper Image.

I disapprove of The Sharper Image, which is a shop devoted to the pointless. There is not a single item for sale here that anybody actually needs. This is where you shop for those who have everything. This is where you will find the trivial made epic, such as a full-size replica of a petrol pump from the 1930s or a suit of armour – $4000 each. For half that price you can have a massage bed or a massage chair, and – again, in a display of that easygoing openness that Beverly Hills blends with its expensive exclusivity – you can play with all these toys without being blasted by the management. Indeed, it's expected that browsers will spend at least half an hour being shaken up by a massage machine as it melodiously ripples and bumps and grinds, or fiddling with the electronic toys, the digital memo pads and instant translation machines.

The city even has its own supermarket. Juergensen's has moved out to Pasadena, but Mrs Gooch's remains, a discreet presence on Crescent. The walls are wood-panelled, as are the check-out counters, which resemble booths in a smart restaurant.

Mrs Gooch's is rigorously health-concious, eschewing harmful additives and favouring organically grown produce. Above each display of moist endives or radicchio or carrots a label indicates the number of calories per serving and lists the main nutrients, a boon to those who eat by numbers. 'Our meats', the signs declare, 'are prepared without the use of nitrates and nitrites.' In Europe organically grown vegetables tend to be unshapely, gnarled, and undersized, reflecting the struggle between vegetable growth and the unkindnesses of climate and predators. Not at Mrs Gooch's, where the displays of fruit and veg are impeccable, gleaming, inviting. Piles of red and green apples alternate in a rush of designer grocering. Prepared foods are mouthwatering: Szechuan tofu, salads, sandwiches using approved breads, and party platters for the impromptu office lunch. No need to make the long journey from office to shop: Mrs Gooch's supplies fax forms so you can speed your order through.

Yet a glance at the fish section shows that aesthetics has won over flavour. All the shellfish is frozen with the exception of bay scallops; all the fish is filleted except for trout, whitefish, and salmon. No sign here of the bloodied eyes, the slithery scales, and the guts on the floor beneath the fish stalls in Grand Central Market. The cheese section is equally disappointing, with few imported cheeses and most of those chilled down to impede their natural decay into aromatic, pungent, oozing ripeness.

Mrs Gooch's offers complimentary tours, as a flyer printed on recycled paper explains: 'Melissa Abehsera, your personal shopping guide, will share valuable information on different goods and products we carry so that you can reach your goal of feeling fit and looking your best.' Not a word about quality or taste.

I wandered down to the high school one afternoon just as the children were leaving for home. A few walked through the gates, past the security guards, and down the street; a few were met by mothers parked outside. But most of them had their own vehicles, which came thundering down the ramp towards the street. The fashions of the year in teenager personalised transportation are four-wheel-drive vehicles and curvacious Japanese sports cars, as well as junkier, funkier cars for the underprivileged. When these children grow up, they may well end up in the entertainment industry, and that means they will do lunch at Jimmy's, a chic restaurant just up the street from the school.

Walking past Jimmy's car park one lunchtime, I saw seven cars tucked away near the entrance. Five of them were Rolls-Royces – evidence that a deliberate decision is made to park the most ostentatious cars in the most favoured spots. Jimmy's thus colludes in the fawning fiction that the more expensive your car, the more important and deserving of consideration you must be. Such pitiful exhibitionism typifies Beverly Hills at its most infantile. (There is a crumb of comfort, however. Prosecuting United States attorneys in Los Angeles County have stated that the Rolls-Royce is the car that the great majority of Southern California's white-collar criminals prefer to own.)

As is well known, all this privilege and pampering and ceaseless gratification of whims is a highway to misery, though a more agreeable road than poverty and deprivation. The city caters richly to lives that have gone awry. Parallel to Rodeo Drive is Bedford Drive, known to the locals as Couch Canyon in tribute to the 200 or so psychotherapists who offer their consolations here in this Harley Street of ego, id, and derangement. Among the discreet office blocks and boutiques there used to be a place where you could drop off your kids while shopping or shrinking, but it has now closed.

No. 436 Bedford is a smart new building by the fashionable Jerde Partnership. Green windowframes set against a facade of pink stone face the street. Light fittings are attached to the exterior; dull gold in colour, they resemble wastepaper baskets and thus symbolise the wished-for repository for your therapist's weekly bills. Within are the offices of various outriders of medicine: psychiatrists, dermatologists, physiotherapists, and practitioners referred to as ob/gyn, so familiar a branch of medical peeking and probing that a contraction suffices to identify it.

In Suite 301 I found the Beverly Hills branch of BodyTone. An ad in the *LA Weekly* had encouraged readers to visit the facilities. Even though I enjoy a perfect body, I am not complacent and occasionally feel the need to work just a little harder at preserving its admirable proportions and suppleness. I already had an appointment at Los Angeles' most exclusive gym, but Body-Tone's ad suggested I could maintain perfect physical fitness without doing all the sweaty stuff: 'Gyms and health clubs can be intimidating, time-consuming, and not up to your sanitary standards, and if you're out of shape you risk muscle injury. So where do you go?' BodyTone had the answer: 'BodyTone is effortless, effective and designed for your lifestyle. So if you're willing to spend a few hours a week working on your muscles, our medical staff will personalize a program for you.'

I explained to the receptionist that I was interested in pursuing a course of effortless treatment. She led me off to a 'treatment room'. Here there was a couch and a machine the size of a stereo turntable. Attached to it were a dozen wires, and each outlet had separate controls. The wires were connected to pads resembling shoe heels.

'These are the flex and relax pads. We attach them to various parts of your body, your leg, your arm, your stomach, wherever there's some fat you want to lose or muscle you want to develop. Every three seconds the pads vibrate, and over a period of time you will lose weight and improve your physical fitness.'

'How long a period of time?'

'Each session is forty-five minutes, and we like you to come in three times a week.'

'How many weeks?'

'That depends on you and your physical requirements. I forgot to mention that we can also do an optional bodycomp analysis. I just did one for myself.'

'What does that do?'

'It's a body fat composition analysis that helps us to establish the right goals for you in terms of exercise programme and diet. You'll find it's covered by your insurance plan.'

'Hey, what's this about exercise? I thought I could dispense with that.'

'It's up to you. But the bodycomp analysis will give you a cardiovascular report that we can tie in to an exercise programme at the gym.'

'Do you have a proper gym?' I asked, affecting the insolence of the ultra-fit. I wanted her to understand that I was no novice at the Nautilus but an old hand at the pull and strain, the heave and grunt.

She showed it to me. Gleaming steel machines, with their cranks and pulleys, tubes and grips, seats and stirrups, rose from a thick carpet of green and pink. An overweight black man stumbled about on the treadmill, seeping sweat.

'Hey, Bette,' he puffed, 'bring me a towel, willya? Don't forget now. Thanks.' She ran out, ran back, towel in hand. Calvin mopped himself while keeping one eye on the television. The gym and the treatment rooms are all equipped with television, so you needn't miss your favourite laugh-track while improving your physique.

I was entranced by everything Bette had shown me, but deterred by the cost, especially as I was probably the only person in Couch Canyon who didn't have whatever-the-bill-we'll-pay-it medical insurance. Twenty sessions would set me back $500, and I decided that the money could be better spent on pizza or a Filipino massage parlour. So I said goodbye to Bette and her charming colleagues, and left Calvin to drip.

6

PIGS WITH WIGS

Hi. . . . It's coming up to the top of the hour and Janey and I are getting ready to bring you the first lines of this new chapter. We'll be updating you on all the latest plot developments, and we have a few real twists and turns up ahead.

You bet, Steve. Say, you seem kinda throaty this morning?

Guess I got a cold comin' on.

O-oh.

Not good news. I think it's that mutt's fault. Remember how we got that new dog last week, Janey?

Yeah.

Well, he got lost in the yard last night and I had go out in my nightshirt and find the little crittur.

What kind of dog you got, Steve?

Not a real dog. One of those little Yorkshire terriers.

Oh, a kick dog.

You got it. Anyhow, it's hard to put in a good morning's keyboarding when you keep reaching for the Kleenex. But a man's gotta do what a man's gotta do.

You bet. Don't go away now, as we'll be bringing you the latest word on the weather here in Maida Vale, and a traffic roundup.

I hear there's a real snarl-up on Randolph Crescent?

You said it. Mr Chipperfield double-parked his brand-new Jaguar, and some guy clipped his wing. And there's a fender-bender in the mews.

O-oh. Any other big stories comin' up this next hour?

You bet. Gotta do some file retrieval on the old disk, and some copying onto the new one. And while I'm fixin' a fresh pot of coffee, maybe there'll be time for a little printing-out.

Sounds like a great hour ahead.

We gotta great one.

We'll start with today's big chapter headings:

Knott's Berry Farm

I went there out of puzzlement. Why should a berry farm be a major tourist attraction? Its propaganda department helped to explain: Knott's Berry Farm was 'America's Oldest Themed Amusement Park'. Scholars of PR prose may be able to detect a subtle semantic difference between 'theme' and 'themed', in which case, go ahead. I was just happy to be getting out onto the freeways again. A friend had warned me: 'Knott's Berry Farm is visited by people who are too dumb to find the way to Disneyland' – blistering stuff. But I had not been deterred.

As I drove towards the freeway I saw what would become a familiar sight at the foot of the ramp. A man was standing very still, holding up a sign that read: 'Will Work for Food or ?. Thank You for Your Consideration. Vietnam Vet.' I pressed eastwards, then south down the Santa Ana Freeway. I whizzed past the Citadel Corporate Park, with its immense walls designed in castellated Assyrian, and wondered how any theme park could compete with such straight-faced fantasies. Then I crossed into Orange County, and knew I was close to my destination.

Walter Knott settled in these parts in 1920. A rhubarb farmer by trade, he was persuaded by a neighbour to abandon this comic profession and cultivate, and then market, the new-fangled boysenberry. It was a hit. Mrs Knott opened a restaurant and brought to the site in Buena Park some replicas of the Old West to help draw in the customers. At first there was no charge for the decor, but as the sets and props accumulated, the entertainment business began to supersede the fruit business, and the Knotts had it made. The fruit is still important, as you discover soon after arriving at the farm. Having parked your car, you walk through the arcaded California Marketplace, where you can buy clothes, Christian inspirational goods, toys, and souvenirs. A large sales area is devoted to the local products, the jams and syrups, mixes and relishes. You'll also pass Mrs Knott's Chicken Dinner restaurant, where the old lady's recipes are still served up, but you have to pay extra for white meat. This is the Angeleno's closest acquaintance with farming: jars instead of bushes, cash registers instead of hoes.

At the ticket booths, a taped announcement welcomes us to the farm. Cash dispensing machines wink nearby. A mysterious sign by the booths warns: 'Dress and Appearance Standards Will Be Followed.' I am sensitive about this kind of thing. Just a few weeks earlier some goons at the Naval and Military Club in London had refused to let me into the building to attend a private wine-tasting on the grounds that I had chosen not to twist a narrow strip of cloth around my neck, and we had nearly come to blows. The authorities at Knott's, bless 'em, gave me no trouble.

At Knott's Berry Farm the theme of themes is the Wild West, loosely interpreted, and the park combines rides and diversions with reconstructions of buildings saved from ghost towns and the demolition gang's punch. Interspersed among all this are fast-food booths and ice-cream stands, to keep you brimming with energy, and more serious face-stuffing takes place at the Dining and Shopping Village. I was strolling past the Wagon Camp Wild West Stunt Show, when a gun-toting cowboy herded me and a few other visitors onto the bleachers in a kind of amphitheatre. Someone was selected from the audience to participate in the stunts, a giggly man who apologetically claimed to work for Disney World in Florida – gasps of horror: a rival in the compound. He was on his honeymoon, a revelation that prompted some routine ribaldry. He was – yes, yes – part of the stunt team, as became obvious when he was thrown from an upper window onto the stage.

The show over, I wandered on, past the Chinese laundry, the barbershop, the brothel – a daring inclusion – and the smithy. Unlike Disneyland, where the entire conception is an exercise in fantasy, some of the structures here are authentic; others are reproductions. I passed up certain attractions: the amusement arcades, the dodgems, the miniature trains, and the trip over the rapids (sponsored by Alaska Airlines). Nothing could persuade me to sample the cardiac-arrest rides, such as the Sky Jump, a simulated parachute drop from a considerable height, or Montezooma's Revenge, which propels you around a 76-foot loop at 55 mph, then swoops you up a near vertical 140-foot rail, before repeating the whole journey backwards. The Boomerang is just as sickening, spinning you upside-down six times in a minute. I watched as a little girl accompanied her sadistic father on the Sky Jump. As they ascended in the basket, the tot clutched her father's leg with her little fingers. Descending, the waif had her arms wrapped around his leg. I was tempted to turn him over to the child abuse police.

On the Kingdom of the Dinosaurs ride, I chugged into a huge laboratory, while the voiceover lamented that he couldn't prevent us from going back in time, oh no! Clock hands rotated wildly in the unfamiliar direction, and the air conditioning was turned up savagely to create a primeval chill. We passed between growling beasts, giant slugs and beetles, and overweight prehistoric monsters. Music and the thumping of drums added to the amiable terror. I quite enjoyed all that, and then headed for the steps marked Exit, which led directly into an amusement arcade.

I bought something sweet and horrible to drink and watched the happy folk wandering to and fro. At California theme parks the visitors can be more bewildering than the rides and exhibits. A long-haired, scraggily bearded youth approached clad in black Mitre trainers, lilac and black shorts with a skull and crossbones pattern, a grey T-shirt beneath his NFL Giants jacket, an LA Lakers cap, and yellow plastic wraparound goggles. Around his neck he wore a pendant. To my paranoid imagination, the lad radiated threat and imbecility, an unnerving twinning. At Knott's Berry Farm, after all, there is no distinction between real and bogus, between imitation and reconstruction. The gun-toting cowboy turns out to be an underemployed actor, and the innocent in the audience turns out to be his roommate. So why should I take the visiting thug in his sartorial riot of sporting regalia at face value?

I returned to my car, and drove slowly up Route 39 on my way back to the freeway. In Los Angeles museums come in gangs. On the right I found the Museum of World Wars and Ripley's Believe It or Not, and on the other side of the highway, the Movieland Wax Museum. Opposite the military museum was Heritage Square, which when decoded is American for single-storey arcaded shopping mall with faintly Victorian motifs. Next door to Heritage Square is the Buena Park McDonalds, Western-style with shuttered windows and paired 'gas lamps' in the car park. Spoiled for choice, I could have lunched instead at the PoFolks restaurant and sampled its 'All You Can Eat Speshuls'.

And returned in the evening to the fortress-like Medieval Times Dinner and Tournament opposite.

I hit the freeway, punched the radio buttons, standard routine. Barbara was on. I settled in for a drive of rage. Barbara De Angelis is the host of a counselling programme on KFI with a bad case of *folie de grandeur*. The moment I hear her invite the callers to pick up that phone – 'I want you to let this program change your life' – my blood heats up. What's she up to now? Ah yes, a woman whose boyfriend 'is not meeting my needs'. And why not? Because, listener, he is a reserved kinda guy and she's an outgoing kinda gal.

'You need to go back into therapy.' That was me speaking, not Barbara. Barbara and I have this arrangement: in exchange for having to listen to her, I am allowed to guess what she's going to say next.

'You need to go back into therapy.'

Bingo!

'You gotta tell him you need to see him working on his past, and you need to see some progress within a certain time-frame – '

Me: 'Six months.'

Babs: 'Say, three months – '

Me: 'Damn!'

'Three months – or that's it. I know it's hard, but that's why you've got to tell him. Listen to me, I'm giving you good advice.'

Well done, Barbara. Another troubled relationship brought to crisis point over the airwaves. Now the poor schmucks have to live with the aftermath of your advice for months to come, while you move on to the next caller.

I stayed on Route 5 until I passed downtown, then turned up the Pasadena Freeway. This, the first freeway to be completed, back in 1939, is also the most challenging to drive. It has real curves that require drivers to slow down, which any self-respecting freeway king is loath to do. Most thrilling of all are the exits at which you must make a right-angled turn. To do this without risk of accident, signs advise you to reduce your speed from the freeway maximum to a snail-sprint 5 mph. This goes against the grain, but if the advice is ignored, your car is likely to be wedded forever to the guard rails.

I was on my way to the Huntington Library, which I first visited in 1965. How on earth I managed to get there from Beverly Hills without a car I cannot imagine, but I did, and I remember finding the gardens at the Huntington as beautiful as any I had ever seen. The estate is the legacy of Henry Huntington, proprietor of the Pacific Electric Railway, a network he founded at the beginning of the century; he was also the largest landowner in California. His 600 'Big Red Cars', as the trolleys were known, linked the various parts of an urban area that was already dispersed. With 1164 miles of track, Huntington's network was the largest such electrical system in the world. The burgeoning automobile industry gradually supplanted Pacific Electric, and the last suburban rail service within greater Los Angeles petered out in 1961, although the route linking Long Beach with downtown has been revived.

Henry Huntington had railways in his bloodstream. His uncle, Collis P. Huntington, had been president of Southern Pacific. After Collis's death, Henry, who had failed in his attempt to succeed him as the head of Southern Pacific, set up his own company in 1901. Over the next decade he made a fortune, but not just from selling rail tickets. The elite who then ruled Los Angeles were clever speculators, whose business interests allowed them to control the pace and location of urban development during the boom years. Huntington knew perfectly well that railway lines encourage suburban development, and by buying undeveloped land and then providing rail services to it, he could watch his property investments increase in value over and over again.

As his fortune grew, supplemented by the independent fortune of his art-collecting wife Arabella, he resolved to turn his estate in San Marino, adjoining Pasadena, into the finest private park in the United States. The local architect Myron Hunt built the Huntington mansion, which is now the art gallery, and an equally large building was constructed later to house Huntington's collections of rare books and manuscripts, indisputably one of the finest in the world. Despite the size of the principal buildings, the grounds are large enough to conceal most of them most of the time. The landscaping skilfully gives the impression that the estate is in the depths of the countryside.

The library building is lined with blind paired Ionic arcades against the long blank walls. Here we are among temples, except that their walls have been sealed against the California heat and light. Within, the only sounds are the murmurings of visitors and the soft hotel-room swish of air conditioning. There is much to admire: the Ellesmere Chaucer manuscript, one of twelve surviving Gutenberg bibles on vellum, Caxton's Chaucer, the Polyglot bible of 1517, early scientific books and herbals, Shakespeare folios and quartos – the Huntington owns more early editions of Shakespeare than any other library – and the double-elephant folio of Audubon's *Birds of America*. That's just some of the books. The manuscript displays change regularly, but on my three visits I was able to see the earliest surviving manuscript of the Chester cycle of mystery plays, the eleventh-century Gundulf bible, sheets by Pope, Dr Johnson, Shelley, and Swift, Mrs Thrale's Thraliana manuscript, and autographs by Walt Whitman, James Joyce, and T. S. Eliot. These are mere minims and crotchets extracted from the symphony. Stacked away on the shelves, most of them out of sight, are 340,000 rare books and over two million manuscripts.

The main house is a chilly neoclassical mansion, its stiff ostentation more appropriate to Newport, Rhode Island, than to the West Coast. The Huntingtons' passion for things English has filled the rooms with mostly eighteenth-century furnishings and paintings, though a collection of Italian renaissance bronzes adds a more sensuous note. In the main salon tapestry chairs, Chinese vases, magnificent carpets, and Beauvais tapestries are viewed from behind ropes strung waist-high along neoclassical fluted wooden posts. Portraits of well-behaved children by Reynolds and Romney fit perfectly into this bloodless setting. In other rooms, among the Chippendale and the gleaming silverware, are fine paintings by Constable, Hogarth, and Lawrence.

Tacked on to the mansion is a long gallery devoted to eighteenth-century English painting, notably Reynolds' portrait of Mrs Siddons as the Tragic Muse and Gainsborough's celebrated *Blue Boy*. The individual distinction of these paintings is oddly muted by the military precision of their hanging. Their marshalling suggests determined acquisition rather than a passion for art. The long high gallery depresses me, and, perhaps because of the lighting, the paintings appear flat and drab. In a different and more appropriate setting, the Adam halls of Kenwood House in Hampstead, a similar collection, exposed to daylight and the whims of an English climate, seems far more brilliant and joyful. Another hall combines a rescue operation with a re-creation, by gathering within its walls panelling from Castle Hill, Devon, a mantelpiece from Grove House, Chiswick, and doors from a

Mayfair mansion. Other rooms are filled with French eighteenth-century paintings by Greuze and Boucher and other sickly sentimentalists, a collection redeemed by a single Watteau, just as the upstairs collection of sugary crowd-pleasing English portraits is brought to life by a group of Van Dycks and by an intense shriek of light emitted by a Turner over the fireplace.

It's a relief to emerge into the gardens from this gloomy palace. The formal mood lingers on in the extensive rose gardens, and in the steep grassy bowl that forms the Japanese garden. First planted in 1912 and exquisitely maintained, it is focused around a lofty cat's-back lacquered bridge. On another visit here I saw this garden through a gauze of rain. Beads of moisture clung briefly and in vain beneath the petals of cherry blossom, buds of wisteria were clamouring to open and admit the nourishing wetness, and the pale lime-green willow looked even more than usually fragile set against the dark wooden solidity of the reconstructed seventeenth-century Japanese house on the slope opposite. Near this Oriental exercise is another gallery, built in a style modelled on the original mansion. Opened in 1984, it is devoted to a representative collection of American painting and a hall devoted to the exquisite furnishings of Greene and Greene, two local architects with whom I was to grow increasingly besotted as my acquaintance with their work deepened.

The most sensational of the fourteen gardens has to be the desert garden, the largest outdoor garden of its kind anywhere; with no fewer than 5000 different species, it offers a festival of spines, a panoply of penetrative tortures to furnish an entire circle of hell. The subsequent rain would also transform the desert garden, and I would find many of the cacti in improbable bloom, their domestic-looking flowers rising from a dense enclosure of prickles. The Huntington is proof that in California, given enough water, you can, horticulturally, do anything. The genteel, high-toned orderliness of an English rose garden flourishes just yards away from the stiff desiccation of the desert garden.

When I got back to West Hollywood, there was a message on my answering machine: phone Richard. I did so, and heard his answering machine playing Leadbelly's 'Jump down, turn around, pick a bale of cotton . . .' It faded out and I expected a witty request to leave word, but heard instead a weary: 'Yes, it's me, leave your message.' I identified myself and invited myself along to his roving Sit and Spin disco, which that night was occupying a club called the Black & Bloo on Sunset. Los Angeles, like other American cities, has spawned underground clubs. Technically illegal because they are usually in breach of licensing laws, they outwit the authorities by shifting venues from week to week, while a hard-core membership alerts potential visitors to the next address.

Richard Glatzer's Sit and Spin is not strictly an underground club, though it has more in common with them than with Los Angeles' well-established discos and music clubs. He founded it out of an exasperation with the majority of gay clubs in the city, and has made a point of encouraging women and straight men to turn up too. The club always provides some kind of entertainment, but of a kind that won't disrupt the main activity of the place by forcing people to stop dancing.

In New York anyone hoping to attend a club has to endure paroxysms of anxiety: am I wearing the right clothes, are my shoes the wrong colour, am I too old, will I be turned away at the door? No such worries in Los Angeles, where I never saw anyone being humiliated by scrutinies at the door. I found myself in a dark cave, lit only by thin strips of blue and red neon, and by lights that had the effect of turning all white fabrics, such as my shirt, phosphorescent. A podium was occupied by two boys-a-go-go clad only in white underpants; they were twisting and twirling with as little evident exertion as if they had been taking an afternoon stroll. The clientele favoured T-shirts and ripped jeans, and one T-shirt bore the legend: Nobody Knows I'm Lesbian. There were a few women in the crowd, and two men in drag, one of them with a startling blond wig and a feather boa draped around his neck.

While the deafening music thundered on, the boys-a-go-go held up a sheet between them to form a screen, and a film show began. The movie was entitled *Twisted Revenge* and featured two drag queens, ineptly got up, and the essentially picaresque plot was obscure. The arrival in one sequence of a youth with a pizza led to a memorably messy scene. Then a slight change in cast and a new title: *Pigs with Wigs and Twigs*. The plot, again, was impenetrable, and consisted principally of shots of the two queens in a state of alarm and surprise. The audience loved it and shrieked with delight at episodes that were meaningless to me, but evidently these home movies delivered a succession of in-jokes.

Sit and Spin is a gay club in the AIDS era. No debaucheries or back rooms here, no reek of amyl nitrate, no chains and leather. A peck on the cheek was as intimate as it got. If anybody had come to the club primarily to pick somebody up, they were being extremely discreet about it. Indeed, most people had arrived in groups, giving the club the atmosphere of a private party. Richard insisted it also differed from most West Hollywood gay clubs in ignoring the cult of the body. You don't need to be thin or good-looking to get in here. As an inspector rather than as a reveller, I couldn't help but feel awkward and isolated standing about nursing a can of beer. A vision of hot cocoa began to dance before me, which I interpreted as a bad sign, and I went home.

7

RODNEY KING DRIVES TOO FAST

Because Los Angeles County embraces over eighty municipalities (plus dozens of unincorporated districts) and almost 100 school districts, citywide planning becomes virtually impossible, especially since three other counties have jurisdiction over different parts of greater Los Angeles.

So the governance of Los Angeles gives rise to quite a few headaches. Indeed, it's quite difficult to discover who is responsible for running the city. The mayor is assisted – some would say ruled – by a fifteen-person city council, which represents the 3.4 million residents of the city. The county, however, is governed by a five-member board of supervisors who represent its eight million residents.

However, the great majority of Angelenos take no interest at all in city or county politics, except when it directly threatens their locality. The citizens of Glendale or Compton or Santa Monica are mildly interested in how their own community is governed but can't work up much enthusiasm for the larger bureaucracies from which they long ago declared their independence. The one issue that can stir heated debate is the pace of growth and development. Foremost among those willing to fill the campaign coffers of local politicians are property developers, who have most to gain from keeping elected officials sympathetic to their interests. By and large these tactics are successful.

The slow-growth movement, and its handmaiden environmentalism, employ a self-righteous discourse in the service of self-interest. The last thing a middle-class community wants is any serious influx of people or changes in land use that might alter its character or exclusivity. Thus in the name of 'preserving the quality of life' you can maintain a firm grip on your privilege and your property values. Not that there is anything reprehensible in seeking to protect your neighbourhood from a pulverising new freeway or a ghastly Piggly-Wiggly shopping development. Nor is the humbug exclusive to the slow-growth advocates. The pro-development forces have their own mealy-mouthed discourse. Developers, as we know, aren't *primarily* interested in making money; their main concern, as they keep reiterating, is to provide cheap housing for the yearning masses and to serve the community as a whole.

The opponents of slow growth have contributed to political language a charming acronym describing the philosophy of their opponents: NIMBY – do what you want or need, do it anywhere you like in this great big city of ours, but Not In My Back Yard. But from behind the Alamos of their communities, the slow-growth activists have retaliated with an acronym to express their contempt for pusillanimous politicians: NIMTO – Not In My Term of Office. For all the ill-disguised self-interest behind many of the arguments, it is hard not to sympathise with the slow-growth enthusiasts. The laxness of building controls has led to the despoiling of much of Westwood and the loss of its former character as a charmingly dozy university town. Nor is it difficult to cheer on the environmentalists who battled against such potentially disastrous projects as Armand Hammer's proposal to drill for oil in the Pacific Palisades.

Presiding over this seething mass of conflicting vested interests is the mayor. One would expect Mayor Tom Bradley to be an immensely powerful figure, yet his authority seems to be diminishing with time rather than increasing. Electing a black ex-policeman as mayor in 1973 did much for the prestige of the city, and helped undo the damage to its image inflicted by the Watts riot of 1965. Bradley had won the electoral support of millions of white voters, so his victory was seen as a unifying force that would restore good government to Los Angeles. Although Bradley has clung to office, the enthusiasm, both his own and that of the electorate, has waned. Some of the spark left him after he failed to become governor of California in 1982. More recently, he has dithered on crucial points of policy, and suggestions of financial conflict of interest at City Hall have further damaged his authority. Nor was his position eased by the fiscal crisis that affected California as a whole in 1991. Bradley's budget for 1991–2 proposed cutting about $100 million in expenditure and increasing taxes to raise a further $77 million. A freeze on new hiring would reduce the size of the police force and the fire department. All this on top of the usual arguments about commercial development, new highway construction, the collapse in educational standards, and environmental issues.

Such momentous local issues should have stimulated the citizenry to make sure that, when the time came, its voice would be heard. But in the local elections in April 1991, the voter turnout was a wretched 15 per cent. The city's two principal newspapers, the *Los Angeles Times* and *LA Weekly*, couldn't work up much enthusiasm for most of the candidates either, and failed to endorse candidates for most of the races.

I asked Harold Meyerson, the politically acute executive editor of *LA Weekly*, why there was so much apathy. We met in the lunch room at the newspaper offices, where he was manipulating the microwave in an attempt to make his wife's vegetarian gumbo horror palatable. In between mouthfuls of the glop, which he appeared to be enjoying, Meyerson did his best to explain:

'What's striking about Los Angeles is that its politics have been depoliticised. Municipal government here is nonpartisan. Earlier in the century the two main parties were both perceived, rightly, as being in the pockets of Southern Pacific. So power was deliberately diffused by means of councils and commissions. There are no political structures here comparable to Tammany Hall in New York or the political clubs of Eastern cities. What passes for politics in Los Angeles is essentially neighbourhood organisation, which by definition has no citywide focus. This makes Bradley's position inherently weaker than it would be for mayors in other major cities, and his position is weakened further by talk of financial misdeeds. But the truth is that people here don't want an all-powerful mayor. Most migrants who settled here came out of the Midwest, and the last thing they wanted was to establish another set of political machines and tyrannical big-city mayors.

'The system has worked reasonably well because both the city council and the board of supervisors have succeeded in representing the interests of the Anglo majority. Corruption is probably less of a problem here than in other cities, and patronage is not a well-developed art. The proliferation of neighbourhood organisations and new cities has led to a very serious problem, however. The city services that remain in the public sector increasingly cater to minorities – especially education. There is no longer a sense in this city that the people as a whole have a stake in the way Los Angeles is developing. There is plenty of goodwill and cash available on the Westside for good causes on the left, but hardly anybody would think of devoting them to local problems. It's a familiar and justifiable gibe that politically conscious people in Los Angeles are more knowledgable and concerned about what is going on a few thousand miles away than about what is happening on their doorstep. The poor are notoriously invisible in Los Angeles.'

In 1991, however, there was one local issue that did, for a while at least, grip the city and inflame passions. One evening in early March a black man called Rodney King, an Altadena resident with a conviction for second-degree robbery, was being chased by cops. It was originally stated that King was speeding at 115 mph, but these allegations were later toned down, especially when local car dealers affirmed that Mr King's Hyundai wasn't capable of such speed. Eventually five police cars stopped King. Exactly what happened next is not clear, and it is certainly possible that King, about to be arrested, did not take kindly to the notion, though he himself pointed out that when you have five guns pointing in your direction you are not inclined to argue. The police used a Taser stun gun to calm him down; the usual effect of this stun gun is not dissimilar to electrocution, and its sole purpose is to induce extreme passivity.

There is no doubt about what happened next, however. With methodical violence, three or four policemen beat Rodney King to within an inch of his life, even though speeding on the Foothill Freeway is not yet a capital offence. He sustained almost sixty blows with nightsticks wielded with a swing more usually exercised by baseball players hitting home runs. In addition, he was kicked while lying helplessly on the ground and his neck was stomped on. There were about a dozen witnesses in nearby apartment houses, none of whom saw King offering any resistance after the beating began. King's skull was broken in nine places, and surgeons would later express considerable surprise that he had survived at all.

We know all this because a witness, George Holliday, filmed

the entire scene on his new video camera. Holliday made his film available to newsmen, and within a few days there was hardly anybody in the United States who had not seen, repeatedly, the incriminating tape. The situation was compounded by the fact that of the other officers present during the beating, only one made any attempt to control his nightstick-wielding fellow officers.

For years there have been allegations of police brutality on this scale, but they were often dismissed as the whingeing of wrong-doers who, if they hadn't been up to no good, would never have attracted the possibly overenthusiastic attention of the forces of law and order. However, the fact that in 1990 alone the Los Angeles Police Department (LAPD) paid out $11.3 million in damages to settle law suits brought by victims of police brutality suggests that such cases were merely the tip of the iceberg and that police harassment and beatings were just as prevalent and random as those at the receiving end, mostly blacks and Hispanics, said they were. Only Detroit had a worse record in this respect. Disciplinary proceedings against officers who had used excessive force – or, in the vernacular, beaten the shit out of people for no good reason – were rare.

Recently the LAPD has had the misfortune to mistreat citizens of some repute, whom the media were more inclined to believe than some nonentity at the wrong end of a nightstick. The former LA Lakers basketball star Jamaal Wilkes found himself hand-cuffed against his car on the peculiar grounds that his car registration was *about* to expire. A baseball hero, Joe Morgan, was roughed up at the airport by police officers who believed him to be a drug courier, which he was not (a case that cost the LAPD $540,000). These were men of influence. Rodney King was not, and one can only speculate about how much notice would have been paid to his injuries had Mr Holliday's camera not been whirring.

Enter Daryl Gates. This gentleman became police chief of Los Angeles in 1978. He is a West Coast version of the Southern good ole boy, a physically fit redneck whose frequent political and social pronouncements reveal him to be reactionary and mean-minded. Gates was rather slow to respond to the outcry that greeted the nationwide airing of the King tape, but eventually someone jiggled his arm and he got round to declaring that the beating was a bad thing. But he insisted it was an aberration, a deplorable but almost unprecedented lapse, while all the evidence suggested that this was far from being the case. He also offered an apology to Rodney King for the behaviour of his officers, but did so 'in spite of the fact that King's on parole and a convicted robber', with its obvious implication that King's shady past made his beating less heinous.

There was no doubt that some disciplinary action would be taken against the officers who had assaulted Rodney King, but what began to be interesting was the fate of Daryl Gates. He had made enemies over the years, and the King incident boosted their claim that Gates had to accept overall responsibility for the behaviour of his officers and resign. Gates's supporters argued that the chief could hardly be held responsible for the acts of every one of 8300 LAPD officers. Gates himself made it clear that he had not the slightest intention of resigning.

Gates had found himself in hot water before and had survived the rumpus. Soon after he became police chief he had observed that some Latino police officers were 'lazy', which didn't endear him to that community. In 1982 Gates told his staff to find out why so many blacks had died after being held in a chokehold by arresting officers. 'We may be finding,' mused Gates, 'that in some blacks when [the carotic chokehold] is applied, the veins or arteries do not open up as fast as they do on normal people.' The black community just loved that use of 'normal'. After a jury awarded $90,000 to a man whose nose had been broken by police officers during a search of his home, Gates gaily remarked: 'How much is a broken nose worth? Given the circumstances in this case, I don't think it's worth anything.' His finest moment came in 1990 when he declared to the Senate Judiciary Committee in Washington, not exactly a forum for off-the-cuff remarks, that 'casual drug users ought to be taken out and shot'.

For many, the King beating was the last straw. Radio talkshow hosts, political commentators on the right as well as the left, the LA Weekly, and various civic groups called for Gates's resignation. After some fence-sitting, so did Mayor Bradley. But for the Los Angeles city council, on the brink of municipal elections, the issue was seen as an untimely embarrassment. Only one councilman, Michael Woo, called for Gates to resign; even liberal members of the council such as Ruth Galanter kept mum, while the remaining members argued vociferously in Gates's favour. Harold Meyerson had a little fun at the hapless council's expense in *LA Weekly*: 'The King beating has confronted the city council in particular with a series of choices – between accountability and invisibility, between good and evil – for which they were plainly unprepared. "We had explicit assurances that matters like these wouldn't come before the council," an indignant Zev Yaroslavsky fumed. "We're here to apportion City Hall parking spaces and we're damned good at it." The exception here is Michael Woo . . . who political scientists now speculate is not really a council member at all. "Woo was probably elected to a more serious body – the State Assembly or the board of directors of the Auto Club," said one UCLA professor. "There's obviously been some mistake."'

I went along to one of the anti-Gates demonstrations outside the downtown police headquarters. There were about 200 in attendance, a motley crew of little old ladies of Quakerish demeanour, men in bizarre costumes such as top hats, men and women in kerchiefs and baggy trousers, men in T-shirts emblazoned Veterans for Peace. They walked up and down with their placards: End Apartheid in LA; LAPD Racism No More; Community Control of the Streets; and the cumbersome Throw The Gestapo Chief Out, Take Down the Barricades and the Whole Police State Program. The Spartacists had their own placard: Break with the Democrats and Republicans – Build a Class Struggle Workers' Party. The parade chant was a variant of a traditional favourite: 'Hey hey hey, ho ho ho, Daryl Gates has got to go.' Some passers-by honked their horns in support of the demonstrators.

On this occasion the King beating had become just another rallying ground for the angry left. The Orange County Coalition for Peace and Justice, which had organised this particular demo, issued a bulletin that read in part: 'Innocent people were victimised by a disproportionate and illegitimate array of forces resulting in atrocities against humanity and a descent into barbarism on the part of the perpetrators, the US and the LAPD, respectively.' This attempt to draw parallels between the recently victorious American forces in the Gulf and the thugs who beat up King was crude, to put it mildly, and might have been less irksome had some reference also been made to the ungentlemanly practices of Saddam Hussein.

If this was the best that the anti-Gates forces could do, the chief had little to fear. Not that he was above using the recently concluded Gulf War for his own purposes. When Gates returned to his offices, a 'spontaneous' demonstration took place. His supporters, employees of the LAPD in this instance, greeted him with a display of yellow ribbons. The tying of yellow ribbons to trees, door knockers and car aerials had been a way in which Americans expressed solidarity with their troops in the desert. Yellow ribbons in the chief's offices suggested that he too was returning in triumph from the wars, except in this case the battle had been waged against the citizenry he was pledged to protect.

Calls continued for Bradley to fire Gates, but the mayor had no authority to do anything of the kind. Nor could the city council have ousted him, even if that supine body had wanted to. The police chief was a civil servant and enjoyed a kind of tenure that made it virtually impossible to fire him. The mayor then went into a backroom huddle with the city's Police Commission, which suspended Gates on full pay for two months while investigations into the King incident continued. Gates was furious at being offered a long paid holiday, and the city council shared his wrath, because they felt their authority, even though they were reluctant to use it, was being usurped by the unelected Police Commission. The council, in a rare burst of energy, overruled the Commission and the courts also supported Gates in this matter.

In the meantime a grand jury brought serious charges against King's assailants, who were brought to trial in February 1992.

Up in Hollywood, meanwhile, studios were releasing onto Sunset Boulevard posters for *Out for Justice*, a new film starring Steven Seagal, the ponytailed karate virtuoso. Ads for the film ran the following copy: 'He's a cop. It's a dirty job . . . but somebody's got to take out the garbage.' Seagal's character's means of taking out the garbage usually involves multiple feats of extreme violence. If police brutality is endemic in Los Angeles, then it is not the LAPD alone that bears the responsibility.

Gates held out until August, when, for predictably high-minded reasons, he offered his resignation.

8

HAMMER HORROR

I woke to a repetitious pinging that was not my alarm clock. I lay still and listened. It sounded like the pink of a mandolin. Hollywood sound-effects technicians would have rushed to record it for later use in Chinese water torture scenes. Then I tracked down the source of the noise. It was rain. Water was dripping steadily from a gutter onto some piping.

I took it personally. Southern California had let me down. I had abandoned my family, flown 6000 miles, endured jet lag, airline food, security checks, and a humiliating failure to get myself upgraded to first class, all in the expectation that the months ahead would be spent beneath perfect azure skies. Now it was raining. Not just a few random splashes from a rogue cumulus, but steady stuff, the kind of rain that makes lines as you peer at it and dribbles diagonally down the windows. There were puddles on the patio. I turned on the radio, which confirmed, in weathermanspeak, the evidence of my ears and eyes: 'Today we have a sun outage advisory.' I headed for the door to retrieve my newspaper from the mat. I spotted my landlady at her kitchen door, nose tilted up to receive the fresh tingle from the skies.

'Rain!' she beamed.

'Rain,' I scowled. 'What a bloody nuisance.'

'What do you mean? This is wonderful!'

She explained that California had been suffering from drought for five years, that various measures had been introduced to reduce water consumption, and substantial rainfall might just

obviate the imposition of even more draconian measures. I
replied that, as far as I was concerned, drought was an ideal state
of affairs.

I returned to my quarters, ingested more coffee, and confronted the day. What, after all, was there to do in Los Angeles
in the rain? The entire city is predicated on the assumption that
the sky is blue. Under the present appalling conditions, I could
either stay in and read a book – a suspect occupation for a
fledgling Angeleno – or I could go to the movies or visit a
museum. The latter appealed most, and to fill in the hours before
the County Museum opened its doors, I decided to go for a drive
to enjoy a rare glimpse of a sodden Los Angeles.

I whizzed up La Cienega and crossed Sunset, following a car
with the licence plate HYSTRCL. I continued up into the hills.
After half a mile of twists and turns, I sensed that I was making
a mistake. The road had turned into a torrent, and it was
becoming difficult to distinguish the soft mushy shoulders from
the hard tarmac. Descending traffic was hugging the middle of
the road. Even parked cars became hazardous, as cascading
water dashed against their tyres and threw up constant walls of
spray that briefly blinded me. Palm fronds blown from the
treetops floated down on the tide, and since some of them were
six feet long they too presented motorists with problems. Roadside earthbanks were dissolving before me, and mini-torrents,
like newborn springs, sprang brown and muddy from the slopes.
Oh Zsa Zsa, where was your firm hand on the wheel in my hour
of need!

The rain didn't let up, and more water fell from the skies
during those twenty-four hours in February 1991 than had fallen
in the eight previous months. And it kept on raining, copiously,
dumping four inches in fewer days. Since the average annual
rainfall of Los Angeles is fourteen inches, this is by local standards Bengali weather. TV weathermen chuckled, old ladies
beneath umbrellas used for their original purpose rather than as
sunshades smiled at strangers, and every householder in the city
gibbered like yokels of the glories of rain and how their gardens
were lapping it up. It wasn't all good news, of course, as the
downpours inflicted a fair amount of damage on a city unaccus-
tomed to monsoon conditions. A tornado even touched down in
Orange County and tore up a garage or two. The Santa Monica
Bay had to be closed to bathers not because of pollution but

because a tide of mud and debris from the canyon roads had poured into the bay, with garden pesticides and other poisons tucked under its arm. One Angeleno complained to me: 'We can't even enjoy the refreshing sprinkle of rainfall here. All we get is mud-slides, tornadoes, and light devastation.'

Local attitudes were understandable when you consider the efforts the city fathers had taken to ensure that Los Angeles would always have an adequate water supply. The Southern California valleys and coasts were semi-arid regions, with no flowing rivers and deep lakes; without abundant water agriculture would collapse, swimming pools would become extinct, and the vast residential acres would shrink into villages huddled around a spring or river. William Brewer, observing the Los Angeles basin in the 1860s, wrote: 'We are on this plain, about twenty miles from the sea and fifteen from the mountains, a most lovely locality; all that is wanted naturally to make it a paradise is *water*, more *water*.'

The city fathers a century ago were well aware that only the lack of a dependable water supply impeded the infinite growth of the city. Droughts in 1902 and 1903 confirmed the uncertainty. There was ample water in the sierras, but no means to bring it to the thirsty city at the Pacific shore. Some of the most powerful figures in Los Angeles property and banking circles worked out that the most logical source of water lay in the Owens Valley, some 250 miles to the northeast. Unfortunately, farms and settlements in the hundred-mile-long valley were already tapping the local water supply. A senior official of the US Reclamation Service in California, J. B. Lippincott, went off to tell the farmers that the government had ambitious schemes to irrigate the valley, which would greatly increase the amount of land that could be cultivated. But their cooperation was required. All the government wanted was for them to relinquish their present rights to the water. This would allow the government to proceed with its schemes, and then, for a nominal cost, the farmers would be able to acquire large tracts of this newly irrigated land.

In the meantime the bankers and real-estate men of Los Angeles, including Henry Huntington and Harrison Gray Otis, the publisher of the Los Angeles Times, were buying up land not only in Owens Valley but in the sparsely inhabited San Fernando Valley. The tycoons realised that once the city's water supply was assured, the Valley would become ripe for development and property values would rise steeply. Lippincott succeeded in getting the farmers of Owens Valley all excited, but having done so, he stepped into a magic closet and re-emerged not as chief engineer of the US Reclamation Service but as the assistant to William Mulholland, who ran the Los Angeles Water Department. Furthermore, he announced that the US Government was no longer interested in the ambitious irrigation scheme he had promoted; indeed, there was reason to suspect that it never had been.

Everything was now ready for the rape of Owens Valley. The farmers had lost control of much of their land; when the city of Los Angeles announced that they had come up with a new wheeze, namely the construction of an aqueduct to bring the Owens water directly to the city, the politicians and businessmen were already holding all the trump cards. When the city announced a bond issue to finance the aqueduct, which would cost $22.5 million, the citizenry voted it through overwhelmingly. There is evidence that the city fathers deliberately engineered a water shortage shortly before the vote in order to encourage the electorate to support the bond. There was one potential hitch: not all the water rights of the Owens Valley were controlled by the city. Then Gifford Pinchot, head of the US Forest Service, obligingly declared that much of the valley would henceforth become a federal forest, thus putting an end to future agricultural use. Owens Valley, once fertile and prosperous, reverted to wilderness.

The building of the aqueduct and its 142 tunnels was a marvel of engineering, yet after five years the waters poured not, as one would have expected, into Los Angeles itself but into the San Fernando Valley. The wildest expectations of the syndicate that had promoted the whole scheme were fulfilled, and their 108,000 previously worthless acres in the Valley acquired incalculable value as steppe was speedily transformed into suburb. The whole episode was a brutal piece of political chicanery and manipulation, an elaborate hoax by which the resources of one valley were purloined for the benefit of another – and for the particular benefit of a handful of businessmen. As one drives along Mulholland Drive, the beautiful road on the crest of the mountains and the only spot from which it is possible to view both Los Angeles and the San Fernando Valley, it is worth remembering that it honours one of the masterminds of the whole unsavoury operation.

The American West has not forgotten the fate of Owens Valley, and when the lingering California drought of recent years sparked debate on how to ensure the state's water supply in decades to come, those parts of the West with abundant water instinctively put up the barricades against possible predators from Los Angeles. One of the guests at McKee's tennis party was a water engineer, who insisted that there was in reality no water shortage at all, despite the drought. The problem was a political one, since Southern California was dependent on Northern California for water and there is little love lost between the two regions. The cultivated Northern Californians have long considered the Angelenos as little better than barbarians, not a view calculated to engender cooperation.

'Water is easy,' said the engineer. 'We know where it is, where it flows, how to transport it. The problem is solely one of distribution. Southern California has 60 per cent of the state's population, perhaps more, and thus more political clout, which the north would like to limit. Some of the industries in the north, especially in Silicon Valley, use enormous quantities of water, and the north doesn't want to jeopardise its industrial base. After all, many of those industries are now being wooed by other states such as Oregon, and Northern California doesn't want to do anything that might lessen the economic viability of its industries. You'll hear people telling you that housing uses a great deal of water, but the fact is that agriculture uses much more. An acre of farmland uses far more water than an acre of tract housing with all its sprinkler systems and pools.'

Despite the February rains, Los Angeles was forced to impose further restrictions on water use. The Metropolitan Water District, the body from which local authorities in greater Los Angeles contract their supplies, asked for a 50 per cent cut, which if implemented would severly affect landscaping and gardening. Other Southern Californian cities, notably Santa Barbara, had for some time been experiencing a far stricter regime. Santa Barbara had modulated from a city of green to a city of brown, although the spring rains had temporarily restored the verdure. Officials were keen to dampen expectations that the heavy rains of early 1991 would make a lasting impression on the state's water supplies. Reservoirs and ground water reserves remained depleted, although less severely than before.

*

It was still pouring as I slithered down Sunset Plaza Drive to the more level ground of Sunset Boulevard. I drove along Sunset, then down La Brea in the direction of the Los Angeles County Museum of Art (LACMA). At the corner of Fairfax I passed the Macy's store built in 1940, its golden drum, as shapely as a hatbox, dominating the intersection. Alongside the museum are the famous La Brea tar pits, still bubbling, and decorated with lifesize models of mammoths and other animals whose fossilised remains were discovered here after a submersion that lasted 100,000 years.

I had first come to LACMA in 1965, shortly after it had opened. It was then the city's newest attraction and my friend Peter Shireson was eager to show it off to me. We approached one of those modern American sculptures composed of a car wreck and while we were contemplating it in silence, a diminutive Jewish couple trotted up and made disparaging remarks. 'They call this art? – A child with a hammer could do this – They could find nothing better to spend their money on?' – and so forth. When they had finished, Peter, adopting a faint German accent, mumured: 'So. You laff at my vork?' The elderly couple fled.

Since then the museum has expanded. The Anderson building along Wilshire is an addition of 1986, and no more distinguished architecturally than the earlier buildings. Its stepped walls of sandblasted limestone are decorated with bands of green terra-cotta and fluted milky glass square panels. It resembles an epic interpretation of a maximum-security public lavatory. The entrance to the galleries is located in a courtyard reached along a lengthy glass-canopied passage leading from the Wilshire pavement. On the right the charcoal-grey Donors' Wall, separated from the walkway by narrow pools of flowing water, lists the founders and sponsors, donors and benefactors, all the nuances of munificence and tax write-offs. Because the museum has been put together piecemeal, with new buildings added on when a benefaction permits, there is a clash of styles, nowhere more apparent than in the courtyard.

The principal collection is housed in the Ahmonson building, its galleries ranged around a four-storey well. In addition to superb Oriental exhibits and a seemingly eclectic collection of Egyptian, Greek and Persian antiquities, the Ahmonson houses a mercifully unique collection of mosaics, most of which are either Roman work of the eighteenth and nineteenth centuries or

Florentine *pietre dure*. These are technically intriguing, especially the miniatures, but artistically of little interest. Another room contains collections of monumental English silver such as wine cisterns and candelabra, and two extraordinary silver-gilt gates from a Ukrainian church.

In a room full of English paintings, the sole Turner was obscured by five Japanese visitors lined up in front of it while posing for a photograph, commemorating the occasion on which they gazed at a camera rather than at a Turner. Some of the halls resemble auction galleries rather than coherent collections. One moves swiftly from Assyrian artefacts to Greek amphora, then to medieval carvings and stained glass. The paintings are diverse too, and include a lovely Hans Baldung Grien, a striking De La Tour of Mary Magdalene, and portraits by Rembrandt and Hals. The Rodin collection is magnificent.

The presence of a Hammer wing reflects the many connections the elderly oil man and philanthropist had with the County Museum. Having lent LACMA many paintings, he had let it be understood that he planned to bequeath his large private collection to the museum. Not long before he died he entered into negotiations with LACMA officials and insisted, among other conditions, that all his paintings should be exhibited together and the collection staffed separately. The museum told Hammer such conditions were unacceptable. Hammer stalked out, and the next day unveiled designs for his own museum. Since it was unlikely that any architect could have come up with these detailed plans overnight, it seemed obvious that his falling out with LACMA had been premeditated. To add to the fun, the County Museum filed a lawsuit against the Hammer estate on the grounds that his written assurances that his collection would be left to LACMA had dissuaded curators from bidding for certain works which, had they not been promised comparable works by Hammer, they would have definitely sought to acquire.

Howard Fox, LACMA's curator for contemporary art, told me that Hammer's volte-face set a bad precedent. 'In New York major donors feel it's a privilege to have their paintings hanging in the Metropolitan Museum of Art. In Los Angeles collectors want vanity museums.'

I later took a look at Hammer's own museum, which opened in November 1990. It's a striped building mostly of Carrara marble attached to the offices of Occidental Petroleum on

Wilshire. The Huntingtons extended their home into a museum; Hammer did the same to his office. The galleries are arranged around a cloistered courtyard, arcades and loggias on both storeys providing shelter and space to wander. I could make no sense of the way the exhibits had been arranged. Walking into the first room I found myself in front of some nineteenth-century Russian paintings, probably a reference to Hammer's origins. Then a Gilbert Stuart portrait of George Washington, a sugary Thomas Lawrence that must have escaped from the Huntington, an Eakins portrait of a cardinal, and an elegant Sargent portrait. The next galleries looked back to Titian and Tintoretto, then jumped ahead to Rembrandt and Rubens. The collection's strengths lie mostly in late nineteenth-century works. There are, of course, the usual representative paintings by Corot and Boudin, Monet and Sisley, Pissarro and Renoir, Vuillard and Bonnard, but the exceptional paintings are by Van Gogh, Toulouse-Lautrec, Ensor, Degas, and Odilon Redon. Manet, Gauguin, and Cézanne are here too, but those paintings are hardly leading examples of their work.

The highlight of the Hammer Museum is the Daumier collection, which is stupendous. The bronzes are extraordinary, like sketches or vignettes, although of course each one is brilliantly crafted. The lithographs are famously satirical and impatient of pomposity and procedure, but the little bronze portraits capture every nuance of complacency, stupidity, vanity, vacuousness, and pigheadedness. Hammer had also bought a codex by Leonardo da Vinci, the only example in the United States, and the manuscript is cosseted in a room that has the necessary dim lighting. After spending twenty minutes poring over the pages of this codex, I discovered that there were limits to my fascination with flowing water and lock gates, the topics that particularly engaged the master's attention on these densely scribbled sheets.

The Hammer Museum is a great disappointment. Of course there are fine paintings here, and the Daumier collection alone makes a visit worthwhile, but there is little to suggest that the collection was so individual that it required its very own museum. Hammer hadn't helped his case by donating about fifty remarkable Old Master drawings to the National Gallery of Art in Washington in 1987. Controversy had also dogged the construction of the museum, as shareholders of Occidental Petroleum sued Hammer and other executives, charging that corporate funds had been used both to purchase the Codex (for which Hammer paid £2.2 million in 1980) and to finance the construction of the museum, said to have cost close to $100 million. The case has yet to be resolved. Visiting the Hammer Museum I was more aware of the oilman's vanity than of his acuity as a collector.

These days of rain and wind were unwelcome to Morris and Theresa Cerullo, who had recently arrived in Los Angeles for their three-day Miracle Explosion 'crusade'. There are many who feel alarm at the persistence of American evangelism. I for one deeply miss Jimmy Swaggart and Jim and Tammy Bakker, and all the other defrocked preachers who provided so much free entertainment on Sunday morning television. Their unmasking is, of course, just part of the natural cycle. You ride high, and then you crash to the ground. The great survivors, such as Billy Graham and Robert Schuller, are also the preachers who take the fewest risks. Swaggart gave full value every time, falling to his knees and weeping with orgasmic fervour.

Showbiz abhors a vacuum, so now there was a chance for second-raters such as the Cerullos to wiggle into those empty shoes. The Crenshaw Christian Center on South Vermont is not, shall we say, in the most exclusive part of town. The congregation was a mixed one, with a sprinkling of Asians and Latinos and Anglos among the predominantly black faces. The centre is an impressive structure, like a theatre in the round, with the seats fanned out in front of the stage. On these occasions I like to sit apart, just in case I feel like talking in tongues or enjoying a quick spasm or two. But the ushers, aware that the auditorium would be only half-filled on this inclement evening, herded us together. I found myself between two elderly black women, both clutching their bibles. A white couple on stage were doing a bouncy warm-up number and most of the congregation was already on its feet, clapping and singing along. There was a party atmosphere, and I was ready to play. Then a change of mood: the jaunty couple stepped back, a black singer came on to croon a more reflective recitative, and the audience, evidently moved, raised its hands like antennae to winkle down the divine vibrations.

The main musical entertainment was still to come. The mournful singer retreated to give way to Jesse Dixon from Chicago, another black singer but in a striking white suit.

'How many of you here know that Jesus is alive?' he yelled. Judging by the response, everybody knew except me.

'I want you to jump to your feet and say: Glory!' They jumped.

'He's alive!' screamed Jesse.

'He's alive!' the faithful responded, and repeated the routine a few more times.

Jesse then segued smartly into the musical number 'Jesus Is Alive Today'. Hands clapped, arms waved, and when it was all over the old ladies next to me struggled to their feet and shouted 'Praise the Lord!'

Until this moment I had got off lightly. Nobody had asked me for money or to stand and identify myself as a first-time visitor. My luck was about to run out. Jesse asked us to turn to our neighbours and tell them that Jesus is alive. I'd have thought he'd made that point exhaustively by now, but you can never have enough of ringing affirmations that contradict the evident facts of the case. The crones pumped my hand and yelled the formula, and I did my best to smile and look acquiescent. I don't think they were convinced.

'Hallelujah!' That was a woman in the row behind me. I glanced back and identified the enthusiast as a rather beautiful black woman in a fur jacket. While Jesse rambled, she burbled, throwing out a 'Thank you, Jesus' or a 'Jesus is alive' whenever the mood took her, closing her eyes and directing her face heavenwards to expose a very shapely throat that begged for a string of pearls.

After another few dozen cries of 'He's alive!' from the platform, the hysteria in the hall was sufficient for Morris and Theresa to make their entrance, hand in hand. Morris has been preaching for forty-four years in 153 nations. Not surprisingly, he has become rather hoarse, and his voice has developed a curiously grainy high-pitched squawk. Theresa, who from the distance looked much younger than her husband, was evidently a peach. How do they do it, these busy evangelists?

What we were going to do on this crusade, Cerullo informed us, was 'take back what the devil has tried to steal in this territory'. This went down very well, though as a programme it seemed rather vague. Where's the beef, Morris? He now made us go through another round of telling each other 'Jesus is alive and well', having no doubt made an excellent recovery after his bout on the cross. I found the strained smile harder work second time around, and the matron on my right was eyeing me suspiciously, and I can't say I blame her.

Cerullo, performing in duet with his wife much as two newscasters hand each other cues at the end of each sentence, talked about how Morris had been allowed to ramble on for hours on a Russian news programme, bringing the good word to the Soviet people.

'Wasn't that something, sweetheart?'

'It was just amazing, honey, a real blessing from the Lord.'

Theresa had her own message to give, in the form of an exceptionally long prayer, which inspired some strange gabblings all around me, either the sound of congregants speaking in tongues or racing tips in Korean.

Back came Morris with a quick prayer and the money pitch. On entering the hall we had all been handed the familiar envelopes that crackled with thirst for cheques and dollar bills. Cerullo confided to us that he had spent $100,000 organising this three-day crusade. Since it had been his idea, I couldn't see why he was troubling us with his invoices but he did his best to turn his problem into ours.

'The Lord kinda dropped this in my heart today,' he croaked, as if an urge to beg had come over him quite unexpectedly. He asked us to place our hand on the envelope while he tried a prayer on us.

'Anoint us, anoint us with the anointing of something special.' And more such eloquence. When it was over we were allowed a couple of minutes to fumble in our handbags, while a plump lady in white at the electric piano played special bouncy chequewriting music.

The sermon began. Cerullo spoke so slowly that my concentration lapsed, lulled by the soft organ whooze that accompanied his ruminations. As Cerullo increased his own vulume, the organist followed suit. When the preacher used a harsh word like 'crushed', the organist ventured a discord. I began to pay more attention as Cerullo became more excited and screechy. On pronouncing the word 'saved' he jolted into a higher gear. Most evangelist sermons are journeys from code word to code word, each sparking a new round of excitement, which becomes cumulative. After 'saved', we had 'victory'. Cerullo carried the device to an extreme by making us repeat certain words over and over – 'purpose' and 'spirit' – probably to keep our attention pitched high and to give him a little extra time to work out where his ramblings were headed.

He told us how awful our lives were. 'You are hurting. You are hurting, and you can't find the answers, the solutions.' Actually I felt fine. 'The son of God,' he continued, 'was made manifest to destroy the works of the devil. The same spirit that baptised Jesus is blessing us. Jesus will heal you of your crushing.' Theologically, this struck me as weak, but Cerullo was now on a roll, jumping up and down with excitement, not a dignified sight given his great age and small stature.

I don't respond gratefully when people scream at me, so I left, disappointed that Cerullo's sermon had been so lacking both in intellectual content and in entertainment value. Driving back towards Hollywood on the Harbor Freeway, I flipped into the tape-deck a treasured cassette of the great unforgotten Jimmy Swaggart that I carry with me on my travels.

His voice sang out: 'When you walk up to a movie theater and lay your two dollars or four dollars or whatever it costs to get in that thing, and you go in and watch what Hollywood or whoever offers, you have just joined communion with demon spirits that's behind that trash, rot, and filth. You hear me? You listenin'? I'm talking about Christians. Lady, lady, when you dress or undress yourself' – Jimmy being an authority on this topic – 'in a way that is provocative or indecent – yes, times change, but God's laws never change – you are taking communion with demon spirits that foster lust, lasciviousness, concupiscence and all the powers of hell. Twenty years ago I sat down at a professional football game in Houston, Texas. I sat there for twenty minutes. I couldn't stand it. They were drinkin' all around me, they were drunk or gettin' drunk, the profanity filled the air until it turned blue. That was the first professional game I ever been to, that is the last professional game I ever been to. Some of you are saying, Now, Jimmy Swaggart, you're hittin' my pet.

'I can't help that. It's just my business to deliver what I hear.'

9

ARMED GUARDS ARE WATCHING
OUR PLANTS

On Pico Boulevard a few blocks from the ocean the shelves of Vidiots, an alternative video shop, are lined with foreign films, documentaries, black-and-white classics, New Age movies, and cereal commercials. I'm in Santa Monica, and Vidiots, catering to a trendy, well-educated, thoughtful, yet fun-loving clientele is typical of the town. Santa Monica might have been very different. Decades ago proposals to build the principal port of Los Angeles here never materialised and the port facilities stayed further south in San Pedro, Wilmington and Long Beach. Yet Santa Monica was not fully integrated into Los Angeles until the freeway was completed just over thirty years ago. Until then the beach was somewhere you went to on outings, not a place where you lived. No longer. Santa Monica has become just one of a number of prosperous beach communities between the Palisades and Palos Verdes.

I walked north along Ocean Avenue. Shore and avenue are connected by walk streets, lanes closed to traffic that lead to cottages set within small fenced gardens. Closer to the ocean itself the Castle Apartments are decorated with an immense mural depicting whales. Above it there's a pious inscription: 'We Did Not Inherit This Earth from Our Parents, We Are Borrowing It from Our Children', as though the two formulations were mutually exclusive.

I walked past the Loew's beach hotel, a postmodernist fantasy in soft peach and lime colours. Beyond the hotel and a cluster of smaller motels, sandwich shops, and a Mexican deli, I came to the pier. From here there's a perfect view of Santa Monica Bay. Leisurely breakers begin their roll a hundred yards out to sea, and the shoreline surges, yet it's soothing in the regularity of its restlessness. To the north the protective mountains rise steeply behind Malibu, and to the south the other beach towns march down the coast.

The pier is everything a pier should be, slightly raffish, cosily shabby, studded with cafés and amusement arcades and a gaily coloured hand-carved indoor merry-go-round. The pier restaurants also sell live shellfish, Maine and California lobsters, Dungeness crabs and rock crabs, live conches, cherrystone clams, species that by defending themselves defy us to eat them, and lose the wager. Telescopes point towards the mountains and convert small change into close-ups. At the end of the pier, where tarmac turns into boardwalk, anglers sit patiently above the curling breakers. Signs posted in English and Spanish warn against eating mussels and white croakers, and advise that delicious scallop corral be discarded. With my back to the ocean I can wide-angle the shore through a fuzz of haze and spray. Walking back down the pier I almost tripped over a black preacher cross-legged on the boardwalk, a tambourine resting next to his bible, while he croaked 'Lord lifted me' over and over.

Beyond the pier, palm-shaded gardens overlook the beach and provide a dormitory for the homeless, many of whom are sprawled along the benches, their carrier bags and stained blankets filling supermarket trolleys parked alongside. Elderly couples in smart tracksuits stumble contentedly past on their morning walk, benignly overlooking the destitute who are all around them, ransacking the rubbish bins. A shuffleboard enclosure is marked: Senior Citizens Only.

Opinions are divided about the presence of so many homeless people in Santa Monica. Some point to the soup-lines on Ocean Avenue, and excoriate the city council for turning a blind eye to this eyesore. Matt Kramer, a club owner who takes a keen interest in the town, was more sympathetic. Some time ago, he explained, elderly people who had long rented apartments in Santa Monica found themselves being squeezed out of their homes by rent increases. They reacted by organising themselves politically and began winning seats on the council. Even in modern entrepreneurial Los Angeles, Santa Monica remains one of the few places where you can still find rent-controlled, low-income housing. As a corollary, the council takes a more indulgent view of the homeless, providing shelters and soup kitchens with a generosity that leads some citizens to suspect that other cities put their homeless population on buses and tell them to get off at Santa Monica. If one is condemned, for whatever reason, to be without a home, then there are worse places to end up than in this oceanside park.

There is more to Santa Monica than pier and beach. Two blocks inland, Third Street has been pedestrianised and dubbed the Third Street Promenade. There are grumbles about gentrification and yuppies, but they are mean-minded; the Promenade is one of the few streets in greater Los Angeles where it's a pleasure to walk and where the shops actually sell something worth buying. Sidewalk cafés spill onto the promenade. Lone guitarists croak dimly remembered sixties hits while perched on benchtops. Between Wilshire and Arizona there's a spurt of bibliophilia: among other bookshops, the radical Midnight Special Bookstore, its windows plastered with antiwar notices, announced vigils and meetings to protest against hunger, homelessness, and thuggish cops. I was untempted by the branch of the yogurt chain Humphrey Yogart with its yukyuk cuteness, but succumbed to the Congo coffeehouse, which is furnished like a students' union with low hard armchairs of stimulating discomfort, worn coffee tables, and sallow linoleum.

The King's Head pub is the unofficial headquarters of a segment of the sizeable British community in Los Angeles, many of whom live in Santa Monica. A car was parked outside with the succinct licence plate: BRITUSA. Inside, the pub was a passable copy of a British original, serving chicken pie and fish and chips and English ales. Beer-burly men in T-shirts sat around watching the froth on their pint mugs, and two slimmer specimens were stabbing away at a dartboard.

Behind the apartment blocks and hotels facing the ocean are a few commercial blocks, and then the town's residential areas, which are for the most part modest and architecturally unexciting. As in other middle-class neighbourhoods of Los Angeles, plaques planted on front lawns threaten intruders with 'Armed Response' in the form of a man with a gun who eventually turns up to see why the alarm has gone off. A civic designer appears to have cornered the market on coral trees, with their bright orange-red blooms peppering San Vincente and other city streets. On the northern edge of Santa Monica, handsome houses along the escarpment of Adelaide Drive look onto Rustic Canyon and the Palisades. Built onto the cliffside is the skeletal metal frame of a large house that, if completed, would have partially blocked the view. On Sunday mornings Adelaide Drive is thick with joggers and cyclists, and I overheard one panting athlete, resting against a wall, telling another how he and other community activists had put a halt to this house's construction.

One evening I accompanied Matt Kramer to a gallery opening on Broadway. The owner, a precise balding Russian called Lev Moross, attributed the rash of new art galleries in Santa Monica to the success of the Third Street Promenade, and to the town's proximity to Venice, where many artists still have studios. Lev explained that he also ran an art printing and publishing business and owned the gallery next door.

'At my other gallery we concentrate on contemporary fine art, whereas here I put on more commercial shows and the prices are lower.'

'How low?'

'Five to twelve thousand dollars, in the case of this show.'

I gulped – the work on the walls was amateurish – and he added severely: 'This is not just a gallery, it's a concept.'

Everybody talks like that in Los Angeles, and after a while you learn to pay no attention. After all, running a gallery is a high-risk enterprise in Los Angeles, and many recently founded galleries on Melrose and elsewhere have now closed, mostly, according to Lev, because they were under-financed, though an alternative hypothesis would be that nobody wanted to buy the art they wanted to sell. With a concept as well as four walls and the stockroom, you have more to offer.

Santa Monica was also playing host to the American Film Market at Loew's Hotel. This event coordinates the marketing of films made by about 200 independent production companies that work outside the studio system. Clients flock here from sixty different countries, and in the main they are not searching for masterpieces. Europe is the principal purchaser, accounting for 65 per cent of sales, but Japan, with 21 per cent, has a growing appetite. Unlike the Cannes Film Festival, nobody comes here for the glamour. They're here to buy and sell distribution rights, and do so with such fervour that the American Film Market has become the world's largest film sales event.

They wouldn't let me in. The press office was up on the gallery overlooking the lobby, but the security men wouldn't let me near the place because I didn't have a pass. They acknowledged the absurdity of the situation, but still wouldn't let me through. While these fruitless negotiations were taking place, I spotted another staircase leading up from the lobby to a spot closer to the press office. I descended, climbed the other staircase, and the security man posted there was more obliging.

Not that it did me any good once I got inside the office. A gorgeousness with padded shoulders told me she needed three copies of my writing.

'What writing? I've published over a million words.'

'The writing you're planning to do here.'

'How can I give you copies before I've written it?'

'What paper you with?'

'No paper. I'm doing a book.' The moment I uttered the word 'book' I knew I was doomed. A book is a despised commodity only of value as the basis for screenplays. The shoulders angled in towards me as she launched into a lengthy speech about the role of the media in reporting this particular event.

'I think what you're trying to say,' I offered helpfully, 'is No.'

She nodded. 'That's about it. But I can give you a regular day pass if you want to cover the event.'

'Will that cost me?'

'Yes.'

'How much?'

'Two hundred and fifty dollars.'

'Goodbye.'

On my way out I whipped some catalogues and brochures and, dodging the vagrants, headed into the gardens to read what was on offer to prospective purchasers.

What choice! I select a mere handful: *Journey of Love* (which the producers annotate as follows: 'An old married couple embark on a journey to the sea which they have never seen, following the course of a dried up river'); *Stone Cold* ('For centuries he has blazed a trail of death and destruction as Ghengis Khan, Jack the Ripper, or Dracula. When death is imminent, he withdraws into a coma-like cryogenic sleep only to awaken fifty years later to continue his reign of terror'); *The Adjuster* ('An insurance adjuster goes beyond the call of duty in his attempts to repair the lives of others, but fails to see his own life falling apart'); *Struck by Lightening* [sic] ('A serious comedy set in a sheltered workshop for disabled adults'); *976 Evil – II* ('Two students are forced to look for a brutal killer who may very well be one of their teachers under the influence of a direct telephone line to hell'); *Terminal Bliss* ('Accidental suicide, necro-masturbation, the death of the Yuppie, this is a disturbing true story of nihilistic and materialistic American youth'); *Pigs Gate* ('A transplant specialist's mind is implanted into a pig by a sadist surgeon, who in turn is implanted into the body of the specialist'); the apposite *London Kills Me* ('Clint may be homeless but he and his friends know how to have fun on the streets'); and the much-acclaimed *A Nymphoid Barbarian in Dinosaur Hell* ('Deadly dinosaurs have arisen from a nuclear holocaust, and all of them are hot for the last woman alive'). All of which may be coming to a cinema near you, especially if you live in Lima or Kyoto.

Some weeks later I sat in on a meeting of the board of directors of the Santa Monica Convention and Visitors Bureau. Matt Kramer was on the board and invited me along. An item with a permanent place on the agenda was the need to differentiate, and persuade visitors to differentiate, between Los Angeles (sprawl, smog, gang warfare) and Santa Monica (surf, sun, friendly folk). A Japanese travel catalogue which featured Santa Monica separately from Los Angeles was applauded and passed round the room. The main item under discussion was the success of the Film Market which, after five years in Beverly Hills, had moved to Santa Monica. There had been minor problems, but the bureau's director announced confidently that the Market 'proves we can handle a big blue-chip event'.

Matt's club, At My Place, is one of the most congenial in the city, and the repertory changes nightly. Matt's tastes are fairly catholic, so nobody is likely to find all the acts to their taste. I had a little trouble with Michael Krieger and associates, who were performing the night I went. Their material was distinctly fey, songs about 'the beautiful planet' ('lovers of light, upward they glide') and 'good friends' ('life goes up, life goes down, we stick together').

I'd had more fun in Santa Monica in the late 1970s. My cousin, then living in Marina del Rey a few miles down the shore, had taken me to a place called the Fox Inn. This bar had raked seating, and we occupied a bench along the top row and ordered beer by the jug. Entertainment was provided by the grinning proprietor, who at the drop of a hat would stand on his head and consume, in one gravity-defying gulp, a glass of beer. Tipplers in the audience would attempt, unsuccessfully, to match this feat. I dimly recall a spotlit blackboard on which the words of a German drinking song – all JaJaJa and slap-my-thighs – had been written. The proprietor, pointer in hand, took us through the lyrics a line at a time, then invited us to join in while he sang the song at his clattering piano. The sheer eccentricity of the Fox Inn was captivating, but it closed years ago.

Beverly Hills, so rich, so status-conscious, so conventional even in its dissipations, would never have spawned, and certainly not tolerated, a Fox Inn. It even had difficulty supporting a decent bookshop, while Santa Monica could offer at least half a dozen that were not commanded by national chains. To the horror of more staid communities Santa Monica's liberal-minded rulers had assessed the disturbance caused by hundreds of homeless people along its prized asset, the shore, and found it tolerable. If Santa Monica was a reaction against the pervasive materialism of much of chic Los Angeles, then I was all for it.

A local architect cautioned me against taking too romantic a view. 'Because we have rent control and low-income housing, there's a broader social mix here than in most other parts of Los Angeles. A keen business sense is not seen as incompatible with a social conscience. This is one part of Los Angeles where you can live comfortably even if you don't have a colossal income. But that only applies to people who have been here for some years. It's much harder for newcomers to break in. You usually have to pay about $4000 before you can move in to a rent-controlled apartment. It's illegal to demand fees, but it happens all the time.'

Santa Monica attracts artists, left-wingers, academics from UCLA who can't afford to live in Westwood or Brentwood which are closer to the campus, as well as plain folks who like to live in an easygoing beach community. One of its best-known residents is Frank Gehry, an architect of Canadian background who has had a tremendous impact on the look of Los Angeles. Gehry at his most ingratiating can be experienced close to the Promenade at Santa Monica Place, an enjoyably zany shopping mall with more than its fair share of visual surprises, its angular lines mitigated by cheerful Mediterranean colours. Southern California has its own colours, notably salmon pink and the baby blue known locally as teal blue, offered in gently sun-bleached tones.

Gehry's own house on 22nd Street is more typical of what he has been up to. The core of the house is a conventional wooden frame house of no pretensions which he adapted in 1978 by adding on sections composed of his favourite materials, which include glass, corrugated iron, and, a Gehry trademark, chain-link fencing. He likes tacking on shapes in the form of a tilted box, and a side wall of corrugated iron is punctured by an angled rectangular gap that allows passers-by to glimpse a cactus garden within. Gehry juggles with different forms of enclosure, with half the length of the side of the house lined by a conventional white picket fence, while in the front, the uncultivated garden is boxed within a wilfully ugly low blue-green wall.

Gehry loves adapting industrial materials for domestic purposes, though I'm quite happy to see a distinction between the two. He is at his best in structures such as the downtown Temporary Contemporary, a commercial building that he transformed into a large informal space for modern art exhibitions. Gehry's refusal to prettify the building and his retention of its heavy beams contributed to the eventual design, and the manipulation of the space is undeniably expert. His museum designs, such as the California Aerospace Museum at Exposition Park south of downtown, are also innovative, cheerful, and eye-catching. It's his domestic architecture that raises doubts. Gehry remains very much in vogue, and has been selected as the architect of the Walt Disney Concert Hall that will eventually be built on Bunker Hill.

Gehry is perfectly capable of producing attractive, joyful buildings when he wants to. There's a large house on South Roxbury in Beverly Hills, essentially a large pink box jazzed up on top with a sprinkling of playful elements that resemble multi-coloured children's building blocks. He plays with different patterned tiles and various sizes and styles of glass panels, and the spatter of textures and colours brings a charm and sunniness that blends suprisingly well into the staid respectable designs favoured by most developers in this part of Beverly Hills.

Frank Gehry has been making his mark on Los Angeles for so long that his innovations no longer seem startling. The torch of radicalism has been passed to the often unsteady grip of architects such as Eric Owen Moss and the group practice known as Morphosis. The Beverly Hills restaurant Kate Mantilini is one of Morphosis's most accessible designs. The rectangular cream-coloured interior is cheerfully decorated with boxing motifs. Opposite a counter that runs the full length of the space is the equivalent of a blank-windowed aisle, with booths in place of chapels. The design of the Comprehensive Cancer Center at the Cedars-Sinai Hospital must have presented Morphosis with a greater challenge. A corridor leads to a roughly plastered white and blue wall, from which some of the plaster has been removed, leaving a jagged gap through which one can see a model of part of a house, just as an X-ray reveals the masonry and joists of the body. To the right of this gap is a four-foot-high blue door, but here the symbolic programme becomes obscure. A balcony over-looks an unashamedly hi-tech interior two storeys below, with scanning equipment screened from a seating area by an aquar-ium. Hi-tech fun and games and coy analogies, whatever their aesthetic appeal, don't immediately strike one as the ideal setting for cancer treatment, but the very few accounts I had of the place as a medical environment were approving.

Morphosis's designs are somewhat vitiated by their whimsical-ity. For modern architecture that can be seriously weird you should head down to Ince Street in a drab district close to the Culver Studios. Here Eric Owen Moss has built a small office complex that features slanting roofs, half-columns with half-vertical sections missing, a row of stubby pillars with one at a slant (echoes of the fey Viennese artist Friedensreich Hundert-wasser here), a false façade, and studded broad wooden noughts-and-crosses in place of shutters. The wall facing the parking lot is hung with chains and pulleys and plexiglass squares attached to the breezeblock wall with rusted metal bolts, and rung ladders that go nowhere. There's homage to Gehry in the use of industrial materials and sly references to sculptural minimalism in their choice and placement, but also a fatigue of the imagination in the dogged employment of inappropriate materials to create an impression of novelty and freshness. Moss tones down the grimness in a house he designed in the Palisades at 708 El Medio. Here a box, painted white and baby blue, has had a diagonal green grid imposed on it; walls project out to nowhere, and other happy-go-lucky ideas give the house its unconventional cheerfulness.

There's vigour and novelty in all these recent designs, but often the wilfulness and whimsicality and aggression of Gehry or Moss seem a petulant counterdevelopment to the rigidities of the International Modern Style. The avantgarde designs of the late 1980s seem fussy and lacking in conviction, substituting shock tactics and cute eye-catching detailing for the sweep of a grand design.

I urged the architect and interior designer Dan Freund to define a California style in architecture.

'I'm not sure there is one, but there certainly is a California look, even if it's difficult to pin down. After all, people come here from Japan and Europe to commission architects and designers to reproduce it for them. The lightness of the look has something to do with the climate here. There's no winter corrosion, no high wind loads to worry about. I think it's true that nowadays we're not seeing a great deal of adventurous innovative architecture, though people like Morphosis and Moss and Gehry are obvious exceptions. The problem is that in this profession you can only go as far as your clients will let you. People here have no deep understanding of the vocabulary of the past and so they feel free to reinvent it, which usually results in awful buildings.'

Back at the turn of the century Los Angeles was mostly a city of idiosyncratic wooden houses such as can still be seen in Angeleno Heights. The rambling Craftsman style flourished in Pasadena and, in a more debased form, in the suburbs of South Central. By far the most popular style was the Spanish Colonial Revival. Its picturesque qualities lent themselves perfectly to composition in large or small volumes. The addition of wings around a patio could expand a modest house without wrecking the architectural balance. The same elements could compose a bourgeois cottage or a nobleman's villa; only the scale and the landscaping need differ. The best examples, such as those in Pasadena, or the Meade House on June Street just south of Wilshire Country Club, are rambling yet not diffuse, and vividly varied in their elements, the rustic chimneys, the richly pantiled roofs, and their exquisitely laid out gardens.

It was a central European invasion, however, that would create a domestic architecture specifically geared to the Californian climate. Rudolph Schindler was born in Vienna in 1887, trained as an architect, and came to Los Angeles in 1920, followed by other younger architects such as Richard Neutra. In Vienna Schindler had been exposed to the works of Otto Wagner and other *Jugendstil* artists, but he hadn't been in Los Angeles long before the break with their work seems complete. In 1922 he built a house for himself and one other family, the Chances. Now surrounded by apartment blocks, the asymmetrical Schindler house has survived – miraculously, since the West Hollywood site on Kings Road must be worth a fortune.

Schindler took advantage of the Californian climate to blur the difference between outdoor and indoor. The walls are concrete, but replaced here and there by large wood-framed windows, many of which slide open, exposing the rooms to the open air. The rooms are divided, but also linked, by sliding doors of wood and canvas. Patios with exterior fireplaces suggest that the Schindlers and the Chances spent as much time as possible outdoors. Up on the flat roof are the half-enclosed porches that Schindler called 'sleeping baskets', as he liked people to believe that the residents spent most of their nights sleeping up there, but contemporary witnesses were sceptical.

The design of the house is functional, lucid, unornamented, logical. Some original wood furnishings remain, but the interior too is austere. It is hard to love. The concrete walls are left unfinished on the inside, which hardly promotes warmth and intimacy. Moreover the fabric is visibly deteriorating: some exterior beams are worn and cracks are appearing in the joints; the windows don't seem waterproof. The only inhabitants were a cat and her offspring, but the house was poorly stocked with nooks and crannies, corners for ambushing, and the other amenities required by play-demented kittens. I find it hard to share Reyner Banham's enthusiastic description of the house in his book on Los Angeles as 'perhaps the most unobtrusively enjoyable domestic habitat ever created in Los Angeles'.

Yet the Schindler House remains an important precursor of a style that would dominate progressive domestic architecture in Los Angeles for decades. Later practitioners of the International Modern Style, such as Soriano, Neutra, Eames and Kappe, varied in their use of materials, often using plain steel frames rather than wood to define the shape of houses that were essentially glass boxes, but the governing principles of their designs were the same as Schindler's, notably the interpenetration of indoor and outdoor light and life. Lautner's houses in the Hollywood hills enrich the style with his own zestful inventiveness.

Los Angeles' cosmopolitanism meant that it could not be unaffected by the more brutal manifestations of modernism. Not far from the Schindler House, at the junction of Melrose and San Vincente, looms the Pacific Design Center. It aroused controversy when it was built in 1975, and in some quarters still does. Its scale is overwhelming. A 600-foot-long box, it is sheathed in cobalt-blue glass, and in 1988 another box in an equally dramatic deep green colour was added on. From San Vincente the roofline is gently humped and sculpted, but these are the only soft lines other than the half-cylindrical drum that projects onto Melrose. Those who object to the building do so principally because of the way its bulk lords it over the mostly residential modesty of West Hollywood.

The Argentinian-born architect Cesar Pelli, who has designed a number of innovative buildings in Southern California, was responsible for the Center, now nicknamed the 'blue whale'. Its colours are gorgeous and sensuous, yet the building is wilfully excluding, and it is impossible to discern from the exterior what the building is for. The glass panels that look so striking from the street are apparently backed by sheet rock, which means that the panels are opaque and lighting is from within. Its aesthetic distinction can't disguise the insensitivity of its location. The subliminal message to the neighbourhood is: Keep Out.

The same is true of an even more massive intrusion in West Hollywood, the Beverly Center at the junction of Beverly and La Cienega. Beverly itself is a gentle boulevard of specialised shops – nail salons, feather suppliers, tailors, florists, and a fitness studio with plate-glass windows that offer passing drivers a view of straining bodies in leotards – but its mom-and-pop-store blocks are brought to a sudden halt by a great blob the colour of nuclear winter: the horizontal thumb of Beverly Center. A casual visitor would be forgiven for assuming that the Center is a high-security prison, so relentless is its exclusion of the outside world. There is no formal entrance, although cars can enter ramps marked Parking and More Parking to repose among five levels of space, each marked with a different pastel shade, the only dab of colour on the Center's exterior.

For pedestrians, a minority species, the entrance lies up an external escalator, a glass hutch reminiscent of the Pompidou

Centre in Paris, an isolated playful note that makes the barbarous crudity of this building all the more painful. Above the parking floors are three levels of franchises and chain stores, ubiquitous mall fodder. On the ground level are scoff-it-down restaurants such as the Hard Rock Café. Descending from the shops in search of the ground-floor California Pizza Kitchen, I found myself among the cars, and traversing the grim deserted concrete bowl was like walking along the bottom of a sump, dodging oil leaks and garbage bags, squeezing between pillars and jeeps. (The Kitchen is a link in a highly successful chain of pizzerias, presenting in an inexpensive form the innovations of Wolfgang Puck, the German chef credited with the invention of the California pizza, which offers toppings such as duck sausage, grilled teriyaki chicken, shrimp pesto, and southwestern burrito, that are more appetizing than they sound.)

Fortunately the Beverly Center is not typical of Los Angeles. On the contrary, it is an intrusion on the gentle urban pastures of the city, a clumsy invasion from the suburbs, a brutish piece of commercial self-assertion, snubbing the cosy inefficiencies of the one-at-a-time shops and businesses of Beverly and the other boulevards. Fortunately the essential blandness of the mostly flat, grid-defined city forgives such excrescences. Except in the newer tracts of the Valley and the counties to the east, Los Angeles, contrary to popular belief, is not a city of uniformity. The houses of Alvarado Terrace or Chester Place are as fanciful and stylistically chaotic as their builders could make them.

After the Second World War, the individualists took to the hills, especially the canyons between Hollywood and the Valley. Their houses were usually smaller than the Spanish Colonial haciendas of the interwar years, with the striking exceptions of the largest estates of Bel Air and Beverly Hills. Only the exceedingly rich could afford to rearrange the landscape in the radical way required to build a mansion on a hilly site. This is where the architects of the International Modern Style came into their own. The principles laid down by Schindler found new life in the cheapness, availability, and flexibility of new materials. The lightness of steel-framed houses with their expanses of glass were perfectly suited to hillside sites, and extensive earthworks could be avoided by simply cantilevering the houses out on stilts. Glass walls and wooden decks built out onto cantilevered horizontals could exploit the view and the relative purity of the above-the-smog air, while the roadside façade could be kept modestly undemonstrative, since the residents had no wish to gaze out on traffic anyway.

There are some admirable examples of this kind of house in Silver Lake, not far from downtown, and in the Hollywood hills. At 9038 Wonderland Park Avenue, off Laurel Canyon, is a house by Pierre Koenig, one of the famous Case Study houses of the late 1950s. Its clean, almost boxy lines and effortless elegance are enhanced further by a moat, which is not a neo-medieval pretension, but a device which reflects and strengthens the limpidity of the design. Close to the spot where Rustic Canyon meets the Pacific shore, a neighbouring valley provides a sylvan setting for the Eames House and Studio of 1947, two tall elegant boxes set within a dell beneath a eucalyptus grove. Visible, just, from the foot of the drive, the Eames house employs the simplest industrial materials, yet creates a magical rapport between the luxuriant vegetation of the site and the sympathetic translucence of the house and studio.

The technique for building on seemingly impossible hillside sites was swiftly mastered, but there were always those who sought other solutions. Perhaps the most remarkable of all is John Lautner's so-called Chemosphere house, high up in the hills off Mulholland Drive. It's a glass-walled polygonal structure of 1960 perched on a tall concrete pedestal, from which struts radiate out to the base of the dish. Thus the house, often likened to a flying saucer, appears to be floating on air, even though it is securely anchored to the ground. The pedestal is not only a crucial support for the dish above, but the source of the house's power supply.

Lautner clearly specialised in dramatic modern houses. The Carling House of 1950 on Pacific View and Mulholland is especially exhilarating, a sprawling composition with immense jutting roofs and decks. You can get close to the Carling House and Chemosphere House is easily visible from afar, but some of the most fascinating modern houses up in the hills are thoroughly concealed, and their owners intend to keep them that way. I found the driveway to John Lautner's Bell House on Woodrow Wilson Drive, but was immediately confronted by the following sign: 'WARNING – DANGER. These premises are protected by trained guard dogs, electronic signal devices and armed security patrol guards.' Here, then, we have an architecture that is deliberately open and accessible yet cowering within a conception of property that is exclusive but fearful.

In other circumstances it can be paranoid. On Beverly, just east of the Beverly Center, there's an unremarkable restaurant called the Carriage Trade. Above some blossoming shrubs is the following sign: 'These Plants, Flowers and Shrubs are Under Video Surveillance. Our Armed Guard is Aware and Watching. Theft is Punishable by Law. You Will Be Prosecuted. We Know Who You Are. Stop Stealing These Plants. Thank You.' The thanks scarcely mitigate the aggression, which seems directed at the innocent as well as the guilty. The bluster is evident, since if the owners know who we are, why are they being so slack about taking action against us?

For many people, with or without justification, the serenity of life under the endlessly blue California skies is constantly shadowed by alarm, anxiety, threat, and unease.

10

OLD ROPE

'Excuse me, but are you trying to play cricket?'

'Yah.'

That wasn't much of a welcome to a compatriot far from home, but perhaps my mildly sceptical tone of voice made an unfavourable impression. Still, the sight before me was rather peculiar. A cricket pitch had been improvised on the polo ground at Will Rogers State Park. Stumps stood upright in the ground, but there were no bails. A solitary batsman faced the bowler; there were no fielders, unless the gentlemen sprawled across the benches just up the slope from the pitch were performing that function.

'Excuse me, but aren't you supposed to have *two* batsmen in cricket?'

A sigh from my informant. 'This is just a practice round.'

'Do you have other teams to play against?'

'Not really. Well, yes we do,' he explained.

Another young man, unmistakably British in his merchant banker's drawl yet trailing a spicily Californian ponytail, turned towards me: 'We don't mix very well.' Which I translated into the local lingo as 'Beat it'.

I left. You'd have thought the Beverly Hills XI or whoever they were would have been grateful for a little support from an evidently well-informed enthusiast, but apparently not.

The leisured classes were also at play further down the slope at the practice polo field, where a chukka was in progress. While Argentinian playboys were whizzing about on their horses,

Abby, a young woman with long fair hair and dark glasses, was coolly cantering around the arena with a prong with which she was picking up stray balls. During a subsequent chukka, when Abby was off duty, a Miguel or José tried to pick her up. He was, he informed her in a gentle Spanish accent, a bachelor.

A few yards away, leaning against the netting, two middle-aged Californians in riding gear and boots were working up a froth of indignation by spotting all the fouls that the referee was missing.

'Hey, Walt, forgot to tell ya. You see that movie *Scenes from a Mall*? New movie with Woody Allen and Bette Midler? Yeah, well, the first minute of that movie was shot right in front of our house.'

'No kidding.'

'Hey, Walt, if that wasn't a foul, I'm going blind.'

I didn't hang around, though I was curious to see whether Miguel would get his gal. I wandered past the horseboxes and the station wagons (licence plate EQU9LUV among them), and made my way to the ranch house. The humorist and entertainer Will Rogers had lived in this verdant, wooded corner of the Pacific Palisades, and had for a time been mayor of Beverly Hills, an unexacting office usually reserved for worthies in the movie industry. Although Rogers died in a plane crash in 1935 he remains a much-loved character in these parts, and not only because his bequest provides the Westside with one of the few open spaces other than the beach. His homespun saws have acquired epigrammatic status. Some of them are framed within the little museum attached to his former home. For instance: 'You got to sorta give and take in this old world.' And perhaps his most famous, and fatuous, dictum: 'I never met a man I didn't like.'

Just beyond the house I found what I had been looking for: the Wild West Arts Club. It sounded like a gathering of painters in spurs, but these arts were of a different kind. Members had come from all over the country, and a few had even crossed an ocean and a continent to get here. At the registration stand you could buy videos demonstrating rope tricks or sign up for the knife and whip accuracy contests. Near the stage a clown was stomping around in an oversized sombrero, keeping a few children politely amused. Seated on the grass were a dozen long-haired teenaged girls dressed identically in shiny fringed shirts and red slacks and black stetsons; embroidery on the back of their jackets identified them as the California Cowgirls. After the clown retreated, it was their turn to divert us. They announced a rope trick involving four separate strands.

'I gotta tell all you folks,' said the master of ceremonies, 'I ain't never seen a trick quite like this before. It's really something.'

It sure was. One of the girls kept dropping her rope, causing all the other strands to tangle and knot, like Medusa's perm, into an earthbound heap. Eventually she got it right, the ropes twirled, another cowgirl walked into the middle of the circle created by the ropes and twirled her own rope, and then did some adroit hopping beneath and over the other ropes. Nevertheless we applauded. Then somebody performed a rope trick while bouncing about on a unicycle. In the distance I could hear the cracking of bullwhips as artists in the whipping event practised for their contest later in the afternoon. Back came the clown, tottering on stilts, and I took a break, heading off in search of the closest hallucinogens.

I once spent a day in Amarillo, Texas, talking to a man who, despite having lost both his legs beneath bulls during rodeo contests, was still riding the beasts. That's my idea of Western arts, not pussyfooting about with old rope. But there were still the evening's festivities to come, and no doubt the Western aficionados, agreeably weary after a day spent throwing knives and flicking whips, would be letting their hair down and whooping it up at the annual dinner.

Wearing my finest embroidered shirt, my Keep On Truckin' belt buckle, and my incredibly expensive cowboy boots from Amarillo, crafted from sensuous calf and the finest endangered-species ostrich hide, exquisitely mottled by the darker spots from which the quills had been tugged, I sauntered into the Westwood Holiday Inn, where the banquet was to be held. The hotel overlooks Wilshire where it traverses Westwood, the only spot in Los Angeles where the urban landscape aspires to Manhattan's Park Avenue. Characterless blocks twenty or thirty storeys high with status-redolent names such as the Regency or Westwood Towers stand alongside hotels such as this. A less suitable setting for a cowboy knees-up it was hard to imagine.

I found my way to the windowless conference room where we would dine together. My heart sank. Next to each place setting was a coffee cup. Not a glass in sight. I took my place at a thinly occupied round table, which gradually filled up. My fellow guests wondered what an Englishman was doing here in cowboy boots with subtly bevelled riding heels, and I muttered that long spells in Texas had acquainted me with the ways of the West. On my left sat an expert in tomahawk-throwing; to my right sat a bullwhip cracker and his father. The tomahawk man regaled us with folkloric tales from Oakland, California, and amused us exhaustively by showing us the many different ways in which a napkin could be folded.

My new-found friends were dressed even more splendidly than I was. They were wearing stetsons, which stayed on their heads throughout the meal, and sported splendid manly jewellery, neckchains and bracelets and rock-sized rings hewn around glittering rhinestones. The wives at my table were real double-baggers. (Lexical note: A 'double bag' is when you're out on a date with a girl so ugly that you need one bag to cover her up, and another to cover your own head so you can't possibly see her.)

Napkin-folding is one sure way to work up a thirst, so we took it in turns to mosey on over to the table where we could help ourselves to cans of Coca Cola, Diet Coke, Fanta, and Sprite. Meanwhile the musical entertainment got under way. White-bearded Andy Anderson diverted us by playing the guitar and singing out of tune. Another fellow had constructed a fiddle out of a bath plunger – the artistry of the Old West lives on – and he played upon it with a bow decorated with the semblance of a splayed chicken. It sounded like vivisection.

Food! On came the salad, which I supplemented with a roll, the kind that grows stale within two minutes of the first incision. The main course was turkey, accompanied by mashed potato with gravy, candied yams, and, an original touch, a bed of catfood beneath the turkey slices.

The tomahawk man wasn't happy.

'I axed for vegetarian, so I bet all I get is a plate of steamed vegetables,' he whined, gazing with longing at the predigested glop on my plate. As if on cue, a waiter arrived with a plate of steamed vegetables, which looked far more appetising than my dish.

'Wad I tellya?'

'If you don't want vegetables, there's not much point being a vegetarian, is there?' In the West we don't take no crap from no one, least of all some wimp that won't sink his teeth into a pound of T-bone or a tin of Felix.

The California Cowgirls, who had changed into formal evening wear of black jeans, proved they could do more than drop rope. They could sing, in a manner of speaking. They put on a karaoke act, three at a time. The youngest of the group, a Cowchild whom we were invited to greet 'with a big hand because she is only eleven years old and this is only the second time she has performed in public', was on next, followed by six Cowgirls who sang, in honour of the troops returning from the Gerlf, 'Proud to be an American'. At the conclusion of the song they produced little American flags from behind their backs and waved them.

I was very moved, and scarcely noticed the approach of the servants with their soft cry, 'The white jug's regular, the brown jug's decaff'. I moved away from the vegetarian tomahawk maestro and occupied an empty seat next to the tallest and, I hoped, oldest Cowgirl. We talked.

The next morning I was up early to go to church. The Saturday edition of the *Los Angeles Times* lists so many different species that the choice is as perplexing as at a Hong Kong fish market. I'd heard good consumer reports of the West Los Angeles Church of God in Christ on Crenshaw, and when I mentioned this possibility to a friend, he claimed to have heard of it. 'That's the place on Crenshaw and the South Pole.' To him, all parts of the city south of the Santa Monica Freeway are Antarctic.

Driving east along the vacant lanes, it was hard to credit this freeway with its wild reputation. Thomas Pynchon in *Gravity's Rainbow* has best formulated the personalities of the freeways: 'The Santa Monica Freeway is traditionally the scene of every form of automotive folly known to man. It is not white and well-bred like the San Diego, nor as treacherously engineered as the Pasadena, nor quite as ghetto-suicidal as the Harbor. No, one hesitates to say it, but the Santa Monica is a freeway for freaks.'

The Crenshaw district is in fact one of the most prosperous black neighbourhoods, with a healthy concentration of spacious well-cared-for houses. Publicity about riots in Watts and gang warfare in the ghetto has obscured the fact that, by the turn of the century, many blacks had made fortunes in Los Angeles. It is as a commercial centre that the Crenshaw district shows the

strain. There are too many empty shopfronts and closed businesses. Many black neighbourhoods of Los Angeles are pleasant
enough as residential districts, but nobody wants to invest in
them.

With difficulty I found a parking place within commuting
distance of the church, and joined the hundreds of others
queuing outside while waiting for the previous service to end. I
felt embarrassed, not because I was almost the only white face
around, but because I was dressed in my customary casual attire,
as is appropriate in Los Angeles. But this congregation was
dressed to kill, the women in silks, the men in suits, the children
festooned with bright ribbons in their plaited or primped-up hair.
Under their arms they carried bibles couched cosily within
morocco wrappings.

I took a seat towards the back, but wasn't exempt from the
Recognition of Visitors routine, in which first-timers are asked to
stand and submit to the blessing of the congregation. A slinky
woman in dashing purple silk kicked off the show with a few
shouts of 'Praise the Lord' and a spirited version of 'Sing Unto
the Lord a New Song' while, on her recommendation, the
congregation waved the order of service papers to and fro, sprang
to its feet and clapped. Matrons in floppy hats jiggled up and
down in time to the syncopated rhythms as the choir, clad in
emerald-green robes, launched into 'I do rejoice for He hath
made me glad'. Despite the tremendous racket, the little girl
seated next to me was fast asleep, itself a miracle of a minor
order. The exuberance was infectious, and I was suprised to find
myself enjoying the service, all the more so because references to
religion were kept to a minimum. I hadn't been to a singsong as
good as this since the publisher David Godine gathered his house
guests round the old upright, and banged out Anselm's Ontolog-
ical Proof of the Existence of God to the tune of 'Waltzing
Matilda'.

Of course the fun had to stop eventually. A minister appeared
and reproved us with a long sermon, lightly speckled with
humour. His peroration was a cunning piece of oratory, laden
with leitmotifs such as 'Hold on to the Lord' and 'God ain't
through with you yet!' But ten minutes later He was through,
and we were free to file out into the shimmering sunshine, where
another few hundred congregants were awaiting their own
rollicking turn.

I found my car, and drove north to West Adams Boulevard. At the turn of the century this was one of the grandest streets of the inner suburbs. Some of its mansions survive, such as the astounding Fitzgerald House of 1903 by Joseph Cather Newsom, which is dominated by an immense but irregular stone chimney in the centre of the façade. In front of the gables knots of looped wood form a kind of screen, a rustic fantasy of swirling growth imposed on a stately home. The whole design is thoroughly bizarre, yet vigorous and exploratory, jumbling vocabularies in an attempt, albeit botched, to devise a new decorative rhetoric. Sunday morning is a good time to visit this part of town, as many of the mansions have been converted into churches: an Hispanic Assembly of God church from which sounds of singing and clapping came soaring through the open window, a Mormon tabernacle, the Polish Parish, the headquarters of the Korean World Evangelisation Crusade. A licence plate on a parked car echoed the theme of the boulevard: 2PRZGOD.

Now a preponderantly black section of town, West Adams used to be exclusive – in the literal sense of exclusively white. Restrictive covenants kept out those racial and ethnic groups of which the homeowners did not approve, but such stratagems were outlawed by the Supreme Court in the 1940s. Whites began moving out soon after, gradually forsaking inner city suburbs for the greater safety of the prosperous outlying districts. The present population did not take kindly to being told how to deal with property that whites had first barred them from owning and then forsaken, and while I was in Los Angeles a furious row developed after a church decided it wanted to tear down a West Adams mansion. The house, designed by Myron Hunt, had belonged to the founder of Pepperdine University in Malibu, and was thus considered of historic interest.

The Holman United Methodist Church, which owned the property, wanted to develop the site. The local conservation society, the West Adams Heritage Association, wanted to save it. Many of those active in the association are white families who have recently bought and restored their houses. Their campaign was rewarded with accusations of racism by the minister of the church, accusations themselves couched in racist terms as he stereotyped those who had moved back into the area and were contributing to its modest revival. Moreover, the minister was using the injustices of the past to gloss over his own rancour, which, no doubt, was largely motivated by the commercial interests of his church. He fiercely, crudely inveighed: 'The West Adams Heritage Association is a white organised and led organisation. They are largely the sons and daughters of the generation which did not want ethnic people in this area, formed housing covenants to keep us out, and burnt KKK-type crosses to scare us away and then fled as we continued to buy housing to suit ourselves.'

A mile or so to the east, just north of the campus of the University of Southern California (USC), is another enclave packed with interesting buildings, such as the church of St Vincent de Paul, with its exuberant Churrigueresque tower and its wildly fanciful tiled dome. Not far away stands Chester Place, now a college campus but originally a twenty-acre private estate enclosing thirteen huge houses, of which a few rambling examples remain. The scale of the development eclipses even Alvarado Terrace, and its exclusivity is apparent from the elaborate gates at either end. 'Gated communities' are nothing new in Los Angeles.

Incongruously positioned on the fringes of the ghetto is the University of Southern California, an expensive private university, and there are uneasy jokes about its location. Of course the university has colonised much of the neighbourhood, and fraternity houses and restaurants and fast-food places that cater to students and faculty are close at hand. Nonetheless, everyone seems slightly embarrassed by the proximity of this bastion of middle-class privilege to South Central. In contrast the 383-acre campus of the state university, UCLA, sprawls among some of the most expensive acreage in America: Westwood and Bel-Air. In recent years this university has eclipsed the once exclusive USC, as the cost of private college education has risen. To send a student to Stanford, for example, costs about $21,000 each year. So even professional middle-class families, confronted with a university education bill of close to $100,000 per child, have balked. It has ceased to be axiomatic that top students will attend a private college, and UCLA is the beneficiary. Moreover, this branch of the University of California, like its sister in Berkeley, has always set very high standards.

An old acquaintance took me to lunch at the faculty cafeteria, and then we strolled through the campus. Since East Coast Ivy League colleges had monopolised the Colonial style, with the exception of Yale with its fondness for Oxonian Gothic, the designers of UCLA went for something completely different: North Italian Lombard Romanesque. A new structure, the Fowler Museum, has been built in a similar style but lacks the very decorative elements that make the older buildings so attractive. The museum is ranged around a two-storey cloister, which is oddly lit by Iranian-bathroom-style bronze lanterns.

'The trouble with this building,' I remarked, 'is that it's been deprived of its ornament.'

'The trouble with this building,' Al retorted, 'is that it's been deprived of its money.'

The physics building, identifiable from the mosaic of equations on the side, overlooks a small plaza with a fountain, or a latent fountain, since the water had been shut off as a conservation measure. The bed of this fountain consists of large stones and, off-centre, a cistern. When the fountain was being planned, a physicist with a view observed that wind currents across the plaza would blow the jets of water beyond the edge of the fountain and their loss would make it difficult to keep the pool filled. The problem was taken to the university chancellor, who suggested that the water should be directed down rather than up. Hence the peculiarities of its design. This is not so much a fountain as an ornamental drain.

Al's reference to the financial restraints imposed on the University reflects the acute crisis in which the state of California finds itself. In March 1991 Governor Pete Wilson had pointed out that the state could close its universities, empty its prisons, shut down the parks, and the budget would still be in deficit. At UCLA capital expenditure had continued more or less unabated, which meant that new buildings had been put up, even though the university may not now be able to recruit the students needed to fill them. Promotions of faculty to the next grade of the professorial hierarchy were allowed to proceed, but the beneficiaries were denied salary increases. Students were affected too, with basic fees almost doubling, so that most students would need to come up with about $3600 each year, even though the state university is supposed to be a free institution.

On a spring morning there was no sign of the tension and concern that was gripping the university. Smiling faces were everywhere, and those I approached with an appeal for directions – UCLA is a confusing campus to negotiate – were helpful. An adorable young woman majoring in Judaic studies even mistook me for a fellow student as she guided me to my destination. She led me into the Murphy Sculpture Garden, one of dozens of courtyards on various levels scattered across the campus. Here an art show is combined with an arboretum, and figures by Rodin and Maillol pose beneath jacaranda, white alder, fern pine and oak. Hepworth, Moore, and Lynn Chadwick are given plinth space here, as are Arp and Lipchitz and the girders of Anthony Caro. As a terrible warning to the students, large figures by Gaston Lachaise depict women who have neglected to work out.

11

TAWNYA'S HELPING HAND

Which reminded me: I had been neglecting my own physique, and the scales shrieked that I had put on at least half a pound since my arrival in the city where nobody walks. Off, damned flab!

Sports Club LA opens at 5.30 each morning, but that was too early for me. I set my alarm for a sensible hour, woke brightly and flicked on the radio. By now I had discovered KLOS. Today the hosts, Mark and Brian, were persuading construction workers to wear lacy lingerie on the job. Hard hat on head, boots on feet, and silk round the hips.

'While you jackhammer,' wheedled Mark or Brian – I could never tell them apart, 'we want to hear how it feels to have that silk against your thighs.'

Some of the construction workers were ready to climb onto their scaffolding, in view of passing traffic, clad in lacy scrotum-hugging undergarments. But there was a hitch. The team was two men short. Mark and Brian were not fazed, and immediately set about twisting the arms of their colleagues. The weatherman refused point-blank to wear lingerie, and neither would the Skylord, the station's traffic reporter.

'There's only one possibility left,' said Mark (or Brian, whose names will from now on be used interchangeably).

'Roger.'

'Yup. Roger the security guard.'

'Let's dial him right now.'

Roger was having none of it. He sounded quite serious, and even showed signs of bad temper on the air.

'Roger, you are our first choice.'

'You are our number one. Numero uno.'

'No way, guys.'

'Roger, what would you say if we gave you fifty dollars – '

'No.'

'Roger, we don't want to push you into doing something you don't want to do – '

'Yes, we do.'

'No way. I'm not doing it.'

'Okay, Roger, you're letting us down. We understand.'

'If you're feeling insecure about your sexuality, fine, we understand.'

'Maybe you're not really committed to this show.'

'We understand.'

I never did learn whether Roger made the transition from uniformed security guard to half-naked beauty queen on a construction site, as I had to make some important, executive-style phone calls before leaving the house. Then I drove along Santa Monica to Sepulveda, parallel to the San Diego Freeway, and was soon approaching the large pink box that houses the club. I swung the car into the parking bay, jumped out, and tossed the keys to one of the three parking attendants, who were all dressed in white like hospital porters. Sports Club LA offers valet parking, which saves you from having to walk all of fifty yards from the multi-storey car park adjoining the building to the entrance. A friend remarked, 'You spend thousands of dollars to become as fit as possible, then you drive up to the club and are instantly treated like an invalid.' (You can tell he comes from New York and just doesn't understand.)

My Geo was driven off to snuggle against a concrete wall alongside Porsches and Mercedes with customised licence plates, such as ILUVTAN and FITDUDE. I strolled through the glass doors of the club to find myself in a quintessentially Southern California interior, an airy space decorated in peach and blue pastel shades. I was about to work out, of course, at the city's most expensive and exclusive club. It cost $28 million to build in 1987, and looks it. Unlike most health clubs in Los Angeles, membership is restricted, in this case to 6000, so its facilities are rarely overcrowded. The fanatics arrive at dawn, so that they can be sure of getting the same locker and the same machines every time, and it gets crowded in the early evening, when those unfortunates who go to work stop by to exercise. The elite, of course, don't work in any sense that requires going to an office and being let out at five, so we like to turn up earlier.

The club claims to have the best qualified staff in the city, with bundles of college degrees in kinesiology and exercise science. They are also encouraged by the management to be good at name recognition, so that we feel at home here. Sports Club LA is essentially a resort with Nautilus machines. We can meet our friends at the LA Grill restaurant, or in the special room where parties are held to watch the Oscars or the Rosebowl on the big screen. The Sidewalk Café offers more informal fare. Some of the cakes looked dangerously rich, but Tawnya, who takes care of me at the club, assured me they were prepared on a strict dietetic basis. There's a hair salon too, so you can incorporate a manicure or tanning session into your fitness regime.

If you don't know what to wear, a shop within the club will sell you 'top-of-the-line designer workout gear', Tawnya tells me. I gave a lot of thought to my outfit. My best workout clothes were too precious to be taken out of England – my Bruno Magli trainers with lizard inlays, my two-toned Chanel sweatshirt, my David Emanuel lace sweatbands – but my cousin came to the rescue by allowing me to raid her husband's closets. Since my beloved Fozzy Bear T-shirt would be considered a touch louche at Sports Club LA, we settled instead for one of William's ecologically sound Save the Bay T-shirts. My suggestion of wearing beige socks was too shocking, and I was persuaded to stick to convention and borrow William's woolly whites.

Tawnya bashfully waved goodbye at the entrance to the men's locker room. These are carpeted and the lockers are wood-veneered, but this is not good enough for some of the members, who crave executive membership (waiting list only), which entitles you to a permanent locker and free laundry service. After I had changed I wandered into the gym, which is laid out on two floors. At the main desk you can take advice from someone with a BA in bicep management on how to structure your fitness programme.

Tawnya appeared by my side to introduce me to Greg, my consultant for the afternoon. I asked her why people paid $2000 here when they could jog round Beverly Hills for free.

'Exercise,' she intoned, 'gets rid of stress, and you feel better about yourself.'

'The balcony is lined with beautiful young people of twenty-two. Don't they feel good to start with? If I looked like they do, I'd feel ecstatic.'

'It's not so simple,' replied Tawnya patiently. 'We have lots of models and actresses, people who need to stay in shape. LA is a competitive city, and everybody wants to look their best. People like the feeling that they're getting in better shape with every day. The trouble with jogging is dealing with smog, with traffic. You don't have that here.' And as the brochure explains: 'You may be the ideal weight according to the many height and weight charts, yet still be overfat. A body composition test measures lean muscle mass and body fat and is available at the Club.' In other words, you may look like Madonna and still be a flab-bucket.

Tawnya added: 'It's also a social thing. We're one of the few clubs to organise business networking.'

Indeed, Sports Club LA publishes a networking directory for its members. Bernd Stevens, accountant, will give you a 15 per cent discount, and you can get up to 50 per cent off if you order from Bill Ring's 'advertising specialities business'. There's discounted dry-cleaning from Stephen Geary, and Dancing Barry the magician will knock a fifth off the bill. Molly-Ann Leikin offers Polishing and Marketing Contemporary Songs, at 15 per cent off to members. I used to think networking was crass, but of course I'm prim and British. I've come round to the view that networking is indeed crass, but at least Americans are open about it. In Britain we do the same thing but pretend not to, which presumably is why people join the Freemasons, hoping we'll believe that their real reason for joining is a passion for hopping on one foot or an inability to make a charitable contribution without a support group.

Greg overwhelmed me with choice. The overlong menu included the Cybex machine for the upper shoulders, an upper back machine, the Military Press and the Seated Chest Press. All these machines, he explained, were isokinetic, and involved pulling and tugging fixed weights. I found all these exercises easy enough, until Greg altered the weights, at which point they became much too difficult. Moving down the body, there were Leg Extension (kick up) and Leg Curl machines. An Ergometer allows you to pedal with your arms, though why anybody would want to I can't imagine. Electronic monitors are attached to all these machines, so you have to punch in your weight, the time you wish to spend on the machine, the desired speed, and so forth.

One of the machines had to be adjusted according to my weight.

'How many kilos?' Greg wanted to know.

'No idea.'

'Pounds?'

'Not sure. We work in stones.' I estimated my weight in pounds for him, but to my annoyance he raised an eyebrow and added on another ten for good measure. Bad move, Greg. Just wait till your Christmas box comes round.

The treadmills were very boring, although you can adjust the elevation as well as the speed to vary the routine. The Gauntlet simulates stairs, while the ClimbMax has alternate treads which increase the difficulty.

'I think I'll go cycling today, Greg.'

'Okay. We'll set you up here. Whatdya say to fifteen minutes of Rolling Hills and then fifteen of Gentle Climb?'

'Sounds great. Push those buttons.'

While Greg was priming the machine, I unfolded my newspaper and propped it up on the stand. I'd forgotten my water bottle, for which a rack is thoughtfully provided beneath the seat. As I climbed aboard, Greg admired my calves, which are certainly among my most inspiring features. While I pedalled, I polished off the *Los Angeles Times* in about ten minutes, so I tossed it aside and watched the satellite TV, for which the sound is beamed into your Walkman along special frequencies.

When my time was up, Greg helped me off the machine and carried me downstairs. Tawnya was on hand to lend me her arm as we walked past the various sports facilities, the basketball, volleyball, squash, and paddle tennis courts. We moved on towards the aerobics studios, where one class was engaged in Steep Reebok, very popular this year. This involves stepping up onto a box and down again. It's great for the calves and bum, but does little for the mind. Needless to say, the facilities are fabulous. As the brochure relates: 'Our state-of-the-art aerobics floor provides excellent shock absorption, rebound, and foot stability. This scientifically engineered floor utilises coiled metal springs placed under two layers of wood.'

Back in the locker room I called through to the front desk.

'Just want to know if my car is ready. I asked for an engine shampoo while I was working out. Mine's the Geo, the one with the plastic fascia.'

'Not yet, Mr Brook.'

'No sweat. I have to do my laps anyway.'

These I performed in the spacious swimming pool up on the top floor. I dried off on the sun deck, listening to the distant murmur of traffic, the growl of landing planes at LAX, the padding of wet soles on tile. Then, stepping carefully over the starlets working on their nipple tan, I returned to the manly arena of the locker room and changed into my Dunhill underpants, my Gordon of Salford socks, my street-vendor-of-Delhi vest, and my Toshiba cotton slacks with the retractable flies. Then, mindful of my appointment with Mike Silverman, loped out into the lobby and whistled for my car.

'I came out here from New York in 1949 as a graphic artist. I had six dollars in my pocket. One night I met a drunk in a bar and the next morning I woke up in the real-estate business.'

Mike Silverman is still in it. From behind his polygonal desk within a glass booth at the back of his offices on Canon Drive in Beverly Hills, he surveys his team of agents, for whom the ear is an adjunct to the telephone. Our talk was interrupted by frequent phone calls. The real-estate market was terrible, which was all the more reason for the likes of Silverman to be on their toes. I eavesdropped.

'When we took on this property we put some stupid price on it because you always do just to get the ball rolling. I'd say it's overpriced by one and a half, two million. . . .'

'Listen. Do a real song and dance. Why? On the theory that enthusiasm is contagious. Tell the client I'm a proven success, which I am. Do a lot of pump on him. . . .'

'Have I heard from Zach? No, and if I had, I'd have got you out of bed in the middle of the night. . . .'

Silverman was philosophical about a market he described as the worst he recalls in over thirty years. By the end of the 1980s the market was simply saturated, and prices were unarguably too high. The recession in the late 1980s and early 1990s didn't cause the slump in the property market, but it certainly exacerbated it.

'In the 1980s someone once asked me how high the prices were going to rise. I replied: "Until they repeal the law." "What law?" he said. And I replied: "The law of supply and demand." That's what it comes down to. A few years ago it was wild out there. You'd have buyers sitting in their cars outside the property bidding against each other. Now it's very different and people are finding it very difficult to sell. This opens the market to scavengers who are looking to buy properties at the bottom of the curve. Of course there's always been this kind of speculation.'

Silverman confirmed that there was still no shortage of foreign buyers, especially those seeking property in prestigious areas such as Beverly Hills.

'But it goes in cycles. When it looked as though the Shah of Iran was in trouble, I put out an ad in Farsi in Teheran and flew there for a few days so people could come and look at our portfolio. Then the next wave of foreign purchasers were from the Orient, though many were looking for investments rather than homes. But don't get the idea that the domestic market is dead. The movie and TV business can create instant millionaires. Write a great script or direct a hit movie, and a deal can put millions into your pockets overnight.' The passion of foreign buyers for Los Angeles mansions remains so acute that one large real-estate company, Coldwell Banker, employs a sales staff with twenty-four languages at its command, including Tagalog, Hebrew and Farsi.

White-haired but trim and energetic, Silverman exudes showmanship. 'I was the first to show properties by helicopter. It was a gimmick and it generated lots of PR. But it also gave the clients an idea of the area they were thinking of moving into – how far the freeways were, the layout of the land, where their neighbours were located, and so forth. So I was able to build up a corporate image of colourful dealings. I sold sizzle, not the steak.

'You heard of John Kluge? Communications billionaire? We were having lunch one day, and John heard that I had Frank Sinatra's house for sale. He said he was looking for some real estate round here, and was interested in Sinatra's house. I said I'd show it to him, but he had no time. So he made an offer. I took it to Sinatra, and Sinatra said yes. So Kluge bought the place sight unseen. Some time later I sold Sinatra a house in Bel Air, and two years later he called me up and said: "Mike, there are two things I want to get rid of, Mia Farrow and the house." He wanted his old house back. So I called Kluge. He was about to get divorced and wanted to sell the house too. So that deal worked out well. There's a lot of this kind of trading. I once sold Tony Curtis's house to Cher. Turnover is quite rapid, often every five or six years. As people make more money or have more children, they want to trade up. Divorce is another big factor.'

'What kinds of features are buyers looking for?'

'Different buyers are looking for different features. Security is very important. Many buyers don't want any windows visible from the street. They want gates and cameras. They want to minimise the risk of kidnappings.'

This is in addition to the private police forces that towns such as Beverly Hills and Bel Air hire to patrol the streets night and day. Taking a walk down Crescent one morning in 1965 I was stopped by a private cop who did his best to discourage me from such exercise. The point of these private police forces, now said to employ more patrolmen than the LAPD, is not only to look out for suspicious characters or circumstances, but to act as a constant discouragement to outsiders. While immigrant populations swirl and overflow through districts such as Koreatown and Fairfax and Huntington Park, in the richer communities paranoia and anxiety take quantum leaps. Entire districts are now gated and privately patrolled, allowing access only to residents and accredited visitors.

Architectural quality seems a low priority for most purchasers, although one real-estate agency does list some houses in its *Los Angeles Times* ads under the heading 'Architecture', citing designs by Craig Ellwood and Wallace Neff, among others.

I asked Silverman to translate some terms I had encountered in the real-estate ads. He did his best. 'Fabulous architectural tri-level' was comprehensible if bombastic; others were more baffling. 'Etched glass accents' turned out to be engraved glass doors and panels; a 'media room' is the one with the hanging TV, the stereo system, the video, and so forth; a 'unique trophy property' is one so unusual that it was acquired for more than it ought to be worth, and is thus being sold at a premium too.

'Atrium garden?'

'I guess that's a garden inside an atrium.'

'Chaufferised motor court?'

'No idea.'

'Motorised sky dome?'

'Beats me.'

The house that had everyone talking in the early 1990s was the one built by Aaron and Candy Spelling on Mapleton Drive in Beverly Hills. Utterly without architectural distinction, the winged mansion is designed in a vaguely French neoclassical style. A friend of mine who is an architect thinks of it as a kind of domestic Pentagon, and its bloated grandiosity makes the comparison apt. There are conflicting accounts of its size, but the interior has an area of 56,000 square feet, making it the largest modern house in town, even surpassing Beverly Hills' previous best effort, Greystone's 46,000 square feet. Candy Spelling's clothes closets alone occupy 4000 square feet.

The house, like everything else in this image-conscious town, is intended to make a statement, but who is making it? Who are the Spellings? Aaron Spelling is a television producer, probably the most successful in the history of the industry. For twenty years, his shows – which included *Charlie's Angels*, *Love Boat*, *Starsky and Hutch*, and *Dynasty* – came in convoys over the airwaves. Frequent reruns filled the moneybags not only of the networks and actors but of Spelling – until the late 1980s when revenues diminished so rapidly that he actually lost control of his production company, although he remained an active partner in it.

By all accounts, the Spellings revelled in their riches. Snow was trucked in to guarantee a white Christmas for their progeny, and Candy Spelling was famous for her who-cares-what-the-price-is shopping sprees. The house on Mapleton Drive was just one more manifestation of their passion for conspicuous consumption, and it was Mrs Spelling whose tireless energy found ways to fill the indoor acreage. The house contains a full-sized bowling alley, as well as the legendary his-and-hers closets, but the zoo and indoor ice rink, Candy Spelling insists, are figments of excitable journalists' imaginations. The Spellings feel not the slightest embarrassment about their elephantine appetites, as though in their real lives they need to eclipse the fantastical splashiness of their televisual creations in, say, *Dynasty*. Candy Spelling once told a reporter from *Los Angeles* magazine: 'When I can't sleep . . . I'll go in and colour-coordinate Aaron's closet, from the whites to the beiges, and then I'll do mine.' The divorce should be fun.

Not everybody can afford to build their own palace, but many Angelenos can afford to erect a passable substitute by the process known inelegantly as 'mansionisation'. This simply consists of building on to an existing house, adding rooms, storeys, or service wings as the need or the mood takes you. Proposition 13 has increased the incentive for homeowners to stay put rather than move to a larger house. A new house might cost you five times what you paid twenty years ago for your present house, and your property taxes would increase by a comparable factor. Mansionisation is good news for the house owner, but often bad news for the neighbours, who suddenly find that the modest ranch house next door has acquired an additional storey and a cathedral ceiling which keeps their garden in shadow for half the day.

It you're a failure in life and don't own a large house, you can take vicarious pleasure in the foibles of those who have more money than imagination. The open house has long been an institution in the city, and each Sunday morning the *Los Angeles Times* lists the houses which the public may view that day. I started off just after lunch with 'a luxurious new Mediterranean Villa de Provence', located on Somma Way in Bel Air, and priced at $5.9 million. It proved to be part of a little development of similar villas, though each has its own private driveway. The views are lovely, peering down into Stone Canyon from a considerable height, but the pool, shaped like sunglasses with a jacuzzi at the nose-bridge, was small. The Provençal note was struck, I suppose, by the hand-hewn beams that looked as though they had been dusted with flour. There was a vast master bedroom, the obligatory walk-in closets, and a grand spiralling staircase. Despite a total area of 7800 square feet, it did not feel immense. Wasting space is part of the luxury, and in any case the average Angeleno doesn't have a great deal to put into his house, at least not until the decorator has gone on a shopping spree to the Pacific Design Center.

As I was the first visitor of the day, the agent from Rodeo Realty seemed very pleased to have someone to talk to. There was an even warmer welcome from the woman who opened the door at a house off Benedict Canyon on Green Acres. The house, set back from the road, was on a smaller lot than the Somma Way villa, but not an inch of space had been wasted. As always in these houses, bathrooms outnumber bedrooms, of which, in this instance, there were four, as well as garage space for four cars. This house was almost as large in area as the Provençal

villa, but considerably cheaper at $4.8 million, though it later
became obvious that if I could bring myself to offer $4 million, it
would be mine.

'I'm so pleased you stopped by,' gushed the smartly dressed
woman, designer scarf flung round her throat, 'especially since
this is my first open house.'

The proprietorial tone led me to assume that Marie was the
owner but she soon disabused me.

'This house belongs to an actress, and it's on the market
because of a divorce.'

'The usual story.'

'That's right. That's why you'll see all these boxes stacked up
in various rooms. Michelle's husband has moved out, and as
soon as we can find a house for her, she'll be gone too. In the
meantime a lot of her stuff is still in the closets, but feel free to
open them so you can see how much closet space there is. You
can walk round on your own, and I suggest you start here with
the masculine-motif den.'

The den was separated from the double-height living room by
a pair of mounted elephant tusks. Within the den the chairs were
covered with leopardskin-patterned cloth, tiger heads snarling
from wall-brackets, and a bar equipped with four stools and a
popcorn machine. This home safari tent was as tasteful as it
sounds. For more formal entertaining there was a startling deep-
green dining room with a mirrored wall to reflect the glitter of
the hosts and guests. Staff were accommodated in two maid's
rooms. The back yard consisted of a small patio, a handkerchief
of grass, a pool and jacuzzi, and a tennis court. You could almost
hear the sigh of relief that the inventory had been crammed in
with only inches to spare.

Upstairs I wandered into the master bedroom. It had a fireplace
– Marie couldn't remember exactly how many fireplaces there
were in all – five, six. An exercise bike stood alongside the bed,
and bedside reading matter consisted of professional journals
such as *Variety* and, prominently displayed, the scarlet CAA
catalogue. Creative Artists is easily the most powerful agency in
Hollywood, and Michelle clearly wanted to pass on a message to
those who would be trooping through her house. Marie came
rushing in to make sure I didn't miss a single closet. They were
immense, especially the one she described as the Imelda Marcos
closet, with layers of stiletto-heeled shoes toe-first against the

walls. One closet was devoted to the fur coats, and the dresses were so numerous that wheeled racks bearing surplus stock were parked in the corridor. These vaults for the outer person were somehow connected with the bathroom – the layout became labyrinthine at this point – which had two separate lavatories, a dry sauna for the ex-husband, showers and jacuzzis. Another door led to *his* closets, now invaded by stacks of boxes marked SCARVES or BIKINIS or SCRIPTS.

Another bedroom was Michelle's office. Posters confirmed that her profession was that of a very tall actress. A third bedroom was now the gym, lavishly equipped with weights and machines. Taped onto the closet was a calendar listing her daily routines, and on separate sheets, headed 'Butt work' or 'Thighs', more detailed exercises had been prescribed.

I asked my Hollywood acquaintances whether they had heard of this Amazonian actress, she of the magnificent butt and more shoes than hairs on her head, but no one knew of her. That means nothing. There are more stars in the firmament than any human being can glimpse in a lifetime.

Downstairs I bumped into a quiet man in his forties who was also surveying Michelle's domain. He had come from Fort Lauderdale and was 'in stocks'. He told me he found prices in Beverly Hills very high, and wondered how they compared with those in London. I had to confess that I too found them high, and indeed this particular house was slightly more than I could afford.

'But,' I pointed out to Marie, anxious to maintain my Bel Air street cred, 'you need to look high, you need to look low, so as to get a clear idea of what's available within each price band.'

She couldn't agree more.

'I've just had an idea,' she said thoughtfully, and her voice gained excitement as the narration progressed. 'A fella just walked out of here, and he told me he has three houses in Bel Air. He's looking to trade, with a little cash to make up the difference. Now that could be an interesting solution! Only the judge wants a settlement quick, and I'm not sure the trade would work for my client as there won't be much cash involved. But if you figure that each of his houses is worth about two million, then if he gets some kind of deal worked out, he may want to dispose of one of those houses to a separate party. Now that might be something for you!'

'Ingenious. Worth thinking about. Of course we haven't seen his houses, have we?'

'No, we'd have to look into that. And if this neighbourhood is too high, there are other areas of the city – we only list the best areas – such as Cheviot Hills where the lots are larger and you're getting more house and land for your dollar because it isn't called Bel Air. I'm sure I can find you a nice property there that would suit. Or possibly a fixer house.'

'Fixer house?'

'Place that needs to be fixed up. Listed cheap, but you may have to put on a new roof, or new landscaping, pay an extra $200,000 or half a million, depending on what you want to do. But they can be bargains. If I may ask, what's your budget? See if I can help you.'

'I'm not sure yet. I'm still based in London and I'm waiting for a few offers to come through before I do any serious house-hunting. I don't like to get too caught up in this kind of thing until the contracts are signed.'

'You're so right. But it never hurts to look around.'

'Absolutely.'

As it happened, a few days later the big deal materialised for me, and I signed on the dotted line. As a result, I earned £300 from a Sunday newspaper. At this rate, Bel Air would be within my grasp by the year 3000.

12

THE SONY SIDE OF THE STREET

Hollywood is not in Hollywood. The Hollywood on the map is a slightly seedy sprawl just south of the mountains. The Hollywood that is shorthand for the movie industry is in Culver City to the south, Westwood to the west, and, above all, in Burbank and Studio City north of the mountains. To the west, where Hollywood adjoins West Hollywood, the streets climbing the slope towards Sunset Boulevard are lined by small apartment blocks and the apartment courts that range from the tacky to the utterly charming. A true sense of community was established around these courts, which invariably overlooked gardens. Some became associated with political groups, others with states from which the residents had migrated to the West Coast. Hollywood is particularly rich in Spanish Colonial Revival examples, wrought-iron decoration curling elaborate arabesques against whitewashed walls and beneath rust-red pantiles.

The major boulevards, Sunset and Hollywood, become more sleazy as you move eastwards, with their unappetising souvenir shops, their street corners and parking lots where bikers and drug dealers congregate, where bemused tourists in search of glamour pick their way between bums and prostitutes. North of the boulevards, topography brings exclusivity, and in these hills striking modern houses jut out over the canyons. In Los Angeles height brings prestige, seclusion, and a view down onto the fumes of the plain.

Tucked obscurely into a corner of Hollywood is Whitley Heights, east of Highland and west of the freeway, a charming

area of narrow twisting roads, along which Spanish Colonial
Revival houses outnumber a handful of fine Streamline Moderne
examples. The Heights are happily cluttered with loggias and
terraces, palms and flowering shrubs, walls in mellow brick and
dappled stucco. Attached to one wall I saw a sign that read
MASERATI PARKING ONLY. It may have been tongue-in-cheek,
but in Los Angeles you can never be sure. Cars are too important
to be joked about. Anyway, the humour of the rich-and-proud-
of-it is rarely side-splitting, as a Rolls-Royce licence plate I spotted
in the canyons smarmily confirmed: 4CHOON8.

The steep streets and confusing layout of Whitley Heights
deter casual visitors, yet paranoia has recently set in here too,
and many residents are campaigning for a set of eight gates to
seal the roads that lead to the little colony. Pedestrian malefactors
are not common in Los Angeles, at least not in residential areas
where taking a walk constitutes immediate grounds for suspicion.
Seasoned observers deduce that the real reason for wanting to
gate Whitley Heights is not to deter criminals but to confer an
aura of exclusivity on the neighbourhood that will have a beneficial effect on property values.

The northern fringes of East Hollywood adjoin Griffith Park,
4100 acres of mostly wild hillside dotted with cultural and
sporting oases such as the Greek amphitheatre, and the observatory, from which the views onto the city are as good as the smog
du jour permits. Among the winding streets just south of the park
entrances stands one of Frank Lloyd Wright's great Los Angeles
houses, the Ennis House of 1924 on Glendower. There's another
Wright house nearby in Barnsdall Park which is now a gallery
and thus more easily visited, but the Ennis House is arguably his
masterwork in the city, tremendously powerful in a city where
good buildings are often deliberately low-key. In complete contrast is an apartment court on Griffith Park Boulevard that
pretends to be an organised row of rustic Norman cottages. It is
often remarked that Los Angeles buildings resemble film sets,
and nowhere is this more true than here. The wooden roof tiles
simulate wear and tear, and the stucco has been peeled roughly
away from the walls to reveal brick – a century of decay created
with a few flicks of the trowel back in 1925.

Few visitors to the topographical Hollywood come here to
admire domestic architecture. They are drawn to the icons that
relate the Hollywood of the map to the Hollywood of the

imagination. Mann's (formerly Grauman's) Chinese Theater draws the lines of vision upwards and downwards in vertiginous competition. On the ground are the famous concrete paw prints of the movie stars, inscribed and signed. Above are the phantasmagorically Chinese whirls of the roofline: the tapering copper obelisks capped with what could be a representation of darting flames; the Polynesian flourishes of the roof ornaments; the medallions over the scarlet columns flanking the main entrance that seem pseudo-Hellenic rather than Oriental in inspiration; the hanging bells, the friezes, the hard bright colours. Symmetry alone keeps the riotousness in check. Within the courtyards are gift shops, a display of Oscar winners, and booths offering tour tickets and free admission to the recording of TV shows. The cinema advertises reduced prices for 'golden agers'.

As a monument to Tinseltown the Chinese Theater is perfect: exuberance, boldness, artifice, drama. If the founders of Hollywood, Horace and Daeida Wilcox, were to be spirited back to the boulevard they would surely be horrified. When they bought these acres in 1887, they had in mind a Methodist retreat. After the city was incorporated as Hollywood in 1903, it was a haven of clean living. Neither cinemas nor alcohol were permitted here. By 1910 Hollywood voted for annexation with the city of Los Angeles, largely because it lacked sufficient water to sustain its own development. Once annexation had taken place, the upright character of the town was soon overwhelmed by the big-city values the Wilcoxes had hoped to keep at bay.

The early filmmakers found Southern California ideal for their purposes because of the steadiness of the climate and the diversity of the landscape: grasslands, sierras, and ocean were all at hand. Even in the early days Hollywood was not the principal focus of the movie industry. Universal Studios was founded in 1915 on the northern side of the hills. Other studios followed suit. By 1920 Hollywood had a population of 36,000 and about 100,000 people were employed in the burgeoning industry. The speed of the growth both of Hollywood and moviemaking was phenomenal. Most of the industrial expansion was taking place outside the town, with only RKO and Paramount maintaining studios in Hollywood itself. MGM was in Culver City by 1923, as were David O. Selznick's studios. The Fox lot was just south of Century City, and still is, and Warner Brothers built studios in

Burbank. By 1926 Hollywood was, in term of gross earnings, the fifth largest industry of the United States.

The major studios still wield the power in this industry. Few independent production companies can match the breadth of expertise and the depth of the coffers of the studios. Agents are growing in power, assembling packages that studios will find irresistible, but this also reduces the roles of the studios to those of bankers and distributors. The more prestigious the actors and directors linked in such a package, the greater the chance that they will exercise more control over the final product than the studio would normally wish to see. There is an inevitable tug-of-war between the various participants in any deal, but the studios, with their control of marketing and distribution, can still make or break a film.

The character of the studios has changed since the days when single personalities such as Sam Goldwyn or Louis B. Mayer dominated them. The constant complaint now is that the studios have fallen into the hands of accountants, financial wizards fresh from Harvard Business School but with no experience of the film business, and hence no nose for the magic that leads to daring, imaginative and commercially successful moviemaking. Even when studios are controlled by men with precisely this kind of experience, as in the case of Columbia's co-chairmen Peter Guber and Jon Peters, their puppet-masters keep a vigilant eye on the proceedings from afar – usually Japan. Columbia is owned by Sony, who paid $3.4 million for it, and Universal is a subsidiary of MCA, which was bought for $7.5 billion by Matsushita Electrical. The Japanese have also been funding individual producers and smaller companies, which suggests they have quite a shrewd grasp of a very complex market.

It was the screenwriter William Goldman who coined the adage 'Nobody knows anything'. By which he meant that it is impossible to predict the fate of any movie. The annals bulge with accounts of minor movies, ill-treated by the studios and underfinanced, that went on to become highly successful, and there have been innumerable costly ventures with all the desirable ingredients – stars, special effects, well-proven themes – that have flopped. There are sequels that out-performed the originals, and sequels that proved disasters. Richard Schickel once observed that 'the question of whether a movie works or doesn't work is determined largely by 1000, 10,000 instinctive decisions people make under pressure'.

Turnover is rapid in the higher echelons of the studios, and executives find that they are more likely to survive by exercising caution than by taking chances. Hence another frequent complaint: that executives are conditioned to say no. The worst consequence of turning down a project is that another studio will pick it up and the film will be a hit; the worst consequence of giving the green light to a project is that the film bombs and the studio loses $40 million. And then the finger will be pointed at the hapless executive who said: go ahead, we're behind this project all the way. Of course if you take this principle too far it may dawn on the studio bosses that the executive has produced nothing for the company and ought to be fired. But if he loses his job, he has a good chance of replacing another executive in another studio who has moved on for similar reasons. Even if an executive green-lights a script that turns into a hit, there is no guarantee that he or she will get much credit for that decision – there are too many other people with their fingers in the pie, including the producers, the director, the stars, and the heads of the studio.

Studios need financial wizards because the movie business has become incredibly complex. Box-office revenues are still vitally important, but are only one of many ways in which a studio recoups its investment. Sales to cable television and home video companies are important, and studios strive to sell ancillary rights to films before they are put into production. Advance foreign sales can raise much of the money required to make the film in the first place. The same process also benefits independent producers, who have fewer assets and less borrowing power than the large studios. In addition, studios promote sales to television of films in their 'library', their backlist. Other studios, notably Disney and Columbia, are active in other aspects of the entertainment business, whether it be theme parks or recordings.

Indeed, Columbia are now taking a leaf from Disney's book, and there is talk of a new theme park to be called, uninvitingly, Sonyland. Peters and Guber have been running Columbia with the swagger of the old-fashioned media moguls, paying and receiving huge salaries, renovating former studios in Culver City, and spending handsomely on new deals. Peter Guber has *Batman* among his credits, though for Warner Brothers not Columbia, and he and Peters are gambling hundreds of millions on projects that they hope will have the same kind of appeal and the same rampant success. But since nobody knows anything in Hollywood, it is impossible to say whether their projections are accurate. The Hollywood insiders are sceptical, but they too know nothing, and can only back their hunches, just as the studio moguls have done. Back in Tokyo, the masters at Sony are watching, watching. One day there will be a reckoning, and for those of us on the outside the thrill of it all is that the outcome is so unpredictable.

I drove into the Warner Brothers lot in Burbank and gave my name to Sonny at the gate. He told me to park next to the writers' building, a two-storey structure ranged around a courtyard. I climbed the stairs to Dimitri's office. I found a dark-complexioned man behind an empty desk contemplating a bottle of 1984 Château Palmer. An associate had cancelled a lunch date for the third time, and sent over the bottle to make amends.

Many of those who work within Hollywood have come from the inside. Countless directors, producers, and executives have ended up in the movie industry because that's what their fathers did. They grew up among a sea of scripts, and the jargon of the business has always been as familiar to them as charts are to a sailor. Dimitri, however, spent his teenage years not in the luxurious confines of Beverly Hills but among the street gangs of the South Bronx. Thanks to his own energies and some timely patronage, he became an actor, studied as an opera singer, and traded in antiques. A protégé of Mel Brooks, he was persuaded to come out to Los Angeles both to act and to write.

He was being employed by Warner Brothers on a term deal, producing material that the studio can either develop for its own use or sell to another studio. 'Sometimes term-deal writers are asked to do some work on other scripts. This is not part of our deal. If we say no, then the executive is likely to say, "Isn't your contract coming up for renewal soon?"' The benefits of the arrangement include not only a salary but an office and secretary and a parking place at the studio.

Dimitri didn't fancy the food at the Warner Brothers cafeteria so he recommended we go over to Columbia about two blocks away. The journey took fifteen minutes, as we had to find his car, drive about 150 yards, and then search for a parking spot. I followed him into the smart new Columbia building, still not entirely at ease in his company. Swarthy, and with jowls slightly puffed by treatment for recurrent asthma, Dimitri emitted blips of menace among the amiable flow of his talk. He struck me as a man one should not cross if it could be avoided. He combined the confidence of the professional actor with the louche swagger of the street kid grown up; there was a stud in his ear, and his bushy greying hair was gathered into a ponytail.

An immense television set almost blocked the end of the corridor that leads into the cafeteria.

'See that? A Sony set. That's just to remind the guys at Columbia that we're Japanese-owned now, and you'd better not fuck with us.'

'Is there any resentment that the Japanese are buying up Hollywood studios?'

'There is, though I hear that Sony have kept their hands off Columbia even though they own it. There's virtually no interference. But people do resent it. Look, movie stars are American royalty. For the Japanese to buy a studio here is like them buying the Tower of London. TV's less important. Television is seen as nouveau riche, but movies, that's royalty.'

As we walked in, two young men, separately, came up to Dimitri, hailed him by name, and gave him a brief resumé of their recent careers – 'I'm working for Jim Belushi now, we really ought to get together before long, have a talk' – and handed over their business cards. Dimitri was very affable – 'You bet – take care' – but as we headed towards the food, he turned to me. 'Not bad for a guy who's never seen those two before. Jerks.'

The cafeteria was lavish, with separate counters for hot breakfast foods and grills, for salads, and for hot dishes that didn't look too convincing.

'What's good here?'

Dimitri shrugged. 'Think I'll go for the Desert Storm Salad.'

'I'll try the Mother of Pastas.'

We found a small unoccupied table. No sooner had we sat down than someone else came up to Dimitri and asked him whether he had ever been in a television show, the name of which I didn't catch, about fifteen years ago in New York. Dimitri nodded sadly, and, pleased, the man drifted off.

'About six years after that show ended, I was in a restaurant in New York with a friend. There were two girls at a table nearby. I could see they were looking at me and whispering, one nodding, the other shaking her head. I felt good. They were clearly discussing me. Eventually one of them came up to me. Are you Richard Dimitri? I said I was. And had I been in that show? Yes, I had. I felt great. Any moment now, they'd be asking me whether I could handle two women at the same time. Then one of them said, "I knew it was you. We're really into trivia." Trivia! So I turned to them and said, "And I'm really into small weaponry. Get out of here!"'

Writing scripts is a depressing way to earn a living. Even the best of scripts are invariably rewritten and repeatedly altered, not only by other writers but by directors and actors. The final screenplay may bear little relation to what the writer originally put on paper. I asked Dimitri whether he found it frustrating working in such circumstances.

He shrugged. 'You accept it. At best, you can see what happens to an original script as a form of collaboration. At worst, it's just bullying. Everybody knows that whether a script is accepted or rejected has nothing to do with its quality. Often studios make defensive acquisitions. CBS, say, will buy an idea for a television script that is nothing like the kind of programme they want to make. But they want to make damn sure that another network doesn't buy it and actually put it into production.

'You learn the system after a while. If an executive has been reading my script and we're having a meeting and he says to me, "Dimitri, I don't think this character works," I'll look at him patiently and ask him to tell me what he thinks is wrong with it, what suggestions he has for making it better. In the beginning, the temptation is to grab the guy and say, "What the fuck do you know about scripts and characters?"

'You can still be blackballed in this town. Not for political reasons, but because if you start arguing with the studio executives, they'll look at each other when you leave the room and say, "Good writer, but difficult to work with, difficult to work with." And they'll make sure the word goes round.

'One of the first rules when discussing your script with studio executives is never refer to character psychology. Use that phrase in front of a Disney executive and you're dead meat. So you tend to go along. Having your script toyed with doesn't seem too high a price to pay if the rewards are good enough.'

'You mean money.'

'Sure I do. Writers also rationalise being part of this system by believing that if they go along with it, they'll somehow acquire greater freedom within the studio and that will give them greater power to write what they want. It hardly ever works out that way. But writers are beginning to work on spec more. They'll come up with a good idea, and if they can get a studio interested, they'll start a bidding war. The studio executives are smart, and they usually end up with the script for exactly the money they think it's worth, but sometimes the bidding war works, and a writer can end up with a million bucks in his pocket.'

In Hollywood there is no conception of an author retaining rights over the material he has created. Once a studio has bought a script, they own it forever. The contract will offer additional payments to the author if and when the script is developed further and made into a movie. The Writers Guild, the screenwriters' trade union, lays down elaborate rules for dividing the spoils, both in terms of movie credits and payments, among the various writers who contribute to a script. Another screenwriter was soon to tell me that the best script he has written in twenty years was purchased by Disney and never made. There are vague promises that the studio will get round to making it when the commercial context seems appropriate; the writer has no way of knowing whether he is being strung along or whether, at some point, the studio may indeed decide to develop his script.

'What's difficult about this business,' said Dimitri, 'is that executives change hats all the time. There's an executive I know who thinks I'm great. He loves my ideas, we've developed things together. Recently he moved over to Disney. Now you mention my name to him and he'll say, "Who?" That's because of the kind of studio Disney is. They're into demographics. They've worked out the kind of movies that work with Midwestern family audiences. That's their market and they're very successful. Executives, when they move to another studio, they have conversion experiences. It's worse than born again. But one day that executive will leave Disney and go to work for a studio that likes my stuff, and he'll start telling everybody how great I am. Of course, when you're on the receiving end of this kind of thing, you can go nuts.'

'After you've written and delivered a TV comedy script, who actually reads it?'

'Two trainees, to start with, then the director of comedy, then the vice-president for comedy, then either the vice-president or the president of production. And they may get opinions from other people too.'

'Is it like a hurdle race? Knock one down and you're out of the race?'

Dimitri nodded. 'Knock a hurdle down and you're definitely in trouble. Studios need team excitement. You have to remember that executives aren't interested in the *quality* of your work. They're interested in the longevity of their careers. So if most of those who read the script think it's okay but not great and the president of production thinks it's fabulous, within minutes everyone all the way down the line also thinks it's fabulous. Look, in this business if you have brains and sensitivity, you have to try hard to lose them.'

I asked Dimitri, who is in his forties, whether writers had limited shelf-life.

'There's a definite ageism in Hollywood. The people who run the studios believe that if you're selling to a sixteen-year-old, then the best person to handle the material should be sixteen. And in a way they're right. The drawback is that there is no concept of becoming mellow and wise with age. Most writers are finished by the time they're forty. I'm an exception.'

As we were walking down the corridor towards the exit, Dimitri made a detour into a room filled with Sony merchandise in glass cases. We peered at some answering machines in a vitrine.

'That's what I'm looking for,' he said, tapping the glass, 'a top-of-the-line answering machine.'

He looked around for assistance. A young Asian woman was placing some goods in a neighbouring showcase.

'Excuse me,' Dimitri smarmed, 'do you work here or are you just stealing things?'

13

INDIAN CUCINA

Once a week I ploughed through the two food sections of the *Los Angeles Times* hunting for the restaurant reviews. The restaurant under the spotlight that week was The Muse. What caught my eye was the phrase 'this '80s museum', especially since the 1980s were within the memory span of a five-year-old. The reviewer, Jonathan Gold, continued: 'If you'd held a candle a couple of inches above one entrée on a recent Thursday night, this is what you might have seen: white beans; black beans; radish sprouts; carrot batons; carrot shreds; spaghetti squash; black sesame seeds; grilled eggplant; chives; zucchini; broccoli; cauliflower; cilantro; tomatillos; red bell pepper; red onion; red cabbage; honey-Dijon-mustard-marinated pork tenderloin. The dish tasted like pork 'n' beans. . . .'

Trenchant stuff. Gold went on, with sublimely confident and expert condescension: 'The menu here is pretty interesting, and from it . . . you can trace the broad outlines of the pre-Spago California-cuisine era. You can see evidence in the salads: a cucumber-avocado macédoine . . .; a fashionably pale salad of Belgian endive, ground almonds and Stilton. . . . There's evidence in the entrées too: tasty medallions of rare ahi tuna, served with asparagus in a green peppercorn sauce; decent sautéd sturgeon served under a lump of mustard; grilled salmon with tomato and basil and extra-virgin olive oil. In twenty years, this is what nostalgia restaurants are going to be reviving instead of macaroni and cheese.'

This is the archaeology of California cuisine, and the phrase 'pre-Spago' is the key to Gold's lofty amusement and makes it comprehensible. Spago is the famous restaurant founded by the German chef Wolfgang Puck, who also established other pace-setting Los Angeles eating places such as Chinois on Main and, more recently, Eureka. This superbly designed restaurant, enriched with gleaming copper and with engraved glass panels, incorporates a brewery. When Puck came to California, he reinvented its cuisine. It is Puck you can thank for the California 'gourmet pizza' that is rapidly becoming available worldwide. Today Spago is more famous for its clientele – a nightly spattering of Hollywood celebs – than for its food.

I ate out as often as I could, because Los Angeles restaurants are fairly priced and the cooking in the best of them is both inventive and refined. Most of those I tried seemed happily embedded in this pre-Spago era. The chefs whose cooking I enjoyed didn't seem to care any more than I did whether their dishes looked 'fashionably pale'.

Puck was not the only force for change in California. Up in Berkeley Alice Waters was creating her own unique style at Chez Panisse, while in Los Angeles Michael McCarty was busy from the late 1970s in changing the way Angelenos dined out.

I went to see McCarty at his Santa Monica restaurant, Michael's. This is one of the prettiest, and most expensive, restaurants in the city, elegantly strewn with glassware and cutlery of good quality, colourful bouquets on every table; there's a charming patio with a rock garden at the back. McCarty has an ebullient manner; dark hair sweeps back from his forehead and races over the top of his head and down again. He gives the impression of being a man not assailed by serious doubts.

'You have to remember that "modern American dining" is only about twelve years old. Until then, expensive restaurants in any large American city were French. They were formal. We had virtually no restaurateurs. The smart exclusive places like Chasen's in LA and the "21" in New York were gathering places. The owners were personalities, and going there was like walking into someone's living room. What's more, cooking or running restaurants were not considered suitable careers for young middle-class males in America. There were no cooking schools in America. I grew up near New York and my parents entertained a lot. They enjoyed the revelry. Their food was excellent in the sense that the meat and fish were always the best quality, but they were prepared simply. Entertaining was about camaraderie. Nobody would have remarked on the food, except to say that it was great and then continue with whatever the topic of conversation happened to be.'

McCarty went to France to study cooking, and opened a small restaurant in Paris just as *nouvelle cuisine* was catching on. This style, with its willingness to combine ingredients in an inventive way, would have great influence on California cooking. McCarty's parents moved to California in 1976, and he followed them out West.

'By then I knew I wanted to be a restaurateur, but the major problem here was obtaining ingredients. I solved it by running a farm, from 1976 to 1978, but that didn't work out too well. I started persuading suppliers to improve the quality of their produce and to plant new varieties. I opened Michael's in 1979, quite self-consciously as a modern American restaurant. Hanging art in a restaurant wasn't a novel idea, but I resurrected it, and bought work by Stella, Hockney, Cy Twombly, Jasper Johns, that's still hanging on the walls downstairs. I went for a well-defined look. The restaurant was light and airy, and we had a garden. It was amazing that so few other restaurants had places where you could eat outside. Most restaurant owners here had come from Chicago or Boston or places where you wouldn't dream of eating outdoors. Michael's was casual but sophisticated. Ralph Lauren was a friend and I hired him to design staff uniforms that were relaxed but professional. We had a youthful staff – I was only twenty-five when we opened – and no intimidating maitre d' on the door. Plus there was the novelty value, the glamour element of a young American chef opening a restaurant here. The whole thing clicked for a lot of people.

'Before long the kind of thing we and Alice Waters were doing was labelled California cuisine. We had new ingredients, we were open to influences from Italy and Spain and the Orient. In Paris I'd studied alongside Japanese trainees and I was amazed by the attention they gave to the presentation of food. I saw my role as being in the front of the house, as being an ambassador to the clients. We've been very successful.'

I asked him to elaborate on the distinctive features of California cuisine.

'I'd say there are two schools of chefs. The first I call the chemists. These are people who live in their kitchen, producing the whackiest food they can create. They are usually well educated and well travelled, and are always introducing new ingredients, new combinations, new ideas. The palette of ingredients available to a cook in California is immense. It's not Oriental food, but Vietnamese, Thai, Chinese, Japanese. Not just Mexican, but Argentinian, Brazilian, Guatemalan. The chemists are the avant-garde, and there was a period when they went overboard with all these combinations. It was absurd. But they don't stay in that stage for very long. They mellow out, and eventually devise a formula that works, a style of cooking that evolves, but evolves slowly. Any good chef develops his classics. Michael's is famous for its goat's cheese salad. We still have it on the menu, because people expect to find it here. People come to Michael's with certain expectations, and it would be crazy to throw out my menu every year or so. Of course our menu keeps changing, if only because the seasons impose changes. Right now we're beginning to get our hands on the new season's shad roe, pompano, baby red snappers.'

Michael's greatest success is to have survived. The restaurant scene in Los Angeles is extraordinarily volatile. The institutional restaurants, places such as Chasen's that fill a social rather than a gastronomic niche, survive without difficulty, but innovative restaurants seem to be participating in a kind of lottery. I asked McCarty why so many Los Angeles restaurants closed only a year or so after opening, even though the food was good and the critical reception favourable.

'Often it's because of some crisis. A divorce, or partners splitting up. That means the management deteriorates, jobs don't get done properly. Many of the people who own restaurants have no experience of the business. They're casual investors. In the 1980s there were thousands of people with a few grand to spare, and they liked being able to tell their friends they owned a piece of a restaurant. Restaurants were a kind of theatre, places to see and be seen. People in this town don't have time to entertain at home very often, so restaurants become extensions of their business and social lives. Some people who open restaurants are fine cooks, others are good businessmen. It's hard to find someone like myself who can combine the two. Both aspects are important. If either is neglected, you're unlikely to survive.'

Promising chefs bounce from restaurant to restaurant. Michael's is highly unusual in having retained its chef for twelve years. Most spend a year or two gaining experience, then either move on elsewhere or start up their own place. Good cooking is in demand as never before. Everybody acknowledges that the farms and oceans of California provide a marvellous array of ingredients, easily supplemented by spices and herbs and techniques brought to Los Angeles by diverse groups of immigrants. Californian wines, once blockbusters with very high alcohol, have been slimmed down so as to complement a wider range of dishes. In recent years Californian wine producers have opened restaurants and cooking schools, stressing that wine and food are inseparable twins of gastronomy.

'Twelve years ago restaurants were not news. They were mentioned in gossip columns, but only because they were locations, settings. Michael's became news because of the art on the walls as well as the design and the food. Today there are many good food and wine magazines, and the reviewers are very important to us. Whether they're reliable is not, for most clients, the primary consideration. People who eat out a lot tend to be very busy. Restaurant reviews simplify matters.'

The proliferation of food magazines and restaurant reviews does encourage diners to experiment, but it also leads to fickleness. Similarly, good word of mouth, that essential ingredient in making a new movie successful, is just as important in the restaurant business, but it doesn't promote stability. Just as you've grown familiar with the food at the Purple Urchin, a magazine raves about the Green Mole; for two months you had to fight for a table at the Urchin, but overnight the place is empty. Food is chic in Los Angeles, and you like it to be known that you've been to Katsu or 72 Market Street, but that doesn't mean you need to dine there regularly. So the clientele is as volatile as the styles of cooking.

'That was especially true in the 1980s. Less so now. The thousands of well-paid young couples with no kids encouraged new restaurants to open up. Now we're seeing a more conservative, regular clientele. People don't want to stand in the street in line for an unknown quantity. They like to come to a place they know is reliable. The cuisine has settled down too. The present attitude seems to be: why fix it if it's not broken? We're into a refinement period now.'

McCarty has, like many successful restaurateurs, been tempted to build his own empire. He also owns restaurants in Denver,

New York, and Washington. I suggested it was hard to maintain high standards when he is necessarily absent from three of his restaurants at any one time, but he didn't agree. 'It's a matter of communications and training. I talk to all my restaurants every day.' The restaurateur Bruce Marder has been less fortunate. His Westside restaurants Rebecca's (new-wave Mexican and decor by Frank Gehry) and the West Beach Café (costly Californian with Italian influences) have been very successful, but when he opened DC3 at the Santa Monica Airport, the buzz and the chic didn't last long, despite an exciting interior design. Marder's restaurants seemed infected by the Hollywood notion of 'high concept', a clever idea that's easy to grasp yet grabs the attention. Marder has managed to create wildly successful social gathering places, but has found it more difficult to sustain them.

Another restaurateur, Fred Deni, is sceptical about this kind of empire-building. 'Restaurateurs dream up a new idea for a restaurant, then they collect a few investors. New ideas rarely come cheap, and they don't always work, and I have a feeling that the 1990s will see a big shakedown in the Los Angeles restaurant scene.' Even now he estimates their failure rate at about 80 per cent each year. Deni himself makes no claims to offer great cooking. His restaurants, including the only one actually on the beach at Santa Monica, about a mile up the Pacific Coast Highway, provide simple dishes at modest prices. Deni prospers by catering to a casual clientele in busy locations. He has deliberately avoided trendiness, being only too aware of the speed with which fashions tumble. Californian *nouvelle cuisine* is now *passé*, he assured me, as is 'Southwestern', a shorthand for elegant Mexican cooking. He discerns a move back to home-style cooking, to mashed potatoes and meat loaf, the kinds of dishes Kate Mantalini's serves. Good bread, impossible to find in Los Angeles until about five years ago, is now very chic.

It's not just the cooking that makes or breaks a restaurant. There are many different ways in which a restaurant becomes trendy. In some cases it's the presence of a star chef such as Wolfgang Puck or Joachim Splichal who owns the superb Patina. Sometimes a famous actor, such as Carroll O'Connor, is the owner whose name appears in neon over the door, and this will draw a certain clientele. In the case of Deni's own beach restaurant, the location is crucial. Elementary psychology can come in handy too. I ate at the

Lebanese restaurant Al Amir in the Wilshire Courtyard building. Because the owners originally wanted to attract a wealthy Middle Eastern clientele, they dressed the waiters in tuxedos. This beamed a message to lunchtime escapees from nearby office buildings that Al Amir was too pricy and formal for the likes of them, and they ate their lunches elsewhere. A quick change of costume took place one week, and the same waiters reappeared in green Polo shirts; pizzas and salads were added to the lunch menu, with exotic and high-priced Lebanese fare mostly relegated to a separate menu. Al Amir began to fill up.

If Los Angeles restaurants have a generic fault, it is that many of them are abominably noisy. Even in Michel Richard's fine restaurant Citrus, with its high ceilings and well-spaced tables, it can be impossible, on a busy night, to hear what your companions are saying. I asked a local *bon viveur* why this was so. 'The traditional explanation,' he told me, 'is that a high noise level has to be maintained because most diners in Los Angeles have nothing to say to each other.' Neatly cynical, but a less probable explanation than the flimsiness of building materials. In the benign climate of Southern California thick walls which can cushion sound are superfluous, but lighter materials help noise to reverberate.

Fred Deni is critical of many restaurant reviewers, and Jonathan Gold seemed just the kind of writer he had in mind when he told me: 'Too many food writers seem out of touch with the customers' interests. If a new restaurant opens, the reviewer may become ecstatic on discovering a rare ingredient in a sauce or garnish. That's showing off, letting your readers know how skilled you are. I often hear friends who eat out a lot telling me they're disappointed with restaurants that have had rave reviews, because the writer has ignored factors such as noise and ambiance.'

Nor are the restaurant review pages always as dispassionate as they appear. Many papers and journals won't run a review of a restaurant unless it is prepared to advertise in its pages. Deni told me: 'A friend of mine who's a restaurateur was approached by a radio station and told that the presenter wanted to review his restaurant, and would he take out an ad. He said no, and the offer to review his restaurant was withdrawn. I call that extortion. My own restaurants don't need that kind of publicity, as word of mouth has been excellent, but that kind of extortion can work against a smaller restaurant that doesn't have a large enough budget to advertise and prefers to spend its resources on producing good food.'

Michael Daniels, a lawyer with offices in Beverly Hills, dispenses with newspaper reviews when he wants to indulge his serious passion for dining out. He turns instead to his desktop computer. He sat me beside him as he plugged in a programme called Prodigy.

'Name a city.'

'Los Angeles.'

Punch, buzz, whirr.

'Okay. Here's the menu. You want Shopping Tips, Hotels, Wining and Dining, or Inside Scoop?'

'Wining and dining.'

Punch, blip, whine.

'Okay. You want the latest ratings for the top twenty restaurants in the city?'

'Sure.'

And so it went on. There were wine notes on tap too, and a bulletin board where Daniels had left a message for mega-taster Robert Parker, who had replied with advice on Châteauneuf-du-Pape. Prodigy was clearly a far more interesting pursuit than Litigation, though Daniels seems successful enough as a lawyer. His clerk also had special interests and was summoned into the office to list for me the trendiest clubs of the month.

It was Daniels who sent me off to sample the best Mexican food I was to eat in Los Angeles, at a small neighbourhood restaurant, La Serenata, on First Street in Boyle Heights. It's surprisingly difficult to find good authentic Mexican food in the city. Linda Burum, who writes about ethnic restaurants, suggests that this is because there is no tradition of dining out in Mexican culture. Thus most Mexican restaurants tend to be lunch places or snack bars. The grander Mexican restaurants in town, such as the crowded and enjoyable El Cholo, cater very professionally to American notions of Mexican cuisine. La Serenata, in contrast, dispenses with the theme-park decor and jugs of margaritas, and serves seafood cooked in a variety of spicy styles. I was offered a beer with my meal, but as the jingle so admirably puts it, 'Nothing beats a Bud', so I had nothing.

Some ethnic cuisines retain a fair measure of authenticity after their transposition to Southern California. Others begin an instant mutation. I lunched one day at the East India Grill Too, one of a pair of Indian restaurants on North La Brea, between the Fairfax district and Hollywood. On the window the sign read 'Indian Cucina/California Accent'. In Culver City, where a large number of Indians, mostly immigrants from the professional classes, have settled, the superb Bharat Bazaar stocks all the vegetables and spices and ghee and lentils and rice you would need to fuel a decent Indian restaurant. The India Grill was clearly aiming for something different. The raw materials included Cornish game hen, Australian lobster tail, and squid, and after my meal I could order cappuccino. And why not?

To sit by the window of this clean little restaurant with its hi-tech decor was an instructive and quintessentially Angeleno experience. While mopping up a vegetable curry with some nan, I could observe the traffic across the patio between the two branches of the restaurant. Within this patio is the La Brea Kosher Market, and on the other side of La Brea is the Yeshiva Yashiel Yehuda, a slice of Jerusalem's Mea Shearim or London's Stamford Hill wafted into Southern California. One set of doors at the yeshiva gave admittance to young boys in sidelocks, while another opened to reveal young Orthodox girls in long skirts. There was no clash between the rootlessness of this new-comers' city and the ancestral traditions of a Chasidic community. Powerfully built Jewish matrons wearing heavy wigs were wrestling with the power steering of their station wagons just like any other city mom who was collecting her progeny from school.

Beverly Hills is a Jewish city, and Brentwood, Westwood and West Hollywood also have large Jewish enclaves, but out here beyond Fairfax and in the side streets around La Brea and Beverly are very different kinds of communities. The Westside Jews came, like other migrants to Los Angeles, from other parts of the United States. From the 1970s onwards Jewish immigrants began arriving from the Soviet Union in large numbers. There was a time when Jewish emigrants, having acquired exit visas after tremendous struggle and hardship, arrived at a port of entry within Western Europe, and instead of proceeding to Tel Aviv, headed straight off to New York or Los Angeles.

These Russians, few of whom are religious, settled originally in the Fairfax district, the most overtly Jewish district of Los Angeles in terms of its shops and places of worship. They are not to be confused with the Chasidim who live, often in very splendid houses, a few blocks to the west towards La Brea. Most of these are second- or third-generation American Jews, some of whom come from Chasidic backgrounds in Brooklyn or elsewhere, while others are born-again Jews from secular backgrounds. On Saturdays they emerge in all their splendour, the men in silk gaberdine frock coats and tall fur hats, their wives, usually pregnant and with a row of children in tow, in snoods and swirling silk dresses. Outside the synagogues the men, mostly bearded, stand in small groups, their black and white prayer shawls flung over the backs of their black coats. There is no Mea Shearim shabbiness here.

Nobody knows exactly how many Israelis are living in greater Los Angeles. There would seem to be at least 100,000 and possibly twice that number. Anxious to avoid the accusation that they are deserting their country in its hour after hour of need, Israelis rarely admit that they have emigrated. They often speak of their stay in California as somehow temporary, as a period of study or work experience. Nor is it possible to draw a clear distinction between the Israeli-born and those who may have spent a short time in Israel after half a life in Russia or Morocco before taking the decision to move to America. A number of Israelis live in the Fairfax district, and many others live in smaller pockets in the Valley or in the various Westside communities.

The downfall of the Shah persuaded about 30,000 Iranian Jews to head for Los Angeles. Some of the richer ones were responsible for some notably garish instances of *nouveau riche* vulgarity in Beverly Hills; many were poor but lucky. There was a delightful incident early in 1991, when police were summoned to an apartment building in Santa Monica, and found an impromptu abbatoir in the garage below. The victims included a dozen chickens and three lambs. Fearing that Satanic orgies were taking place, the police made the customary inquiries, only to learn that it was an Iranian-Jewish custom to have a tremendous feast, all under the proper supervision of a rabbi and *shochet* (ritual slaughterer), to celebrate the completion of a building project. The victims of the butchery, the police were reassured, would end up on the plates of the poor.

14

NO HABLO INGLÉS

They had been invited to stay for two nights, the woman explained, but were obviously intending to stay for two weeks. And that wasn't all. They stayed up real late, drank too much beer and then threw up on the carpet. If this went on much longer, she'd have to flee her own house.

She wasn't explaining this to me, but to Mark and Brian. By now I was addicted to their show. These two public-spirited broadcasters regularly offered to intervene in delicate matters of this kind, and the woman was now appealing to them to act as go-betweens. She must have been mad.

'So what's the guy's name?'

'Alan.'

'And we've got the number here.'

'This is your home number. Where are you?'

'I'm at my office. I had to get out of there. Alan's probably asleep.'

'Hey, it's ringing now. . . .'

'Hello?'

'Is that Alan?'

Grunt.

'Alan, this is the Mark and Brian show. We've just had a call from your friend Shirl who's been putting you up? Remember Shirl? Okay, Alan, this is her beef.'

They explained why his hostess was upset. Shirl murmured assent in the background. Alan was not unduly perturbed but was slightly defensive.

'Hey, Alan,' said Mark firmly. 'Here's the deal. You're not welcome. They don't like you.'

Shirl was feebly protesting down the line that she did like Alan and his friend but it was just that they were, you know . . .

'Alan, you don't seem to understand. We're trying to be delicate.'

'That's right.'

'Just quit leeching off your friends.'

'They hate you.'

More squeals from Shirl, claiming misrepresentation. Mark, who was ignoring Alan's protests of innocence with lapses, kept up a stream of fairly diplomatic argument, while down the other microphone Brian was hissing, 'Get out of the house, get out of the house.'

All that domestic havoc put me in a cheerful mood as I left the house. The sky was blue, the traffic was light along Beverly. I drove east through Koreatown and into the Latino districts, until I came to Boyle Heights. A fashionable suburb in the 1880s, it shares a similar historical development with comparable districts in other cities which attracted waves of immigration. It was once a Jewish area, though hardly anything remains to confirm that this was so. There are some older buildings, mostly two-storey wooden houses in a dogged, well-wrought Midwestern style. Street murals are plentiful in Boyle Heights, all part of a programme to provide street art throughout the less salubrious parts of Los Angeles. An exuberant set on Soto Street have survived the depredations of sun and man well enough, but those on Mott Street south of First Street have been wrecked by graffiti. Even though the main streets are packed with cafés and restaurants, mobile food vans, their silver sides scrawled with gaily painted menus, are moored throughout Boyle Heights – and other Latino areas – offering tacos and burritos and soft drinks to passers-by. Many of these vans are parked on the edges of parking lots or gas stations alongside vendors of floral wreaths and vibrantly coloured garden gnomes.

Everybody who has heard of Los Angeles has heard of Forest Lawn, the Cemetery That Wished It Weren't, but in Boyle Heights I came across a serious rival, the Calvary cemetery. As in most Californian graveyards, tombstones are eschewed in favour of simpler plaques laid into the lawn, which thus becomes a park above a humus of corpses. The principal building here is the

Mausoleum of the Golden West. From a distance it looks like a standard Spanish Colonial Revival structure, but the detailing is astonishingly eclectic, with an Assyrian entablature and Romanesque fenestration and arcades. On either side of the pilastered main entrance are five free-standing Corinthian columns, each topped with a statue of a stylised angel. Inside, the chapel, covered with a splendid painted roof, is exotically Romanesque. The side chapels and broad corridors of the interior, lined with up to eight tiers of marble compartments for coffins, are gaudily illuminated by luridly coloured painted windows from the 1920s. Some of the drawers are still empty, awaiting family members not yet returned to dust; others are inscribed Baby Longo or Baby Johnnie or Baby Murphy, prompting giggles among the gloom.

Continuing eastwards I came to Whittier Boulevard in the heart of East Los Angeles, a busy shopping street with some stylish Moderne buildings from the 1930s, cheerful palms flapping overhead, and colourful shopfronts. Whittier is reputed to be the most dangerous street in the city, with drive-by shootings its best-known feature, but on a weekday morning there was no sign of trouble, no tension or threat. I was on my guard nonetheless, recalling that Dimitri, on hearing about my proposed excursion here, had remarked: 'Along Whittier, if you hear a pop, it's not champagne.'

To Westside Angelenos, East Los Angeles is at best a mystery, at worst a place of dread. Any travel east of downtown can easily be undertaken on freeways, so there is no compelling reason to take an off-ramp into East Los Angeles or Boyle Heights or Huntington Park or any other predominantly Latino district. Yet much of the character of Los Angeles derives both from its Hispanic past and its Hispanic present. Despite the great diversity of the Latino community – a jumble of third-generation Angelenos, Mexican wetbacks, Nicaraguan businessmen, South American trainee doctors, and so forth – it is perceived, with considerable justification, as remarkably cohesive. The Mexican community is especially numerous, for obvious geographical reasons, and for half a century Los Angeles has been the largest Mexican city after Mexico City itself. The statistic is matched by the Guatemalans; their 100,000-strong community in Los Angeles is outnumbered only by Guatemala City. And then there are 120,000 Cubans, dispersed throughout the metropolitan area, from Glendale in the north to Long Beach in the south. 50,000

Nicaraguans live here, and at least 350,000 Salvadorans, most of whom have fled from endemic civil war. South Americans are represented too, with about 50,000 Peruvians and slightly fewer Argentinians.

Four-fifths of marriages are contracted within the community; language and customs are faithfully preserved. Some might argue that this constitutes an almost stubborn disinclination to blend into the Anglo community, but I never sensed this was much of an issue. With 3 million Hispanics in Los Angeles County – a third of the total population – Latinos can argue that their culture should be on an equal footing with Anglo culture. Nor is their presence limited to the sprawling tracts of East Los Angeles; there are large Latino communities in Hollywood and the valleys.

These 3 million Latinos are seriously underrepresented on the governing bodies of city and, especially, county. Not all the blame for this state of affairs should be laid at the door of a discriminatory Anglo establishment. Only half of those entitled to vote are registered to do so, and only a small proportion of those who are registered actually bother to vote in municipal elections, presumably because a large Hispanic family in East Los Angeles feels little connection with the somnolent machinations of Anglo-dominated local politics. Immigrants from Latin-American countries also take some persuading that casting a vote will have the slightest impact on their lives. Still, it is now easier for Hispanics to become American citizens, and more and more are availing themselves of the opportunity. If citizenship brings with it a heightened sense of civic responsibility – and power – the political passivity of the Latino community may soon be a thing of the past.

The potential power of the Latino population alarms many Anglos, although it is hard to see what they find so disconcerting about the prospect. There are thought to be 30,000 Hispanic-owned businesses in Los Angeles County, hardly a sign of a community in dire straits, begging for dependency. This question of Latino power particularly interests David Hayes-Bautista, the director of the Chicano Studies Research Center at UCLA.

'People say that within a decade or so Latinos will be a majority in Los Angeles. What I keep asking is: So what? What difference will it make if Latinos outnumber any other racial group in the city? Of course we're not a single ethnic group. We're a civilisa-tion, one that's both heterogeneous and dynamic. It's every bit as complex as Anglo civilisation, so it's not surprising that when the two civilisations have to coexist, there's a clashing of tectonic plates.

'I suppose "minority" has bad connotations for Anglos, and we're perceived as a very large and hence threatening minority. Yet we're a very stable community. If you want to generalise about Latinos you would have to say that a high percentage of the community is employed, that we have a long life expectancy, low levels of drug use – whether we're talking about tobacco or alcohol or hard drugs – and we place great emphasis on family life. This adds up to the inverse of the "minority" model. It's dangerous to generalise, but in terms of community behaviour, we're exemplary.

'But we're also poor. For Anglos, there is a correlation between poverty and immorality – it's part of the Puritan tradition. Yet Latinos behave in exactly the way that conservatives keep urging people to behave. In Latino discourse, there's no connection between poverty and immorality. We don't know we're supposed to be immoral yet! Of course there are problems in our community – there is criminality and there are gangs. But we often find that these turn up in the third generation. Gang members in Boyle Heights aren't immigrants. Joining a gang is not characteristic behaviour for Latino immigrants. It's true you'll find immigrants hanging out at MacArthur Park peddling drugs, but they're often involved with crime and drugs precisely because they are here alone, without their families, without the support structures that lead to the stable productive life that the great majority of immigrants seek by coming here.

'Anglos are often puzzled by features of our community that are simply cultural. I'll give you an example. We have a very different sense of space. Anglos, blacks too, like to have their house with a lawn around it. To live in that way is unimportant to Latinos. We derive from urban or rural environments where nobody has lawns.'

I wondered about the ways in which this enormous community was changing, and Dr Hayes-Bautista, who specialises in demographic projections, had some answers.

'Twenty years ago three-quarters of Latinos were second- to fourth-generation. Today about the same proportion are immigrants. We're experiencing a continuous infusion of new people, a reinforcement of the culture. At our Center we've been conducting a study of Latinos' sense of identity. We've distributed packs of cards, each with a different term printed on it, and asked people to throw out the cards they felt didn't apply to them, and to rate the rest in order of priority. We found that the values they identified with most were, in order of priority: family relations, national origin, Catholicism, and the Spanish language. The respondents weren't just immigrants. In fact most of them were third-generation. Yet they would consider themselves Americans. So what we have here is a community that is genuinely bicultural and that is reluctant to assimilate. In East Los Angeles I can show you a singles club for Spanish-speaking Jews. There are Jewish communities in Argentina and Mexico and elsewhere, and when they emigrate to Los Angeles, they stay Jewish, but they also stay Latino.'

Everybody knows that there are millions of illegal Latino immigrants in Southern California. Nobody knows the exact number, but Dr Hayes-Bautista thought that up to a third of the immigrants were illegal. An amnesty has helped to legalise about two million who came here before 1982.

'Illegals face plenty of problems. They consume few public services and receive no retirement benefits, even though they pay taxes that are deducted from their pay cheques. Private clinics in California love illegals, because they pay cash and never initiate malpractice suits. So in many respects illegal immigrants are model citizens. Of course they can't vote, which lowers the proportion of voting Latinos. But among the second and third generations, I don't see much to indicate that they're politically less interested than Anglos. Latinos may feel they have fewer avenues for political expression, and gerrymandering makes it more difficult for Latinos to get elected – the deck's stacked against them. But give them the opportunity, and they'll go for it. The same's true of education, and third-generation Latinos have similar levels of educational attainment to Anglos.'

Statistics for the educational success of Latinos as a whole were far more discouraging. Only about 16 per cent of Hispanic high school graduates fulfilled the criteria for admission to the University of California. The average was 28.6 per cent, and an astonishing 55 per cent of Asian students met the requirements. Perhaps it was too easy to squirrel oneself away inside the community.

'Here in East LA,' a doctor at the White Medical Center told me, 'you need never learn English, not even in school. Many immigrants can also thrive without ever learning English, though doing so will often help them get better jobs. Los Angeles has become pluralistic, and everybody recognises it. Just look at the advertising in this city, not only in English and Spanish but in many other languages too. There are two Spanish-language television stations in the city, and many more radio stations.'

Before 1965 60 per cent of immigrants to America came from Europe. Today 80 per cent are from Latin America or Asia. Los Angeles accurately reflects this diversity. Zena Pearlstone, in her book *Ethnic L.A.*, notes: 'Between 1982–5 the ten immigrant groups admitted/processed in the District of Los Angeles in descending order of frequency were Vietnamese, Koreans, Chinese (from Taiwan, Hong Kong, and the People's Republic), Filipinos, Mexicans, Iranians, Cambodians, Salvadorans, Soviets and Indians. . . . Los Angeles is the second-largest Mexican, Armenian, Korean, Filipino, Salvadoran and Guatemalan city in the world, the third largest Canadian city, and has the largest Japanese, Iranian, Cambodian and Gypsy communities in the United States, as well as more Samoans [60,000] than American Samoa.' Court interpreters have to provide translations in eighty different languages. In Los Angeles you can buy five local newspapers in Chinese, four in Korean, three in Japanese, not to mention publications in Armenian, Farsi, and Russian. By the end of this century, demographers calculate, Latinos and Asians will constitute 56 per cent of the population of Los Angeles County; 11 per cent will be black, and the remaining 33 per cent will be white.

The prospect seems more thrilling than threatening, yet I would find most of these ethnic communities inaccessible. I recall pleasant conversations with the owner of the city's main Armenian bookshop, and talks with Dr Flores at White Medical Center and other professional members of the Latino community, but the Koreans, despite my determined attempt to make contact with the community leaders, remain a closed book. My experience is not unique. Steven Milukan, an editor at *LA Weekly*, which has its ear to the ground as much as any citywide publication, shared my bafflement.

'The many ethnic communities here are mostly phantom communities – they're invisible to most of us. Their cultural aspirations don't intrude on ours. They don't annex any of our cultures. I live close to a number of ethnic groups, and I have no idea what they do to have a good time. In part that's because I can't read their newspapers and posters. So we have a society that's genuinely multi-ethnic but also impenetrable.'

Howard Fox, a curator at LACMA, took a similar view: 'The various ethnic communities don't knit together. They seem to be leaderless – at least I have no sense of who their leading figures are. Los Angeles is not a melting pot. Instead it's fractured, with a frail superstructure. There is no sense of connection between the different parts of the megalopolis, whereas in New York there is no space within the city to avoid that connection. In Los Angeles the problem is partly geographical, because the city is so dispersed. So I think it's highly unlikely that LA will ever become a homogenised city.' Yet he valued highly the notion of culture that ethnicity imports. 'One can speak of culture as a received body of knowledge or custom that is transmitted through the generations – only the ethnic communities have that kind of culture. In America as a whole the sole unifying factor is television, not the sense of the past. So instead of culture we have a constantly shifting consensus. One month we're all talking about Berlin, then about Iraq, then about the Baltic states. Thus the only real culture is ethnic, and that is not part of the American collective experience.'

It's not only the foreign-born who have flocked to Los Angeles in their millions. Most of the American residents have come from elsewhere ever since the last century, when wave after wave migrated from the Midwest and elsewhere. A British friend who had lived in the city for a few years found this aspect of its culture consoling. 'It means that nobody can look down on you. There are no tedious rituals of admission to the citizenry. There's no elite here other than the possession of money.' Society, in any recognisable sense, only exists in a few corners of older communities such as Pasadena and San Marino, and its values are either ignored by the rest of Los Angeles or regarded as a quaint irrelevance.

Richard Dimitri, an immigrant from the South Bronx, also noted the ease with which one can gain functional acceptance in Los Angeles.

'The difference between Los Angeles and New York is that in New York people accept your own identification of yourself. You arrive in the city with a suitcase and a cheap suit, you buy some cameras and tripods, and you announce that you're a photographer. Or you rent a studio in Tribeca and say you're an artist. Nobody questions that. In Los Angeles you tell someone you're an artist, and they look at you with a smile. They know why you're here. You're in Los Angeles for the same reason that everyone else comes here – to make it. People come here because they want jobs, they want to succeed. This place is openly careerist, and that's its advantage. You don't have to play games. We're all after the same thing.'

Boosterism used to be a feature of Los Angeles. Every American community has its pennants, its mottoes, its excuses for civic pride. In the case of Los Angeles the city's virtues were vigorously promoted in the early years of this century as the city fathers, the Chandlers and Huntingtons and the rest of the vultures hungry for new carcases to batten off, urged Americans in search of a better life to move out to Southern California. Boosterism is less fashionable now, and there is no need to advertise the city to attract new immigrants. Indeed, the city managers would probably be glad to see a slowing down in the rate of fresh arrivals.

Severin Ashkenazy, himself an immigrant from Poland via France, is very much a modern-day Los Angeles booster. His own good fortune has been allegorised into an assurance that Los Angeles is indeed a city of boundless opportunity. When I went to see him in his offices at the Hotel Mondrian, he plied me first with statistics, and then with magazine articles he has collected, their common theme the wonders of Los Angeles, its economic vitality and promise. Ashkenazy does not fit the image of a successful California hotelier. He is a tall handsome man in his fifties, dressed not in slacks and a polo shirt but in a three-piece suit. He is urbane, quiet-spoken, studious.

After I'd entered his office, he offered me drinks and refreshments, which I declined.

'But I would like a glass of water.'

'That's all? How about some iced coffee?'

'What a good idea. Thank you.'

His secretary returned within seconds with two cans of Original New York Express Iced Coffee, a new product fresh from the factory in Singapore. There were cases of the stuff in the office, and clearly Ashkenazy was giving it a whirl, trying it out on friends and clients. This visitor was not impressed by the sugary concoction and I settled for water after all.

Ashkenazy arrived in Los Angeles in 1957 at the age of twenty-one. He attended UCLA and was working towards a doctorate, but gave up his studies after six years and went into the property business. By the time he was thirty-three he had put up a couple of hundred buildings, mostly on spec, and he was rich. Despite recent losses on investments in savings and loan institutions, Ashkenazy and his brother still own four of the smartest and most distinctive hotels in Los Angeles. In addition to the Mondrian, its external colour scheme an act of homage to the painter, they own the Bel Age, L'Ermitage and its annex, the Petit Hermitage, which is an ultra-exclusive and extremely discreet establishment where patients recovering from plastic surgery are comprehensively pampered in complete privacy before their return with reordered features to the world at large. All the hotels offer suites only and the Ashkenazys' most celebrated gimmick is the proliferation of original prints and other works of art throughout the hotels.

Severin Ashkenazy had a conversion experience in Los Angeles. He is the model of the cultivated European who became utterly entranced with his new home, despite its pitiful image as a cultural desert.

'When I arrived here I assumed that all the clichés were true, that Los Angeles is a plastic city, a city that doesn't know the meaning of culture. But after I'd been here a year or so, I returned to Paris and discovered that I wasn't impressed any more by what European cities had to offer. So I came back to LA. One day I was walking through the campus at UCLA and I heard the sound of violins. I opened the doors of the hall from which the music was coming and I stopped dead. There, giving a class, was Jascha Heifetz. Some weeks later I was attending the first performance of a new opera by Milhaud, and was seated next to a man in a wheelchair. We had a long talk before I realised that I was sitting next to the composer. Then there was another occasion when I was in a café, and I heard behind me some people telling the filthiest jokes in Polish I had ever heard. I went up to them after a while and teased them about it, as of course I speak Polish, and I recognised the man who had been telling them. It was Artur Rubinstein.

'And Los Angeles is a cultural desert? I can think of nowhere else in the world where a young man in his twenties could meet artists of this stature, and many of them, including

Rubinstein, became friends of mine. For me, Los Angeles was an intellectual heaven. I have to tell you that after living here, I find other cities provincial in behaviour and attitudes. This is a city that looks to the future. In Los Angeles, to try and to fail is not regarded as anything terrible. Indeed you are applauded for trying. Scandals are forgotten and failures forgiven. You are allowed to experiment here. A couple of years ago everybody was horrified by the Michael Milken scandal. I assure you that in a few years no one will remember it, just as hardly anyone recalls that the studio boss David Begelman was convicted of embezzlement.

'People make the mistake of comparing Los Angeles to a European city. But it's not. No European city has the kind of ethnic mix we have. Los Angeles blends the highly democratic with the pioneer spirit. The pioneer spirit encourages you to do what you want, especially on your own property, but the democratic spirit requires you to have the agreement of your neighbours. There's a clash but it always gets resolved.

'Do you know why Los Angeles is always denigrated? It's because the mass media are located on the East Coast. They've been whipping Los Angeles for eighty years, ever since the movie industry came out here, and they simply can't recognise that Los Angeles has now become the capital of the United States. There is a distinctive California cuisine and art, which is not true of New York, and Los Angeles is a style-setter, which is also not true of New York. You can start here without preconceived ideas, just as I built this hotel, which is now used as a model for hotels in other parts of the States.

'Los Angeles enjoys the most stupendous private sponsorship of the arts. The Getty, the Hammer, the Norton Simon, all these great museums. They are the exact equivalent of the Guggenheim and Frick in New York, but those are old museums. The new museums are not in New York, they're not in Chicago, but here in Los Angeles.

'There are things wrong with Los Angeles. For example, our convention centre is disastrous. But we can shrug off criticisms. This is still a young city busy creating itself. We don't need to fight for business or strive to find an image for ourselves. I know journalists promote the idea that Los Angeles is a city of fads, but in fact it's a city of trends. How many people know that Los Angeles is a world centre for perfumes and cosmetics? And who can deny that a label reading Giorgio of Beverly Hills means more than many labels with a Paris address?'

I could have taken issue with much that Ashkenazy was saying. The days when Stravinsky and Thomas Mann and Schoenberg had hobnobbed in the Palisades had long passed, and I was not convinced that Giorgio of Beverly Hills was as treasurable as he wanted me to think. Nor was the light moral sense that did indeed forgive and forget with casual ease necessarily admirable. But in the main he was right. Jeered at by the American press as a city of airheads and perceived in Europe in stereotypical terms as the domain of surfers and movie stars on the one hand, and of murderous roaming gangs on the other, Los Angeles was far more convincing, far more vital, and infinitely more complex than the condescensions of mostly ignorant outsiders could admit.

15

THE KAREN SALKIN STORY

You can eat quite well at the studio commissaries. Dimitri had introduced me to the routine at Columbia, and now Scott Arundale suggested we meet for lunch at the Fox lot. I was early and waited for him outside, where some employees were munching their salads at tables on a terrace. Another group of employees were hanging around at another set of tables, but didn't seem to be doing anything useful such as eating lunch.

When Scott turned up, all was made clear. 'Those cameras by the door have been set up for the next take of a new Steve Martin movie. And those people not eating lunch are in fact extras who are dressed up as studio employees. Talk of art imitating life.'

We studied the menu. This was organised so that the dishes on the left of the two-page spread were lower in calories than those on the right; the exact calorific content of each dish was specified beneath each entry. An entire section was candidly described as 'junk food'. My eyes moved immediately to the right in a kind of instinctive protest against this tyranny of the dieticians. I ordered a 734.

Scott, by origin a youthful New Yorker who had been educated at a British public school, works on the Twentieth Century-Fox lot not for Fox but for Largo productions, an independent production company run by Larry Gordon. Largo functions as a studio within a studio. Gordon did extremely well with such films as *48 Hours* and the *Die Hard* series, and running his own company gives him the kind of control he presumably wants. So

Largo has negotiated an 'output deal' with Fox, whereby Gordon's overheads – the services he requires from Fox – are charged to him.

Scott's role within Largo was not clearly defined. He screened and read scripts submitted to the company, but also dabbled in other aspects of production, as though serving a kind of apprenticeship. Titles are often meaningless in Hollywood, and serve as sops to egos rather than as descriptive tags. During lunch I mentioned that my cousin was married to an independent producer, and when I told Scott his name it turned out that he had been on the phone to him that morning. This simply confirmed what Scott described as 'the collective unconscious' in the movie business. People are constantly trading information and projects, and favours are offered freely in the knowledge that favours are also likely to be returned. Although the various studios are rivals, the turnover among both executives and projects is so rapid that it is impossible *not* to know what your rivals are up to.

'When a script comes in to a studio, it's usually from an agent who insists it's for your eyes only, and, by the way, he needs a response by Monday morning. The script is given to the creative executives – there are usually between five and ten of them – and to a reader. Few if any of the executives will actually *read* the script, so they'll turn to the coverage, which is the outline together with the reader's comments. The creative people then have three options. They can "pass", which is more polite than saying no. No one in Hollywood likes to say "Fuck you and the horse you rode in on". Or they can "consider" it. Or they can "recommend" it. Unless there's a good deal of enthusiasm, the producer or the studio is unlikely to proceed. After all, everyone has to sell the idea to someone else. The writer to the agent, the agent to the producer, the producer to the studio. If you have doubts, you're probably going to stumble. This whole business is a political minefield. To get anything done, you have to be really tough.

'Producers don't just wait for scripts to come in from agents or writers. Some have representatives in New York looking out for new books and new plays, especially off-Broadway. Everybody reads the box office records every week as if they were following the race track. We want to know what's doing well. The prevailing philosophy, the one thing drummed into me at film school, is that the only thing that matters in film-making is story, story, story.'

There was a brief distraction as I watched a man in a casual fawn jacket cross the commissary to greet a friend at another table. He looked just like Mel Brooks. It was Mel Brooks.

After lunch Scott showed me round his office. A script library filled the tall shelves of a bookcase, and beside his desk a computer was running a programme called TalentBook. This summons up data on everybody who is active in the movie industry, a kind of electronic *Who's Who*. He also showed me a dossier, compiled by agents and handed out to favoured clients, which lists all the projects being developed by other studios. No wonder there are few secrets in Hollywood.

'It's curious,' mused Scott, 'that similar ideas seem to spring up independently at various studios. I'm not just talking about copycat films, but themes that are conceived almost simultaneously. As soon as a project goes into turnaround it is pitched to another studio. So an awful lot of projects do the rounds in the hands of persistent agents, producers, and writers. This means that studios hardly ever initiate projects these days. They are essentially hosts and financiers – the creative energy comes from outside.

'Pitching is really important. Executives don't want to hear a long spiel every time a writer or producer walks into a room. It's best done as simply as possible. Any idea that can be quickly described and quickly grasped is a high-concept idea. For example, somebody once pitched the following idea: "Buddy-buddy movie, but one of them's a dog." It was bought immediately. The result was *Turner and Hooch* and at least one other movie with the same concept.'

A successful pitch leads not to a movie, not initially, but to a development deal in which the studio purchases a script and toys with the idea of turning it into a movie. It's the Hollywood equivalent of industrial R&D. Development can be stalled at any time, and only a fraction of projects that are put into development end up on the screen. It is perfectly possible for writers to earn an excellent living from selling ideas to studios. Since the script will be rewritten and possibly butchered repeatedly in the development process, it is often of marginal interest to the original writer whether the movie is ever made. Of course it's nice, and helpful to the career, to see your name when the credits roll, and to dream about the profit participation clause in the contract that never seems to turn into royalties, but seeing the movie made is almost like the icing on the cake. (William Goldman once wrote: 'All stars command a percentage of the profits and, if they are superstars, a percentage of the gross, profits being like the horizon, receding as far as you approach.')

Compared to the millions of dollars required to put a movie into production a development deal comes cheap. When word gets out that Studio X is developing a high-concept project, it may deter Studio Y or Z from using the same idea, even though Studio X isn't wildly excited about the project in the first place and may well decide not to make the movie. Development deals also make people feel good: agents, directors, writers, actors, all feel wanted, and all will understand if the deal eventually falls through, and no one will mind too much, since almost everyone will get paid something and almost everyone will have other deals in the pipeline.

'That's why,' said Scott, 'everybody in this town has a deal. Or so they say. You have to be sceptical as there's so much hype involved. Producers know that out of ten or twenty projects they may have in development only one will get to be made, so they need far more material than their production resources can handle. A good producer is always trying to generate heat, keeping up interest in his projects.'

One source quotes the Fox executive Susan Merzbach, who estimated that this studio puts up to a hundred projects into development of which only about twelve become movies. A project can be halted, or put into turnaround – a polite way of saying the studio has lost interest and the project is now up for sale again – for a number of reasons. The cost may prove excessive; conflicts or potential conflicts between the stars and directors may seem too tiresome to be tolerated; another studio may have a similar idea under a better team; or the executives who developed the deal may have been fired or hired by another studio and those now occupying their desks may have no interest in their predecessors' projects and prefer to develop their own.

There are different kinds of deals reflecting different levels of commitment on the part of a studio. A so-called step deal allows the project, especially at the writing stage, to be re-evaluated after each draft. 'Pay or play' deals handsomely compensate the big players – the producer, the stars, the director – even if the project goes into turnaround; this provides an additional incentive for the studio to keep the project alive, an incentive that can lead to some dire movies being made that would have been better ditched.

Having digested my lunch at Fox, I made plans for lunch at Disney, this time with a production executive, Jay Heit. Walking through the Disney lot in Burbank I couldn't decide whether the local moguls have a vein of self-mocking humour, or whether it's an earnest piece of corporate marketing strategy to plaster the Disney logo – a colourful drawing of M. Mouse – on every available surface. In the Rotunda restaurant in the new Team Disney building, the salt and pepper shakers and plates have Mickey prancing across them, and the black chairs have cut-outs in the shape of his ears. The Team Disney building is a chunky sandstone structure casing a vaguely postmodernist design, of which the most controversial feature is the pediment supported by figures of the dwarves from *Snow White*. Inside the building, which confuses even those who use it daily by making no distinction between doors that lead to suites of offices and doors that lead to broom cupboards, a forest of stumpy columns breaks up the space, forming in the restaurant an outer and inner ring. Jay and I were seated in the outer circle, but whether this made us very important or less important we couldn't tell.

As everybody knows, all studio executives are the personification of cowardice, duplicity, and stupidity. No one has a good word to say for them. Creatures of the corporate structure, their role is to stifle creativity, cut back on necessary expenses, and protect their own back. One writer of my aquaintance pondered the nature of the studio executive: 'In my experience they range from merely stupid to egregiously stupid. They can treat you very well, but only if you serve their greater purposes. The moment your presence is no longer seen as an ornament to their career, they'll cut you dead and stab you in the back.'

I expressed this view to Jay, thus putting my lunch at risk, but he responded amiably enough. He agreed that it was easier for executives to say nay rather than yea, and added that there was a tendency to fudge all decisions, especially when contentious issues were involved. For example, decisions are made about the shooting schedule that everybody realises are unrealistic. Later, the director, unable to meet an impossible schedule, then calls for overtime, and the expenses end up being far higher than they would have been had a realistic schedule been set in the first place. On other occasions executives send mixed signals, especially if, for example, a package bought by a studio includes a director who may be an unknown quantity. 'In such cases, studios have ways of giving it to him and not giving it to him at the same time.'

Jay is a production executive, not a mogul. He worked his way up through various jobs before being appointed one of ten such executives at Disney. His job is to keep an eye on budgeting and scheduling, and to oversee a project that is in production, usually in conjunction with a creative executive who may have been responsible for developing the project. During shooting, Jay spends every day on the set, both to make sure that the director doesn't start doing things that the budget and schedule don't allow for, and to mediate with the studio if the director or designer or stars or anyone else seems unhappy about any aspect of the film.

It seemed to me that someone like Jay would be as welcome on the set as an Orangeman at an IRA coven, but he seemed to take his responsibilities in his stride. He told me he does his best to be sympathetic to the film-makers. 'I find it easier to dodge the bullets coming from the studio than those of the film-maker and stars on the set.' But there was a temptation for line producers or production executives – all these titles being more or less inter-changeable – to side with either the director or the studio depending on the direction in which they thought their career was heading.

I found the whole notion of the 'film-maker' problematic. Was the director the film-maker, or the producer, or the cameraman? If you read Julia Phillips' brazenly self-serving account of her life in Hollywood, you leave with the impression that she and she alone was responsible for the success of *Taxi Driver*, of which she was one of the producers. But how could any producer, whose role approximates that of an impresario, claim the bulk of the credit for the success of a film, as though directors and actors and technicians were merely adjuncts? Those with practical experience of the movie industry give the *auteur* theory – which in any case applies to directors rather than producers – short shrift, though writers plausibly argue that their contribution can be more crucial than any other. Jay, for one, was not willing to propose any single theory to account for the success or failure of a film.

'It's like setting up a new corporation each time,' he told me. 'Each movie employs a different group of people and has a different balance of power. No producer fulfils the same functions. The first thing they have to be good at is getting their foot in the studio door. After they've got the support of a studio, some producers see their role as bringing together the creative people, the writers, the costume designers, the sound and camera people. Once they've assembled the team, they're content to let them get on with it. Other producers are frustrated directors who try to impose their vision on the film, and this doesn't always blend with the studio's vision of the film they are financing.'

After lunch Jay pointed me in the direction of the offices of Dana Lombardo who is in charge of market research for Disney. I wandered down Dopey Drive and turned onto Mickey Avenue, carefully following directions until I reached her office. I found a large desk behind which sat an attractive, exceedingly well-groomed young woman. The Disney group, under its various divisions of Touchstone, Walt Disney and Hollywood, releases about twenty films each year, and Dana is charged with marketing their theatrical distribution. Videos and other ancillary sales do not directly concern her. Her job is to ascertain what the potential audience is likely to be for any film, to gauge both what's appealing about the film and what may leave audiences dissatisfied. She can only begin work once the movie has been completed, as the shooting script may differ greatly from the finished product.

She'll organise previews, sneak previews, recruited previews, all the techniques of observing the audience, testing its response, and, if necessary, altering the film to boost its chances of commercial success. She described the techniques as reliable, and can think of few occasions when the studio has made a serious error of judgment.

'We knew well in advance that *Pretty Woman* would be a hit, and we also knew that *Scenes from a Mall* wouldn't do particularly well. But we never know how high is up. Over the years we've found that the audiences at previews rarely tell us something we don't already know. If the audience doesn't want the doggie to die, the same idea will have occurred to the people who've made the movie.'

Jay Heit confirmed this view, and said that, contrary to popular belief, marketing people do not wield excessive influence within studios. Their undoubted expertise is usually matched by the equal experience of the creative executives and the studio bosses. When, as in the case of a film such as *Dick Tracy*, commercial expectations in the form of merchandising and other subsidiary rights are built into the film, the goals may be set at a dangerously high level. The film picked up a few Oscars and grossed $100 million, no mean sum, but was still regarded by the studio as something of a disappointment because it was expected to do even better. Some commentators believe that the tail is beginning to wag the dog, that executives, at a loss to predict which of the projects in development are likely to perform best, are turning increasingly to the street-smart nostrums of the marketing people. Dana, understandably, did not think much of this theory, although with so many ancillary rights at stake as well as cinema distribution, it was not surprising that marketing executives should be consulted before a new project is green-lighted.

I asked her whether she could discern any long-term thematic changes. She could, and it was not good news. She foresaw a return to traditional values, not in any hectoring way but as a kind of thread running through new movies, an affirmation, a positivity. Films that revel in conspicuous consumption are also on the wane. I groaned at this vision of a Mississippi of blandness coursing through the cinemas of the world, but Dana reassured me that this would not be the case, that special effects and adventurous plots would keep me interested. Nonetheless for many years Hollywood films have been increasingly vitiated by reflex sentimentality. Potentially interesting and unusual Hollywood films such as *Dead Poets Society* or *Defending Your Life* have been wrecked by the lashings of treacle that are folded in as the film approaches its closing sequences.

After talking half the day about stars and studios, I had to pay a visit to a real star in a real studio. Karen Salkin had invited me to the public access studios to join the audience for the taping of her latest show. She ushered me into the Green Room where the other guests were sitting patiently. I was introduced to a lawyer, a schoolteacher, a writer, a car salesman. We made polite conversation until Karen told us it was time to enter the studio, a blue cube of a room with a platform at the far end. Here Karen positioned herself behind a pink-clothed table on which stood a solitary flower in a square vase. She was wearing a skintight black miniskirt and a splendidly embroidered jacket with gold, pink, and blue designs, and on the back, the antiquated legend: Flower Power.

Karen stood by the table, fussing with her makeup and conferring with the cameramen who knew her of old. Lisa, the principal cheerleader, yelled: 'Hey, Karen, there's a girl at Jerry's Deli in the Valley who looks just like you.'

'Y'mean she's gorgeous?'

'Of course.'

'So what's a gorgeous girl doing working as a waitress at Jerry's?' She turned to more important matters, such as giving instructions to Errol behind the camera: 'I may get up during the show and show the dress, so don't get worried.'

Lisa shouted: 'Karen, I love your nails.'

Karen jiggled her fingers. 'Poppy. It's called poppy.'

'Yeah, that's way more hip than red.'

'Oh, not *red*!'

Karen turned to me: 'Stephen, can I tell about your book?'

'I'm not sure the audience would be enormously interested,' I said, bashfully.

'God, you'd make an awful publicist.'

Cameras rolled, and almost as soon as she went on the air she mentioned that among her specially invited audience tonight there was a writer from England researching a book on Los Angeles. 'I'm trying to be in it. Whether I say any more about it depends on whether he laughs a lot – but since he's English, I don't think we can expect a lot of chuckles from his corner.

'Okay.' Deep breath. 'Okay. I'm going to review a few things straight away.'

We cheered. Karen launched into a long and impossibly elaborate story about visiting some restaurant where the theme of the evening was a murder mystery. She told us about her 'date', who was 'adorable' – Mr X doesn't like going out to restaurants – she told us about the seating plan, about her adventures with some egg rolls. To the woman seated next to her she had said, 'If it's you that gets killed tonight, can I have that fabulous bracelet?', a request greeted with a frosty stare. We in the specially invited audience enjoyed the line, and so did Karen who could hardly control her own laughter.

She reined in her hilarity. 'Anyway. The food's good and it's a very happening place. Okay. I want to show the dress. The jacket I'm wearing is by a friend of mine who is a very talented designer.' She stood, knocking over her chair as she did so. 'I've knocked over the chair,' she informed the camera, 'but the good news is that I didn't break a nail.' We admired the dress and the jacket, noisily.

Karen then continued with the restaurant review. 'Let me tell you, this place had the third best mushroom soup I have ever had in my life. What's the matter, Errol? Do you hate this? I mean, you're standing there next to your camera looking so – yech. You're just standing there? Okay. You see, whenever Mr X goes out of town, I can come here and be abused. And another exciting thing that happened is that Stephen took me to tea and at the very next table was Colin Hay from Men at Work – Oh-oh.'

Karen was staring glassily at the table.

'What's the matter, Karen?' It was Lisa calling.

'It's a bug.'

'Kill it.'

'I can't. It's a very small bug. Look, bug: I do this show *alone*. Shall I leave it?'

'Just leave it. Ignore it.' We were of one voice. 'It's just an ant, Karen.'

'I know it's an ant, but what's it doing on my table?'

The sight of a living creature, however insignificant, reminded Karen of her late dog Bud, and she began a tale of Bud, but cut it short, saying she wasn't going to give us the whole story as she didn't want to start crying, especially since Bud was the most wonderful – 'I'm now going to review a play. No, instead I'm going to review a private party. I have one more minute? Wait a minute. Yes, I just have time to tell you about this party . . .'

Time passed quickly, too quickly for Karen, and a few minutes later we were back in the Green Room awaiting her triumphant return from the studio. Most of her guests left, but a few of us lingered; Lisa, Ian the car dealer, and myself. Ian was a Londoner who had come to Los Angeles to work with computers, but had drifted into more profitable dealing in Rolls-Royce cars. The four of us decided to go out to eat.

'How about that place on Santa Monica?'

'What's it called?'

'I don't remember.'
'How about the Bicycle Shop?'
'It's dirty, I don't like it.'
'There's that Indian place—'
'I hate Indian.'
'I know. The Plum Tree.'
'What's that?'
'Chinese. Really excellent.'
'Okay. Where is it?'
'On Wilshire.'
'Left of Bundy.'
'Isn't it right of Bundy?'
'Could be.'
'How do we get there? It seems stupid to take four cars.'
'I'm not leaving my car outside the studios.'
'Can we get in your car, Stephen?'
'Not in what Americans consider comfort.'
'We'll take mine, and I'll bring you all back.'
'That means I have to leave my car here, and it's a convertible and that's too risky.'

So we each took the wheel of our own car and followed Karen in a speedy convoy to a very modern Chinese restaurant on Wilshire. (Two weeks later, according to the newspaper listing, the Plum Tree was closed down for one day on the grounds of 'vermin infestation and gross contamination of food surfaces'.)

The same indecision marked our study of the menu.

'How about beef with broccoli?'

'I *despise* broccoli.' From Lisa.

Lisa and Ian had once dated. Ian tried to recall in which of the four Rolls-Royces he had owned he had collected Lisa on their first date. Ian's ideal girl had to be dark, short, slender, Jewish, and with a fringe. Lisa had seemed to fit the bill but he had married someone else, and now, after only four months, the marriage was over. We discussed what had gone wrong. We discussed the extent to which Ian had been in love.

Lisa talked to Karen about earrings. Karen talked to Lisa about the friend who designed her jacket. Simultaneously. This constituted a multiple digression to a story Karen had begun to tell about the Price Club.

'We must discourage these digressions,' I muttered, which they found immensely funny.

'She interrupted *me*,' said Karen, defensively.

'I have to interrupt you,' retorted Lisa, 'otherwise I'd never . . . Anyway, what's your book going to be called, Stephen?'

Karen replied on my behalf: 'The Karen Salkin Story.'

16

SKIP EATS AN OLIVE

Dimitri phoned. I asked him how he was getting on with his various projects.

'I had a meeting on Monday at one of the studios. The guy took me into the commissary and I had to do my pitch in there. I didn't know why we were there rather than in his office. He hadn't said anything about doing the meeting in the commissary. I was giving him my ideas and he kept looking at his watch. So I said: "Look, usually there is a connection between the face and the mind. In your case I don't see any connection between what's going on on your face and anything I've been talking about for the past ten minutes. So I don't see much point continuing with this." And I got up to leave. The executive became very flustered, said he didn't understand what I was saying, insisted he loved the idea and was very keen to know the ending. I told him the ending, but also said I didn't think we had much else to talk about.'

'Dimitri, you've told me that screenwriters learn never to be combative with executives, that with experience you learn how to handle them and make the necessary concessions.'

'Exactly. I think I did rather well. I was telling you this story so you can see how well I've mastered the technique of self-control.'

I was doing no better when it came to self-control, and had become masochistically addicted to the hectoring Barbara de Angelis, the local expert at splitting up relationships. On my car radio her advice, instantly given without a moment's reflection, was guaranteed to wind me up and leave me spluttering with rage. Today she was on fine form. She began by confiding to the listeners that even though she wasn't feeling well she had struggled into the radio station anyway. 'Your love will get me through.' Count me out.

A caller was dating a man who was trying with little success to give up smoking. De Angelis, severe ideologist that she is, advised the woman to stop seeing her boyfriend – not because he was a smoker but because they perceived the issue of his fondness for a smoke in different ways. 'Just tell him that you have different values, have different paces of growth, and aren't compatible. When he's sorted this out, he can call you again.' Good. That was another relationship successfully detonated on the basis of a thirty-second conversation.

No time to linger. Next caller's on the line. This one had a boyfriend who wanted to live with her before marriage; she didn't agree with this approach. What should they do? Dr De Angelis wasn't stuck for an answer: 'You need to take relationship classes, get some therapy, and problem-solve the issue. I suggest you set a time limit, perhaps six months, and then evaluate the relationship.' Another caller was having problems with her boyfriend but was also doing her best to see her boyfriend's point of view, to understand what he in turn was going through. De Angelis brushed aside such generosity of feeling with unflinching authority: 'He's not going through anything because he's not working on himself.'

She was to surpass herself as a scourge of the perplexed when taking a call from a woman who had the misfortune to be married to an alcoholic gambler. 'I can tell you,' responded Barbara, she of the flaming sword, 'this is going to get worse. Your children are going to grow up to be alcoholics, or to marry alcoholics. You are dooming your kids to a terrible future if you stay in this relationship the way it is at present. Your kids are going to hate you some day.' I was surprised that the counsellor didn't simply suggest that the wretched woman slit her own throat and have done with it.

I turned off the radio, sated with the miseries of thousands and the certainties of one. Art, unlike advice, is rarely unthinking. It collects, orders, stylises. Even disruptive art, paintings that fragment what is observed or sculpture that distorts the forms of nature, is reflective, considered. It forces the observer inward, it compels a relation between seer and seen. Instant radio counselling is an arrow that pierces. Heedless, it admits no response. So after a dose of Barbara I was ready for the studied assurances of art.

In recent years it seems as though a new museum has opened each year in the city. In 1986 it was the turn of MOCA, the Museum of Contemporary Art, adventurously located just south of Bunker Hill. The building, of red Indian sandstone, is greatly admired. The architect, Arata Isozaki, dug a pit and put most of the building underground. The sandstone walls and pyramidal glass skylights peek up shyly but elegantly among the downtown towers and parking lots. (Isozaki's other architectural contribution to Los Angeles is the Team Disney building, with its playful dwarves and stumpy columns.)

Tom Bradley, reminded that Los Angeles was the only American city of its size to lack a modern art museum, had got to work allocating the funds, and today the museum has an endowment of $30 million. Many of the items in its permanent collection have been donated by local collectors. While Isozaki was at work, Frank Gehry was asked to convert into a temporary exhibition hall a vast former police car garage that the city had leased to the museum for a peppercorn rent. Gehry did a splendid job and this branch, known as the Temporary Contemporary, remains extremely popular.

Not all of MOCA seemed to be in use when I visited the museum. Those rooms that were open were devoted to a show of Edward Ruscha's work. Ruscha is much respected in California, but I find his output pretentious. Its theme, the catalogue says, is 'the mysterious space between word and image'. What this means in practice is that slogans are painted against backgrounds either of pure colour or, in more recent work, of grainy black or grey images of cars or houses or wagon trains. The colours can be gorgeous and many of the paintings sumptuous, but their intellectual content, while appearing provocative, strikes me as negligible. His art is drawn from a single well, its flavouring is uniform. What is one to make of slogans such as 'Safe and Effective Medication' against a background of clouds, 'Sea of Desire', 'Heavy Industry' (just white lettering on a pure black background), 'Japan is American', and the famous Hollywood lettered sign not in white but in black against a glowering grey background? In some later works the space grows even more mysterious, with lettering omitted altogether or replaced by blank white spaces.

I walked over to the Temporary Contemporary, which stands close to Little Tokyo. The immense wooden-roofed interior is supported with steel girders, X-struts, and exposed pipes, which Gehry has left in place and not attempted to prettify with the bold colours of other intestinally exposed buildings such as the Pompidou Centre in Paris. The industrial starkness is modified by the creation of different levels, which provide a variety of spaces for exhibitions. When I visited the museum, it was offering a show that had originated in New York, at the Whitney Museum, although a number of the artists were Californian. The show, 'New Sculpture 1965–75', was a tribute to postminimalism or 'process art'. Since I knew little about postminimalism and hadn't been enraptured by what I did know, I paid close attention to the informative captions. These artists, I read, in 'utilizing non-art materials such as plastics, neon, felt, rubber, salt and video, they engaged in a variety of new expressive sculptural practices which addressed the intrinsic tactility and mutability of their materials'. I did wonder what properties a material had to possess to qualify as 'non-art'. I read on: 'These works emphasized a personal interaction between creator and media' – as though Donatello or Rodin had never given much thought to wood or bronze.

Bruce Naumann's 'Piece in Which One Can Stand' (1966) is a simple two-foot metal ramp. A few feet away stood a small bin on wheels with a plastic bag tucked inside and lapping over the edges. I admired this witty adjunct, with its deft use of non-art symbols, especially the wheels with their suggestion of rotation and mutability. As I peered into the bin, some drops of water splattered onto the back of my head. I yelped and look upwards, where I saw another globule gathering bulk and gleam up on the ceiling before its descent. The attendant told me I was not the only idiot to have mistaken the bin for an exhibit. Why, just the other day she had arrived early in the morning and found a janitor about to sweep away a piece of burlap left in a corner. The artist, Bruce Naumann again, had created this work in 1965–6, which suggests he's a very slow worker. A caption shed light: 'Naumann's sculptural subjects have oscillated between himself and a variety of left-over spaces.' Left over from what? Why are these people trying to mystify me?

Naumann didn't monopolise the show. Elsewhere I found strewn metal scraps by Richard Serra, tangles of wire and wire netting by Alan Saret, and chopped-up felt strips and broken glass, enough of it to fill a small restaurant, by Barry Le Va. This work is entitled 'Discontinued by the Art of Dropping', and the caption helpfully describes the obvious: 'Le Va has scattered variously cut pieces of felt, interrupting and concluding that activity by dropping glass.' Robert Smithson specialises in fretted metal bins filled with rocks. Joel Shapiro contributes a few small cast-iron Monopoly houses scattered across a floor. Richard Tuttle (in a work of 1972) has fixed extremely thin wire, which has been bent into seemingly random shapes, to a white wall, and linked in pencil the points of contact with the wall. This is easy to miss, so attenuated is the wire, so tentative the soft pencil markings. To notice it or overlook it were, for me, equally rewarding.

A few items from the permanent collection had been corralled into 'Perpetual Investigations', an exhibition of higher quality than the travelling Whitney show. I was particularly intrigued by Robert Irwin's 'Untitled' (1967), a disc painted white and affixed one foot away from a white partition wall. Spotlight threw shadows behind the disc, but also managed to manipulate the flatness of the surface into seeming roundness, magically transforming a disc into a sphere.

A few blocks away from the Temporary Contemporary, on the forbiddingly named Traction Avenue, is a more modest museum. Located among desolate warehouses, large parking lots, and industrial buildings converted into lofts, the Neon Museum was founded in 1981. A few precious items form a permanent collection, including glowing script from the marquees of defunct cinemas. The simplest creations were the most successful, perhaps because of the sheer purity of the medium. Kim Koja formed tendrils of neon that emerged from ceramic pots filled with black beans and jelly beans. I then made the mistake of reading her blurb: 'The bean form is used with every pun intended as a symbol of the human being or at least as my means for an autobiographical expression. I find in it elements of the plebeian, of third world diets; its shape has roots from the Korean comma and the Japanese magatama to kidney bean-shaped swimming pools and coffee tables. As an organic pod form it represents potential for transformation, the seeds of future possibilities.'

Who prompts and who approves such obfuscations? At what point did psycho-babble stray from the therapist's office and the pop psychology books? Since the point of the exercise is visual, why muddy the waters with a blur of words? No words were required to decode the complex visual delight of Guy Marsden's plexiglass chambers within which neon streams twist upwards, their random waviness caused by a turbulence within the chamber itself that is generated by electrical current.

I was the only visitor. The museum's location must deter those who might otherwise be intrigued by its contents. And perhaps its theme was too limited to attract heavyweight patronage. The more prestigious Los Angeles museums, such as LACMA, do not find it hard to attract support from the community. Hollywood stars such as Steve Martin are among its most diligent supporters. One evening I attended a meeting of LACMA's Modern and Contemporary Arts Council at a gallery on Melrose. The council consists of donors who contribute to the museum about $1500 annually; in exchange they can attend special events such as this one. The gallery was showing new work by the Texan painter John Alexander, and the council had organised, as it does frequently, a question-and-answer session between Maurice Tuchman, a senior museum curator, and the artist.

Tuchman is a slightly intimidating presence, a rather stiff figure with swept-back black hair and granny glasses and a passing resemblance to Trotsky. But John Alexander wasn't intimidated at all, and leaned back in his chair drawling in a mildly smartened-up Texan accent, flashing a fine pair of cowboy boots. I wasn't greatly impressed by his paintings except for a handful of enjoyable, splashy landscapes that could have been Jackson Pollock reworkings of Monet.

Alexander has lived and worked in New York for decades, but retains a certain detachment from its art scene. He relished a comparison between the New York art world and the Houston real-estate market, both of which, he explained, were subject to booms in value for which there was no rational explanation. A former teacher at a Houston university, he recalled a meeting at which the chairman of the art department announced with pride that the student body had increased from 1000 to 1200. Alexander had leapt to his feet and called for students to be thrown out rather than recruited in ever larger numbers. 'After all, they're only about thirty of them worth a shit.' Alexander sketched for us a typical successful young artist: 'You see this weaselly thirty-year-old in a limo with two attorneys and an accountant on his way to Spago to lunch – this is repugnant to me. It's the fault of the critics, the museums, the collectors. I've long thought that the New York art world in particular consists of the untalented being sold by the unprincipled to the bewildered.'

He noted that in Manhattan alone there are over 500 art galleries, each, it was reasonable to assume, with a stable of about twenty artists. 'That's about 10,000 "artists",' he remarked, and left us to draw our own conclusion. But he was cheered by the thought that the bubble of an overheated art market was about to burst. 'I'm afraid a lot of people in this room are gonna lose a lot of money. I'm kinda glad.' The assembled collectors and donors of Los Angeles were gracious enough to laugh.

Not that the collectors here practised their vice on the epic scale favoured by an earlier generation in Los Angeles. Howard Fox, the contemporary art curator at the museum, later told me that the days of the great collectors with their vast private fortunes were probably over in Los Angeles. Getty and Hammer were dead, and Norton Simon was no longer actively collecting although his sister Marcia Weisman was a formidable collector in her own right, as was her former husband Fred Weisman.

'But there are many modest but sincere collectors, such as the people who came to hear John Alexander. There's a considerable respect for contemporary art in this city from people who read the journals and follow the galleries and have got to know a few artists they admire. This is a serious art-minded community, but what I find particularly exciting is that more and more artists are choosing to live and work in Los Angeles. It wasn't that long ago that Californian artists had to go to New York to advance their careers. That isn't so any longer, as there's an adequate audience for their work on the West Coast. Not that many of them can live solely from their work.'

I went to see one of them. A few blocks away from the Neon Museum lives Skip Arnold, a scrawny performance artist who inhabits a stark block beneath one of the downtown freeways. I knocked on a window and Skip motioned to me to come round to the back. Here he admitted me through a chain-link fence into the compound in which his studio and home are located. Instead of trees there are the graffiti-covered pillars and pylons of the freeway. Instead of grass there is urban detritus and instead of a Mercedes there is an ancient motorbike.

Skip, his head wrapped in a blue scarf, welcomed me in to his hut in hell and looked for a clean space for me to sit while he prepared mugs of coffee. Then he flopped back into a chair, his very knobbly knees visible through the holes in his jeans. The people of Los Angeles have seen a great deal more of Skip than I have, since some of his performances involve stunts such as standing naked on a fountain pedestal as a replacement for a missing statue.

He came to Los Angeles ten years ago and found a place in Venice. 'But then the BMWs came in and the rents went up and up, so I moved downtown. In the early 1980s there were more clubs and cafés here. There are fewer now, as many people don't know about them, or if they do know, they don't want to come all the way down here.'

A former painter, Skip Arnold specialises in 'site-specific activities' that use his body as the medium. He showed me slides and brochures and videos of his work. In 'Root to a Tree' he spent two hours stretched out in a park, his hands pressed against a tree trunk. In another piece he wrapped himself against a telephone pole in a city street. In New York he created piles of dirt, which confused passers-by who took them for earthworks sanctioned by ConEd, the local electricity company. Skip was deeply gratified when on other occasions ConEd's piles of rubbish were mistaken for his own counterfeits. He has imitated models at fashion fairs. When he had himself strapped between two boards with his feet off the ground, he found himself so tightly squeezed in that he could only bear the constriction for forty-five minutes.

'One day I put on a T-shirt with the slogan Shoot Me. I got on my motorbike, and drove through Watts. The cops stopped me, of course, and said, "You're lucky that we're not in the mood to oblige you today." But the gangs thought it was the coolest thing they'd seen, and they got their friends to take photographs of them posing with me. This went on all day.'

I asked Skip whether performance artists suffered from plagiarism.

'It does happen. I register copyright in my pieces and deposit my tapes at archival centres, which gives me some protection.

But I don't worry about it that much. In fact, I agree with the idea of appropriation. Warhol and other artists appropriated commercial images to create their own work. What does bother me more is when, as happened to me recently, a photographer took pictures of my performances and then sold them without giving me a penny. That's not appropriation. That's exploitation.'

Like Karen Salkin, he appears on public access television, but without an audience. He has made 'pieces' specifically for television, which he performed in real time. He showed me a video piece called 'Skip Eats an Olive', in which he used an X-ray machine at a cancer clinic to record the epoch-making event. Another video showed him swinging a rifle and shouting repeatedly, 'Girls in bikinis get fucked all day', which was regarded in certain quarters as ideologically suspect. Skip's slightly flip approach to performance art reflects his own gently jaded feelings about the medium. Happenings, the hard core of performance art, have long been outmoded, and the genre as a whole has been losing popularity. For Skip the excitement lies in the act of performance, so he favours unannounced acts. 'People flip out. Sometimes I get accused of indecent exposure. That doesn't matter. To me the event should be as important as the object.' To add spice to the daily routine, Skip participates in a group called Red Zone. 'We appropriate space, like the time we took over the space under the Fourth Street Bridge. The police took a close interest in that.'

I asked Skip whether Los Angeles was really suited to the staging of performance art. Where does one find the passers-by to provide the response that completes the piece?

'You're right. In many ways I felt more comfortable working in New York. New York is a walking city, a traffic city, people have to rub shoulders. I'm interested in people and their responses, so that's ideal for me. But in LA it's easier to have access to the media, even though there are more opportunities for funding in New York.'

Skip ekes out a living with occasional grants, a few teaching jobs, and by working in art production for the film industry, though jobs are becoming harder to find and wages are now being reduced. Although far from old, he is already beginning to sense himself as belonging to a more senior generation. 'For many younger artists, those coming out of art school now, art has become product-orientated. They're not so much artists as

budget whizzes – it's like training to be a dentist. But all power
to them if they can get buyers to pay large sums of money for
their work. I'm all for that. But many of them are prepared to
compromise in order to succeed financially. I don't do that. But
I'm enjoying a humorous life, I'm digging it. As long as there's
food in the fridge, someone to cook me dinner once in a while –
that's cool, that's cool.'

The club manager Matt Kramer asked me to join him later that
evening to visit a new club opened by Mick Fleetwood. As we
drove east towards West Hollywood, he gave me a running
commentary on the clubs along Sant Monica Boulevard, most of
which had experienced their moments of glory in the 1970s. Like
restaurants, music clubs tend to have brief spluttering careers.
Matt could think of very few that had been flourishing for more
than ten years.

I knew as soon as we arrived that Fleetwood's LA Blues would
not be my kind of scene. There was valet parking, and an
expensive look to the place that the customers would end up
paying for. Located in a stylishly revamped building along Santa
Monica, it offered two blues and R&B shows each night. Suppers
were served below, close to the stage, but upstairs there was a
gallery for less formal entertaining. Rounded columns broke up
the space, which was lit in a dim blueish glow. The manager,
who showed us round, stressed that the club was presenting
classic blues music and 'five-star dining with Mediterranean
cuisine'.

I was looking forward to a glass of wine but Fleetwood's,
probably uniquely among blues clubs in the non-Islamic world,
had no liquor licence. Local residents, on learning that this
building was being converted into a night club, protested to the
licensing board that granting a liquor licence would only lead to
raucous scenes on nearby streets, imperilling virgins and children. The residents won their case, and Fleetwood's was doing
its best to appear sophisticated while accompanying its five-star
dishes with mineral water.

I studied the menu, and flinched. The prices were alarming.
We could have gone to Citrus or Patina for less. Since *ris de veau*
was translated as veal, I opted instead for *Saucisse de fruits de mer
aux truffes noires de Périgord*, which was unexpectedly good and
served with a small tasty cabbage cake. The main course was

duck prepared in two ways, pink *magret* and honey-glazed leg, which we washed down with a lightly *pétillant demi-bouteille* of nonvintage San Pellegrino.

The music was provided by the veteran blues singer Charles Brown. I think Matt was embarrassed that I had never heard of Mr Brown, but I certainly enjoyed his performance, even though he chose to appear behind the piano in a shiny black jacket and a hat reminiscent of a Paraguayan general's cap.

Two weeks later Fleetwood's, dismayed but surely not surprised by small audiences whose idea of a good evening out was not entirely met by apologies and mineral water, closed down. It promised to reopen in the summer, with a well-stocked cellar. It never did.

17

DEVELOPMENT SLUTS

I left London for Los Angeles on the morning that the ground war in the Gulf began. By the time I had unpacked my bags the war was just about over. I had not questioned that thwarting Saddam Hussein was a worthy enterprise, although I experienced the usual disquiet at urging other men and women to risk their lives for my own moral satisfaction. In the event the Allied troops suffered virtually no casualties, while the Iraqis, civilian as well as military, were killed in their tens or hundreds of thousands. Nor was the outcome of the war, the great balance sheet of force, consoling. Hundreds of thousands of Kurds and Shiites, encouraged in the belief that the United States and its allies would protect them as they rose against Saddam Hussein, were left stranded, and the responses of the American administration were, at the very least, hesitant. Kuwait was restored to its previous proprietors, who resumed the same autocratic behaviour they had displayed before the Iraqi invasion.

Southern California was not a good place from which to assess the war and its aftermath. The *Los Angeles Times* did provide exhaustive coverage, and the *LA Weekly* printed lengthy and thoughtful articles reflecting a variety of views. Nonetheless, despite the efficiency and pungency of television news coverage, the Gulf seemed impossibly distant. War and deprivation seemed as remote as they had during the Vietnam War, when it took years of television footage and body counts to persuade a significantly large segment of the American public of the enormity of what was happening. Now, efficient military censorship and news manipulation were keeping the least palatable consequences of the Gulf War at more than arm's length. A murderous clash had appeared, in terms of its public imagery, essentially bloodless.

The proliferation of military bases and aerospace industries in Southern California provided a close tie between the populace and the war, which from here appeared to be a mostly domestic sequence linking the tearfulness of departure, an interim of yellow ribbons, and the proud homecomings. The war, and its human cost, were like an unfortunate interlude in a great patriotic parade in which America, the allied forces and the United Nations had put the world to rights, even if it had been left jagged at the edges. Military analysts on television baffled us with the science of war: 'Inverted spoons,' I heard one say, 'is military symbology for chemical weapons.' I had gone on a brief excursion to some wineries a hundred miles north of Los Angeles. At dinner with Brooks Firestone and his colleagues at the Firestone winery, he was beside himself with excitement. His son was returning from the Gulf that evening and he was about to rush off to a local air force base to greet him.

His emotion was shared by the relatives of hundreds of thousands of other troops, many of whom were now flying home. Their relief and happiness were infectious, but my own soft-heartedness ended once the victory parades began and the great sentimental patriotic revival meeting got under way. Mindless emotional patriotism had become so constant a factor in American self-recognition that it seemed to require frequent ingestions of foreign adventure, whether bogus and suspect as in the case of the invasion of Grenada, or morally justifiable as in this instance. There was a thirst for crusades, as long as the outcome was assured.

As the troops came home, all the old faces reappeared on the television screens to proclaim their American pride. One network staged a Bob Hope special, in which the elderly comic introduced numerous guests. As they trooped on, Hope engaged them in laborious, scrupulously scripted exchanges, all entirely predictable: how wonderful it was to have the boys back home, what a fantastic job they'd done out in the desert. Then a song. Brooke Shields launched into a number that began: 'Stand tall, stand proud, voices that care are all crying out loud. . . .' A singer called Susan Anton was so overcome that she declared with emotion: 'Life is very present now', though I never understood what she meant. The untalented Ed McMahon, who has been put on earth to laugh at Johnny Carson's jokes and to advertise unwanted products, attempted appallingly unfunny remarks, noting that Kuwait now comes in two sections – smoking and non-smoking.

Hope's show was more than a warm-hearted welcome to returning troops. It was another skirmish in the campaign to rehabilitate the tarnished reputation of American military might. It was possible to support the Gulf War without approving of earlier American military adventures in Vietnam or the Dominican Republic or Nicaragua, but to Hope and other unregenerate cold warriors all wars in which Americans had been involved were of equal worth. Thus William C. Westmoreland, the most prominent American general of the Vietnam War, was wheeled on by Hope to give the American public his tuppence-worth on the Gulf. All fighting men were heroes was the subtext, and all American wars were, by definition, just.

The manipulation continued throughout the winter, as each wave of returning soldiers prompted another celebration, another parade, another television spectacular. In late April I endured 'A Celebration of Country' in which country-and-western singers performed patriotically in front of President Bush and numerous political and military dignitaries. Tears dribbled down cheeks as singers belted out songs with lines such as 'America, you know her, you love her, she's been like a mother to you'. A black performer directed an oration towards an image of Abraham Lincoln, and gulped to an end with the words 'Thank you, Mr President' before turning to the present holder of the office, George Bush, and repeating the same words. Here, masquerading as patriotism, was blatant politicking. I nominate the show for the Ceauşescu Award for Shameless Propaganda.

Some of the mindless bilge had little to do with the war; it simply exploited patriotism as a marketing device. An advertisement for Dodge on radio and television bawled out the theme song: 'It's time to discover America', accompanying the words with images of Niagara, men in hard hats, and a group of patriots hoisting up the Stars and Stripes. The appropriation of national symbols for commercial purposes seemed deeply objectionable, yet I was not aware that my distaste was widely shared. But there was unease about giving thanks for a war that had come to such an unsatisfactory conclusion, especially since it was considered unseemly to refer to those aspects of the victory that might mar the general triumphalism. I wandered into a bookshop near Westwood and overheard the owner on the phone: 'Sure we're celebrating. It's like we're Republicans. It kinda sucks.'

I felt more attuned to the response of the popular talk-show host Rush Limbaugh, despite his rightwing views. Limbaugh was pompous and full of conceit, and affected the orotund verbal delivery of an unslurred W. C. Fields. Given the constant barrage of stupid television sitcoms, puerile ads, and manipulative politicians' hogwash, it's not surprising that many Americans are incapable of forming a grammatical sentence. I found it especially irritating when professional 'communicators' displayed the same deficiency. Day in and day out, I'd heard Los Angeles talk-show hosts fumble over words of more than two syllables, using 'capsulises' for 'encapsulates', mistaking 'contingency' for 'constituency', muttering 'trepedition' instead of 'trepidation', coming up with formulations such as 'I'm a little bit different from your perspective' and 'I guess my comment to that is . . .'

Spokesmen for organisations or pressure groups were equally ill-educated. A representative of the John Birch Society said: 'I think we should factor that in with the other inputs you have . . .' A gay film director defended his latest film as 'an analytic perspective to various forms of violence'. An anti-pornography crusader droned to the interviewer: 'It's a strategising time, and I'm into systems change advocacy. . . . I find this discrediting to women, but I'd be happy to dialogue with you on that.' A politician blathered: 'This is beginning to affect the economy on a negative scale. . . . This is something I want to be at the front edge of the process.'

Limbaugh could not only string words together lucidly, but he had wit and the ability to poke fun at himself. When a writer in the *Los Angeles Times* dubbed him, on account of his staunch Republican views, 'the most dangerous man in America', Limbaugh was thrilled and proudly repeated the slur at every conceivable opportunity. He was, he often informed the audience, the man whom thousands of American mothers were hoping their daughters would some day marry, unless, that is, they were harbouring similar fantasies on their own account.

Limbaugh's contribution to the end of the Gulf War was to cast his forthcoming production of *Gulf War I: The Mini-series*. Each day would see new additions to the list, which Limbaugh used as a genial way to settle some political scores. Clint Eastwood, unobjectionably, was cast as President Bush; James Earl Jones would play General Colin Powell, while Rush Limbaugh himself would take the role of Norman Schwarzkopf. As Mrs Norman Schwarzkopf he cast first Teri Garr and then replaced her with Bo Derek (murmuring 'love blooms in the desert' as he imagined the as yet unwritten script of the series). Ringo Starr would play Yassir Arafat, Marlon Brando was cast as Mikhail Gorbachov. The parts of the news reporters Peter Arnett, Bernard Shaw, and Ted Koppel would be taken, respectively, by Jack Nicholson, Whoopi Goldberg, and the children's television character Howdy-Doody. Roseanne Barr would have a role as Saddam Hussein's mistress, British Prime Minister Major would be played by Steve Martin, State Department spokeswoman Margaret Tutwiler by Kathleen Turner, and antiwar senator Dick Gephardt by ET. Two other inspired pieces of casting: the New Kids on the Block as the 'elite Republican Guards' and Bea Arthur as 'the Iraqi woman who speaks perfect English and runs from bombed Iraqi building to bombed Iraqi building yelling about America at the cameras'.

Here was something to give offence to everybody. Yet Limbaugh's levity was a sign that as the war receded from centre stage, the public's focus could return to domestic issues such as the environment and education. Schooling was undoubtedly the number-one peacetime topic of conversation in two-television households. It was widely believed that over the past decade or so the public-school system had deteriorated to such an extent that no child should be subjected to it. There were exceptions: some suburban communities and towns such as Beverly Hills had good schools. But the wealth of the community did not guarantee sound education. California as a whole ranks forty-ninth among the states in terms of expenditure on education per capita. In many communities only a small percentage of the school population is made up of local children; most pupils are bused in from other, usually less salubrious, neighbourhoods, which lowers the schools' social cachet. I could see why education was an urgent issue in Los Angeles when I flicked through *LA Weekly* and came across an ad for the California Healing Arts College that had been 'approved by Department of Postseconderary [sic] Education'.

The introduction of a multi-track system into public schools was also worrying some parents. This new system has been devised so that school facilities can be used and teachers employed year-round, thus reducing overall costs. It seems sensible as a cost-cutting device, but parents worry that their children could be on different tracks, which would complicate the planning of vacation periods and family holidays.

To send a child to a private primary school costs at least $7000 annually, and secondary education comes with an annual tag of at least $10,000. But nobody seems to flinch. Like car insurance, private education is simply a necessary cost, and the anguish of British middle-class parents of liberal disposition who forsake the state system for expensive private education is not widely shared in Los Angeles. Here the problem is not one of conscience but of competition, as there is a shortage of good private schools. At dinner parties I would hear over and over again how parents connive to secure a place for their offspring at a decent school. At some schools there are 150 applicants for each place. Interviews take place with parents as much as with the kids, and heavy hints are dropped about the need to top up the building fund. The parents of successful entrants are not discouraged from making contributions to the school over and above the tuition fees.

The best schools – Harvard Westlake, Marlborough, Windward, Curtis – are no doubt excellent, and many of those with the highest reputations ensure that they are not Caucasian ghettoes that enclose the pupils in a cultural quarantine. Many offer scholarship programmes so as to broaden the social mix, to dilute the proportion of children from the families of moguls and millionaires. Lesser private schools, according to one friend, 'are places where you pay 6000 bucks to get what your public school ought to be providing and nothing more'. He had no scruples at all about enrolling his daughter at a top private school. In his view, the state of California has allowed the public-school system to become so run-down that no parents who actually care about education can contemplate entrusting their children to it. 'The problems with the public high schools, though there are a few exceptions, are over-enrolment, hardly any language tuition – at Marlborough, in contrast, the language programmes are hooked into UCLA computers – poor arts tuition, little after-schools activity, and gang warfare.'

I asked Harold Meyerson of *LA Weekly* why educational standards had been plummeting.

'I think there are two factors that have led to the virtual collapse of public-sector education,' he told me. 'From the left, busing for purposes of integration led to opposition from many parents, especially in the Valley. And from the right, Proposition 13, which led to a general decline in public services. California used to show up well in statistics about educational performance in the 1970s, but we soon had the largest class sizes in the country. All the surveys suggest that people favour spending more on education, but the problem is that nobody trusts the legislature to do so wisely.'

The statistics are certainly depressing. Of roughly 700,000 children living within the Los Angeles United School District in the late 1980s, 100,000 attended private schools, and of the remaining 600,000, 500,000 were non-white. The point is not a racial one, but confirms that the public schools are now dominated by black and Latino children, many of whom come from poor backgrounds in which social problems are rife. Yet only forty years ago a Los Angeles booster, Ralph Hancock, was writing: 'Nowhere else are public schools so opulent and well attended by rich and poor alike, nor are there more college students in proportion to the population.'

Of course, the lesser private schools, in addition to offering a standard of education not appreciably higher than that available in the public schools, are also poorly equipped and drug-infested. A high-school headmaster told me that many children have been removed from the private system by their parents and returned to the public one.

Whatever the parents say, social climbing also plays a part in the decision to opt for private education. I recall a party where many of the guests were discussing which schools their children attended. The actor Josh Mostel, who does not live in Los Angeles, turned to me and mused: 'Curtis, Buckley, Westland . . . all these Wasp names. I guess Schwarz Academy doesn't sound so good.'

One morning I visited one of the city's better high schools, University High, just east of Santa Monica. A couple of decades ago it was a mostly white, mostly Jewish school, drawing students from districts such as Brentwood and Bel Air as well as the slightly less ritzy local neighbourhood. Even in those days, the principal insisted, the school had been multi-cultural – he knows because he first taught at Uni in 1959 and his two sons attended the school – and today it is even more so. 34 per cent of the students are white, 32 per cent Hispanic, 17 per cent Asian, and 17 per cent black. One third are bused in from black neighbourhoods such as Crenshaw and Baldwin Hills, and from Latino districts such as Huntington Park. Forty-four languages are spoken by the school's 2500 students. The principal, Jack Moscowitz, assured me that some of the children, whatever their colour, came from the homes of highly qualified professional people, while other kids were unequivocally poor.

Moscowitz did not deride those who had become disaffected with the state system, nor did he dispute that the public-school system had deteriorated. Indeed, he shares the worries of those who see a dual system emerging, one for the moneyed and mostly white middle classes, the other for the rest. But not all the signs were negative: he favoured the growing trend towards decentralisation and pointed to the excellent academic record of his own school. He has no trouble recruiting good teachers. On the other hand, there is undoubted overcrowding, with classes of up to thirty-five pupils. Attendance rates are only about 85 per cent and declining, a worrying development which Moscowitz blames on the distractions available outside the schools: television, drugs, family problems, and so forth.

Moscowitz walked me through the school. 'We had some problems last year with gang members, but we managed to clear that up. Colours and any other gang symbols are not allowed here. And we're having to deal with a serious graffiti problem. Last year we had 700 linear feet of graffiti sprayed on the buildings by kids who broke into the grounds one night. But they were caught, and we sent their parents the bill for repairing the damage, and I think they're still paying it.'

'So how's discipline?'

'They're pussycats.'

Which, no doubt, is why Uni High, in common with other city high schools, employs a full-time policeman to protect the students, the teachers, and the campus.

In the art class the ponytailed teacher, Jerry Citron, was helping the pupils to devise personal logos. 'They're also having their first air-brush experience.' His courses offer life-drawing, advertising design, and art history, as well as mucking about with paints.

In a biology class, the students, many of whom were Asian, were eviscerating frogs laid on their backs in baking pans. I didn't visit any language classes, but Moscowitz was proud of the fact that Uni offered, in addition to Spanish and French, courses in Latin and Russian. Three years of study of a foreign language are an entrance requirement for UCLA. Because of the high Latino enrolment, there is much bilingual instruction too, as well as 'sheltered' English-language classes where pupils are given support in their native language.

'I know some people are sceptical about bilingual instruction,' said Moscowitz, 'but you have to remember that some kids come to this school illiterate not only in English but in their native language too.'

The principal explained, with no great enthusiasm, that much of the school was attending a special assembly to mark Earth Day. 'Want to take a look?'

'Sure.'

Inside a hall a young woman from UCLA was waffling on about goods the students shouldn't buy for environmental reasons and how to preserve the rain forests. Worthy stuff, but her delivery was stumbling and the hundreds of doodling students in the hall were restless and slack of eye. Moscowitz could tell I wasn't impressed, and neither was he. We did not linger.

Moscowitz wanted me to meet a social-science teacher, Rick Takagawi. We found him sitting alone in his deserted classroom while sipping a bowl of clam chowder. Takagawi, Moscowitz implied, was one of the school's more interesting teachers.

Indeed he was. The previous term his students had been directed to found their own religion, and then abide by its dogmas and practices throughout the following term. He has also been teaching dream psychology in his lessons, drawing on Jung and Joseph Campbell, and required the pupils to write a dialogue between themselves and one of their dreams.

'That was fairly weird even by my standards. I try to give them interesting things to do rather than just lecture them. In one of my government classes I gave the kids a case that was coming up before the Supreme Court in Washington and told them to argue it pro and contra.'

'What about the time,' interjected the principal, 'that you asked them to produce copies of the Constitution?'

'Oh yes. I gave them this project and none of them did

anything about it. I then gave them an extension. Still they did nothing. So I told them I was deducting fifty points from their credits. The class was furious. So I told them to sue me. So they did. They hit me with a suit for "arbitrary assignment", and argued their case with the help of witnesses from outside as well as inside the school. We appointed a "court" to rule on the case, and it decided I had had the right to give the class the assignment, but not to penalise them for their failure to perform it within a specified time. If you ask me, I still think that judgment was flawed.'

'Why don't you appeal, or at least sue your students in return?'

'Hey, not such a bad idea. I'll think about it.'

I lunched with the teachers, split among smokers' and non-smokers' tables. I was advised that although the air was foul at the smokers' table, the conversation was usually better. I munched on a miniature pizza, then headed for the open area behind the dining rooms where many of the students were gathered. Most of them coalesced into groups united by language or background, but Moscowitz insisted that there was very little racial tension on the campus. While he went off to try his luck at arm-wrestling with some of his charges, I chatted to an Iranian boy. His chin sprouted a fledgling beard, while his thick black hair, shiny with unguents, was slicked back from his forehead. He had left Iran seven years ago and been taken to live in Germany. He and his family came to Los Angeles two years ago and joined the other 300,000 Iranians in Southern California. Here he had begun to learn English, which he now spoke extremely well, in addition to his other languages of Farsi, German, and Turkish. Looking at him and talking to him, there was no way I could deduce his economic and social background.

After lunch I had to dash away. It was Oscar night and I needed to consult the oracles before making my own predictions of the winners in each category. Since the Angelenos are always eager to welcome newcomers to the best society, I had been deluged with invitations to Oscar-night parties. Many of them were charity events and called for a large financial outlay, which was not what I had in mind at all. On the contrary, I intended to emerge from the evening with a handsome profit. The price of the ticket usually includes dinner and prizes, but drinks are sometimes extra ('no-host bar' in cryptic code). These parties invariably include a contest that rewards the guest whose predictions are the most accurate. One party (tickets $150 per head) featured the presentation of some award to Ginger Rogers and James Stewart; there was free champagne (but how much of it?) and a top prize of a round trip to London. Karen Salkin had invited me to a bash at which she was a 'celebrity hostess', but after deliberating for five seconds I decided to accept the invitation of potential mogul Jay Heit (entrance fee: a bottle or two of wine).

Jay just happens to be married to one of my oldest friends, Zoe Leader. After decades of exciting countercultural adventures, she has settled down into a semblance of domestic life with a kind husband, a fluffy baby, and a well-paid job. I arrived at six. The television was on, and the four-hour ceremony was just beginning. As the other guests arrived, each one had to chuck five dollars into the kitty. Since the pot would be awarded to whoever predicted the largest number of awards, the atmosphere was tense. A number of women, all of whom worked for studios, flopped on the floor close to the set. ('Who did they work for?' Dimitri wanted to know, when I reported to him later. 'I don't know, but they were mostly in development.' 'Ah,' he replied knowingly, 'scum. Development sluts.')

If he did them an injustice it was hard to tell. Slaves of the movie industry, they preferred to talk among themselves: how X had called them last week or how they had called Y, or how Z was either the sweetest guy in the whole world or the worst sleazebag they had ever met. They exchanged notes on what a particular director was like to work with, and which actors were especially 'hot' that month. The movie industry was indeed all-absorbing, and it was hard for me to imagine a group of publishers talking about nothing but authors and agents for an entire evening. But this was Oscar night, so I had to be indulgent.

The award ceremonies were fairly dull, especially when the most obscure Oscars were awarded – best makeup in a foreign documentary about a coal mine, or most tearful scene in a movie about someone dying from an incurable disease – but they picked up when Michael Blake won an award for best screenplay for *Dances With Wolves*. He introduced a note of Hollywood piousness by bringing onto the stage a woman called Doris Leader Charge, who was prevailed upon to translate his acceptance speech into Lakota, which must have pleased the two or three living Lakotans who still have a little trouble with the English language. Judging from later press accounts, we were not alone in speculating as to whether this beaming Indian woman was indeed translating correctly, or whether she was giving her Lakotan chums a choice commentary on the occasion.

During the ads and the dancing routines the women in development gossiped furiously. There were useful tidbits about Kevin Costner, all from impeccable sources and all unprintable, and much discussion of the hair styles of the stars. Kim Basinger was disapproved of, and Madonna had a mixed reception.

Joan, a development gal, was especially indignant that Gérard Départieu had been nominated for an award for best actor: '*Cyrano*'s a foreign film, for God's sake!' I pointed out that the film was fully eligible for nomination in this category, but she was having none of it. Of course the film's star, Départieu, was not especially popular in America at that moment; he had admitted to an interviewer that at the age of nine he had raped women. If true, this is unsavoury indeed, though I found it hard to envisage a nine-year-old rapist. The National Organisation for Women did not, and called for him to be refused admission to the country. I had heard the head of the local chapter of NOW on the radio, insisting that Depardyoo's confession – no American seems capable of pronouncing his name correctly – told us all about his 'realisation of women', which told me all about her ignorance of the English language. He was a dangerous man, she declared, and she appealed to the members of the Academy as 'men and women of conscience' (surely she was joking there) to ensure that 'rapists are not rewarded'. When her interviewer pointed out that thirty years had elapsed since the crime had been committed, she retorted, 'We don't see men growing out of that kind of behaviour', thus dooming all nine-year-olds who behave viciously to a lifetime of contrition and exclusion from public esteem.

Depardyoo didn't win.

After the final Oscar had been presented and all of Zoe's excellent food had been eaten, it was time for our own awards. Joan, jaw clenched, was confident that, with eleven correct guesses, she had scooped the pool. I flicked my card in her direction.

'Foreign entry. Twelve correct guesses.' And reached for the kitty.

18

HUBBA HUBBA

Most cities with a shore as broad and sandy as that of Los Angeles would have stacked its fringe with resort hotels. But Los Angeles is no Miami, no Torremolinos, no Blackpool. At the shore the city simply stops. The ocean is a treasured asset, and environmental groups struggle to protect it from effluents and oil derricks, but the shore is regarded as a delightful adjunct to the city, not its defining feature. The beaches are the principal parks of Los Angeles.

A century ago, greater Los Angeles had its full share of resort hotels for rich Easterners escaping the rigours of a Philadephia or Cleveland winter. But these hotels were in Pasadena or Riverside. There was a resort hotel just north of Santa Monica, the Ocean House Hotel, that used to be the palatial beach house of the Hearst family, but it was razed in the 1960s. Plans to replace it with a modern 350-room resort hotel were put to the voters, who said no. Santa Monica has plenty of hotels, and the city would like to be regarded as a beach resort, but only the Loew's is close to the beach. The waterfront remains the preserve of promenaders, the fishermen and children on the pier, and a few hundred down-and-outs. The towns to the south, from Venice to Hermosa Beach, have never been developed as tourist resorts. Now it is too late. Zoning restrictions, the tenacity of the thousands of people living in cottages close to the water, and parking restrictions that prevent the towns being swamped with outsiders, have kept the towering hotels at bay. Almost the entire Los Angeles coastline, except for a few enclaves at Malibu and elsewhere, is accessible to the public and any moves by hotels to reserve portions of the beach for their use would be fiercely resisted, which may be another reason why tourist developments are almost nonexistent here.

The beach communities come to life at weekends. From early in the morning the few parking areas along the Malibu shore fill up with cars as their occupants head for the surf. But until recently few people wanted to *live* by the shore. Even today the shoreside town of El Segundo is hardly the loveliest spot in Los Angeles, and the gentrification of its neighbours to the south, Manhattan Beach and Hermosa Beach, is restrained. The only major development along the bay has been Marina del Rey, created in 1968 as an artificial marina community of small apartment and condominium complexes and flashy seafood restaurants, aimed mostly at young singles with money to spend and beds to share. One of the more boring evenings I have spent in Los Angeles was passed in a singles bar in Marina del Rey in 1979.

Venice, the most intriguing of the beach towns, was its precursor as a planned community. In 1892 a businessman called Abbot Kinney first conceived the idea of an American version of Venice. Kinney was a rich man, his fortune derived from the manufacture of Sweet Caporal cigarettes, and property dealing brought him the ownership of this rather undesirable tract of shore. Because the land here was marshy, drainage was essential before any development could begin. Kinney turned this to advantage by converting drainage channels into fifteen miles of canals. These were dredged and bridged, weeping willows were planted alongside them, gondolas and gondoliers imported from Italy plied the waterways, and proud civic buildings and hotels modelled on Venetian-gothic *palazzi* formed a dignified town centre. By 1904 this act of homage was completed.

This ridiculous yet touching urban experiment proved short-lived. Decay set in early. In 1912 the state board of health declared the often stagnant waterways a health hazard, and Kinney began to transform Venice into a more conventional pleasure resort of piers and roller coasters. He provided free transportation to Venice to publicise the resort. The amusement park proved a far greater draw than the 2500-seat concert hall he had also built along the shore. When oil was discovered here in 1929, the thirst for black gold swept all before it, and Kinney's dream-vision, and the pleasure grounds that supplemented it and debased it, gave way to derricks and lumbering commercial structures. The lagoon at the heart of Kinney's Venice was filled in, and many of the canals suffered the same fate. (Kinney's other great venture was the Eucalyptus Crusade, which covered huge areas of Southern California with this Australian species, an achievement that proved more enduring.)

A few canals survived a few blocks inland. The waterways are fringed with untidy grass verges and blocks of cactus that provide a home for ducks so tame I could walk within a foot of them without any sign of alarm on their part. The houses facing the canals come in sizes large and small, grand and shabby, weathered old clapboard or shingle alongside modern stucco and glass. Bridges of alarming ricketiness arch over the water. The animal population seems to outnumber the human: dogs and cats flop in the small front gardens among scattered chairs and hammocks, umbrellas and beach towels.

Hardly anybody who comes to Venice today notices the few remnants of Kinney's vision. But visitors do come in their thousands, especially at weekends, to enjoy the nonstop carnival of the boardwalk. Local residents often keep their distance from the hubbub of the boardwalk, and gather at haunts such as the Rose Café on Main Street, patronised by a fluctuating crowd of out-of-work actors, body builders, artists, and university teachers. On the corner of Main, opposite the Rose Café, over the entrance to the North Beach Bar and Grill, a huge and very silly statue of a transvestite clown arthritically kicks his foot out into the air.

The famous boardwalk is little more than a street between the last row of houses and the beach itself. The cottages along the walk streets are scruffier than those in the other beach towns, matching Venice's bohemian image. The boardwalk doubles as a market for cheap jewellery and T-shirts. Somebody has counted twenty-three boardwalk shops that specialise in sunglasses, and every one of them is Korean-owned. The T-shirts are ornamental and some seek to be amusing. I couldn't raise much of a smile for the T-shirt that read 'Shut Up Bitch', until I saw, a few shops down, one that trumped it with the slogan 'Shut Up Stupid Bitch'. All the shops have display racks by the entrance featuring postcards of thinly clad beauties of both sexes. Nearer the beach are impromptu stalls and tables manned by the readers of tarot cards and palms.

Along one of the side streets a bright mural, entitled 'Endangered Species' and dated 1990 depicts a stylised Venice beach, with two large porpoises in the foreground. A crouching woman holds up a 'Will Work For Food' sign, which is an everyday sight in Los Angeles, especially at the foot of freeway ramps. Tanks are riding over human bodies, and an arm reaches out from beneath the treads. Scavengers root through the rubbish bins in one corner of the design, and in the other stands a prostitute. This apocalyptic view of Venice is 'sponsored by the Social and Public Art Resource Center'.

A shop called Venice Rock is richly scented with leather and copiously stocked with studded armbands, psychedelic T-shirts, sew-on patches, metal badges, and all the other paraphernalia of machismo and moustache, swagger and sweat. But this is Venice and this is the beach, and there was no threat in the air, no smouldering disorder in the shop, just an impeccably neat little bazaar for house-trained bikers. It even stocks pretty tie-dyed fabrics. The nearby Magnet Hutch sells representations of food, portraits of politicians, and name plates, all of which are intended to be attached to your refrigerator door. It seemed extraordinary to find a whole emporium devoted to such a minor activity, yet if the range of items on offer strikes you as insufficient, you can have your name stamped on it. As the sign says, 'We Can Personalize Almost Anything.' Genteel mutilation is available at numerous ear-piercing parlours.

There's another mural on the Beach House Market, this one depicting a sign-painter as he slaps the word Venice on the wall, a pleasingly self-referential design. The Sidewalk Café bustles all day long, its tables packed beneath a splendid Venetian arcade that faces the water, while inside there is a spacious bookshop. A stall opposite solicited signatures for a petition to legalise cannabis – I signed – and another that demanded the firing of Police Chief Gates. Girls in labia-hugging Lycra shorts gravely read the petitions, while perambulating German tourists in unbuttoned shirts gravely glanced at the girls and their clefts and crevasses.

From the market stalls near Windward Street an awful smell of incense wafts onto the beach. Other stalls peddle Ray-Bans, wind chimes – 'from cathedral bells to Nu-Wave' – and cheap clothing. Opposite the market, on the beach side, boardwalk portraitists offer instant sketches, and balloon-twisting clowns chortle at the big-eyed tots gazing up at them. A turbaned guitarist glided by on skates, one more spectacle in the Venice carnival. Another stall was selling feelgood T-shirts – 'All One People', 'Save Our Oceans', 'Save the Rain Forests' – until a police jeep rumbled along the boardwalk. The stallholder, presumably lacking the appropriate licence, muttered 'Oh shit' and kept her head down until, to her obvious relief, the jeep had lumbered past. Beyond her the tails of kites were swooping and gliding along the horizon.

Behind the stalls are some of the few remains of Kinney's grand design. A replica of a small Venetian *palazzo* is now the Venice Beach Hotel. But the architecture, derivative to be sure yet eye-catching and charming, no longer stands alone. The muralists have been at work. The lower half of the hotel facing the ocean is decorated with 'Venice Reconstituted 1989', depicting the boardwalk and wittily starring Botticelli's Venus on skates. On the top floor there's a *trompe l'oeil* mural of a woman looking out of the window.

On this particular morning the main attraction along the boardwalk was Perry Fernandez, Prime Minister of Limbo. A lithe man in his late thirties, his only ostentatious feature, his abundant fuzzy hair, was kept in check with a red and gold headband. His routine consisted of balancing a glass of water on his forehead while ducking under the bar, and then lowering the bar and repeating the act with two trays of water glasses, one in each hand. Perry Fernandez soon made it clear that he wasn't entertaining us just for the fun of it.

'Gimme some juice,' he yelled. 'I'm workin' my ass off here!'

So we applauded and cheered. But this wasn't enough for the prime minister.

'Talk to me! You want the bar down? Talk to me!'

More cheers as Perry lowered the bar to no more than one foot off the ground.

'I share my culture with you,' he proclaimed in his politest Trinidadian tones, 'and I want you to share your culture with me.' He rubbed his fingers together so that there could be no misunderstanding, and he ran around the perimeter placing plastic buckets in each corner. 'C'mon, guys, make my day. Keep comin'. Let's see those tens and twenties.'

Trays in hand, Perry wriggled beneath the bar, the sides of his bare feet flat on the ground. As he bounced upright again, someone shouted: 'Hubba hubba!'

'Hubba hubba, my ass!' retorted Perry. 'Put some money in the box!'

He then made preparations for his next act, jumping barefoot onto a mound of broken bottles. Too squeamish for this, I moved away and continued down the beach. I came to a children's playground, to basketball and paddle tennis courts, and to ropes and bars used for athletic training. To my disappointment, the body builders who have made Muscle Beach famous were nowhere to be seen. I paused at one of the less repulsive fast-food stalls along the boardwalk: Jody Maroni's Italian Sausage Kingdom. Forget hot dogs and frankfurters. This is where you come to munch on *boudin blanc* and excellent Portuguese fig and pinenut sausage. While I ate I watched a vendor of mechanical toys. What particularly caught my attention was a model of a GI in fatigues wriggling along the ground, the Stars and Stripes tucked under his arm and flapping over his head. Only five dollars for this Desert Storm souvenir!

Further down the beach I found a rival to Perry, an athletic black man wearing an elegant Noble Weed T-shirt. He was urging us to clap, to cheer, to stamp our feet.

'It's the oldest trick in the book, but it always works. People hear that noise, and they think some hot shit's goin' on. So give me a cheer. And you black folks, give me a whoo. Ladies, throw your underwear in the air.'

He rehearsed the crowd a few times, but as it never became clear where this was all leading, we began to slip away. I found another attraction in the form of the Echo Man, whose rap incorporated its own echo. A neat trick, to be sure, but after you've heard it for thirty seconds it loses its appeal.

Frank Gehry's Norton House ornaments a quieter stretch of the beach. Steps in tile and metal rise up on both sides of the severely recessed façade. From the terrace above the ground floor a pole supports a square room like a crow's nest, accessible only by ladder. The windows front and back have shutters suspended from beams laid across the flat roof. It was a breezy, nautically inspired design, perfectly fitting for a beach house.

Yet town planning and architecture have now become incidental to Venice. Only Abbot Kinney's neo-Gothic arcades and the pleasant backwaters of the surviving canals retained their charm. Venice was carnival and parade, full of let-your-hair-down vulgarity and all-American cheerfulness, its hippie-ish echoes curiously quaint and tolerated by the police, who no doubt were well aware of their commercial importance to the community. My original interest in Venice had been architectural, but had been sidetracked into something more antiquarian. This old Venice was dead, but the new Venice, tawdry and boisterous and exhibitionist, was very much alive.

I spent another afternoon wandering along the shore from Manhattan Beach to Hermosa Beach. The bohemian elite of Santa Monica and Venice look down their noses at these southerly neighbours, which they view as bedroom communities for young families no longer able to afford Westwood or West Hollywood and as hangouts for beer-drinking airheads. Manhattan and Hermosa are linked by their main streets, which follow the line of the shore. There's a proliferation of shops selling beachwear and workout clothes. Cafés struggle to maintain separate identities, and in Manhattan Beach I found a mysterious Australian bistro. There's an 'environmentally conscious store' that only sells products that are 'cruelty free', for those who want a dash of self-righteousness with their cold cream. The houses in Manhattan Beach were larger and newer than those in Hermosa, and Manhattan is undoubtedly the smarter community, yet I preferred the slight seediness of Hermosa to the flash of Manhattan.

Walk streets connect the beach and the main shopping streets, which are the preserve of boutiques and cafés, while the larger-volume supermarkets and garages are a few blocks further inland, where they are less obtrusive. Anyone who derides Los Angeles as formless should take a look at these beach towns, which manage their precious spaces in an exemplary manner. Along the walk streets cottages sit dumpily behind waist-high walls and fences. The assumption here is that if you live along a walk street you must sacrifice your privacy. Residents sitting out in their gardens almost welcome the gaze of a passer-by, and respond cordially to a greeting.

From the small pier on Hermosa Beach, where Latino fishermen clutch their lines, you can look north towards Manhattan Beach and the Santa Monica Mountains. There is no public parking on the beach, which effectively keeps the bucket-and-spade hordes at bay. Indeed, the little town is self-consciously civic-minded, promoting campaigns to keep its beaches clean. The most public area of the beach is the Strand, the continuous concrete path that follows the bay northwards. Cyclists, skaters, and pedestrians use the path, but at Manhattan cyclists are separated from pedestrians, which is a relief to both.

I was planning to learn how to skate, but Karen Salkin told me that skating is now 'out', so I changed my mind. This definitive statement had not reached entire families in Hermosa Beach, who were queuing up to rent the necessary equipment. Four-wheelers are still popular, but the most fashionable and skilful practitioners of the outmoded recreation favour in-line Roller-blades, which provide no more support than a pair of ice skates. The rest of the gear includes knee and elbow pads, wrist pads, and helmets. Some cyclists pedal along the Strand with low-slung baby carriages in tow, while skaters and joggers push tricycles in which the infant bobs along in a sling. Skin-tight Lycra is still worn by cyclists, though it looks to me like a natural breeding ground for noisome crotch bacteria.

From Hermosa there is a good view south to the wooded lion's-back hump of Palos Verdes, the most prosperous of the coastal communities. While the atmosphere at Santa Monica or Manhat-tan Beach is cosy and villagey, Palos Verdes has the grandeur of the exclusive suburb, with large houses sometimes hidden behind walls and foliage and an even more exclusive enclave in gated Rolling Hills. Hermosa and Manhattan are easily explored on foot, but Palos Verdes was designed with the car in mind, preferably one for each family member. Palos Verdes Boulevard climbs gently to Malaga Cove, a shopping plaza built in the 1920s as the hub of the community. With its brick arcades and loggias, it is loosely modelled on an Italian Renaissance square, complete with a replica of a Bolognese fountain. Some of the detailing is coarse, but the overall effect, enhanced by rows of pepper, cypress, eucalyptus and Moreton Bay fig trees filling the fourth side of the square, is charming and even intimate. Nearby are the community's handful of public buildings, designed in a vaguely Spanish Colonial Revival style by Olmsted and Olmsted, a style also worn by many of the villas along the slopes.

Palos Verdes is an intensely planned community, and none the worse for it. The Olmsteds, in conjunction with Myron Hunt, gave Palos Verdes a distinctive personality, a spaciousness that is both luxurious and luxuriant now that the plantations have matured. The look, the atmosphere, and the exclusivity of Palos Verdes are tightly maintained by community regulations, and Rolling Hills is even stricter in the leeway it denies its residents. A friend who grew up in Rolling Hills told me how every detail was regulated: the heights of houses, and the colours they were to be painted. It was, she thought, like a police state for the rich.

The Italian borrowings in Palos Verdes include the street names. Behind Malaga Cove, Via Campesina zigzags up to the spacious golf course, a landscape contoured and planted with trees when the course was laid out. Opposite the club, at 3456 Campesina, is Lloyd Wright's weird Bowler House of 1963, designed like a ship's prow and embellished with blue glass sail roofs. There's another nautical house by the same architect at 504 Paseo del Mar. The main road follows the twists of cliff and shore; you can stop to gaze out over the rugged coastline, and from Point Vicente you can watch for whales. Beyond Lunada, another beach and shopping centre with a neo-Renaissance fountain, the houses become more modest.

Between Point Vicente and the port of San Pedro is the most fascinating building on the peninsula, Lloyd Wright's Wayfarer's Chapel, set among gardens planted with species mentioned in the bible. From stone walls about five feet high rise glass walls that are ribbed with immense redwood and metal beams. Symmetrical in design, this Swedenborgian chapel is dominated by two large glass circles over the entrance and over the altar. Since the chapel was completed in 1951, trees have risen around it and their branches rest softly on the glass roof, creating a natural bower without depriving the chapel of too much marine light. Inside I watched a young Chinese couple in bleached jeans as they stumbled through their wedding rehearsal.

This idyllic peninsula is, however, under a long-term threat, not from rapacious developers but from its own physical disintegration. For decades houses have been sliding into the sea, and many others have been damaged by landslides and shifts in the earth's crust. The unstable roads are constantly under repair, as the town pays expensive homage to the eccentricities of California's geology. With the descent into San Pedro, the danger recedes but so does the visual excitement. In this port you can find concentrations of ethnic groups that are otherwise scattered in Southern California, such as Portuguese and Samoans and Yugoslavs, many of whom work at the harbour.

Down on Cabrillo Beach is the marine museum designed by Frank Gehry in 1981. It's a series of blockish buildings, linked overhead by the chain-link fencing that is one of Gehry's hallmarks. The architect deliberately chose an industrial style, with an unfinished-looking interior, as he wanted the museum to blend with the craggy harbour outlines of docks and cranes. The museum is unexpectedly fascinating, dividing its exhibits according to their habitats: rocky shores, sandy beaches, and open ocean. Fish are shown changing colour as their habitat alters; the mottled turbot switches from white to black depending on the colour of the nearest bank of sand. The I'll-scratch-your-back school of marine existence is exemplified by the moray eel, which allows red rock shrimps to nibble away at the parasites that cling to its skin, although occasionally the shrimps turn into lunch. The tiny jaws of sea urchins and abalone palpitate against the glass sides of aquariums. At the artificial tidepool, visitors are encouraged to reach down and touch slimy urchins and stubbly starfish.

I continued towards Long Beach, a city best known for its tourist attractions, the *Queen Mary* docked forever on Pier J and the Howard Hughes mega-aircraft, the *Spruce Goose*. Long Beach performs a more vital economic role as the principal port of greater Los Angeles, which handles a greater volume of shipping than any other port in the United States. Driving east towards the district called Naples, I encountered some unexpected street theatre, as an old man crossed the highway in front of me, pushing a wheelchair from which an American flag was flapping in the breeze; in the seat was propped a stuffed toy in the form of a red lobster. I passed through an area of oil wells and refineries, in the middle of which were some surprisingly elegant and well-designed shopping malls, such as the Market Place, embellished with a curving lake and a grand Mexican-style fountain. The disjunction of finding this well-groomed amenity right next door to a jungle of oil wells is not remarked upon.

Naples today is what Venice must have been like after it was built. Its network of man-made waterways is laid out symmetrically within the sheltered harbour of Alamitos Bay. The Rivo Alto canal winds through the district, and cottages line the waterside. Cars are banished to alleys behind the houses, freeing the lanes between the houses and the canal for pedestrians. Boats, bobbing in the canal, are moored outside their owners' houses. These houses come from an inexhaustible catalogue of eclecticism – Wedgwood Gingerbread, Bourbon Street Suburban, Spanish

Revival, Manoir Stucco, Malibu Southwalk with awnings. But under a blue sky with palm fronds flapping overhead, who can object?

It is one of the confusions of Los Angeles that shabby Venice should be called Naples, and that spruce Naples, its canals intact, should be called Venice. They were designed at roughly the same time, and it is odd that Naples should have prospered while its conveniently located sister community collapsed. Closer to the ocean another broader waterway reminded me of the Giudecca canal, its banks lined with larger, grander houses, and boats to match. In the heart of Naples is an island, in the centre of which a grand fountain splashes within a small park. It's not Italian, but it's very Californian.

The sea air whetted my appetite, and that evening I took myself off to ChaChaCha. The seafood here is prepared in a liberally interpreted Caribbean fashion, and I wolfed down some wonderfully succulent and spicy prawns. When it opened at the unfashionable end of Melrose near Vermont, ChaChaCha was an immediate hit. Gratifying queues formed outside the door and hundreds of covers were served each day. The bright colours of its cabin-like interior contributed to the charm. ChaChaCha is no longer so chic, but the food is very good, even though *tarte tatin* isn't what one expects to find in a Caribbean restaurant.

The owner, Toribio Prado, is a very handsome young man with a bushy ponytail. His story is intriguing, but often varies in the telling. A collated version I have assembled from various sources, including his own mouth, suggests he was born in Havana of a Mexican father and Italian mother. He came to Miami and worked there before moving to Los Angeles, where he found a job as a busboy. A talented cook, he was 'discovered' by the owner of the Ivy restaurant, and hired. He left the Ivy to found ChaChaCha and, more recently, the more elegant Prado's. Since he is still in his twenties, Toribio's journey from poor immigrant to successful restaurateur and lecturer on cooking at UCLA is almost complete. What next? In Los Angeles few find it comfortable to rest on their laurels.

19

LIVES OF LEISURE

Here's a pretty tale of Dean and Joe, and it all unfolded on live radio while I was driving along the freeway. First, Dean called Mark and Brian. He explained that Joe, his roommate, had a habit of coming home very late at night and playing on his pinball machine, thus waking up Dean and wrecking his sleep. So, said Dean, he'd had enough. He'd positioned the pinball machine on the balcony of their apartment and was planning to tip it over the edge, an event he wanted recorded on the air.

Mark and Brian were perfectly willing to do this, but thought it would be a richer experience if Joe, the owner of the machine, could listen in too. They tried Joe's work number, and he was soon on the line. Joe didn't feel thrilled about the imminent destruction of his toy, and before Dean went ahead he thought the listeners might like to know how Dean spent his Wednesday evenings.

'Tell us!'

Well, Dean liked to go down the street to where Linda the boss's daughter lived, but only on Wednesdays when the boss was never home. And Dean would come home awfully late.

'Is this *true*, Dean?'

'Yeah, but Linda and I are just friends, y'know.' The remark met with a snort from Joe. Dean insisted on the purity of the friendship.

'What about the video?' said Joe

'What video?' yelled Mark and Brian.

And Joe told the world about a video that committed to

celluloid Linda's eighteenth birthday party, an anniversary the young woman had celebrated by removing most of her clothes in front of the camera. Joe, moreover, suggested to Dean that if his pinball machine went off the balcony, he would send the video to Mark and Brian.

'Why confine it to Mark and Brian?' said Mark, generously.

'Maybe the boss should be brought into the picture,' said Brian. 'Can we talk to the boss?'

Joe had the number, and Mark and Brian dialled it. Joe explained to the boss how Dean passed his Wednesday evenings. Mark and Brian, fine investigative reporters that they are, wanted to know how the boss felt about this. He was 'kinda disappointed'.

'Who with?' asked Joe, naively. 'Not with me, I hope. I'm just your conduit of information.'

'Look at it this way,' said Mark. 'It's great that your daughter wanted to share what she has.'

This did not console the boss.

Brian decided to be constructive: 'Let's look at your options.'

'Yeah,' said Mark, 'you could fire Dean.'

They went back on the line to Dean, who reckoned he had little to lose at this stage. The pinball machine went off the balcony.

'He did it! Wow.'

'I guess Dean and Joe are even now.'

'That's right. Joe is avenged, while Dean has thrown off the pinball machine—'

' – *and* he's thrown down the boss's daughter.'

There you are, a complete three-act playlet between West Holly-wood and Pasadena.

To enter Pasadena is to enter part of the history of Los Angeles. Downtown Los Angeles has older buildings, and so do West Adams and Angeleno Heights, but their presence is patchy, an accidental survival. Pasadena is quite different, as its genteel exclusivity has continued uninterrupted for a century or more. The town was founded in 1875 as an agricultural cooperative by Mid-western farmers, and some present-day residents would be horri-fied to think that their mansions are built on the site of a socialist experiment. By 1907 the population had grown to 30,000 and the town was a major resort, renowned for its beautiful gardens. The classiest sections of the town, and its equally moneyed neighbour San Marino, are havens of solid prosperity. These suburban acres are copiously planted with lovely trees, and the houses sprawl across generous lots set well back from the broad roads along which occasional traffic cautiously glides in the automotive equivalent of tiptoeing.

The Pasadena Freeway twists and turns through the hills of Highland Park that separate downtown from this sedate suburb. South Pasadena greets the arriving motorist with a sign. This is a separate municipality, striving to distinguish itself from both vulgar Los Angeles and snooty Pasadena. South Pasadena, if a resident family is to be believed, still operates a curfew, whereby youths younger than sixteen are forbidden to be out walking the streets after 10 p.m. After the age of sixteen, they will be in their cars and thus no longer capable of the lawlessness of the pedestrian. Pasadena itself opts for a different form of benign nannydom: the city operates 'photo-radar speed traps' which consist of concealed cameras that photograph speeding vehicles, and, aided by computers, identify the naughty owner of the car, who then receives a speeding ticket. The resourceful citizenry have responded by removing their licence plates or by ignoring the tickets on the grounds that they are probably not enforceable in the courts.

Downtown Pasadena is a bit of a mess, and the imposition of a brutal modern shopping centre in the middle has not helped. But it does contain some sensational buildings, including one of the last surviving resort hotels of Los Angeles. Green's Hotel, an oriental-style building that wouldn't look out of place in Bombay, is adorned with cupolas and turrets and friezes, and its most extraordinary feature is a bridge that lurches out onto the pavement, ending in a polygonal cupola'd pavilion. Green's is no longer in use as a hotel, and is somewhat delapidated. Further up Raymond Street, St Andrew's Church resembles an Italian basilica, and is most impressively furnished with iron screens, dark stained glass, massive wooden doors, and splendid arcades of coloured marble piers. All derivative, to be sure, but borrowed with such assurance. Deservedly well-known are the public buildings of the city, which easily eclipse those of Los Angeles: the renaissance *palazzo* that houses the post office, the grand Italian baroque design, complete with dome, of the city hall, and the renaissance-style public library.

Pasedena is divided by the Arroyo Seco, the mostly dry riverbed that the freeway follows as it winds towards Los Angeles. Still wild and steep, the Arroyo is one of the few places in the city, other than Griffith Park, where taking a walk has the character of hiking. My friends who live in South Pasadena are encumbered with a large dog that requires regular lopes, and I joined the family as it set off to accompany the hound on its regular sniff and scrabble, yelp and bark, leg-up and hunkerdown, in the wild grasses of the Arroyo.

I was able to give them some valuable information. Their dog was one of 1466 hounds out of the over 200,000 registered in the city to bear the name Bear. A daft name for a dog but clearly a most popular one. The *Los Angeles Times* had obligingly printed a brief article on the subject. There are thousands of dogs boringly called Blackie and Tiger and Duke, but more revealing were the showbiz names. There were no fewer than fifty Elvises and thirty-seven dogs called Zsa Zsa; Madonna was making a respectable showing with nineteen dogs named after her or her immaculately conceived namesake, and Woody Allen, as was appropriate for a man who loathed Los Angeles, was the source of one dog name only. Communications outscored even Hollywood as a source of nomenclature, with no fewer than 150 dogs called Freeway, as well as mutts called On-Ramp and Tail Light.

It is no hardship to walk in Pasadena. Wandering along Columbia Street towards the Arroyo, we passed the Tanner-Behr house of 1917, which the architect, Reginald Johnson, modelled on a Tuscan villa, set among luxuriant gardens and surrounded with a sensuous, and purely Mediterranean, pink wall. Pastiche it may be, but how beautifully it fits into this serene landscape and balmy climate. The grand houses of Beverly Hills shine with newness, even when their adopted style is a historicist borrowing, but in Pasadena the houses, mellow with their greater age, persuade the observer that they have always been here. By 1930 most of the great houses of Pasadena, and there are dozens of them, had been completed, and it is astonishing that the little town should have attained such fixedness, such stylistic purposefulness, before it was even fifty years old.

We tramped up the gentle incline of the arroyo. On the other side of the concrete channel, where the water still trickles after a downpour, were horse trails, and we had to keep the dog on a lead so as not to frighten the colts and fillies. This regulation is enforced by mounted police who issue tickets to the owners of free-range dogs. Beyond the archery range we came to two enormous bridges spanning the arroyo. The more distant was the Ventura Freeway, the closer a now disused bridge known locally as Suicide Bridge, for reasons that are self-explanatory.

The object of our hike was the Gamble House, the most famous of the many houses designed by the brothers Charles and Henry Greene. The only difficulty was dissension among my hosts as to the house's precise location. Since we were standing at the foot of the arroyo, and the Gamble House stands on a plateau above it, the argument was of some consequence. We eventually agreed on a path that climbed the cliffsides and brought us into a part of Pasadena that looked vaguely familiar. But was it close to the Gamble House? At that moment a car stopped nearby and its occupants pored over a street map. We recognised the bearded gentleman as Professor Larry Lipking of Northwestern University, and correctly deduced that he and his wife Joanna were also hunting for the Gamble House. We rattled the door handles of their car until they admitted us, and moments later we were at our destination.

The Greenes were Midwesterners who trained at MIT and settled in the late nineteenth century in Pasadena, where they set up an architectural practice. There was no shortage of wealthy clients, both among the full-time residents and among those, such as the Gambles, who spent the winter in California rather than the icy Midwest where they had their principal homes. Turn-of-the-century Pasadenans, with leisure as well as money, developed their own 'Arroyo culture', combining a passion for Arts and Crafts with poetry and gardening and health fads.

The early houses by Greene and Greene were not remarkable. They had absorbed the teachings and styles of fashionable architects such as H. H. Richardson, and only in the early years of this century did they develop the luxurious variant of the Craftsman bungalow style for which they are best known. The hallmarks of the style were dark wood and shingle exteriors, expansive rooflines, a daring use of beams and overhangs, and a meticulous attention to detail. The brothers liked to control every aspect of a project, the commission, with Charles creating the interiors by designing the furniture and commissioning carpets and Tiffany lamps and other fittings. The houses' other feature was expense.

The craftsmanship, especially the joinery, was impeccable. The finest hardwoods were used in contrasting ways, and the layout of the houses was practical as well as aesthetic. Broad doors slid open to permit cross-ventilation, a thoughtful device in these days before air-conditioning. These are arguably the most exquisite houses in America, dashing and flamboyant yet in irreproachable taste. Architectural historians like to argue about the influences on the two brothers. Some see Arts and Crafts as their precursors, others find Japanese echoes, others discern the structure of a Bavarian chalet. All these, and other, elements are present, but Greene and Greene are unique. All influences have been absorbed and transformed into what Reyner Banham described as 'a poetic and romantic summary of the kind of wood-building traditions that Europeans had brought to the United States from their home lands'.

The garage of the Gamble House, almost as exquisite as the mansion it once served, is now a bookshop and ticket office for visitors to the house. We bought our tickets and wandered over to the house itself, where a lady named Emily Newton was waiting for us. The Greenes' attention to detail became apparent even walking up the driveway, which is raised into a central mound to allow water, on its rare appearances in Pasadena, to drain off easily.

'Now you folks will be going on the three o'clock tour. May I suggest you go round back and take a look at the fishpond and the gardens? I'll come and get you before the tour starts.'

You don't argue with Emily, and we took the prescribed stroll, then sat on the porch, shaded by the tremendous projection of the eaves; jutting out from those eaves were long beams with softly rounded edges, hardly worn after eighty years of exposure to the elements. The copper drainpipes were decorated with a nailhead pattern that reminded me of the Viennese *Jugendstil* architect Otto Wagner.

Emily fetched us, and passed us to her colleague Millie. 'Millie will be your docent' – an American genteelism for volunteer guide – 'and first she will give you a short orientation.'

I didn't pay too much attention to Millie because the interior was so dazzling and richly detailed that I needed all the time allotted to the tour to stare and touch and absorb. I found the gleaming beauty of the woods ravishing, and the finish of the joins and beams was flawless, as though the wood had been rubbed and rubbed with bands of velvet. The joinery of the staircase is so beautiful it seems to have been woven rather than fitted. All the elements of the house, whether decorative as in the case of furnishings or structural as in the case of rafters, are given equal value and equally luxurious treatment. Ebony pegs varied the colour but not the texture. Most of the structure is of teak, and the furniture mahogany, and both the panelling and the furnishings repeat motifs such as clouds that help to unify this wonderfully coherent house.

Seen during daylight, the interiors of Greene and Greene houses can seem murky; all that polished wood and coloured glass, and ceilings that appear lower than they actually are. Of course these houses, in Californian fashion, extended the living area out onto verandahs and decks and 'sleeping porches'. The Greenes sited their houses carefully so as to exploit the climate and the daily arching of the sun. For light and board games in the Gamble House, you could always go up to the attic, where windows on all sides offered glorious views onto the high San Gabriel Mountains. I can only imagine how sumptuous these interiors must be at night, lit by Tiffany, filled with intimate corners and lamplight softly reflected against the surfaces of the walls and furnishings.

Millie treated us to vignettes of Gamble family life. 'The Gambles had two servants, but they didn't call them servants. Instead they called them "the girls".' Well, that's all right then. The girls had separate quarters on the ground floor, including their own dining room, furnished not by the costly Greenes but by the more rustic designer Gustav Stickley. Expensive hardwoods were superfluous in the kitchen, where pine and maple were used instead. There are other woods upstairs, cedar in place of mahogany, and guest appearances by black walnut in the master bedroom. Another bedroom was the precinct of Aunt Julia, whose photograph still hangs on the wall.

'As you can see,' explained Millie, 'Aunt Julia was a sweet little lady, and her main interest was in teaching Sunday school.'

I peered at the photograph of this dumpy beaming woman in a long uncontoured dress and corsage. Joanna Lipking was staring at it too, and voiced what I too was wondering: 'Is that *all* she did?' – to which Millie had no answer.

We took a stroll down the lane, and passed the Neighborhood Church next to the Gamble House, a Unitarian-Universalist all-things-to-all-persons church presided over by the Reverend B. Lovely. A few blocks away on Prospect Crescent the Millard House stands bunkerlike in an overgrown garden. This was built in 1923, fifteen years after the Gamble House, by Frank Lloyd Wright, and is said, by those lucky enough to have been inside it, to be one of his finest houses in Los Angeles. Its striking but ugly exterior is composed of cubed concrete blocks, embellished with highly stylised designs; the construction technique appears to be the massing of cinderblocks in a repetitive design of Mayan inspiration. The Millard House is unequivocally modern both in its composition and its materials. There is nothing modern about the Gamble House, but neither is it reactionary. Instead, it is a refinement of centuries-old techniques applied to the most traditional of materials.

Prospect Crescent is a spur road along Prospect Boulevard, an especially lovely residential street; a parade of gorgeous camphor trees extends along it, leading at either end to fine gateways designed by the Greenes. Not far away on North Grand is another splendid house by the brothers, the very complex Duncan-Irwin house of 1906. But it would be misleading to suggest that the sumptuous streets of Pasadena are lined with Craftsman houses, as many of the grandest mansions use Italianate and Spanish Colonial Revival styles. The principal elements of the Craftsman style were adopted by countless architects along the West Coast. Few could match the splendour of the Greene and Greene houses, for the obvious reason that their owners were not heirs to the Proctor and Gamble fortune. All over Los Angeles, especially in some older districts in South Central, you find modest Craftsman designs with overhanging roofs and verandahs, put up in batches by speculative builders. On La Loma and South Madison in Pasadena are grand Craftsman houses by architects other than the Greenes. The proliferation of the style inevitably led to its debasement. The Greenes' best work had been done, with very few exceptions, by 1914, and although architects such as Arthur and Alfred Heineman built a number of splendid Craftsman bungalows, the fashion faded as more conservative historicist styles became popular. The superb Wallace Neff houses along Lombardy Street in San Marino, designed in discreet yet elegant Spanish Colonial Revival style, were all the rage in the 1920s.

Pasadena is rich in fine houses, especially in the compact Oak

Knoll district, where the tranquillity is enhanced by the abundance of mature trees, such as the lovely oaks that arch over South Madison. Only in patches will you find ostentation on the scale of Bel Air. On South Oakland mansions sprawl on vast lots set on a kind of plateau, so that the house can boastfully dominate its neighbours. 1290 South Oakland was a building site, so I felt free to wander in. A huge house was under construction among acres of formal gardens, and the foreman told me the story. The previous house, a mere 11,000 square feet in area, had burnt down and was being replaced with this new if unadventurous design which would provide double the space. The foreman told me that the minimum construction cost per square foot is $250, but, depending on the choice of materials, can be twice as high. We did our sums. To build this boring but grand stuccoed house, the owner was spending at least $5 million. Carpeting extra.

Hillcrest is probably the finest street in Oak Knoll, crammed with houses by Greene and Greene and others. The Blacker House is one of their jewels, a dashing composition of sweeping eaves and huge decks. It was bought in the 1980s by a Texan millionaire who promptly sold off most of the original fittings and furnishings. There was an outcry, and the Texan gentleman was required before putting the house back on the market to replace the missing items with accurate reproductions. Also on Hillcrest is a Greene and Greene house quite different from anything else they built. The Cordelia Culbertson House is restrained and self-effacing; only the Japanese garden furniture, the muted green tiles (so different from the ubiquitous pantiles of Southern California), and the exquisite proportions and finish of the house suggest who the architects were.

All these houses are easily visible. The moguls and stars of Bel Air hide behind their security fences and oversized gates, but here in Pasadena, where everyone is quietly rich, houses stand companionably among their lawns and shrubberies and patios. It's no different in adjoining San Marino, where some of the streets are broad enough for six lanes of traffic, even though you can wait five minutes before seeing a single car in motion. These rich suburbs are oddly empty of people. Nothing stirs in the houses, except, very occasionally, for the purr of a Cadillac down a driveway. This is not Porsche country; this is where doctors and lawyers and hereditary executives sleep and play cards.

There are few modern designs in Pasadena, but at the other

end of town, on the north side of Arroyo Seco, is Craig Ellwood's Art Center College of Design, completed in 1977. Set high up along Lida Street, the college is like a black glass bridge, ribbed and framed, that rides the contours of the hills.

It's unfortunate that an architect of Ellwood's skill and adaptability wasn't found for the Norton Simon Museum, close to downtown Pasadena, as this has easily the finest collection of paintings in Southern California, surpassing even the Huntington. One moves in astonishment from a superb Paolo Veneziano to an El Greco and to Giovanni Bellini's first portrait, and then to a lovely group of Flemish masterworks. Giorgione, if the attribution is to be trusted, is represented here, and there are portraits by Rembrandt and Hals, and a brilliant example by Goya. The Hammer collection lists many of the great names, but few great paintings by them. No one could level that accusation at the Norton Simon Museum.

The Impressionist and twentieth-century rooms are equally superb, and great twentieth-century sculpture is scattered indoors and out in the gardens. For good measure there's a beautifully lit Oriental collection. Down in the basement I visited some special exhibitions, all drawn, astonishingly, from the reserves of the Simon collection. On the day I went, I encountered more bronzes and pastels by Degas than I had ever seen gathered before in one room, and no fewer than forty Picasso lithographs of women and thirty-nine etchings by Salvator Rosa. By now these items will have been put back into their boxes and a fresh batch of treasures shown to the public view.

I joined my South Pasadena friends for dinner one evening, and accompanied them on an expedition to acquire the necessary provisions. We went to Bristol Farms, one of those chic American supermarkets where shopping is a subsidiary activity. A stall by the entrance offered Sita's organic burritos, rich in low sodium, hi-fibre, and everything else likely to promote personal immortality. Other free samples included cheese spreads and Mexican salsas. No need to spend money on lunch when you're close to Bristol Farms. They even give you free coffee, different flavours each day. I had Amaretto-flavoured coffee, but it might have been Pina Colada or Macadamia Nut. Not only are there decaffeinated coffees here, but some teas too have been bleached of the life-sustaining drug. The prepared foods include Chinese chicken stir-fry, many varieties of sushi, quiche lunch packs, polentas with sausage and peppers, and pan-blackened chicken. The rare-vegetable section included humble parsnips and Brussels sprouts cutting a rustic caper alongside exotic okra, punchy chillis, Belgian endives, and woodsy chanterelles. For Bear the dog there's Avo-Derm, a vegetarian chew packed with nutritious avocado meal. No surly, pimply, innumerate checkout girls here. At Bristol Farms you have check-out lads named Jason in fetching gingham shirts.

During dinner, butter was grudgingly produced, alongside the household favourite of Shedd's Spread. The label, weak on grammar, claims to have one-third 'less' calories than margarine and no cholesterol, and boasts: 'Butter's finally met its match!' It didn't taste bad at all, I had to admit. The chicken we ate was plump and juicy, but underseasoned. I asked for some salt.

'Salt!' cried my host. 'Salt! We normally keep salt in the poison cabinet.'

20

AN ENCYCLOPEDIA OF LIFE

Ever since as a seventeen-year-old I was taken to tea at All Souls College, Oxford, I have had a weakness for unashamedly elitist institutions. To listen at such a tender age to some of the greatest historians and classical scholars in the universe arguing solemnly for fifteen minutes about the origin of Garibaldi biscuits was a rare comic treat. There are fewer satirical possibilities at Caltech, the California Institute of Technology, although the much lamented late Richard Feynman, a Nobel-prizewinning physicist and exuberant solver of problems great and small, must have provided a personal warmth and humour you don't usually associate with institutes of stratospheric learning.

The institute was founded in 1891, taking on its present form in the 1920s under the leadership of the physicist Robert Millikan. In the following decade Charles Richter invented the Richter scale at the seismological laboratory here, Theodore von Kármán directed the aeronautical laboratory, Carl Anderson discovered the positron in 1934, and Linus Pauling did the work that was to win him the first of his two Nobel prizes. Robert Oppenheimer was on the faculty, and Albert Einstein a frequent visitor. More recent luminaries include Murray Gell-Mann, the discoverer of the quark, Roger Sperry, who observed that the brain is split into left and right spheres with different functions, and John Schwartz and Michael Green, who devised the fashionable 'superstring' theory. Over the years the faculty has picked up twenty-one Nobel prizes.

The faculty comprises 280 professors, 380 research faculty, 300 visiting faculty, and 1000 graduate students. The superlative research facilities keep drawing scientists to the institute, and it is those facilities, manned by some of the world's outstanding scientists, that attract a mere 800 undergraduates to Caltech. It is hard to think of any other teaching institution with a ratio of three students to each teaching faculty member. The competition is intense and, even after they have been selected, some undergraduates are unable to withstand the pressure. There is a fairly high dropout rate, and students sometimes complain that they are being used as cheap lab assistants. Inevitably, some students find themselves working on projects that turn out to be dead ends, a frustrating way to begin a scientific career. Success or failure for a Caltech student is a matter of luck as well as ability.

The pressure may be slightly relieved by a campus-wide fondness for pranks. A few years ago, during a football match at the nearby Rose Bowl, the electronic scoring board was fixed to show a decisive victory for the lousy Caltech team over its rival MIT in defiance of the facts. Since the 1930s the seniors desert the campus for one day in May, and 'seal' their rooms by posing problems for would-be intruders. The rest of the students feverishly try to break the code or master the computer programme or do whatever else is necessary to entitle them to enter the senior's room and claim their reward, which is usually bottled. The story goes that on one occasion the successful students considered the reward too miserly, and took their revenge by taking apart the senior's sports car and reassembling it in his room.

There is a traditional distrust at Caltech of 'big science', those billion-dollar projects that involve huge numbers of researchers scattered across the nation. The Jet Propulsion Laboratory in nearby Altadena began its life as a big-science department of Caltech, which still 'manages' the complex, but it is now essentially a branch of NASA, overseeing space probes and other complex projects. At Caltech itself, individual scientists are given a free rein and individual genius, when encountered, is nurtured and fostered. No one here distrusts a certain zaniness, as the career of Richard Feynman illustrates. Departmental lines are vaguely drawn, encouraging what one faculty member described as 'fluid interpenetrations' between the academic disciplines. A small but high-powered humanities department helps to keep the students sane and literate. Its faculty is pampered just as much as the scientists. Larry Lipking, visiting from Chicago, told me that he regarded a spell at Caltech as immersion in Lotusland, an opportunity to work uninterruptedly. To Professor John Sutherland, working at Caltech was 'like being smothered in silk cushions. After a while you start to long for a contentious Monday morning staff meeting. But of course such things don't exist at Caltech.'

The Spanish Colonial Revival campus blends well into the residential neighbourhood around it. Bertram Goodhue designed some of the buildings, which are graced with arcades and sporadic Churrigueresque ornament. The more recent contributions to the campus are fairly appalling. Most of them are named after Arnold O. Beckman, a Caltech chemist who invented the pH meter before going on to make his fortune; he is now one of the institute's major benefactors. Shortly after I visited the campus, Caltech celebrated its centenary with a banquet. During the opening speeches, a friend of mine attending the dinner spotted one of the administrative assistants dashing from the hall, and assumed that she had been overcome by a gastric emergency. She later learnt that the aide, noticing that Beckman's hearing-aid battery had lost its juice, had rushed out to find a replacement. Since the main purpose of the evening was to persuade benefactors to keep writing the cheques – another guest, Betty Gordon, had recently handed over nearly $17 million – it would have been disastrous if Beckman himself had been unable to hear the appeal to his continuing generosity.

Glenn Wyne showed me round the computer centre and did his best to explain its marvels to me. He was particularly keen on the Intel parallel-processing computer, which, he told me, 'has the neatest flashing lights in the room'. To me it looked like two filing cabinets with lights. Its novelty is that it works on problems not in sequence, but by dividing its chores among forty-eight boards, each of which can communicate with every other board. This speeds things up tremendously, and, needless to say, its special 'message-routing' chip was designed by Charles Seitz of Caltech.

I returned to Caltech at the ungodly hour of eight in the morning to breakfast with Carver Mead. We met at the Atheneum, the sumptuous Tuscan-style faculty club. Beneath a huge porte-cochère a double staircase rises to the main entrance. Within there's a large wood-panelled lounge with an open fire, and tables are laid out in the cloister as well as in two dining rooms. Among the regular patrons are tall stooped gentlemen of advanced age who do not resemble nuclear physicists. These are local residents or alumni who may use the Atheneum in exchange for a substantial membership fee. It is one of the obligations of a Pasadena gentleman of means to endow his local institute of learning.

When I arranged to meet Professor Mead I explained that I was unlearned in the sciences, and begged him to be gentle with me. His appearance was further cause for alarm. He has a thin face, pinched and furrowed, and a goatee beard adds a disconcerting Mephistophelean note. His choice in open-necked check shirts with large flaps suggested a greater concern with the life of the mind than with sartorial harmony. The man's brilliance shows in his eyes, which are penetrating and by turns fierce and twinkling. Mead clearly has the power to intimidate, should he wish to use it. His has been the inventive mind behind some of the most radical developments in computer technology, and when we met he and his team of graduate students were working on a rudimentary retinal chip as a first step towards finding ways to simulate the way the human brain works.

Mead ordered a substantial breakfast, while I restricted myself to bracing liquids so as to be able to concentrate on what he was telling me. When I expressed my amazement at the continuing miniaturisation of computer components, Mead gratifyingly said he shared it, and found it extraordinary that computing was becoming better and cheaper and faster and more efficient as chips became ever smaller.

I wanted Mead to begin by explaining how far we had come in the brief history of computing. He obliged.

'People speak of generations of computers. That's a mistake. What we have is generations of technologies. The fifth generation, parallel computers, is about how standard integrated circuits are being replaced by custom circuits. Every element has its own custom circuit, which means that there is a decrease in the number of elements, of bits and pieces that need to be assembled. The more difficult the assembly, the less reliable any piece of machinery is likely to be. So this simplification has also led to greater not lesser reliability.'

'And are you putting these technological advances to new ends, or using them to simplify the existing problem-solving process?'

'Until recently we've been building computers that perform functions similar to the left half of the brain. That is, they seek to duplicate sequential rational thought and perform symbolic manipulations. What we're doing now is working on the kinds of things that happen in the right half: perceptual systems. This intuitive function is not amenable to digital technology, but this is how the brain works. This intuitive function is also amenable to electronic manipulation, but if you approach it digitally you'll find it's like swimming in a sea of molasses, because computers have been designed to plod through all conceivable possibilities. Computers approximate rational thought, but that's only a small part of what the brain does. That a process is not logical does not mean it can't be performed by a computer.

'We need different kinds of hardware underpinning for the two kinds of computation. For logical thought we need what we think of as a digital circuit – though in fact all circuits are analog circuits, but it's the way we use the circuits that makes them digital by forcing them to make decisions. The other kind of underpinning is an adaptive analog, which is similar to what the brain does. The brain uses relative not absolute values, which favours adaptation over precision.'

'So how can you achieve any degree of certainty?'

Mead was unfazed. '"Certainty" applies *after* you've made a decision. What I'm talking about is perception, which is not a system of measurement.'

'But you've admitted that perception can be very vague. I've seen an article in which you wrote that the silicon retina device you've developed can't even recognise your grandmother.'

'That's because recognising your grandmother is a very complex and difficult procedure.'

'Because it calls on memory and other functions?'

'Not only that. Computers and retinas can measure and analyse light, but light isn't a function of the object being viewed. To identify an object you need not only light but the faculty of perception. Seeing is more than measuremnt. The retina device illustrates this principle. What I'm talking about is neural processing that derives its data from the real world, not just from other computers. Most of this processing is done well below the level of conscious thought, even though it appears effortless. What we're aware of is the end result, not the process. A child routinely learns how to do this kind of thing by the end of his first year, but in fact it is one of the hardest problems to grasp, far harder than chess, say.'

'What neural functions will you be working on next?'

'We're working on depth perception, perception of motion. I've also been working for a long time on the auditory process. All this adds up to a nice start, but the fact is that we haven't got very far into the brain yet.'

'Doesn't this require considerable knowledge of biology as well as computer technology?'

'Of course, and I work very closely with biologists.'

'It's admirable to be able to work towards replicating the function of a retina, but what is the real point of this research, apart from its intellectual challenge?'

'It is only by trying to build a system that you can understand how it works, and thus how biological processes work.'

I wondered whether there were any practical applications that might follow from all this research.

'You're asking now about prediction, but there are predictions I feel quite happy to make. For instance when my friend Federico Faggin invented the microprocessor, I had no doubt whatsoever that one of the offshoots would be the personal computer. No doubt at all, and I was right. What I failed to predict was that the microprocessor would also be used in microwave ovens, cars, all kinds of appliances. If you're asking me to look ahead now, it's obvious to me that we will be developing systems that will be able to understand speech and read handwriting. That will be important, but there will be other more subtle implications that in aggregate could be far more important. I can't predict what they are likely to be. All I can say is that you can look forward to being surprised.'

'You're not only a research scientist. You've helped develop companies that make use of your research. Isn't it difficult to keep a clear boundary between the two activities?'

'It's very frustrating to devise a new technology without being able to deploy it. Students can't be involved in that kind of deployment. They're not development engineers – that's not why they've come to Caltech. So there are limits to what universities can do. If I want to make any real contributions beyond invention, I need to work with smaller companies set up to put the ideas into effect. Of course I can't allow my students to work on these commercial projects, both because that's not their purpose in being here, and also because in a commercial setup you must usually keep quiet about the projects you are working on, and students must be able to discuss their work.'

'How do you set about your research? Computers are incredibly complex, but how do you develop your models? With pencil and paper, or with other computers?'

'First comes the imagining, then perhaps some doodles, and eventually this distils into a way to realise the idea. I can use computers as tools for simulating a system, for checking things, and I can use mathematical tools to analyse. But sometimes we're not even sure what questions to ask. We're working on a uniquely neural process, how we learn, how we wire up the brain.'

'But the learning process is an extremely contentious area, surely. Hardly anybody agrees about it. How can you be ready to develop computer technology that simulates it?'

He smiled. 'It's only by building learning systems that you can figure out what questions to ask.'

'Is there much rivalry?'

'Not really. There is so much to be done that no individual can grasp it all anyway. In fact there's a tendency to collaborate.'

Students sometimes seemed invisible on the campus. Immersed in their studies and research exercises, were they really able to assist scientists of Mead's calibre in their work?

'They are absolutely essential. They bring freshness, they ask questions, they stimulate. Without students to work with, life would be dismal. That's another attraction of working at a university. In small companies you may have a group of brilliant people with a great idea, but after ten or twenty years they're still there and their thought processes have frozen. This is far less likely to happen in academia, because of the presence of students.'

I asked whether science and technology had become so complex that soon, if a breakthrough occurred, only a handful of other scientists would be able to grasp what it was all about.

'That's a very important question, which I ought to be asked often and am asked very rarely.' Mead certainly knew how to flatter me. I was flattered. 'I don't have the exact statistic, which varies from field to field, but every six or eight years as much new scientific knowledge is generated as was generated in the entire previous history of the discipline. You may wonder how it's possible for any one to get an education any more, as we can only grasp an ever decreasing fraction of that knowledge. But as you learn more deeply, things get unified that used to be seen as separate. Specifics multiply, but ideas do not. Our grasp of fundamental principles is deepening, and distilling knowledge into frameworks we can all grasp is an essential purpose of academia. Otherwise we'd just be compiling a catalogue of information. Companies are lousy at this sort of thing. They subdivide and have experts running their divisions, but what they are bad at is unifying their knowledge. What they're doing is applying their knowledge to a single goal.

'There has been a danger, and it was particularly apparent in Britain, to view science and technology as oppressive. It's essential that we view them as a human, not a depersonalised, activity. Science is creative, it does touch people. Just look at information technology! That's been a liberating force, not an oppressive one.'

'With computers in use as very powerful tools, has some of the magic gone out of scientific research? Or is it a romantic misconception to suppose that scientists experience the elation of breakthroughs, the kind of thing we read about Watson and Crick going through with DNA?'

'No, there are still moments of discovery after struggle. It's not a misconception at all. The course of one's work is never predictable, and sometimes we seem to be getting nowhere and have to put the project to one side. And then one day the problem that has brought it to a halt seems to vanish. Just this morning I woke at five and an idea came to me, not a big idea, not a breakthrough, but something I need in order to make progress with something I'm working on.'

I found Mead dazzling, draining. The power and clarity of his mind were apparent to me, as he responded to my elementary questions with lucidity and grace. The comforts of the Atheneum, its armchairs and menus and scattered periodicals, seemed better suited to the leisurely ruminations of the humanist than to the brain-buzz of the typical Caltech scientist. Mead, tending his own fields both in conjunction with his research teams and with the private development companies he has helped to set up, surely typified precisely the kind of individualistic, idea-driven scientist that gives Caltech its distinction.

Later that day I talked to a scientist associated with a very different kind of research, a project that requires organised team effort. Leroy Hood, with the help of about sixty research students, only some of whom are working exclusively on this project, is applying his skills to the genome, decoding the genetic information stored in chromosomes. The project was born in 1985. A collaborative enterprise, it engages the energies of six major teams at various universities as well as smaller groups. Duplication of effort is strenuously avoided, and competitiveness vies with collaboration. The project is controversial, in part because it smacks of the kind of 'big science' research that Caltech has traditionally been wary of. Moreover, the programme may well cost up to $3 billion, no mean sum, which means that Hood has to spend much of his time lobbying those with political and financial power, such as the National Institutes of Health and the Department of Energy. His appeals stress the economic benefits to the biotechnology industries of America. Others criticise the genome project because it seems on the surface to require perseverance rather than the intellectual creativity for which Caltech is renowned.

A robust man with greying hair, Leroy Hood was wearing a bright check shirt of a kind more usually found on the backs of farmers. He received me cordially, too polite to let on that he had probably grown weary of explaining to the ignorant what the human genome project was all about.

'Our chromosomes contain the genetic information that is responsible for our development. The genome project sets out to decipher this genetic code in the language of DNA. There are four elements in DNA, each known by a different letter. Think of it as four colours of beads, and think of DNA as a long string of beads. What's important is their order or sequence. The units of information on chromosomes are genes – 50,000 to 100,000 for humans. Most genes encode a protein. Once again this is a string, this time with twenty different coloured beads. The order of the beads determines how each protein folds in three dimensions to generate a molecular machine. The proteins catalyse the chemistry of life and give our bodies shape and strength.

'The genome project is developing tools that will do this decoding job, which would otherwise be impossibly laborious. It has two major goals – one is to map the chromosomes and the second is to sequence them. Genome mapping and sequencing will provide an encyclopedia of life, equivalent to 500 volumes of

1000 pages each. To analyse all this information will take centuries, even with the development of new computational tools.' In an article, Hood had pointed out that it had cost $150 million to isolate the gene for cystic fibrosis; with a map of the genome, the same task could be achieved for perhaps $200,000.

'What would you do with this encyclopedia once it's been compiled?'

'Medicine is the most tangible application of this research. But it will also revolutionise biology, because in five years we should be able to sequence DNA ten times more rapidly. At the moment we're spending a huge amount of time on sequencing, but once the sequencing throughput has been increased, it will allow biologists to concentrate on real biology. The research will also revolutionise biotechnology, leading to new industrial opportunities.

'The medical implications centre around disease prevention. In twenty years we will have identified perhaps fifty genes that predispose to common diseases – such as heart disease, cancer, allergies. We will fingerprint the DNA of newborns to identify their "bad" genes and institute therapies to circumvent the deleterious effects of these genes. Hence medicine in the next century will keep people well rather than waiting until they are sick and then attempting to make them well. In twenty years you'll be able to have your complete genome on a compact disk. By manipulating the immune system we should be able to prevent the onset of the diseases that each individual will be susceptible to.

'This will have enormous legal and moral consequences. If we can both predict a child's medical fate, and can also intervene to prevent those diseases, does, for example, an insurance company have the right to have access to the information? If we make the analysis prenatally, under what circumstances will abortions be permitted on the basis of that information? Can we patent a gene? And can we intervene in other human traits revealed in our analysis?'

'You mean personality disorders?'

'Yes.'

'At present it sounds as if you're involved in little more than a huge cataloguing project.'

'But at the same time we're developing important tools that speed up the process, such as robotics that will remove human intervention from the sequencing. It's true that the project is not intended to discover fundamental principles. But it will allow biologists to define all of the genes – the most basic elements of life. To begin to understand such processes as consciousness and learning you need a biologist to understand the networks of life. The genome project takes a powerful first step towards analysing these networks. This could open up new vistas in ways we can't today conceive. Here at Caltech it brings together engineers, mathematicians, chemists, computer scientists. We have twenty people working full-time on this, and many others involved part-time. Our students play a role too. They can be wonderfully creative. The more senior scientists such as myself can organise and administer, but the students will often say things such as "Isn't there a better way of doing this?" and they'll be right. And every few years we have a completely new batch of graduate students, again with new ideas.'

I asked whether the results of advanced research in biotechnology were so arcane that only a few people could grasp them. Leroy Hood's reply was not dissimilar from that given by Carver Mead.

'Not really. In biology, the general principles remain simple and powerful. It's the detail that seems infinite and complex.'

21

CHAPTER WITH ORANGE SLICE

It's all very well having these splendid scientists up in Pasadena transforming our understanding of the universe and making revolutionary technological advances, but for thousands of residents of Los Angeles the problems begin at a lower level of academic attainment. They speak no English, and in some cases cannot read or write in any other language either.

In the unlikely setting of Bel Air, the Bellagio School is one of two city schools that educate children for whom the English language is all fog and mystery. Once immigrants are 'processed' on arrival, parents of school-age children are given the option of sending the kids to this special school.

When I arrived there I was left to cool my heels for half an hour in the office. The principal, Juliette Thompson, was having a few problems with a 'parent conference' on disciplinary matters, so I kept my head down until she had finished. Possessed of a charm and vivacity not widely encountered among school principals, Mrs Thompson showed me around the modest facilities. I asked her what the point of the school was, since the children would presumably fit in to any other city school, where minority cultures and languages are unavoidably represented.

'It's not just the language. The children have grown up in completely different cultures. If they attended a regular school, they'd stick out like a sore thumb. They don't know the games, they don't know the cafeteria routines. The first thing we do here is not put them in front of a teacher but give them orientation classes so they know what's happening around them, so they can function here. With the Asian girls, for instance, they're used to squatting in toilets – we have to teach them about Western toilets and about soap and towels. Other kids have to be taught that in Los Angeles it's not customary to throw your garbage out of the window.'

82 per cent of the enrolment is Hispanic. Many of the classes are taught in Spanish; others require the help of interpreter aides who speak fifteen or so other languages. I expressed some doubts about whether bilingual classes would lead to proficiency in English. Mrs Thompson disagreed.

'We've found that in immersion classes, where only English is spoken, Hispanic kids can learn to speak English pretty well. But they find it much harder to read and write and analyse in English. The only way these kids can acquire such skills is in their primary language, and some of them come to the school illiterate even in that. But the goal of the bilingual system *is* to have kids proficient in English. Of course, it's more difficult for the non-Hispanic children, but they get primary language support from aides. Many Asians have bilingual programmes after school in their churches and community organisations, which gives them a great advantage.'

She was understandably keen to show the school in the most positive light. Clearly there were problems too, including absenteeism. She blamed not the children but the social disorder in which they lived, often among one-parent families or with parents who might both be alcoholics, too smashed to ensure their children are scrubbed, fed, and dispatched to school each morning.

'I try to resolve disciplinary problems by inviting the parents to conferences, like the one I had this morning. But some parents aren't even sufficiently together to come into the school to talk to me. In such cases there's very little we can do. It's terrible, because everybody knows that such children are the most vulnerable of all to gangs. We had one little boy here, his mother was a housekeeper, away from home too much to look after him properly. So she sent him to live with his uncle, who was a gang member, and of course it wasn't long before the child became involved in gang activities. We can't prevent that from happening. All we can do is try to give the kids who come here a positive first-year experience so that they'll start life in America on the right footing.'

There was no attempt to homogenise the children. On the contrary, their varying backgrounds were respected, even honoured. In the classrooms each child was represented by his or her photograph and by the flag of the country of origin. As I wandered round the classes, I found, among the numerous Latino and Asian faces, a blond boy from Russia, and children from Armenia, Poland and Bulgaria. I would have given much to learn their stories, how and by what route and in what circumstances they left their grim housing estates in Kiev or Sofia and found themselves, still in mid-childhood, in this soft fluid city of sunshine and dreaming.

Any European, from east or west, would have had experience of some kind of centralised civic administration. In Los Angeles the only citywide organisations one was likely to encounter were the police and the school department. Politically, Los Angeles was diffuse; neighbourhood counted for more than city. The Olympics gave Los Angeles a temporary cohesiveness, but by the 1990s it no longer seemed relevant. Mayor Bradley, once a commanding figure in the city, retained his dignity but not, it appeared, his authority.

The only daily newspaper of consequence, the *Los Angeles Times*, was deliberately localised. I received the English-language Westside supplements, while other parts of the city received local supplements in whatever language was appropriate. This was sensible enough, serving both the interests of readers and of advertisers, who could target their sales pitch more accurately. *LA Weekly* gives deeper coverage of the political life of Los Angeles, exposing the perplexities of the mayor and council, the ceaseless battles between developers and no-growth activists, between the ocean and pollutants, between arts organisations and their bank overdrafts. The other citywide publications make little attempt to cover this ground. The dismal monthly *Los Angeles* had, in the period when the Rodney King beating had gripped the nation, run its lead story on swimsuits, plus pieces on Hawaii and the real-estate slump in the city, and an excerpt from a book about the Queen of England's visit to California – in 1983. *LA Style* is a much classier act, a lush, flashy, large-format monthly composed mostly of ads for goods that only the ultra-rich can afford to buy. Its articles can, however, be of considerable interest, and I encountered worthwhile pieces on industry and architecture, as well as on the latest hot musicians in town or the latest upsets within the studio hierarchies.

The offices of *LA Weekly* are surely the creation of a Hollywood studio art director. Crammed into a crowded and messy building in Silver Lake were offices spilling over with boxes of manuscripts, bulging In and Out trays, computers and phones and Rolodexes on every desk, scraps of paper with phone messages on the bulletin boards, posters, cartoons, phone lists, calendars, memos, and schedules. Clipped to wastepaper bins were boxes proclaiming: 'I'm a Recycler'. 125 people work in this warren to produce a thick tabloid with a distribution of 170,000, although of course the readership is far higher.

I asked the weekly's publisher why there was only one daily newspaper to serve over 13 million inhabitants.

'This is not unusual in American cities,' he replied. 'Most cities have only a single daily paper, and we did have the *Herald* until 1989. But this is a city with little street life, with few news stands, a city that really isn't galvanised by information. Even local TV news is fairly weak in Los Angeles. The *Times* is the only daily paper, but it's astonishing how many people don't read that either.'

Like many papers with leftish leanings, *LA Weekly* has been accused of taking a greater interest in the rest of the world than in the city it serves. The editor, Kit Rachlis, conceded that there had been some truth to the charge. He became editor in 1989, after years in New York as second-in-command at the *Village Voice*, the granddaddy of 'alternative' papers. Under Rachlis the *Weekly* runs editorials only on special occasions; even during the Gulf War there was no single editorial line, which left some members of the staff unhappy. In the mid-1980s the *Weekly* became 'knee-jerk conspiratorial, and it was probably true that we covered Nicaragua more effectively than Watts. I don't think that's true any longer, and I want the *Weekly* to be a writer's paper, without too many editorial constraints.'

Harold Meyerson, the paper's political editor, said that the niche the *Weekly* occupies as an alternative newspaper is in many respects self-defining. The paper can't compete with a daily in terms of news coverage, but they have good connections in high places which provide them with occasional scoops that elude the *Times*. Although the paper has sent out correspondents to cover stories in Russia and Vietnam, it is trying hard to concentrate more on what's happening locally.

'I sensed a need for a paper of ideas that took the city seriously,' said Kit, 'that assumed the intelligence of its readers, that was consciously on the left but also aware of the inadequacies of the left, that was avowedly intellectual despite the fact that intellectuals seem to have lost touch with a mass audience. The fact that the paper is a free sheet meant that I was less dependent on whether a particular lead story would appeal. So I could reinvent the paper every week, especially since it already had a stable identity. Of course there are always certain events that can't go unheeded, such as the Daryl Gates story, especially in a one-paper town. We also know our limits. We can't be exhaustive in our arts coverage, but we know the culture of the city and are willing to go against the grain. I suppose what we're trying to do is to frame and thus anticipate the cultural conversation of Los Angeles.

'Most other city publications' – he was probably referring to *LA Style* and the wretched *Los Angeles* – 'are essentially adjuncts of the movie industry. Fortunately, lots of autonomous cultural centres have been developing, and I believe the *Weekly* has been a vehicle for this trend. After all, of all American cities, Los Angeles is surely the great social urban experiment of the twentieth century. That's not a bad story to be covering.'

Another great social experiment was to take place that evening. My wife Maria had flown out to Los Angeles to ensure that I wouldn't overlook her birthday. By happy coincidence our friend Erik, a screenwriter who lives in Berkeley, had phoned to say that he was coming to Los Angeles at the same time.

He told me what he had been up to, the projects he was working on, and added: 'I've also been writing a novel this spring. Unfortunately nobody's bought it. Or rather, a lot of people haven't bought it . . .'

He asked me which evening we would be free.

'I can do either Tuesday or Wednesday.'

'Either is good for me. Let's do neither.'

'Perfect.'

Eventually we agreed to meet up on the evening Erik was due to see Dimitri and his wife Rosanna, and all dine out together.

Neo-prohibitionism has taken a terrible toll in the United States, especially in Southern California, where wine-drinking has always been regarded as slightly suspect, although I expect

Diet Cristal would go down a treat. The happy consequence of the new alarmism is that wine shops, those few that exist, are desperate to sell good bottles, and I had been able to pick up 1983 vintage champagnes for about the same price as British supermarket champagne. I rarely drink the stuff, but my wife is partial to it.

So we arrived at Dimitri's flat in Beverly Hills with a half-empty bottle of 1983 Philipponnat Blanc de Blancs, which we decided to polish off at the restaurant. As we sat around making impolite conversation, all that petillance began to tickle my bladder and I asked Dimitri where I would find the comfort station.

'Just down the corridor.' He pointed. 'I'll turn up the speakers.'

I recall Erik making a similar joke when we were schoolboys. At parties he would follow a girl as she moved towards the lavatory, wait for the door to click shut, then place his mouth over the keyhole and leer: 'I'm listening . . .' Erik and Dimitri were the best of friends, even though they pursued the same profession in a cutthroat world, yet there was an element of competition between them that clearly stretched back to a time when they hadn't even been aware of each other's existence.

As we rose to leave for the restaurant, Erik found that his leather jacket had not been hung up but lay tossed into a corner. 'Jesus, Dimitri, you threw my jacket on the floor!'

'You said it was a flight jacket, didn't you?'

We decided to eat at Larry Parker's Beverly Hills Diner, not because the food was particularly good but because it was an example of Californian excess that I was keen to experience. Its menu features 1000 items, including sandwiches, omelettes, fish dishes, Mexican food, salads, desserts. Every dish is named, as though an extra-culinary association would validate it. We could choose between Fred's Burrito, Joe's Baked Potato Delight, somebody else's Dijon chicken. Prices were high, but portions were immense. Stickers with snappy slogans or the names of Hollywood stars were slapped on the walls. Since in Beverly Hills you usually eat while working, each booth is equipped with a telephone, so that you can call your agent while forking in the pasta. Larry Parker's looked like the kind of place you would design if, a thousand miles from Beverly Hills, you wanted to invent a diner that overplayed the showbiz card. Appearing bogus, it was authentically theatrical.

As we argued about the menu, Dimitri began his celebrated

impersonation of an effete queen who is ineffectually trying to conceal his camp homosexuality. He affected not to understand why we were all laughing so hard.

I reminded him that we had some champagne to drink, and he prevailed upon our obliging young waiter to bring some glasses. The waiter couldn't have been nicer about it, even though we hadn't bought the fizz at the diner. Seconds later he was back at the table, spreading the glasses around.

Dimitri gazed at the young man with misty adoration and murmured, 'I think we've just bonded . . .'

Earlier that week Maria and I had spent two days visiting wineries in the Central Coast region north of Los Angeles. Dimitri and Rosanna were curious to know how we had fared. I assured them that the trip had gone well, despite torrential rain.

'And the hotel?'

'Ghastly. One of those bed and breakfast places Californians find so winsome. Crumbling Victorian gingerbread house expensively converted into ten rooms, each with a cute name, and no phone, no television and a three-figure room rate.'

Dimitri groaned. 'Doilies everywhere?'

'Worse. Potpourri. Dolls and figurines. Photographs of stiff-collared bankers.'

'I know the kind of place. Two elderly lesbians – "This is my sister Amy,"' he simpered, 'and different decor in every room. "We did this all ourselves . . ."'

'No lesbians but otherwise correct. Our room had a butterfly motif. We could have opted for a baseball souvenir and pennant design in another room.'

'Makes you want to throw up.'

'And on arrival you have to meet all the other guests over complimentary wine and cheese in the drawing room. And at breakfast you have to share tables and be polite to old biddies who love London, and you have to pass them the decaff and tell them how much you adore California.'

'Worst of all,' Maria recalled, 'as we were leaving, the owner's wife said to me, "Part of the deal is that we get to have a hug before you go," and then her husband insisted on hugging me too.'

'How did Stephen take all this?' Erik wanted to know.

'I backed away fast. No hugs for me.'

'I'd have mentioned,' said Dimitri, 'that I was a walking Petri dish of communicable diseases. And the food?'

'Interminable cooked breakfast. Date bread, like eating marble. Watery cheese flan.'

'An orange slice on the plate?'

'Yes! There was!'

Dimitri beamed. 'This is California. You go into a shop to buy a Rolex watch, and it comes with an orange slice attached.'

Our food arrived: bowls of steak chilli, immense salads, burly breads. An additional feature of this diner is the presence of video screens suspended from the ceiling. I had managed to ignore the one near our table, but an argument was developing between Erik and Dimitri.

'It's Dion.'

'No, Erik. This is a cover version of the song.'

'It's Dion.'

'Don't keep saying that. I know Dion when I see him. This isn't Dion.'

'It's definitely Dion.'

'I'll bet you your next development fee it isn't Dion.'

'No way. I like to bet on a sure thing.'

'It's not Dion.'

'It is.'

Rosanna said this was becoming tiresome. Dimitri agreed that we needed to settle the issue once and for all. He summoned over the waiter. Did he know?

'Could be Dion,' said the waiter, before being overcome by doubts, 'but I'm not certain. I'll go find out.'

He returned and broke the news: It was not Dion. Dimitri crowed. Erik shook his head and fell silent, staring at his chilli, cowed by defeat. The conversation turned to other matters.

Then Erik raised his head. He looked perky again. 'Why should I trust some guy in the kitchen? It's Dion.'

Our groans shut him up.

'I have to change the subject,' I said.

'Thank God for that.'

'Don't take it amiss, but do any of you know a plastic surgeon?'

Dimitri nodded.

Rosanna looked surprised. 'You do?'

He nodded again, looking at me soulfully. 'How do you think I got to look like this?'

Dimitri is swarthy, his eyes intense and pouchy, his jowls broad. Dimitri is a striking man, but Paul Newman he is not.

'My plastic surgeon only does one face. This is it. You're looking at it.'

'The colouring,' said Erik, 'is that his work too?'

'Absolutely. Part of the job. In and out.'

Erik, known to be clever, was assigned the task of dividing up the bill. It was agreed that Dimitri and I should pay two shares each, since our wives could reimburse us later. The conversation purred on while Erik wrestled with the documentation and scratched his temple as he did his sums.

'Fifteen bucks each.'

We didn't argue, but Erik seemed troubled. He returned to his calculations. This went on for some minutes.

'Everything okay, Erik?'

'I think I goofed.'

'Should it be more or less?'

'More, of course.'

'How much more?'

'Forget it. It was my mistake.'

'No, no, tell us, we'll pay the difference. Don't want you to be out of pocket.'

'It's nothing. Just a few dollars.'

'How many?'

'Five per couple.'

I handed over five singles. Dimitri did likewise. But Erik was still staring at the bill.

'Hey, wait a second,' he cried, 'I think it was okay.'

'You mean you didn't need the extra ten?'

'No.'

I took back my singles. Erik looked up.

'It's only three extra per couple, not five.'

'Fuck it. Talk to your accountant.'

We left. I was in a good mood, having come out of the evening three dollars ahead, which doesn't often happen when Erik is doing the sums. We walked down Beverly Drive to the car park, where Dimitri retrieved his Mercedes. Rosanna told me how, when she had first come to live in Beverly Hills, she had been astonished by the number of Rolls-Royces and Mercedes in the streets, but she seemed to have come to terms with them without too much pain. Dimitri engaged in some genial chitchat with the Ethiopian parking attendant as he paid the fee.

As he glided out onto the road, he softly remarked: 'Ethiopians have such wonderful faces.'

We murmured assent.

'Not him, though. Yech.' And Dimitri was off, explaining volubly how the attendant wasn't an Ethiopian at all but a Liberian named Sean who'd originally been Irish 'until I sent him to see my facial surgeon'.

A few blocks further on we found two police cars parked diagonally across the street. There had clearly been an 'incident'. Dimitri slowed down, and we had a good look at three youths seated on the kerb, all handcuffed and squinting under the powerful beams from the squad cars.

'Is this before or after the beating?' I asked my companions.

'Before, before. They're still setting up the lights.'

Dimitri looked concerned. 'I sure hope those guys aren't overweight. In Beverly Hills we have a strict weight code.'

As we parted company at Dimitri's flat and headed for our separate cars, Erik took me aside.

'So how's it going with what you laughably call your research?'

'Not too bad, but being in Los Angeles just doesn't feel like being at work.'

'Of course not. In LA we frown upon work.'

'And I keep worrying that I don't have enough material.'

'I wouldn't let that worry you. It's never stopped you before.'

22

TERMITES IN THE VALLEY

It's a long drive up the freeway to the Valley, so I turned to Mark and Brian for diversion. The blood drained from my face as I realised it was their wedding day, and I had probably missed most of the ceremony.

Let me explain. Mark and Brian, realising fondly that they had been on the air together for six years, decided to 'renew our vows'. This they proposed to do in a large car park in the lovely industrialised municipality of El Segundo. For days they had been begging callers to help them to organise the wedding. The listeners had been lavish with advice.

'You need a few cases of really cheap wine with the labels changed to suggest it's fancy stuff, and you have to have matchbook covers with your names spelt wrong.'

'Jeez, you're right. We forgot all about the matchbook covers. Let's go to Line 6. Hey, Lily, what've you got?'

Lily had a cake, or rather the bakery she worked for had a cake, but Mark and Brian wanted a free cake—

'I got to talk to my boss . . .'

'You can't come on the air and give your bakery a free plug—'

'Not unless you give us a free cake—'

'I got to talk to my boss.'

'We're kinda cranky today.'

'We're cranky 'cos we're horny.'

'We're so horny.'

'He's so horny you can hang the car keys off him.'

'The one thing, the only thing, we haven't yet organised—'

'Apart from the cake—'

'– is the guy with a six-foot unicycle riding along doing a Tarzan yell.'

'Okay, let's go to the phones. Line 3! Who've we got on Line 3?'

'What d'you have to offer for the wedding, man?'

'I've got a six-foot unicycle and I can do a Tarzan yell.'

'Yes, man!'

And today was the wedding day, broadcast live from the parking lot in El Segundo. I'd missed the preliminaries, but was in time for the vows. Mark and Brian read together some cod Kahlil Gibran gibberish, ending with: 'Da-da-bda-bda-da-da-err, the right stuff', an arcane reference to a smash hit mumble by the New Kids on the Block. Brian had a little trouble with the phrase 'until parted by death', which he amended to 'until parted by death or the ratings'.

It was heartening to find traditional values reaffirmed on the air as I glided down the slopes towards their finest embodiment: the San Fernando Valley. But there was a dark side to this suburban paradise. It was hard to generalise about the Valley. The home of respectable households, it was also the capital of the American pornography industry. The Valley was part of the city of Los Angeles, but it differed from the rest of the city in many ways. It lacked the proximity to the ocean, and its climate was different, hotter in summer and cooler in winter. The wild heights of the Santa Monica Mountains were both a physical and a psychological barrier between the Valley and the older city to the south. Much of Los Angeles south of the moutains is a conurbation of neighbourhoods and industrial zones, but the Valley is relentlessly suburban, a patchwork of shopping malls and tract housing, with more expensive and less monotonous developments in the foothills. Its expansion had taken place after the Second World War, when the Valley's population grew many times over, until by 1960 there were almost a million inhabitants.

From the air the Valley looked splattered. When in the film *Earth Girls Are Easy* the aliens look down from their spacecraft onto the Valley, they remark: 'What a mess – a city in ruins.' The Valley worries less about aesthetics than about serving the Californian family. It's a network of freeways and boulevards, a collection of schools and cinemas, churches and synagogues, and strategically positioned fast-food outlets. Unlike the Los Angeles basin, where the avenues and boulevards act as linear magnets, in the Valley the Ventura Boulevard carries the burden of providing a social core.

My cousin had suggested that I should visit the Galleria in Sherman Oaks to gain a complete insight into the Valley phenomenon. I duly went there, but couldn't tell the difference between the Galleria and any other indoor four-storey shopping mall I had encountered. Down on the ground floor a pianist trickled out some tunes, but music or a fountain or a clown have become standard props in malls. I did spot a few Valley girls, aged between thirteen and sixteen, gum in mouth, hips in shorts, brains in early retirement. There had been a time when Valley girls, or their scriptwriters, had made some worthwhile contributions to the language. In *Earth Girls Are Easy*, the young Valley hairdressers gaze into the mirror and moan 'Housewife from hell' or 'Matron on drugs', and there's a fine moment when the heroine Candy bursts into song: 'Girls think I'm snotty/Maybe it's true/With my hair and my body/You'd be too./I'm a blonde, yeah, yeah. . . .'

My only pleasurable reason to come to the Valley was to visit old friends in Tarzana – yes, it was named after the creature – who have a pool, a refrigerator full of chilled wine, a set of *boules*, and two exquisite children. Sooner or later they will turn into monsters, like all children, but right now they were irresistible in their insouciant charm. On my visits, small entertainments would be provided, such as a chance to listen to one of young Jack's stories. Beckett would have admired them, since they rarely exceeded the length of a single sentence. On another occasion, coffee on the patio was interrupted by a shriek from the kitchen which announced the onset of a termite invasion. I was fascinated, never having seen two hundred termites skittishly twittering on a kitchen floor, but my hosts were less pleased. I was glad to have seen them, since, according to Carey McWilliams, 'Los Angeles is the capital of all the termites in America' and it would have been a pity to have left the city without meeting a single one.

The Valley was also the home of the studios and other adjuncts of the movie business. I called in at the Actors Centers International in Studio City, an academy offering courses under the general slogan of 'perfecting the professional actor'. In the camera technique classes 'an exciting array of camera experiences maximises the actor's confidence and uniqueness in front of the camera'. Special classes focused on camera technique for aspiring soap-opera performers: 'Lieux Dressler takes you through the entire Daytime experience, from the cold reading audition to the on-set work. She helps you to understand what "Soap" style is and how you adapt your talents to it.' All of which sounded like a deeply depressing experience. Other classes deal with skills such as audition technique and commercial voiceover technique.

Of course you can acquire all the skills in the book and still not find work. No one will employ you as an actor unless you are a member of the Screen Actors Guild, and once you've managed to join the Guild, which is no easy matter, you must still reconcile yourself, unless you are astonishingly gifted or amazingly fortunate, to frequent unemployment. It's estimated that at any time 85 per cent of Guild members are without work.

The race for work can begin in childhood. I saw an ad for an open call at Warner Brothers, who were looking for a 'bright, energetic and precocious' eight-year-old Caucasian for a lead role in a new series. At the entrance to the Warner lot I found dozens of children, each accompanied by a newspaper-reading parent. They sat on the kerb, waiting patiently for their turn in front of the casting director. They had come prepared for a long wait, with colouring books, magazines, and Nintendo games. From time to time a security man emerged from his office to call up the next batch of boys.

I had already been to talk to a casting director at Warner Brothers, and despite her entreaties I had to turn down the roles she was offering me. Gilda Stratton specialises in television comedy episodes, especially *Night Court*, which had been in session for nine years. To cast a weekly series she has to move fast, auditioning from Tuesday and casting on Friday, one week before shooting. In addition to the fixed characters in the series, there can be up to twelve 'guest' characters in each episode. Gilda will initially use the 'breakdown' service, which deluges her with resumés and photos of actors who may be suitable for the part, say, of the big-breasted bimbo with a lisp.

'Once I send the word out, the delivery guys arrive here with stacks of envelopes. We'll process it down. I'm open to agents, of course, but I don't like "hocking", which is when an agent phones you fifty-two times a day to push his client. I often use new faces, and actors know that appearing on *Night Court* can be a great opportunity for them. There are quite a few stars who got their first real break on the show. Personally, I love the theatre, and I like actors with theatre experience. When I start to audition, I'll see up to forty people a day. They never see the whole script, just the scene with their part. Then I'll shortlist five or six for each part, and the producers will then sit in on the finals. I can also call back people who were in previous episodes, and sometimes the producers will tailor parts specially to suit a particular actor they want to use.

'When you're dealing with the networks, even the stars are required to read. These guys make huge amounts of money for each episode, so the networks want to be sure that they are right for the part. The whole process is much more protracted when you're casting a movie, as the money isn't usually in place by the time the casting is done. There are even some producers who use videos instead of live auditions.'

'You make it sound as though being an actor is a terrible life.'

'Being a Hollywood actor is a terrible life. Thousands are out of work at any one time. If you're in the Screen Actors Guild, they won't issue you with medical coverage unless you earn more than $5000 a year. I'm always getting desperate calls from actors begging for the most insignificant part just to hang on to their medical coverage. To be an actor in movies or television, you have to be truly driven.'

In a spacious house in the southern edges of the Valley in Sherman Oaks I found Patrick Stansfield, who earns his living as a tour manager. I had expected to encounter a sleek, hard-edged slave driver but the man who came to the door was a plump cheerful man with swept-back greying hair. He could have been anything, except, it seemed, what he was, a mover and shaker of the rock music scene, a consummate behind-the-scenes operator. As he brewed some coffee, Patrick admitted that age had mellowed him: 'Let me be immodest enough to say that I am one of the elder statesmen of the music business.'

In the basement, office equipment and computers shared the space with a grand piano and his fitness machines. Posters on the walls portrayed the megastars for whom Patrick has organised tours of America and the world. A Midwesterner, he first worked in the theatre as a stage manager, then moved out to San

Francisco, where he lived in Haight-Ashbury and participated in the pastimes of the district. Interviewed for a job as stage manager by both Kurt Adler of the San Francisco Opera and by Bill Graham the rock tour promoter, he was hired by the latter, which sealed his fate. He began to travel the world, holding the hands of the Rolling Stones and other groups in his capacity as assistant production manager.

Now self-employed, Patrick works for a variety of enterprises, not just rock tours. 'I do all kinds of things: site coordination for Tina Turner concerts, industrial shows, product launches, commercials with concert sequences – anything to do with music on stage, usually in front of a live audience. Part of my job is to dissolve the blood clots that occur in the body of any production. I'm the guy that takes care of the nuts and bolts, who makes sure the crews move in and out of venues on time.'

Los Angeles has become the major North American centre for tour managers such as Patrick, mainly because the spaciousness of the city offers plenty of rehearsal venues; New York can't compete on this level. While the band is rehearsing for a tour, Patrick will be in another building constructing a plywood mockup of the set, while in another studio the actual set is being built. He'll practise taking the set up and down and make sure that everything works properly.

'Once the tour is mooted, the artist's agent and manager will start to book the halls, working their way round sports fixtures and other engagements and jockeying for position. While they're doing this they'll be consulting with me about feasibility – whether the hall is easy to get out of, weather patterns, what the freeways are like between A and B.

'I have very little contact with the artists. Often the manager doesn't have much either. In practice many managers find themselves restricted to six asks a week. If the manager keeps throwing questions at the artist, the artist is likely to get annoyed and wonder what the fuck he's employing a manager for. So the manager has to judge whether, on a matter of extra costs which will be paid for by the artist, he ought to consult him. I keep my distance. I did a tour for Dylan, and hardly ever spoke a word with him. When your lips are close to the artist's ear, your throat is near to the razor. Managers have to know when to show up, when not to. You ask an artist a stupid question, and you can be out of there. If you don't ask the right question, you can also be out of there.

'Once a hall is booked, I'll start working on tickets. Production issues such as lighting and design will encroach on the amount of seating that's going to be available. I'll often work with the manager to put together a shortlist of designers and lighting designers. We'll get the ad campaigns moving, and there'll usually be a media blitz the weekend before tickets go on sale. We'll hit the Calendar sections of the Sunday papers, and we try to pick weekends immediately after payday, especially in military markets. Often booking for a number of cities on the tour will open the same day. The artist's managers will be monitoring those sales constantly, and by noon they'll have enough information from each location to know whether they ought to be scheduling extra shows – that's where the money is on these tours.

'All the time I'm keeping score, fine-tuning. There may be a trade show in the hall till four that afternoon, and I have to know whether we can set up in time, whether we'll have sufficient truck access, that kind of thing. We'll be hiring local stagehands, and I'll send out a detailed "rider" to the hall managers. The rider specifies all our requirements in writing, so we can show that we asked for something well in advance. I'll order the catering, the security, the dressing-room amenities. It's usually a high-class operation, with cable TV in the dressing rooms, phones, office equipment. It's expensive but most good agents and managers know that you don't get anywhere by not thinking big.'

Patrick showed me the rider for a tour he organised the previous year. It specified the equipment required ('2 forklifts must have side-shift feature'), fire extinguishers, a 'labour force of approximately ten qualified humpers', the power requirements, shower facilities and bath towels for the crew, mops and squeegees and golf carts at the production office. It explains the special effects and dry ice required. Catering requirements are listed: two chest-type freezers, three deliveries of ice each day, a skip. The artist 'will receive gratis, for the duration of the engagement . . . 3 12-passenger, chauffeur-driven vans with tinted windows or one 40-seat luxury coach for the artist and party' as well as a luggage van. 'All dressing rooms must be clean, carpeted (preferably in light earth tones), free from odors, comfortable and capable of being locked securely.' Security guards must be provided, as well as a secured parking compound. The rider gives a timetable from three days before the show to showday, specifying the crew required for each stage of the operation. A welcome provision states: 'In the event of unreasonable violence by any security personnel upon members of the public being observed by the Artist or tour staff, the Artist reserves the right to cancel or terminate the show immediately and will be entitled to the full contracted fees.'

'It's also my job to book the hotels. Often the artist and the crew will stay in different places. They're on different per diems and have different requirements. Of course I treat my crew well too. Some of those guys have been with me fifteen or twenty years and their morale is important. I'll advance each location, especially the hotels. I take with me a fourteen-page checklist, which covers everything we'll expect.' The list specifies daily breakfast orders, food and drink for the hospitality suite, accounting procedures, daily newspapers required, whether feather or foam pillows should be provided, thermostat controls, special phone lines and screening, and the assignment of extra keys.

'We always take the whole floor for the crew and production staff. These guys don't want to run into little old ladies and businessmen in suits as they're running up and down the hall in their bathrobes, and the little old ladies definitely don't want to run into a screaming sound technician. Being on tour is like being in a time capsule. Once the itinerary book is issued the tour takes over. Your life goes on hold for a few weeks. Every minute is planned.

'What you've got to remember is that we're not selling music, we're selling seats. A seat in a hall is like a short-term rental on an apartment. A big theatre owner is first in the real-estate business, and only secondarily a theatrical producer. But there's more to it than tickets. These days the big money is made through merchandising. In fact merchandising is fast becoming the tail that wags the dog, and the last Stones tour was bought by a T-shirt manufacturer.'

'Is pricing something you stay out of?'

'Absolutely. If the agent or anyone else comes to me and says the tickets are too high because the production costs are too high, I'll say: "I'll do it cheaper. I'm here to serve you. Just talk to your artist and let me know what he says." That's usually the end of the matter.'

'What happens if the tour is a flop?'

'The manager will cut production. It's the only thing to do if the artist and his manager still want to collect their bread. They may come to me for suggestions, and I'll usually say, "Let's start by cutting some musicians." God forbid. You should see their reactions: "Hey man, if you think you're gonna fuckin' well wreck this show by fuckin' up our band, you're fuckin' well out of your skull." So instead we cut out a few laser effects or amplifiers. Trucks are a huge expense, and if we can cut one of those by having less equipment with us, that'll help too.'

'You seem very relaxed, sitting here sipping tea, with Bach playing on the stereo. Are you like this on tour?'

'Me? I'm a maniac on tour, a real jumper and screamer. Less so now. But in the 1970s . . . That was an amazing time, if you lived to tell the tale. We were a free-wheeling bunch. You'd have guys waking at 6 a.m. after two hours' sleep and serious drug abuse because they had a job to do at 7 a.m., and as they climbed into the bus they'd be rolling their first joint. It's because we're dealing with some wild guys that we need to have everything planned meticulously. There's a saying, and you can quote me on this, that the show is continuous twenty-four hours a day, and at specified intervals we let in the audience.'

23

DEAD FISH PLUCKERS WANTED

Every time my cousin and her husband William produce a successful film, they mansionise: they add on another room to their house. The house they originally bought was modest in the extreme. Now it has cathedral ceilings and a pool. Yet their world is not one of expensive lunches, meetings at the Polo Lounge, mad dashes back and forth across the continent, and screaming down the telephone. William sits in his offices in Westwood, unflappable, sometimes inscrutable, and the movies keep coming, and some of them make a tidy profit. Sometimes writers come to him with ideas; on other occasions William and his colleagues come up with a story line and hire a writer to develop it. One evening at a dinner party, somebody talked of a Wall Street banker who was a serial killer by night. William's antennae quivered, and a year or so later his movie *The Banker* was released.

The films are produced on modest budgets, which means that the production company pays modest fees. Screenwriters who belong to the Writers Guild command base fees of at least $25,000. This is not the kind of fee William likes to pay. For considerably less he hires non-Guild writers looking for credits to beef up their resumés. In return William says he is more generous than most studios in offering profit participation, but I decided not to press him on this point. William and his co-producers keep a close eye on the script and its evolution. They feel entitled to make changes, even radical ones, without consultation. Sometimes they will option a script while they sort out the financing. If the financing isn't forthcoming, the project is abandoned and the rights to the script revert to the writer.

William began his career by directing many of his own movies, but now he tends to hire others, while he stays in the background, monitoring the shooting and the postproduction phases such as editing. The big headache is financing. While the writer is working on the ninety-eighth draft of the script, William is busy finding the money either from private investors or, more likely, from companies that make the investment in exchange for distribution rights. His budgets work out at between $1 and $2 million, not unusual for an independent production, though a trifling sum for a major studio, which spends on average about $18 milion on each movie.

I sat in on a telephone conference between William, a co-producer, and a writer about a script they were developing. Down the line, in a different state, sat the writer, who had been rewriting somebody else's first draft. The producers had sent the writer their notes on the script so far, and he was now responding to the suggestions. He began by giving his 'broad strokes reaction'. He was, he said, 'looking for strong moments in a progressive structure', and expressed considerable dissatisfaction with the draft he had been sent. It was too long, it got bogged down, there were turns of the plot that didn't work. The three engaged in polite arguments about the attitude of the protagonist, who was spoken about as though he existed, whereas at present he was no more than a few hundred much altered words on a page. To these problems the writer proposed 'motivational changes'.

As I was listening to all this, I was wondering how someone who spoke English so badly could actually put together a script. This shows how little I understand about the movie industry, since the script is not a work of literature but a skeleton of words and gestures that will later receive the flesh provided by director, art designer, cameramen, sound technicians, special effects wizards, composers, and all the other chefs with their fingers in the pie.

William's current project was *Martial Law Undercover*, and shooting was imminent. He kindly gave me permission to turn up on the set whenever I chose. Since, to keep the costs down, shooting usually took place about thirty miles away, this was an invitation I couldn't avail myself of too often. The first sequences were shot in Griffith Park, which wasn't too far away. Ringing what seemed to be the location spot were dozens of cars, vans with technical equipment, wardrobe and makeup trailers, bossy production assistants with megaphones, and some psychopaths on motorbikes, who turned out to be actors. A youth who looked vaguely familiar perched on a rock, smoking a cigarette. He looked very bored, and I could see why. Nothing was happening. Various people were in a huddle, the director was nowhere to be seen, William had been and gone, and everybody else was hanging about while the next scene was being set up. In other words, a typical moment on location.

A few days later I tried again. This time I had to drive out to San Fernando, where they were shooting at Pancake Heaven. The restaurant was filled to bursting with actors, camera crew and other technicians. Not wanting to get in their way while they were setting up, I wandered out into the car park. Here I found the bored-looking youth, smoking another cigarette. To my surprise, he greeted me by name. Perhaps he was a groupie reader who follows me shyly round the world? Not at all. It was my second cousin, Nick. I wasn't too surprised to find him here, since, like me, he had family connections with the boss, his uncle.

'What are you doing here, Nick?'

'I'm guarding the door. It's my job to make sure nobody goes in that door while they're shooting inside. This is the shit job and I get the lowest pay.'

'You're lucky to get paid at all.'

Nick was to prove an invaluable informant, keeping me up to date on all the tantrums, resignations, firings, and mysterious couplings that enliven any shoot. The script supervisor was the second person to hold that job in three days; strange things, probably amorous, were going on in one of the trailers. Nick had it in for the assistant director, whose job it was to boss everybody around, and was doing it very efficiently, as I discovered when I snuck back into Pancake Heaven and hid in a booth while she set up the next scene. She wanted the refrigerator switched off, as the noise would be intrusive. The restaurant owner wasn't too happy about turning his chilled batter into tepid sludge. Once the scene was set up – it involved two characters, one of whom was making a phone call – the sound man asked for more time. A makeup girl dashed about taking Polaroid shots to establish the exact position of the main actress and her clothing in case the scene needed to be reshot. Eventually the sound man was happy and the camera was in focus.

'We are locked up,' proclaimed the assistant director. 'No one moves, no one makes a sound. Stand by. Quiet.'

At which point someone spotted a shadow on the doorway near the phone. This had to be fixed.

She tried again: 'We are locked up. Roll sound. Action!'

The sound man groaned. 'We are not locked up outside. We can hear voices.' The problem was sorted out, there were three takes of the scene, and then the cameraman decided to vary the speed, and the sound man decided to adjust the position of the microphone, and a crew member put in puffs of smoke to act as a kind of filter. But the smoke stayed on the ground, so that was no good. A method was devised to blow the smoke in through the open door and waft it about until its dispersal pattern suited the director. During Take 5 a dog barked. Before Take 7 the wardrobe crew came in to touch up, and the sound technicians went into a huddle. I was stupendously bored by now, and I wasn't even getting paid.

Of course anyone with the slightest experience of moviemaking knows that it's an unbearably tedious process. Nor is there any reason why it should be interesting, any more than a writer's typing should be considered a spectator sport. I took one other look at the shooting of *Martial Law Undercover*, this time late at night at the Department of Water and Power plant in Sun Valley near San Fernando. This was to be an all-night session, with breakfast ordered for 4.30 a.m. This particular scene was a martial arts confrontation between a well-dressed blonde heroine with coiffed hair and a good line in karate kicks, her long-haired partner in an oversized raincoat, and a blue-suited Oriental karate whizz. Their opponent – whether hero or villain I never discovered – was bearded and decidedly scruffy.

The action was upstaged by the setting, surrounded as we were by the huge turbines and pumps of the power station. The assistant director didn't have to worry about noise levels here, as the growl and grind of the pumps drowned out most conversation. The crew were in hard hats, which resembled inverted tea cups in bright primary colours, and at this stage in the shooting some idiosyncratic notes had begun to creep in. The director's hard hat sported the inscription Quit Yer Cryin, while the continuity girl with the Polaroid had lassoed hers with a silk scarf which she had tied into a huge bow.

After a number of takes the actors rehearsed, and the victim practised his groans as his arm was almost twisted off by the Oriental karate champ. Out in the car park, trestle tables had been set up and spread with snacks and salads. The continuity girl kept scurrying past, a perpetually glum look on her anxious face. I sipped a beer while chatting to a makeup girl, who told me she had entered this line of work by chance.

Nick appeared and joined us.

'Yo, man. What's happening, dude?' I ventured.

He told me that one of his less tedious assignments had been to hunt for locations in East Los Angeles. He and a companion had been standing on the pavement assessing its qualities as an outdoor location, when a large old car rolled up and stopped alongside them. Two awe-inspiring Latinos climbed out and asked them what they were doing in this street. They explained.

'This is a bad area,' suggested the Latinos, 'and you look like victims.'

Nick escaped unscathed. But if he'd returned from dangerous East Los Angeles to sedate Westwood, home of UCLA and William's production company, he might have run into more serious trouble. A film called *New Jack City* was opening in Los Angeles, and because its cast was largely black, it had considerable appeal to the black population. Soon after it opened, over 1000 youths poured into Westwood to a first-run cinema. There are different versions of what happened next. Some said the cinema ran out of tickets, and people who had been queuing for some time were disappointed; others said the cinema had deliberately oversold tickets, which left many ticket-bearing customers refused admission, which understandably irritated them.

The upshot was that 1500 youths, mostly but by no means exclusively black, went on a rampage, breaking windows, looting shops, and vandalising parked cars. There were those who sought to interpret this disturbance in racial terms, but that seemed a false reading. Since there are very few cinemas in the black ghetto, anyone wanting to see the film had to travel to the mostly white suburbs, such as Westwood, where first-run cinemas are located. This riot, which damaged property and not persons, was scarcely justified by the facts, whichever account one accepts, and it seemed startling because Westwood, thick with placid university students and a prosperous bourgeoisie, seems one of the last places in America where you expect to find youths rampaging through the streets.

Perhaps a few of them found time, in between trashing the neighbourhood, to call in at the Job Factory on Westwood Boulevard. This agency specialises in filling unusual jobs. First you must register, which means you hand over $50, and for three months you are notified of opportunities to perform jobs that pay up to $15 per hour, which is what an attorney charges for ten seconds. The Factory advertises positions as cookie decorators, swimmer's companion, paid airline passenger (which helps corporations qualify for frequent-flyer benefits), dead fish plucker (the profession of removing dead tropical fish from wholesale shipments before they reach the pet stores), bird bather, grave-digger, and – one for connoisseurs – as bad skin model for acne ads. As is so often the case in America, the menu is more enticing than the food, for as the manager told me: 'These listings are mostly come-ons for you guys. Except for sperm donor – that's on the list today.'

'How about singing receptionist?'

'Nothing doing, pal. Haven't had one of those for months.'

'Pool attendant for recently divorced starlet on private estate?'

'Get outa here. Anyway, the pool business is hurting.'

And in Los Angeles that was bad news. In Southern California alone there are more pools than on the entire continent of Europe. But the drought had led to restrictions being placed on pool culture, especially in Santa Barbara, where almost any domestic use of water other than for washing and drinking had been severely curtailed.

The owners of Apollo Pools told me not to believe everything I read in the newspaper. Their order books didn't indicate a serious slowdown in pool construction, and they attributed any decline in business to the recession rather than to drought restrictions. Some county officials had been uneasy about issuing new pool permits, but no objection was raised if the purchasers agreed to haul in the water rather than to fill the pool from the tap, as it were. I asked what it cost to fill a pool.

'Usually about sixty bucks,' said Drake, 'but if you're hauling in water from elsewhere it'll cost you about seven fifty.'

'That's a hell of a lot more.'

'Yeah, but when you're paying thirty-five thousand to build the pool in the first place, an extra seven fifty isn't the end of the world. We're not short of customers. In a tough real-estate market, there are plenty of people out there who want to do everything they can to enhance the value of their property.'

There was a Los Angeles councilman who wanted to see new pool construction banned, but the pool builders had banded together and issued a sensible leaflet on water conservation, which included such salient facts as: a pool uses less water than a lawn of the same size, and pool covers can cut evaporation by 70 per cent, a considerable saving since a pool can lose up to fifty gallons a day in summer.

'It's the maintenance guys who are hurting more. Pool owners aren't repairing their pools as much as before, especially if it means draining and then refilling.'

'What does it cost to have a pool in your garden?'

'Maintenance? About fifty a month for electricity, seventy to have it cleaned, gas for heating the spa comes to about forty-five, repairs average out at a hundred a year, and heating will come to a hundred and fifty.'

'A hundred and fifty?' Drake's partner Al had interrupted. 'You're crazy. It only costs me about fifty a month.'

'Not me. Definitely more than a hundred.'

But the two owners agreed that you needed to budget at least two hundred dollars a month to maintain a pool.

Apollo specialise in custom pools, but there are about seventy-five standardised models that can be installed. There's no great art to installing a pool. You dig a hole in the desired shape, put in the plumbing and pumps and heating and filters, spray the surface with concrete, and turn on the tap. The largest pools they have installed are about fifty feet long, but lap pools, long and thin and shallow, are increasingly popular.

'Diving pools are very costly not because of the construction,' Al informed me, 'but because of the insurance. There have been cases when, after there's been a diving accident, it's the company that built the pool that gets sued.'

'Because we do custom pools,' said Drake, 'we can do special cladding and fancy spas. We get clients who want fountains—'

'That's bad for water conservation,' nodded Al.

'Not if you're recycling the water.'

'Even so, you've got a smaller surface area on a fountain, so the rate of evaporation is higher.'

'We had a client who wanted granite decking.'

'Show him the photograph, Drake.'

It looked superb, I said appreciatively.

'Yeah, well, so it should. At forty thousand dollars, it cost more than the pool. And it's hot on the feet.'

'Are there plenty of cowboys in this business?' I asked Al.

'Some. Probably not as many as there used to be. We're established. We don't just offer installation, we offer service and warranties. But in the old days pool builders operated on small profit margins and invested the sums they were given upfront and that's how they made their money. Unfortunately many of them went bust, but they had a lien on your property and could enforce payment by ensuring that you couldn't sell your property until such debts had been paid. You could have problems not only with the contractors but with the subcontractors they dealt with. These days you're less likely to be taken for a ride by builders. New legislation has doubled the cost of a licence fee to ten thousand, so it's not so easy to start up this kind of business without any capital, relying on your customers to keep you in funds. But you've always got suede-shoes operators. That's why it's best to go with a builder who's been around for many years.'

I had an appointment at another kind of pool: hot alkaline springs at an establishment close to Koreatown on Beverly Boulevard. Given the existence of tar pits in Los Angeles, it's not surprising that there should be mineral springs too. The Beverly Hot Springs, which opened in 1986, is the only urban spa in California, drawing on water that lurks 2200 feet below the ground. It's lavish and luxurious. There's marble everywhere, and in the lobby an artificial waterfall splashes down from the full height of the building. Just beyond the spray stands a grand piano and a double bass, which appear to be the whim of the interior decorator rather than an invitation to chamber music. But then if you're paying $2500 each year in membership fees, you have a right to expect a little class.

Upstairs there's a snack bar where Mike Gonzalez, the manager, took me for a dish of tea. A quarter of the clientele is Korean, and he recommended I sample a strong Korean tea concocted from eleven herbs. Called Sang Hwa Tang, it was black in colour and very concentrated, like a rich broth with pine nuts floating on top. I added dollops of honey to moderate its asperity, but nothing could get rid of the dense bitterness of the brew and its taste of tar, and I had to leave it unfinished. A room downstairs has a herbal counter, where customers, mostly Korean, can buy the ingredients required to make their own versions of these fortifying drinks.

Men and women have separate facilities, and Mike directed me towards the men's changing room and said he would join me later. Naked, I tottered across the wet tiles and slid into the lazily steaming water. In the centre of the pool there was a large fountain that bathers used to slosh water over themselves. Mike had advised me to spend no more than five minutes in the pool at any one time, though I was tempted to linger. The other facilities include a smaller cold spring and hot and dry steam rooms. I was surprised by how many of those using the spa were washing their hair and shaving, as though the springs were an extension of their bathroom.

Half an hour later I was summoned for my massage. I had selected shiatsu, the lighter of the massages on offer, but I still found it fairly brutal. I slipped into baggy trousers before being taken in to meet Chun the masseuse. She instructed me to lie face down on a couch; at one end there was a hole for my face, which allowed me to breathe while Chun did her worst. For forty-five minutes Chun, who was invisible to me as I was either face down or, when face up, swathed in hot head towels, twisted my arms and legs, pulled and stretched, pressed and pummelled. Did it hurt? Yes it did, and a few days later my temples were still tender and bruised to the touch. As I groggily got to my feet Chun handed me an envelope marked with her name. I stared at it uncertainly.

'Tip.'

I returned to the spa, as instructed, removed the baggy trousers and slid into the pool to soothe my battered body. After a few minutes I clambered out and sat in an empty chair, mopping my brow.

'You enjoying it?'

I turned to find Mike, no longer in his well-tailored clothes, indeed no longer in any clothes at all, seated beside me. I must have looked blank.

'Great.'

'A good massage?'

'Very thorough.'

'Just relax.'

I looked around me. When I arrived in the mid-afternoon, the clientele had consisted of a few Caucasians and two very tall athletic blacks. Now there were quite a few Koreans, some of them elderly.

'Who comes here?' I asked Mike.

'We get a lot of celebrities, but I don't want you to think this is a celebrity place. This is a club, and all our members are treated equally. But as you'll have noticed, almost all the staff is Korean, and they don't recognise Hollywood celebrities, which is why such people can come here and feel relaxed, even when they're naked. Here's Sam. I think he's come to fetch you for your body rub.'

Once again I was led away. Since the practitioner was male, there was no need for me to cover up. I lay down on a couch. The masseur sloshed hot spring water over me every few minutes, and while I was glistening with wetness he rubbed me down with a kind of rough cloth glove. Then he soaped me down and scrubbed me some more. All crevices such as inter-toe valleys and shy earholes and other more intimate creases and folds were swamped and scrubbed. This was more fun than the pummelling session, and I emerged twenty minutes later cleaner than I have ever felt before.

I was also clutching another envelope, this one with Sam's name on it. Flopping about with Chun and Sam didn't come cheap. Their combined services cost $80, and the tips would bring that to $100. That's in addition to the basic entrance fee ($25) and the disgusting Korean tea ($5). But as the press handout observed, 'European and Oriental royalty paid premium prices to enjoy the solace and healthy rewards of the baths' – so why shouldn't we?

The spa is just one of numerous successful Korean businesses in Los Angeles. A leader of the Korean Federation, Mr Park, estimated that there were about 500,000 Koreans now living in Los Angeles County, and their numbers were growing daily. Koreans owned and ran about 10,000 businesses in greater Los Angeles. Most of the souvenir shops along Venice beach are Korean-owned, as are many of the nail salons throughout the city. Koreatown is far larger than either Chinatown or Little Tokyo, and Koreans have spread out into all sections of the city, moving eagerly into businesses associated with other ethnic groups, whether Jewish delis or Anglo plumbing companies. Instead of capital, Koreans inject their own incessant labour to stay in business. Mr Park confirmed that the stereotype of Koreans as exceptionally industrious, as the Jews of the Orient, was accurate. Like the Jews, the Koreans place a high value on schooling, and will go to great lengths to ensure that their children receive the best education possible; many of them send their offspring to private schools.

Yet the community is racked with problems. Communication is difficult, since so many of the Koreans here are recent immigrants, and Mr Park believes only about 5 per cent of the community speaks fluent English. After an hour in his company, I wasn't sure whether to include him in that group. The Federation, among other functions, offers legal and other services, often acting as an intermediary between a Korean family and the banks or utilities with which they are attempting to communicate.

The most serious difficulty facing the Koreans is their strained relationship with the black community. Many Koreans have opened, or taken over, groceries in poor black neighbourhoods, and this has led to friction. I would have thought that the host community would have welcomed hard-working people prepared to keep useful shops open at all hours, often in gang-infested neighbourhoods, but instead there seems to be bitterness. Whether this is because of envy or resentment of outsiders, or whether the Koreans are undiplomatic or frosty in their dealings with those they serve it's impossible for me to say. In March 1991 a Korean shopkeeper shot and killed a young black girl whom she believed was stealing some orange juice. There was no evidence to support her claim, and the use of such violence, even if the claim had been justified, was obviously intolerable. Shopkeepers in poor areas of the city are always vulnerable to criminal attack, so it is hardly surprising that the owners are edgy and that dreadful mistakes can occur.

The shooting sparked demonstrations. Small but vociferous crowds of blacks shouted 'We want justice!' and 'This store will never open again!' The Korean community, through its various spokesmen, was profusely apologetic about the incident and reminded blacks that the two communities had a shared history of oppression. In ghastly spokesmen's prose, the Koreans hoped the incident 'would not have a detrimental impact on the positive ongoing relations between the communities'.

This was not good enough for some of the black leaders. One of the more vocal and visible of them, Danny Bakewell, thundered in front of the television cameras: 'We are closing their store because of murder and disrespect on the part of these people toward us and our community.' He declared that African-Americans were tired of Korean shop owners who 'take money out of our community, but who don't live here or hire blacks'. He added that he meant not only Koreans but all merchants who 'show disrespect' for African-Americans. You might imagine that the best way to remove the Oriental hordes who are serving your community would be to set up rival shops that were cheaper and better run, but this has not happened. It seemed unsavoury that a whole immigrant community should be reviled by the likes of Mr Bakewell because of the admittedly unacceptable behaviour of one shopkeeper.

Mr Park saw the problems primarily in terms of criminality. 'If we see someone taking something from a store, we turn them in. Their colour doesn't matter. But if a black is arrested, then we have boycotts and demonstrations, and this leads to racial tension. Koreans also have businesses in Hispanic neighbourhoods, and we have no problems with Latinos. None. Nor are there problems with the Japanese in Los Angeles.'

'But Koreans are not welcome in Japan.'

'Not welcome anywhere.' With a smile.

'Why do Koreans open businesses in neighbourhoods where, rightly or wrongly, they are not welcome?'

'Because of lower rents. We do anything to raise money to start our businesses, but often we must start in these neighbourhoods. But we are risking our lives.'

24

IN THE HOOD

The average paranoid Angeleno is convinced that the city streets are infested with ruthless gangs who prey not only on rival gangs but rob small businesses, torch empty buildings, molest defenceless women, and deal in drugs.

The fact is that the city streets are infested with ruthless gangs who not only prey on rival gangs but rob small businesses, torch empty buildings, molest defenceless women, and deal in drugs. However, this gang activity is usually restricted to specific neighbourhoods, mostly Watts or South Central or East Los Angeles or Compton. Bel Air gets off lightly. But the violence can and does spill over. While I was staying in Los Angeles the killers came to Hollywood. According to the *Los Angeles Times*: '4 teenagers stopped their car in Hollywood to use a pay phone, a random act that cost 3 of them their lives and left another critically wounded. . . . 2 people approached the 4 victims at a service station at Hollywood Boulevard and Bronson and shouted a gang-name challenge. When the teenagers . . . responded with the name of a rival gang, one of the assailants opened fire'.

This shootout was a case of open warfare, and a plague on both their houses, but innocents do get caught in the crossfire. Two days before that particular slaughter, a seventeen-year-old Asian boy had been watching television with his mother in their house in Compton when stray shots unleashed by warring Cambodian and Latino gangs hit the innocent lad, who died in his mother's arms. Others die because they or their parents are too innocent to realise that certain clothes or accessories are identified with certain gangs. Wear the wrong outfit on the wrong street, and you could pay for it with your life. Since gang members in Los Angeles County, whose numbers are estimated at between 50,000 and 90,000, are broadly divided into two mega-gangs, the Bloods and the Crips, it is easy inadvertently to offend one or the other by wearing the wrong bandanna or T-shirt or sports-team jacket.

When I was visiting University High School, I saw the principal move rapidly towards a boy wearing a team hat. He told him to take it off and keep it off. There was no reason to think this particular boy was a gang member but Jack Moscowitz was enforcing the sensible prohibition made by most schools against insignia-bearing apparel. A blanket ban against certain items is the only way to keep up with an iconography of rivalry that makes the complexities of Chasidic garb appear straightforward. There are Crips gangs who wear the caps of the Houston Astros, the LA Dodgers, and the Detroit Tigers. So do the youthful fans of those teams – at their peril. Blue and red are the colours of the mega-gangs, so most schools won't allow their students to wear bandannas or belts or even shoelaces in those shades.

In 1990 there were at least 650 gang-related deaths in the county, so this is not a trivial problem. Nobody has the faintest idea what to do about it. The schools can repress any manifestations of gang activity on their campuses, but there is little they can do to monitor what their students get up to outside school hours. With unemployment sometimes reaching 45 per cent among young blacks in Los Angeles, preaching about the horrors of gang warfare doesn't cut much ice. Among blacks and some immigrant communities, the fragility of family structures – with some Latino parents still in the country of origin, and with many families afflicted by various forms of addiction – offers the best recruiting drive the gangs could hope for. In a world where family ties are feeble or nonexistent, the approximately 250 black and Latino gangs and eighty Asian gangs offer a vision, however bloodied, of solidarity, brotherhood and profitable crime.

The city and county jointly fund the Community Youth Gang Services Project which was founded in 1981 in an attempt to tackle the problem. Project employees give talks in schools, anti-gang rallies are organised, and CYGS cars patrol those districts where gang activity is at its most vigorous. I took a long drive along West Slauson in South Central to the Project headquarters, passing community churches, boarded-up shops, auto clinics, and restaurants such as the Belizean Villa Soul Food that seemed more cheerful than the neighbourhood warranted.

Ed Turley, the director of the CYGS, employs a staff of one hundred in an attempt to keep the gangs in check. A tall, lightly bearded man, self-possessed, quiet but watchful, Turley has no time for most sociological accounts of the problem. His job is to contain it, to patch its outbreaks, to stem its flows and rushes. It's an impossible task, and I couldn't find much evidence that the CYGS has made any significant impact on gang infestation, although Turley claims that there has been a fall in the gang-related murder rate in recent years.

The main business of the gangs is drug distribution in a specific territory. Dealers who are doing well from their trade may decide to expand their operations by encroaching onto territory controlled by another gang, and these clashes can be murderous. I don't know what happens to all those drugs. I wasn't offered a single line of cocaine during my three months in Los Angeles, whereas on previous visits opportunities for a snort certainly presented themselves. A friend recalled how she'd arrived in Los Angeles for the first time fifteen years ago, been invited to a party, tried some of the white stuff, and woke up at lunchtime the next day in a flat ten miles away while a man she'd never met before cooked her lunch. It couldn't happen today. Now all the high-rollers with their fashionable drugs are either dead or burnt out or 'in recovery'.

I asked Turley whether any gangs steered clear of criminal activity.

'No. *All* gangs are involved in criminal activity.'

'Drug dealing?'

Turley looked at me wearily as he slowly recited the litany. 'Drug dealing, arson, extortion, theft, kidnapping, sex crimes, vandalism . . .'

'And does that mean that all gangs are necessarily dangerous?' I was still trying to look on the bright side.

'All gangs are equally dangerous, though some are more active than others. Gangs don't hesitate to use violence when it serves their purpose. There's no such thing as a good gang.'

Boys, and some girls, join gangs for a variety of reasons, including peer pressure and economic self-advancement. In an environment where 'role models' are thin on the ground except in the fantasy world of television or Hollywood movies, gang leaders are perceived as the epitome of style and charisma. Children barely in their teens are sometimes recruited into gangs as Tinies or Peewees, just as if they were in some very junior sports league rather than adrift among thugs. These tots would only be involved in running messages or other simple tasks, but by the time they are thirteen or fourteen they could be engaged in far more serious matters. Gangs vary in size from about twenty to 1000 or more, but in the very large gangs only about one-fifth of the members are hard-core activists; the remainder come to meetings and follow the gang's dress code but otherwise may have little active involvement. At meetings the members will discuss what's happening in their territory, what their rivals are up to, who they're going to hit, where they plan to go for the next outing. Since the rundown areas of Los Angeles have few parks or cinemas or other recreational facilities, gangs often pay visits to other districts that are better stocked. Since everyone either has a car or has access to a car in Los Angeles, mobility is no problem.

'Gangs rarely have a single leader,' Turley explained. 'In a gang of 100 there might be four or five, those who are particularly charismatic or quicker to shoot or to act violently. The influence of the leadership is limited. It can initiate activity, but what it can't always do is control the other members of the gang by stopping them from doing something they feel like doing.' By the time they reach their mid-twenties, most gang leaders begin to fade from view. 'Sometimes they just gain some sense of responsibility, especially if by that time they have families of their own. Then they'll begin pulling away, and they're looked upon as OGs [Original Gangsters] or mentors.'

Turley admitted that they could do little, or nothing, to prevent the formation and survival of gangs. 'All we can do is deal with the crimes related to gang activity. We aren't equipped to attack the sources of the problem. We can't unite families, we can't tackle unemployment. We have a job development programme included in our strategy, but that's the only economic element in our approach. What we do is monitor – especially at funerals, when gangs often choose to retaliate – and mediate. We patrol, especially outside schools where there's a lot of recruitment or rivalry or other gang activity, and sometimes we can intervene directly. We know we don't have much impact on hardcore members, but we try to reach kids *before* the gangs get to them.'

'Sounds like scratching away at a mountain with your nails.'

He nodded.

'Aren't the parents eager for you to help?'

'Sometimes. I've seen them come to us and ask directly for our help. But often we'll approach them and tell them their son has just been recruited into a gang and they'll say, "Oh, but he's not like those others." We can only help them if they accept that their son has a problem. Then we may be able to intervene or, if the kid has a drug problem, we may be able to get him off drugs. We have people on our staff trained to educate the community about gang activity and to tell parents how to recognise whether their kids are in a gang. We also encourage parents, or anyone, to keep us informed about gang activities flaring up in their neighbourhood. But many people are afraid of reprisals if they do that.'

'Can't the churches help?'

'They can be a restraining influence, but there are plenty of gang members who also go to church.'

'How about the schools?'

'Unfortunately the schools, which ought to be taking the lead in helping us, are now part of the problem. The LA school district is a failure. Citywide the drop-out rate is well over 50 per cent. In some schools where the gangs are strong, the drop-out rate can be 80 per cent. Where a school has problems of any kind, the presence of gangs just intensifies them. Everybody knows that poor school attendance is often gang-related. Some schools try hard to combat the presence of gangs, but there are plenty of other administrators who just don't want to know. In low-income neighbourhoods there are kids who by the time they are fifteen years old they are lost.'

The following week I returned to West Slauson, and found myself standing in the parking lot adjoining the CYGS building with John Nettles. John, a taut and wiry young man, was a 'crisis intervention worker' who went out on daily patrols through gang territories in a car marked with the CYGS logo.

'You hear that?'

'What?'

'Two shots.' He shrugged.

'We're getting to the dangerous time of day, just as the schools are getting out. We gotta get going.'

I clambered into the back of the car; John and a colleague

occupied the front seats. There were, I discerned, mixed feelings about having an observer with a notebook seated behind them.

'Trouble is the media hype this all up,' said John. 'They don't report the positive things happening in this community. From the media you'd never know that there were gang members trying to stop the killings and get things under control.'

You'd never have thought that two minutes earlier we were listening to gunfire.

I was accompanying one of about forty citywide patrols. Many of them are led by former gang members or pimps or drug dealers, so they know exactly what they're dealing with. No sentimentality here. All the patrols can do is make their presence felt in the hope that it will prevent violence from breaking out. Sometimes of course they themselves are on the receiving end, and bottles or bricks come flying through the window or attempts are made to pull people out of the car or stomp on it.

'Do you only patrol during the day?'

'Yes. We don't work at night, because we don't have bullet-proof vests and we don't carry guns.'

We pulled into a garage. The driver spoke bluntly to the pump attendant: 'Just want the windows cleaned. Can't see shit.' Then we continued on our way, east towards the Newton district which is enclosed by Hoover and Central and Alameda.

John was impatient with the conventional wisdom about colours, which he and Turley agreed were less popular than they used to be. Some gang members are confusing the issue by eschewing colours so as to make themselves less vulnerable to attack. The signals, John seemed to be saying, were rarely clear. 'You need to listen to what's coming out of their mouths before you make any judgment. The gang members that don't use colours are smarter, they're the ones who want to make business. That guy over there, he could be a gang member if you're judging just by his clothes. But he's not carrying himself like he's from a gang. I guess he's just into athletics.'

Approaching Newton, near the 55th Street housing projects, we were in an area both black and Latino. This complicates the situation, as there is a doubling of gangs. On Gage, east of Harbor, we drove past the worst housing I'd encountered in Los Angeles: small houses separated by grubby alleys and no more alluring than a cramped compound of derelict army huts.

A radio message came through; John was needed back on West

Slauson. On our return he was replaced by Mark, a burly man. Like John, he had a strong presence, physical in his case, whereas John fumed with a fierceness barely held in check. With neither man would I have wanted to tangle. Mark was anxious for me to understand why gangs appeal so strongly to the inhabitants of the ghettoes.

'A man may be able to get a job at McDonald's, but he sees that kind of job as a joke. He wants real money, not kid's wages. So he'll get out and sell dope, which gives him enough money to support his family. These guys feel let down by the system. If they can't support their families they don't feel they're the man of the house no more. Gangs give them a bond, a way for people to cling together. What society calls crime they call survival. Government funds don't supply enough for needy families, so people gotta do other things. It's a force situation, one that society's created. You asking me about the crimes and all that, but we can discuss the disease all day, but we got to deal with this situation every day, so you got to go deeper to see what's really going on, what makes a kid a murderer. When the kids read about gangs, or see stuff on TV, that just glamorises it. A few of the gang bangers have mental problems, but others have a lot of heart – I know 'cos I used to be one of them – but they got to do what it takes to survive.'

It was curious how both John and Mark spoke in an almost proprietorial tone about the gangs. The gangs were loathsome but they were also the product, as they saw it, of a cruel and discriminatory society that denied young men their dignity and made it difficult for them to live honourable lives. They wanted me to report not the crimes so much as the social conditions that allowed the criminals to flourish almost unchecked. Mike Davis, in *City of Quartz*, had delivered a similar message in more sophisticated language: 'The deafening public silence about youth unemployment and the juvenation of poverty has left many thousands of young street people with little alternative but to enlist in the crypto-Keynesian youth employment program operated by the cocaine cartels.'

A black sedan roared past us. 'Man, look at those rims. They gotta be Dayton rims. Guys will kill for those. Know what they cost? About two thousand bucks for four.'

'Where do you get that kind of money for wheel rims?'

'Couldn't tellya. But you gotta figure it could be drugs.'

Mark wanted to talk to some gang members he identified on the street, but my presence was complicating matters. A white man in a black and Latino neighbourhood, I could be taken for a cop. But Mark was looking for people he knew, who trusted him. 'We can talk to some of these guys. They respect us, we're strong men, we've established a rapport with them.'

'What happens when the rapport breaks down and a group turns against you? Do you call in the cops?'

'We like to keep the police at a distance. But we'll call the cops if things get out of hand.'

We stopped near Watts to grab some burritos from a mobile Mexican food van. As we ate, Mark told me about his background. 'I got big ears, I had a stutter, I was born out of wedlock, I used to be a Crip. To me, red meant violence. Guys like me, we were lonely and insecure and to us the gang means we got a structure in our lives. In the gang I got shot three times. These kids today watch TV and see someone get shot and then run off. What they forget is when you get shot, you're on the ground and stayin' there.'

We orbited the Markham school in Watts, but it was quiet. Mark offered me a profile of a typical gang member. 'His dad's a wino, his mother's on drugs, and his thirteen-year-old sister is pregnant. Man, this does bad things to your mind. You need to survive any way you can. With kids like that, it's hard to get near to them, inside school or outside it. They're very resentful of authority as a whole.'

A colleague was standing outside the school entrance. Mark leaned out of the window. The colleague reported that there had been three shootings around here the previous night. Kids had been suspended from school. The gangs involved had been the Bounty Hunters (Bloods) and the PJ Watts (Crips).

Mark footnoted this for me: 'That means it's one housing project fighting another.'

The next school we drove past was Drew Junior High.

'Often junior highs are the worst. You got boys turning into men, unsure of themselves, asserting themselves.'

A block away, leaning against a chain-link fence, were some Latino boys, about fifteen years old, ripe for crime. Mark stopped and talked to them, joshing, laughing. The boys looked plump and soft to me, but Mark assured me that although they belonged to a small gang, they managed to get into a lot of fights.

'They look easygoing to me.'

'Sure. They melt. But I know how to talk to them. I have rapport. But they're stupid kids.'

We continued to circle the school. 'We'll stay here a few more minutes, make sure the kids get home safe, make sure no older guys are harassing the younger ones, nobody gets snatched up.'

All was calm. We left Watts, and headed north up South Figueroa. Whores, thighs packed into tight shorts like sausage casings, stood outside the motels.

'Those are the ugliest whores I ever did see. You can get a hand-job for two-fifty from one of those.'

'You can get AIDS too,' said the driver.

'Shouldn't think so. These women don't get too many dates.'

I had only spent a few hours in the ghetto, yet as I drove back towards West Hollywood through the nondescript areas on either side of the Santa Monica Freeway and the lusher pastures of Wilshire and La Brea, I did experience a distinct culture shock. Savage contrasts are not unusual in large cities, but they were especially marked here. To live in South Central or Watts can lead to a surrender to the passivity and hopelessness that these areas breed, a kind of reciprocal dejection. The browning of the grass, the broken bottle in the gutter, the ruff of rubbish stacked against a chain-link fence, the music blaring aggressively from a speeding car, the palms too spindly to offer shade from a blazing sun, the heavily defended grocery stores and garages, traffic lights changing colours on an empty street – all thicken into a desolation that is oppressive and imprisoning.

Eager for some frivolity that would lighten the mood, I took up an invitation from Scott Arundale. Once a week he puts on a silly polka-dot hat and goes down to a tacky Polynesian-style restaurant on West Pico near the San Diego Freeway and runs a night club, the Da Butt Club, which he recommended to me as 'the ugly face of LA at its finest'. Some years ago Los Angeles must have been full of restaurants in this style but only a few survive in their rich exhilarating awfulness. By the entrance there's a fountain constructed of large clam shells and rocks, with coloured lights gently pulsing around it. There are palm trees or their imitations, branches intertwining to form booths, lanterns with fish netting, coconut shells. Additional decor is imported for the night by Scott and his team: the frogman's outfit next to the fountain, the bespectacled desiccated spiny fish suspended from the ceiling, and the fluorescent mobiles bearing the logo of the club.

'Original tropical cocktails', most of which are flammable, are served by waitresses in long dresses and bikini tops; masks of men's faces are attached to the cups over their breasts. There's dancing to Latin and funk in the Coco Bowl, a room attached to the restaurant, but relative calm pervades the booths for those who want to sit and talk. The neighbourhood is a touch worrying, but inside all is sweetness and noise. Shy girls dance with each other, and young Asian couples hover gingerly on the fringes of the Coco Bowl. The Da Butt Club is whimsical more than camp, and, after the derangement of most of the clubs I frequent, its innocence and ease were soothing indeed.

25

HOUR OF POWER

Sunday morning, and I was squatting penitentially in front of the television. Oral Roberts was, as usual, appealing for funds. 'When God lays a specific amount on your heart . . .' he was rumbling, murdering syntax itself in his eagerness to get at my dollars. This year, he told me, he has had a Victory Prophecy, which mentions ten strong enemies and ten supernatural solutions. Prophecy No. 5 is 'a strong attack against your finances'. Lordy, lordy. Jesus, fortunately, knows all about finances. After all, said Roberts throatily, 'didn't he help Peter in his fishing business?' You bet; interest-free loans, special Blue Ribbon overdraft facilities, a line of credit, credit on the line.

On came a woman to give a 'healing testimony'.

'If all you've got is twenty dollars, and you give twenty dollars, then you're giving 100 per cent. I did it and I planted my seed of faith.'

The camera swung towards another member of the Roberts family, presumably Anal Roberts, who praised the woman for this 'seed-faith miracle'.

The church of my choice on this brilliant Sunday morning was Robert Schuller's Crystal Cathedral. It was a long way off, down in Orange County, but I'd seen Dr Schuller and his church on television, and I wanted to experience his mellifluous sermons in the flesh.

Karen Salkin had been very uneasy when I told her I was thinking about going to Orange County. She wasn't squeamish about frequenting some of the more squalid parts of the city, or even about going to the Valley to shop, but she couldn't imagine why anyone should want to drive into Orange County. When I asked her what it was like, she couldn't really say, but she had noticed that people talk more slowly there. 'Like Florida,' she added, cryptically.

Orange County is famously God-fearing, famously white. So it came as a shock when two nine-year-old Cub Scouts refused to utter the word 'God' when swearing the Scout's oath. They were dismissed from the pack, but that was not the end of the matter. Papa, a lawyer, promptly filed a law suit against the Orange County branch of the Boy Scouts of America alleging that his sons' civil rights had been violated, since the BSA is not a religious organisation. The BSA retorted by saying they were a private organisation, and if you don't like the rules, don't join. Their lawyer, George Davidson, stated that belief in God was mandatory for a Boy Scout, but, anxious not to alienate or alarm Muslim or Jewish scouts, he added that they weren't choosy about which particular God you had in mind. The twins were having none of this prevarication. Young William had declared: 'I don't really believe in him. He sort of sounds like a make-believe character.' And his brother Michael concurred: 'I don't believe in him and I don't think he's true.'

Belief in God is mandatory at Crystal Cathedral too, but the God in question is kindly and emollient, just plain nice, a soothe-your-troubles-away deity, a back-patter, a hand-shaker. His emissary Dr Schuller is smarm personified, and some of his fellow preachers can't stand him. The much missed Jimmy Swaggart once declared: 'Religion without a cross is our curse. . . . The greatest attack against the cross today is not coming from the modernist, it's coming from the Pentacostalist. . . . Any time you hear some preacher get up and talk about Possibility Thinking he's attacking the cross. He may not know he's doing it, but that's what he's doing.' You don't have to be a world expert on evangelism to know whom Swaggart has in mind. As usual, I'm on Swaggart's side.

It took the best part of an hour to get from sinful Hollywood to the pristine Crystal Cathedral, where redcoats with walkie-talkies adroitly choreograph the parking. The Chevvy ahead of me sported a bumper sticker – 'My child is an honor student at Portola Middle School'. What was my reaction supposed to be? To dash over to the driver and pump his hand? There were other bumper stickers to admire: 'Control Immigration Now – America First!' And, above small photographs of Hitler, Castro, Gadaffi, and Stalin, the slogan: 'The Experts Agree Gun Control Works'. I walked towards the cathedral, wondering whether the building was entitled to the term. As far as I knew, it is not the seat of a bishopric.

You can be as rude as you like about Dr Schuller, and I shall be trying hard, but you have to admit that his solar-powered cathedral is a most striking building. Designed by Philip Johnson and John Burgee in 1980, its mirrored walls are of glittering glass. As I approached, the carillon was emitting musical saccharine. Inside, the tinted glass walls are supported with white struts closely meshed and resembling netting. The whole effect is fresh and brilliant and sparkling. I went up to one of the two triangular balconies, which are set back into the wings, since the building is broader than it is deep. Opposite the greenery-filled stage the gallery pews are occupied by the choir and a thunderous organ.

On stage sat Dr Schuller and his deputy Bruce Larson, clad in pale blue gowns with purple hoods and flashes on the sleeves, like dons at a recently established university. To Schuller's right a small formally attired orchestra was tuning up. Everything about the cathedral and its service is geared to televisual considerations. The Crystal Cathedral proudly advertises itself as 'the world's first televised global church'; it made its first transmission in 1968 and has gone from strength to strength. Schuller scrupulously avoids the coarseness, the excessive emotionalism, of his rivals, and opts instead for a creamy, fastidious presentation in which the camera is king. Within the church screens are mounted as at a rock concert so that everyone in the hall can watch the show while it is being transmitted. The auditorium is bisected by a catwalk that has no other function than to allow a camera to advance and retreat.

My fellow worshippers were well dressed, in an Orange County sort of way. You don't find the stylishness, the designer frocks, the tear-your-eyes-out nail jobs of Beverly Hills down here. Instead, everyone looks memorably solid, clean, well-coiffed, chain-store shirts as crisp as lettuce, men's haircuts ruler-straight along the nape, ample ties on ample chests, clothing as suitable for the country-club lunch as for churchgoing.

When Robert Schuller rises to his feet, he doesn't need to speak. He just oozes self-satisfaction. 'Thank you, God,' he murmured humbly to the Almighty. The service, typically, was devoid of liturgical structure, and was designed as a concert, with performances by a guest choir as well as by the regular choir, and a hymn, sung in full operatic style by a tenor. After the musical numbers there was applause, and this is not discouraged, as long as it doesn't interfere with the producer's scheduling. The printed order of service even used the word 'Interview' to denote the exchange of niceties between Schuller and his guest gospel singer, Sandi Patti, who had just won a Grammy award. Included in the order of service was the cathedral Family Update, recording marriages and illnesses and 'transitions', a Schullerism for 'death'.

Sandi Patti is a plump unglamorous woman who shines with a brave confidence that is quite winning. Dressed in a generous white blouse and a blue skirt, she is an easy figure for Orange County housewives to identify with. Schuller, currently preoccupied with the 23rd Psalm, said we were all 'going through the valley', and he asked her briefly about her own tribulations, her own valley. Sandi assured us that in times of turmoil, Jesus is the answer, with his message of love, hope, peace. He can calm any storm, be it Desert Storm – loud applause – or the storm in our hearts. Gradually she segued into her song, which wasn't a religious ballad but a kind of recitative, with long punched-out lines such as 'what's it gonna take to show some mercy and compassion' and 'in Jesus' eyes we're all the same'.

Dr Schuller doesn't give sermons. No doubt his market research team has conclusively established that you win better ratings with Messages than with Sermons. He took centre stage and spread his arms wide. 'What a week!' he breathed. Was it the fine weather, or something more momentous he had in mind? He kept us in brief suspense, then revealed all: 'The troops are coming home. Isn't it wonderful!' Schuller is always quiet-spoken and self-assured. He doesn't need to scream and yell and drop to his knees; he isn't converting anyone, he isn't bullying anyone. Instead he's reassuring us, confirming us in our beliefs, offering palliatives when necessary, quietly networking with the Saviour. The man gives me the creeps, with his thin lips, his firm Iowan jaw, his flat profile, his mirthless chuckle. He lets us know how effortlessly he wafts through the halls of power by casually referring to a meeting he had with George Bush shortly after the land war began in Iraq and to a recent visit by J. Danforth Quayle, an obscure right-wing politician who happens to be vice-president of the United States. If Schuller were to confide that he had just had a heartwarming dialogue with the Holy Ghost in the White House Rose Garden, nobody would bat an eyelid.

The message was simplicity itself. 'Valleys' are business or marital problems or, gasp, terminal illness. But valleys are also tunnels, not dead ends, which means: there's always a way out, even though you may have to walk alone through the valley. 'When Jesus needed them, where were the Apostles? They split.' He sped to the end of the 23rd Psalm. '"Thou art with me" – this is the wrap-up' – an intervention prompted by the sign being held up at the front of the gallery that read '1 min'.

'I shall dwell in the house of the Lord forever,' Schuller continued, unruffled. 'The message is that you're going to live forever – like it or not. Find the faith, if you don't have it, and you'll end your life with a win, not with a whine.' These glib formulations are Schuller specialities – 'Stars not Scars' is another – and you either find them cutely apposite or they make you want to vomit.

Back came Sandi to sing 'The Star Spangled Banner'. The anthem is not usually part of a religious service, but these were not ordinary times. As she began to sing, softly enough, ruminatively, a flag larger than a tennis court was slowly hauled from behind the stage to the full height of the cathedral. Her performance became more and more flamboyant, and by the end I no longer recognised the melody as she belted out her lines and the percussion thumped as though Judgment Day had arrived. Mindless patriotism is, after all, an ancient American custom.

Fifty minutes, on the dot, after the service had begun, Dr Schuller asked us, 'Did you all have a good morning this morning?' To which the answer was a resounding 'Yes!' Then we filed out to make room for the next rendition of the Hour of Power.

Out in the courtyards I found the tables of the Adult Ministry, the Women's Ministry, the Career Builders Workshop, all manned by helpful volunteers. Unfortunately the workshop on Designing a Competitive Resumé had already begun. At that workshop Chuck Austin and Jeff Farmer were the 'greeters', Bob Feland delivered the Opening Prayer, and the Power Thought was given by Jeff.

Embedded in the pavement were star-shaped frames with biblical inscriptions and the names of donors, an overt act of homage to the pavement on Hollywood Boulevard. Schuller's Hour of Power is, after all, showbiz with religious flavourings. Behind a white statue of Job the cathedral Gift Shop stocks glass plaques with uplifting messages, videos of bible stories and the Creation Celebration, and tapes of Schuller's Messages entitled 'Positive Ideas for a Happy Family', 'Believe in the God Who Believes in You', and 'Move Ahead with Possibility Thinking'. There are 'God Loves You' bookmarks, 'Jesus Loves You' lapel pins, greetings cards, posters, books, mugs, cocaine spoons.

For my souvenir I took away with me Dr Schuller's latest literary work, 'A GI Family Prayer':

> Hear, Lord, my prayer for my GI,
> so eager to live – too young to die.
> Beneath an alien blistering sun,
> He faces a dangerous enemy gun.
> The storm clouds gather, the horror of war,
> my soldier stands bravely guarding the door.
> Defending justice, peace, and freedom,
> to his Commander-in-Chief give Holy wisdom.
> From wars' alarms, bring swift release.
> Hasten the day of honourable peace.
> On land and sand and sea and air,
> I back my soldier with this prayer:
> 'No matter how far he's forced to roam,
> just bring, I pray, my GI home.'

I spent much of the remainder of this lazy Sunday with my friends in Tarzana. Young Jack told us another story.

'I was in the park.'

'Yes, Jack.'

'I was in the park and there was this girl.'

'Yes, Jack.'

'Yes.'

'That's it, Jack? Is that the end?'

'Yes.'

My friends asked me when I would be visiting the Tropicana, Los Angeles' prime nightspot for cretins, which they had long commended to me. Why, I said, that very evening! This establishment, along a sleazy stretch of Western Avenue in Hollywood, advertises regularly in the city's news sheets. The ads are fetching, since they feature about fifty smiling topless bimbos who delight the audience with displays of mud-wrestling.

The Tropicana is a long shed, with spectators ranged around a rectangular performance area. There was nothing particularly exotic about the decor that would justify the name. Titillation functions in a shed just as well as in a tropical cabana. I leaned up against a counter, nursing an empty beer bottle. I preferred thirst to American beer. While attractive waitresses in miniskirts and halters patrolled the hall soliciting drinks orders, the stage was dominated by the master of ceremonies, a human boulder with a shaven head and a Harley-Davidson jacket. In strategic positions around the hall a few bouncers of comparable bulk waited to deal with any punters who grew too attached to the girls. Music and lighting pulsed in concert, and strobe effects set the heartbeat racing during the theoretically spicier moments.

The show at the Tropicana is of Wagnerian length. The act I encountered on arrival was the auctioning of the girls' wrestling rights. Each girl was introduced individually – Dirty Diana, Alice in Wonderland – and pranced about rather like a prize colt being whipped around the ring at a horse show, gradually shedding her tacky clothes except for a G-string and bikini top. Prices ranged from $40 to $70 and what the purchasers were buying, I assumed, was the privilege of manhandling the girls later. As the girls stripped off they wiggled their breasts, mostly of generous proportions, and their bums, likewise, in the faces of men seated in the front rows. There were few women in the audience.

Once the auction was over, half a dozen girls, minimally clad, made the rounds, each in the company of a minder. A simple transaction then took place. For $1, you enjoy a quick, very quick, cuddle with the girl, who might kiss your neck and then plunge your head between her breasts for a second before pushing you roughly away and darting on to the next dollar-waving customer. Two gentlemen just along the counter from me managed to get through half a dozen girls each, which suggested the satisfaction derived from each embrace was so fleeting that the experience had to be renewed over and over again. Some Chinese punters enjoyed much longer cuddles, no doubt in exchange for more substantial sums. The minder kept a very close eye on the proceedings to ensure that the girl was not actually touched on any part of her body that retained a vestige of clothing.

Then another auction took place, this time for the right to

smear the girls with oil. The going rate was between $20 and $40. After the girls were oiled, half a dozen men were invited to wrestle with them. They were presumably the same men who had offered good money an hour earlier, but I found it hard to interpret these complex rituals. The men were led off and returned wearing only boxer shorts. They were instructed to lie on their backs in the arena, which resembled an empty rubber swimming pool, while the girls poured oil over them. Now both parties were gleaming with grease, as viscous and slippery as a postcoital slick. They then slithered about and pawed each other – oh, wrong terminology: they wrestled. The high point of the group grope occurred when the MC stopped the proceedings and yelled to one of the male contestants: 'Hey, man, yer balls are showing.' Derisive laughter from the hall. 'That's okay, they're pretty small.' Great hilarity, and the bout resumed.

The wrestlers were shooed off to the showers and changing rooms, while attendants came in and spread what looked like damp cat litter into the rubber pool. Some of the girls now wrestled with each other in what was apparently mud. By the time the action, which was fairly half-hearted, was over, the girls looked like mermaids who'd failed to take evasive action as the Exxon Valdez fouled the Alaskan shores. As the girls retreated, the MC announced that the next contest was mud-wrestling between the girls and some other chaps. By this time, and about two hours had elapsed since I'd first wrapped a hand around that empty beer bottle, I was very bored. I can't imagine it's hugely entertaining to slither around with a half-naked girl intent on keeping your pudgy fingers out of her knickers, but it's even less entertaining to watch other people doing it.

Out on the street, especially a few blocks away on Sunset and Hollywood Boulevards, the nightly weekend circus was beginning, as every oddball in Los Angeles headed for the street corners, the bars, the jazz clubs, the restaurants, the Sunset Strip cinemas. There were drug dealers' patches, prostitutes' beats, bikers' stretches. On weekend nights the boulevards of Hollywood breathe heavily, the police patrols intensify, the sirens wail, the drunks stumble with particular abandon, but at least the people are out on the streets, lurking in corners, hailing old friends, settling old scores. Hollywood at night is the freakish sump of Los Angeles, seedy at best, murderous at worst, beating with the urgent tremulous vigour of a racing pulse.

26

WATTS HAPPENING

Mark and Brian, still flushed after the emotion of their wedding, were musing about the desirability of going to bed with two women at the same time. They conducted a rapid survey among the radio station staff, but the first colleagues they asked denied first-hand experience of such a situation.

'How about you, Rita?' Rita dithered, a fatal lapse when Mark and Brian are asking you a direct and intimate question. They pressed her, needled her, wheedled.

'Come on, Rita, we have to know. Have you ever done it with two guys? Tell us.'

'Hey, you guys. I've got to read the ads.'

'Forget the ads. Rita, we need to know. You *have*?'

With so much excitement on the air, I almost missed my turn-off for Huntington Park, which is not a district you stumble across, since it's marooned between the Harbor and Long Beach Freeways without being close to either.

I turned off the freeway, while Mark and Brian were chanting to Rita: 'What a whore, what a whore', and 'Slut, slut, slut'.

'Oh, you big slut! But we like it. Now when was it, Rita? Last year? This year?'

'Last night?'

'We can see you have that special glow about you this morning . . .'

They then directed their fire at another colleague who had been complaining of tiredness because she had been out on a date till the early hours. The lads wanted to know what she had been doing while out so late.

'We talked a lot.'

'Must be hard to talk with your mouth full.'

'Whoah!'

'What we really need to know is—'

'Did you do it?'

'Hey you guys. . . . No, I didn't.'

'We're only asking because we care about you, we're like your big brothers.'

'Did you do . . . IT!'

'Nothing happened. Much.'

'We care.'

'I think we'd better call the dude.'

'Call him!'

The young woman skilfully avoided the showdown by reminding Mark and Brian that they had been planning to phone the Queen of England that morning to congratulate her on her birthday.

'You're right. We're gonna call her. Wish her a happy birthday.'

And they did, and found themselves speaking to a frosty functionary at the Buckingham Palace switchboard. Their affected British accents were deeply unconvincing, and the palace hung up on them. Twice. Mark and Brian found it regrettable that their loyal greetings had not been passed on to Her Majesty.

'How old's the Queen? She must be at least a hundred.'

'Nah. Sixty-five.'

'Really? She's a tight firm babe!'

'She used to be a real horse-face when she was younger though.'

With this blasphemy ringing in my ears, I arrived in Huntington Park. I didn't know what I was expecting to find, since over on the Westside everybody believes the Latino districts are a constant war zone. Yet nothing could have been more conventional, more placid, than the decorous streets of Huntington Park. When I returned one Sunday there was at least some street life. All the shops and restaurants along Pacific Boulevard were open, with shaky racks of clothing clattering on the pavements, where pretty Hispanic girls could riffle through them as they strolled past.

There was high good humour in the air, especially at the Three Crowns Swedish Smorgasbord, with its sign: 'We speak English, More or Less.' The chain stores were those one would find on any suburban shopping street in California; the only real difference was the preponderance of Spanish names and signs and the density of the shoppers.

I turned west on Florence, and after two miles the streetscape changed. The strollers, the bright-skirted children, the teenagers cruising in twenty-year-old cars bought cheap, all vanished. Only around the churches, and there were many of them, mostly evangelical creations of a single pastor with a loyal neighbourhood flock, were there signs of street life, but even that was muted. I had driven into a mostly black area, and heading south of Central for another mile or two I came to Watts.

Watts is flat and monotonous. In the hot months this urban plain has no choice but to sit and bake. Its age shows. Small wooden and stucco houses crouch on lots, usually divided one from the other by chain-link fences. The streets are broad, so that the occasional row of palms or other trees makes little impact and provides scant shade. When Watts was developed fifty, sixty years ago, it was an important community along the railway tracks. Before the freeways, it was a communications centre for commercial traffic and it flourished. When the railways were replaced by the freeways, Watts was left stranded. It looks forgotten, and would have been forgotten were it not for the associations sparked in the American collective memory when its unremarkable name is uttered. The riots of 1965 were an orgy of self-immolation. When it was over, the frustrations of inner-city neglect may have been released, but the price was the destruction of the few amenities, such as shops, that the district enjoyed, and a long-term reluctance on the part of businesses and merchants to set up new ventures.

The strength of neighbourhood associations in Los Angeles works powerfully against those communities at the bottom of the economic heap. With a low tax base, Watts and other poorer districts cannot generate enough revenue to support the social services they so badly need. Of course the poor sections of Los Angeles are not entirely dependent on their own resources to prop them up. However, as the more affluent and mostly white citizens hole up in incorporated communities, they react to the plummeting of standards in the underfunded public schools by growing ever less willing to contribute taxes towards services they have no wish to make use of. Watts is in a rut and seems likely to stay there. There are about a million blacks in the county, but there are many communities with virtually no black residents at all. Some are thriving: within Inglewood, Crenshaw, and Baldwin Hills dwells a large and prosperous black middle class. But not in Watts.

Today Watts is no longer an exclusively black ghetto. Many poor Latino families have moved in. But if there has been some kind of revival in the fortunes of Watts it is not easily discernible. In its drabness and uniformity, with its boulevards dusty with lack of use, its huddled corner shops, its security fences and minimal parks, Watts slumbers on, moody, drained, lethargic. The industrial architectural vocabulary employed as designer chic by the likes of Frank Gehry is recognised by the ghetto dwellers as cheap and nasty. Those who can afford to have replaced the industrial fences with brick walls and modest iron gates, and maintain their houses in a good state of repair. But most of Watts is shabby. The cars, sometimes parked for safety within fenced front yards, are shabby too, old Chevvys and Mercurys, gigantic old Oldsmobiles and Buicks, cheap to buy but costly to run, and the occasional souped-up Mustang or Toyota, chrome polished, hubs gleaming.

The main reason to visit Watts is to see the Watts Towers, a unique piece of street sculpture located just east of the railway tracks. The three towers are shaped like giant ant-hills, but they are skeletal in construction, a mesh of interconnecting ribs with the outer surfaces embellished. The tallest tower is almost a hundred feet high; the shortest is fifty-five. Sam Rodia, better known as Simon Rodia, built the towers as an act of eccentricity, just as other men build grottoes or Meccano monsters in their suburban gardens. Rodia began work in 1921 and was still at it thirty-three years later. The project was infinitely expandable, and the open inventiveness of the design would have allowed any number of additional towers, any number of new links and bridges between them.

What makes the Watts Towers so dazzling is the way Rodia decorated the mortar framework with eclectic ornament. A scavenger, Rodia embedded in the ribs of his towers 70,000 different fragments of pottery, sea shells, porcelain, flower pots, tiles, old plates, and glass. Around the entrance to the towers from the street, an archway is lined solely with green glass recycled from broken Canada Dry bottles. The framework is equally eclectic, but covered over by mortar, so that it is not apparent that some of the ribs are in fact composed of old bed frames, piping, and other bric-à-brac. What his neighbours discarded in complying with America's love of disposability, Rodia refashioned. Their trash became his art.

Irregular in height, uneven in their degree of laciness, the towers, although *sui generis*, are nonetheless reminiscent of flamboyant medieval pinnacles as reworked by Gaudi. The hard surfaces of porcelain and glass resist the bleaching and fading usually inflicted by the Californian sun, and almost forty years after Rodia downed tools, the towers still look brittle and fresh and prickly, great fingers of the imagination, uncompletable rather than incomplete, pointing up into the dusty blue sky.

It comes as no surprise to learn that Rodia was not popular with the municipal authorities. Watts became part of the city of Los Angeles in the late 1920s. Unwilling to grant Rodia a building permit for so pointless a structure, the city tried to have it demolished. Because Rodia scorned scaffolding, it was inconceivable to the authorities that the structure could be stable and safe. The individual and the corporate battled on for years, until Rodia, tired of having to demonstrate to sceptical engineers that the towers were safe and seeking greater repose in which to enjoy his eighty-second year, put down his welding torches and tools for good and moved away to Northern California. He lived for another ten years, but never again laid eyes on his great labour of love.

The towers still stand, one of the unmissable tourist attractions of Los Angeles. Not that too many tourists come here. Angelenos too, made jittery by the grim reputation of Watts, prefer to acknowledge Rodia's eccentric genius from a great distance. The neighbourhood, it is true, is unpromising, and the towers, located in a cul-de-sac, are surrounded by some of the shabbiest houses in this shabby district. One Sunday morning I watched a black family, dazzling in their white Sunday finery and broad-brimmed hats, pack themselves into a bedraggled old car, its springs groaning under the load as they set off for church. From a neighbouring house the jaunty strumming and clacking of Mexican music poured from the windows. In a derelict house opposite the towers, the front yard was strewn with old bottles and broken furniture. Rodia would have known what to do with them.

Who wears a three-piece suit, gold watchband and chunky gold bracelets, and drives a white Mercedes convertible? The answer is Hal Kimbell, the principal of Markham Junior High in Watts. Precisely why and how this school principal has managed to acquire the trappings of a rich lawyer I never managed to work out. Perhaps, given the parlous economic plight of his charges, Kimbell feels compelled to present himself as a model of what a black man can achieve even in the heart of Watts.

I had come to Markham at Jack Moscowitz's suggestion. District officials had arranged for me to visit Bellagio and Uni, but I mentioned to Moscowitz that I couldn't help feeling that these two schools had been selected so as to give me the best possible impression of educational standards in Los Angeles. In that case, he said, why don't you visit a school in one of the most deprived sections of the city?

The population of Markham, one of the schools I had patrolled with John Nettles, is a microcosm of the changing demography of Watts. Ten years ago 95 per cent of the pupils were black; today only half are black, the remainder being mostly recent Latino arrivals. Kimbell is a booster: he was anxious for me to know that his school was the equal of other city high schools, that its location did not imply that its students, however desperate their backgrounds, were mired in failure. The attendance rate, if the school was to be believed, was about 80 per cent, higher than I had expected. Kimbell praised the quality of the teachers at the school. The hard part is getting them to come to Watts for an interview in the first place. Despite Kimbell's enthusiasm, the school's problems seemed immense. Almost all the pupils arrived here with their reading ability considerably below average, and the problem was compounded by the growing proportion of Latino students.

Kimbell asked various senior teachers to take me round to various classes. As soon as I entered a sixth-grade class, a very pretty girl came darting up to me and shook my hand. Her name, she told me, was Laura; she was my 'hostess' and wanted to welcome me to the class. What on earth was going on? I was being greeted like a visitor to a Bangkok nightclub. The only thing missing from the class was a complimentary glass of champagne. Laura told me the teacher's name and described the assignment the class was working on. *Sotto voce*, I expressed my disbelief to the teacher who was accompanying me, but he assured me that a 'hostess' was a regular feature of this particular class. I was charmed.

These eleven-year-olds had been writing essays on the theme: 'What would you do if you were invisible for one day?' Laura, in her essay, longed to be able to doze off in class, but another Hispanic child, less dreamy and more ambitious, said he would nip off to Las Vegas for the day. A black girl wanted to go to amusement parks and eat, but, she added dutifully, she would also build homes for the homeless and make all the houses in her neighbourhood beautiful and create lovely gardens.

In another class, the children were working on Kipling's fables – how did the rhino gets its horn, and the like – and were being asked to create their own. On the blackboard I found the remnants of a previous assignment: 'What are the stupidest rules your parents have about what you can't do or must do?' Elsewhere, slightly older children were being introduced to Shakespeare. The teacher had begun by asking the pupils to write down answers to two questions: 'What do I know about Shakespeare?' and 'What would I like to know about Shakespeare?' The first seemed a reasonable question, the second plain daft since, epistemologically, if you don't know *anything* about him, it's hard to state what it would be desirable to know about him. One girl in the class had read two plays, but for the rest of the students knowledge was limited to 'He was a great writer' and 'He wrote plays'.

We entered a biology classroom. All was hushed apart from the sound of a Brahms symphony emanating from a transistor placed on the rung of a stepladder. The teacher sat among his students, flipping through some paperwork. This was, he told me, a 'dispatch' session, during which the teacher caught up with marking or reports while the pupils wrote material for the teacher to mark on another occasion. Today they were responding to the following questions written on a blackboard: '(1) List four things that happen to the body when stimulants are used. (2) List four things that happen to the body when depressants are used. (3) What can happen to a person who uses hallucinogens?'

When I was their age I had no idea what a hallucinogen was.

Now, apparently, it's as familiar as milk. The function of schools, in part, has become to warn children about the perils of everyday life. Sex education, no doubt, consisted of lectures on AIDS and the more frequently encountered venereal diseases. Of course, such matters are relevant, desperately so, and teachers explained the high absenteeism and drop-out rates to a lack of 'relevance' in school courses. In this biology class there were sixteen children present, and twelve absent. Glancing through his records, the teacher told me he had never laid eyes on six of the kids supposedly in his class, another had been suspended for two weeks, another was absent with asthma.

The pupils need, I was told, to establish a sense of connectedness with the school. To achieve this, the core curriculum was supplemented with 'special interest' sessions, which could be the study of a language, or jazz, or board games, or racketball. I said that no doubt board games were more fun than learning to read and write. The head of this section of the school nodded.

'There are many teachers here who would agree with you. They're content-driven teachers, and they complain that these special interest sessions leave them with even less time in which to instil more academic learning. We find two basic kinds of teachers. Those with elementary-school teaching experience tend to be student-driven, whereas those with a background in high-school teaching are more often content-driven. Often the former make better and effective teachers.'

Other sessions are devoted to keeping the students on the straight and narrow. Once a week two policemen visit the school and talk to a group of students, and I sat in on one of these sessions. These policemen were black, and they began by giving the students a generalised pep talk: 'No one is going to give you anything for nothing. . . . Stay in school and get an education. . . . The world is open to you, a big house, a pool in the yard, a car, as long as you got an education – 'course, just 'cos you got an education don't mean you gonna be a millionaire.' One of the students asked the cops about the King beating. They nodded heavily: 'The cops messed up bad, real bad.' One of them wrote on the blackboard: 'Crips/Bloods' – here was language these kids could understand – and compared the policemen who had beaten King to gang members, 'only worse'. I admired the moral relativism, but the comparison didn't seem particularly apt. 'We should set an example – they did wrong.'

Representatives of the anti-drug programme DARE also visit the school. These are preventative sessions. When actual transgressions take place, both children and parents are required to attend meetings in the so-called Jeopardy programme. Here they are shown slides, introduced to ex-cons, and given a serious talking-to about crime and its consequences. As for truancy, it no longer exists under that quaint Little Rascals name. Now there are Student Attendance and Adjustment Services, and part of their job is to track down parents who fail to turn up to discuss their children's truancy.

I walked through the yard in the company of an assistant principal. Suddenly a black girl pushed her way between us, aggressively and without apology. He immediately called her back, and she turned furiously.

'Look what he done to my pants! He's gonna get his punk ass kicked!'

Her crotch was wet, and she was pointing to a boy standing a few yards away. She accused him of throwing water at her; he yelled back. The teacher told them both to stop 'acting so juvenile'. He told them to stay put while he took out his walkie-talkie and summoned some other school functionary to take the children off to the dean's office for the dispute to be resolved.

I returned to the principal's office, where Kimbell introduced me to a barrel-chested man in a yellow shirt and bowtie. Fred Williams was the driving force behind Common Ground, a kind of reclamation project for school dropouts. Williams is an ex-Crip, a Muslim, aggressive and pugnacious yet all too evidently big-hearted. He claimed to have an excellent rapport with even the most troubled kids and he described to me what he was up against.

'We have a new breed of kids. Later today I'm going to a shower for 150 pregnant teenagers. Often we're talking about kids who are not only illiterate but whose parents are illiterate. They don't even know what education is, or what a family is. These kids have to absorb all the social problems in the environment, yet they're expected to survive. These are kids without vision. I'm talking about kids of thirteen, who are lost, who are confused. What's different nowadays is not that people are doing drugs, but that there is a whole drug culture. Drugs, the money made from drugs, is feeding a lot of babies right now. Drugs are part of the fabric.'

'For some of the parents,' Kimbell added, 'just getting their kids dressed and off to school is a big achievement.' Extended families are rare in Watts, although more common among Latino families, and they provided a more stable environment for children. Poverty forces most of these children to spend their young lives in a very small area, since they lack the mobility that other Angelenos take for granted. Kimbell uses some of the additional funding that the school receives to take its high proportion of impoverished children on trips and excursions, simply so that they can learn that there is a world outside Watts and the fantasies of the television and video screen.

Gangs were an everyday reality. Markham pupils, he told me, daren't walk to the nearby Jordan High School because to do so would mean crossing hostile territory, which they are understandably afraid to do. Indeed, so many children are afraid just to walk home after school that Markham has instituted a Safe Corridors escort programme. Even though Kimbell insisted that only a minority of the pupils at Markham were involved with gangs, he was aware that the potential for gang conflict is constantly present. 'We can't ignore it. We got to stay on top of it the whole time.'

I asked Kimbell what he thought of the white perception that the Los Angeles school system was in serious decline. In reply, he pointed with pride to the success of Markham teams in statewide quizzes. Just because Watts was a rough area, he declared, didn't justify lowering your expectations of what the children could achieve if properly taught.

'Funding's a problem too. The truth is we're even short of papers and pencils. There are budget cuts, but you got to get round them. Of course we need more resources, and the teachers are very worried about the next set of cuts that is on the way, but we won't let these be obstacles. If I don't make a difference to this school by being here, I shouldn't be here in the first place.'

27

ETERNAL LIFE IN ONE CONVENIENT PACKAGE

I pressed the trigger. There was a bang, the desired consequence, and the recoil, the unexpected consequence, and to increase the shock, the two effects were simultaneous.

Robert was indignant. 'You've used a gun before!'

I shrugged, calmly accepting my proficiency with a Smith & Wesson revolver. I'm a peace-loving kinda guy, but when push comes to shove, I can put a bullet right between the eyes of the bull. As it were.

My instructor at the Beverly Hills Gun Club was Robert de Bartelo, a tall man of many chins and abundant stubble. The moment I introduced myself, he leapt to his feet and made for the door. 'One moment, I got to get some ammo out of my car.' No doubt it was setting a poor example for the club members if the manager left rounds of live ammunition on the back seat.

The club is situated in a brick box in a semi-industrial Westside district. The lobby is decorated with posters of movie stars all depicted holding or pointing guns. Clint Eastwood makes the greatest number of appearances. While waiting for Robert to return I browsed through the little shop in the lobby, which offered for sale T-shirts, baseball caps, badges and targets. Meanwhile, over at the gun rental counter some earnest conversations were taking place: 'This one's got a nice slide . . . I almost started rapid-firing out there – I got carried away. . . . On this Ruger model the decocker was cracked – they recalled the semi-autos. But their revolvers are great. . . . As for barrels, this has a nice four-inch, a comfortable grip, but it's a bit big to carry round. . . .'

The club was founded in 1981, and now has over 600 members, although anyone with previous experience can use the club by registering for a small fee and then paying for range time. The first thing Robert did when we sat down was drum into me the safety regulations. The last thing the club wants is an accident, and until now there have been no serious mishaps, although someone did once shoot himself in the hand.

I wanted to know who used the club. Were most of the members paranoid lawyers and housewives from Bel Air, preparing themselves for the Mansons of the 1990s or for Armageddon?

'We get all kinds. Recreational gun users, sportsmen, professional NRA and speed-shooting competitors, cops and FBI. But the self-protection market is growing. I'd say it accounts for about half our membership. We also provide training for private security guards and training in baton use.'

'Just guns? Or rifles too?'

'No large rifles. They'd pierce the armour-plating. Want a lesson?'

'Love one.'

'Okay. First thing is give me your address, so we know where to send the body.' There was a pause while I admired the joke. He pushed two guns towards me, an old heavy-duty revolver and an automatic with a muzzle compensator and magazine feeder. He listed all the stupid things that could occur if I were careless or failed to follow procedures. We went out onto the range, where it was hard to hear Robert's voice above the random staccato snaps and booms of the other guns.

'Don't put your finger on the trigger until you're aiming or you could find yourself adding to all those holes in the roof. Get yourself in position. Legs slightly apart, lean in, not back, and stretch forward, leaning into the gun. Keep your thumb on the side of the gun, not behind, otherwise the recoil will make a real mess of your hand.'

Bull's eye! And Robert's gratifying disbelief, which dwindled after I'd squeezed the trigger a few more times. I did better, overall, with the automatic, with no shots outside the general target area. Even with the muzzle compensator, the recoil was surprisingly strong, as Robert had warned, but a crack shot gets used to it fast enough. After I'd used up a few rounds of ammunition, Robert gave me a club badge as a souvenir, then let me out onto the streets to begin a new life of violent crime.

Many Angelenos might have packed a gun before setting off for the University of Southern California, where I had a lunch appointment with Leonard Stein. The campus forms an oasis at the north end of South Central. I explored the area quite thoroughly, because of the many fine houses and churches in the nearby West Adams district, and I never felt in the least bit threatened. But USC is notorious for being a rich kid's campus inappropriately located in one of the poorer sections of the city. Local wits have dubbed the campus the University of Spoiled Children or the University of Social Contacts.

Leonard Stein, a delightful and rather impish man, directs the Arnold Schoenberg Institute, which operates out of its own, uncompromisingly modern building on the campus. The heirs to Schoenberg's estate insisted that his archives and the institute housing them should occupy a special building, but it was, according to Stein, largely an accident that the collection ended up at USC. The location is apposite, as other archival collections built up by emigré artists, such as the library of Leon Feuchtwanger, are also stored on the campus. Despite a minute budget, the institute publishes a journal, acquires and catalogues new materials, and stages public events such as concerts of modern music, often in conjunction with the Getty Center.

Schoenberg lived in Brentwood from 1934 until 1951, and his studio has been lovingly reconstructed at the institute, preserving not only his piano and desk and much clutter, but tools and book-binding equipment. The heart of the institute is the manuscript collection. Dr Stein let me open the archival box that contains the manuscript of *Moses and Aaron*, where I found not only the score but a little box the composer had constructed to house blocks depicting the tone rows for the opera. Schoenberg's inventions, such as chess pieces composed of model planes and cannons, filled other boxes. Schoenberg was also the inventor of a game he called 'coalition chess', which involves two minor and two major powers locked in conflict. Along other shelves are stacked the composer's personal library, which includes a dedication copy of Mann's *Doktor Faustus*, and I was gratified to learn that I do have one thing in common with Schoenberg: an inability to get through that novel.

Schoenberg the inventor, the doodler, the fiddler, sounded much more fun than Schoenberg the composer. But this was not the place to voice any doubts about the composer's work, especially since his daughter Nuria was in the reading room assisting with some cataloguing work. It was exciting to shake a hand that had been in contact with the great composer's own as a matter of daily routine. For Nuria, it was of course just another handshake.

Driving back to West Hollywood along Santa Monica, I paused at the Sorcerer's Shop. Behind the counter stood a slight, dark-eyed woman called Babetta Lanzilli, who happened to be my local witch. She rules over this deep gloomy shop, selling an immense selection of books, amulets, candles, herbs and roots, incense and oil. She has helpfully placed handwritten placards among the goods, explaining the properties of each ingredient. I learnt that saltpetre adds energy to incenses, lovage increases personal magnetism, alfalfa brings good luck in the home, cloves bring comfort to the sad, and violets reunite lovers. Among the incenses, Fast Luck is self-explanatory, Temple is used to cleanse the ritual chamber, Uncrossing removes negative influences and blocks, and Dragon's Blood removes negatives and draws love. Other notices explained the vibratory influence of colours. All these blends, Babetta Lanzilli told me, were of her own devising, which meant that the same potions found in other witchcraft shops in the city – for hers is not the only one – would probably be differently composed.

I should have taken a few amulets with me when I went, later in the afternoon, to visit Forest Lawn cemetery. Angelenos were always on familiar terms with death. Southern California was a haven for invalids and the retired, who often died a few years after settling here. The undertakers' trade thrived. Although Forest Lawn dismisses the finality of death, it has ironically become famous for its earnest yet lurid passion for exotic mortuary practices. This had given Evelyn Waugh, Jessica Mitford, and others a field day, as they exposed the risibility of Los Angeles' ultimate beauty parlour. An institution that brushed aside death as little more than a disagreeable distraction has ended up by making a cult of death itself. Forest Lawn would like to promise immortality, but its skilful cosmetic disguises have only reinforced the unwelcome realisation that death brings decay.

Not that Forest Lawn is abashed by the rich fun that Waugh, Umberto Eco, and others have poked at it. It is too serious-minded to take any notice of those who find its stage management of our mortality laughable. Its fantasy has become too entrenched, as is only too obvious as you approach Forest Lawn through the unprepossessing semi-industrial zones of Glendale and sweep through the world's largest wrought-iron gates (Amazing Fact) and see ahead of you the tufted hillsides, studded with metal plaques in place of gravestones and planted with mellow eucalyptus trees. To the right a mock-Tudor manor – one of the better Southern California pastiches – presents a reassuring front for the cemetery's offices and mortuary. Brochures invite you to come here to inspect the range of caskets available and promise that you won't be bullied into ordering some fancy velvet and endangered species hardwood job you can't really afford. All prices are clearly marked.

I entered the offices and asked to see the coffins.

The young woman behind the desk looked alarmed: 'Is this a pre-need arrangement?'

'If it were post-need, I wouldn't be standing here talking to you.'

Still flustered, she informed me that I would have to view the caskets accompanied by a counsellor, and there was none available at that time. I said I would call and make an appointment. I didn't. I wanted a coffin, not counselling.

I drove up towards the Great Mausoleum. Alongside the building a large plaque is inscribed with The Builder's Creed, which is signed 'The Builder', an oddly modest signature given the breathtaking arrogance of Dr Hubert Eaton's credo. It begins with an uncontroversial assertion of belief in an afterlife. Then Dr Eaton inveighs against the barbarism of the traditional cemetery: 'I therefore know the cemeteries of today are wrong because they depict an end, not a beginning. They have consequently become unsightly stoneyards full of inartistic symbols and depressing customs; places that do nothing for humanity save a practical act, and that not well.

'I therefore prayerfully resolve on this New Year's Day, 1917, that I shall endeavor to build Forest Lawn as different, as unlike other cemeteries as sunshine is unlike darkness, as Eternal Life is unlike death. I shall try to build at Forest Lawn a great park, devoid of misshapen monuments and other customary signs of earthly death, but filled with towering trees, sweeping lawns, splashing fountains, singing birds, beautiful statuary, cheerful flowers, noble memorial architecture with interiors full of light and color, and redolent of the world's best history and romances.'

Architecture apart, that is exactly what he did. Purely as a humanitarian gesture, you understand. For, as Dr Eaton continues, 'I believe these things educate and uplift a community.' Now the Builder really gets into his stride, as he envisions the joyful masses pouring into his new model cemetery: 'Forest Lawn shall become a place where lovers new and old shall love to stroll and watch the sunset's glow, planning for the future or reminiscing of the past; a place where artists study and sketch; where schoolteachers bring happy children to see the things they read of in books, where little churches invite, triumphant in the knowledge that from their pulpits only words of love can be spoken; where memorialization of loved ones in sculptured marble and pictorial glass shall be encouraged but controlled by acknowledged artists; a place where the sorrowing will be soothed and strengthened because it will be God's garden.' So successful has Dr Eaton been in his manipulation of our extinction that over 60,000 weddings have taken place here.

Within the mausoleum are rooms lined with marble drawers, a great filing cabinet of stiffs whose souls are now improving their handicap at the country club of the afterlife. One room, the Columbarium of Prayer, is marked: 'Restricted Area – Property Owners Only', reminding visitors that in death as in life we are divided into those that have and those that have not, even if the property in question is a jumble of knuckles and shins. Your remains can be disposed of in many ways. There is a 'variety of property available': ground interment, private gardens, wall or lawn crypts, and mausoleum crypts and niches.

The halls are filled with statuary, including reproductions of some of Michelangelo's better-known works. Explanatory panels alongside each one not only certify the authenticity of the reproduction, but instruct us on the appropriate feelings to experience. Against the 'Pietà' we read that 'a symphony of quiet emotion emerges from the stone . . . Here in flawless marble, Michelangelo has created the Psalm of Eternal Life.' Quite the opposite, if you ask me. The Tenders of the Lawn are particularly proud of a twentieth-century statue entitled 'In Memoria' by Ermenegildo Luppi, a stiff work, proto-fascist in inspiration, of a figure with outstretched arms. The placard solemnly explains: 'This heroic figure represents Loving Dignity, Angel of eternal life, standing calm and serene. Because this figure symbolises the Spirit which hovers over Forest Lawn, it was deemed essential that it be created by the world's greatest living sculptor.' An admirable ambition. To achieve it, did the Builder scour the galleries, interview the dealers, visit the churches? No, he wrote to the minister. 'The problem of finding the right man was submitted to the Minister of Fine Arts of Italy. He settled it instantly.' This, as anyone with the slightest knowledge of Italy can confirm, is inherently improbable. If, by some remote chance, this actually occurred, it surely lets a striking cat out of a Gucci bag. If in any country with a long and noble tradition of profound corruption you ask a stranger where you can find a good carpet or the best pizza, an immediate response invariably means that the paragon of merchants to which you have just been referred is a relative of the person you have asked.

But let the Minister of Fine Arts speak for himself. 'Signor,' he said, 'there is only one living sculptor whose bust is beside that of Michelangelo in Italy's Hall of Fame. That man is Luppi. To mention Luppi's name is to take off your hat.' And take your hat off to the chutzpah of the minister, who surely invented Italy's Hall of Fame as a cunning and familiar analogue to those American examples devoted to baseball and other sports. To stand in front of Luppi's work is to participate in a highly successful practical joke.

Another Italian who profited mightily from the earnest Mowers of the Lawn was Rosa Caselli-Moretti, who was commissioned to reproduce in painted glass the *Last Supper* by Leonardo da Vinci. It is concealed, most of the time, by a curtain, and before it hums apart to reveal her handiwork, a taped narrative explains how Dr Eaton, evidently a man of boundless gullibility, was introduced to the humble Rosa, in whose hands, he was assured, rested uniquely the secret of coloured glass manufacture. When Dr Eaton viewed the deteriorating original of Leonardo's great painting, he longed to preserve the masterpiece for ever. He proposed to Rosa that she undertake the reproduction in imperishable glass. 'The suggestion overwhelmed her with joy,' as no doubt did the fee. She decided to base her reproduction not on the fading mural itself but on Leonardo's sketches, thus enabling her to improve on the original, which Leonardo, preoccupied with his pointless inventions and the Codex for Dr Hammer, never got round to completing.

Six years later her work was completed. Her creation is proficient enough, being neither better nor worse than most other early twentieth-century coloured glass windows. Although the light behind the glass is said to be natural, it can be increased in strength for dramatic effect, or dimmed so that only the figure of Jesus remains illuminated. To the strains of Dvořák's New World Symphony, the voiceover gives us a munch-by-munch account of the Last Supper.

I returned to my car and continued up the winding drive, passing green awnings and chairs appropriate for weddings but here employed for all-weather interments. The hills are furnished with monuments such as the Court of David, featuring a large reproduction of the enviably well endowed champion by Michelangelo. A sign warned: 'Flower theft is a crime punishable by imprisonment.' I soon came to the large buildings where more works of art are stowed: Jan Styka's colossal paintings of the Crucifixion and the Resurrection. The former shows the scene at the more cheerful moment *before* the three condemned men were nailed up. There are admirable views of Jerusalem, and a colourful crowd throngs the expansive canvas. The Resurrection is more exciting. Here Jesus, in standard white robe and beard and with an angel PA in tow, stands in a rocky landscape overlooking an immense walled city. Descending from clouds are thousands of Hollywood extras, of all creeds and colours and historical epochs, joining forces in an orgy of positive race relations. Cavaliers rush forward alongside medieval knights and Roman centurions. Behind them is an anthology of famous churches: St Peter's in Rome, St Paul's in London town, Santa Sofia, and, in a little surreptitious patriotic aggrandisement, the Old North Church in Boston.

Next door the museum is filled not, as I'd hoped, with different kinds of embalming fluid, coffins through the ages, and a selection of shrouds and winding sheets, but with more reproductions, including the Crown Jewels of England and Ghiberti's bronze doors from the Florence Baptistry. With manic literalness, every coin mentioned in the Bible is displayed here. History itself is corralled into Dr Eaton's collection of All-Time Greats, the sponsors of noble thoughts that will lift us high above such considerations as corporeality. The souvenir shop stocks plates reproducing Styka's paintings and dwarfish copies of Michelangelo's *David* with a figleaf covering what an elderly clergyman once described to me as 'his bits and pieces'. In the corner of the museum a very gentle sales pitch is lobbed at visitors in the form of coloured photographs of the grounds – and there are branch cemeteries elsewhere in Los Angeles – and my favourite depicted an eager salesman showing a comely young woman the delightful amenities of a vacant plot.

The advantages of being laid to rot at Forest Lawn are numerous. We learn that 'one phone call takes care of everything – mortuary, cemetery, mausoleum, crematory, flower shop, and church'. That's true. Think how much fuss and paperwork and admin are involved in disposing of a corpse. 'Low prices because of one management, and one low overhead. . . . No funeral procession through crowded, noisy city streets. . . . One easy credit arrangement. . . . Self-selection of caskets made in complete privacy.' Even greater savings can be made, I expect, by burying one loved one and marrying another on the same visit. There's even a choice of churches, including a 'counterpart' of the church at Stoke Poges memorialised by that English poet, and the Gaelic quaintness of the Wee Kirk o' the Heather. To mock all this is irresistible, but it's the Protestant sobriety and humourlessness of it all that are most delectable. What's the point in dying if you can't have a good funeral procession, with monks and music and weepers, large black umbrellas, sobbing relatives and disappointed legatees, swaying carriages and black-draped horses? All this is anathema to Dr Eaton and his co-visionaries, who no doubt did as much to take the fun out of life as out of death.

Erik was back in town, this time with his wife Laura and their son Elliot. This visit was the pretext for another dinner excursion with Dimitri and Rosanna, and we were joined by a beautiful actress. There was the usual lengthy debate about where we should eat. Dimitri had a Persian place in mind, but this was vetoed by Erik and myself on the grounds that liquor was banned from the premises. Erik then proposed El Colmao, a Cuban restaurant where no such restrictions applied. This was a diplomatic choice, since Dimitri and Rosanna loved that restaurant. The Actress demurred, but we overruled her.

Dimitri warned us that El Colmao was in a dangerous neighbourhood. 'Just watch out for the drive-by shootings. No, no, it's perfectly safe. They have an armed guard in the parking lot. You'll see, it's a family place, with lots of children.'

'Half of them bleeding,' muttered Erik.

We set off in two cars. Dimitri, recovering from a bout of asthma, was keen not to catch the cold from which I was lightly suffering, so I travelled with Erik, Laura, and Rosanna.

Laura explained why they kept their distance from Los Angeles, even though Erik was in effect employed there. 'Riding in Dimitri's car is going to have a terrible effect on Elliot. He doesn't see why we don't have a Mercedes like Dimitri's instead of a Nissan. When he comes to LA with us he wonders why our house doesn't have a pool. Our furniture is too new, he says. He wants antiques.

'Some friends here were telling us about PTA meetings at their daughter's school. The competition between the parents is ferocious, apparently, in part because Meryl Streep is one of them. Your status in the school is so dependent on exactly where you live and what cars your parents drive. At least in Berkeley nobody cares.'

'No,' I said, 'they care more about more important matters, such as which olive oil to use for bruschetta.'

We turned down Pico, along a section of boarded-up shops and large empty lots.

'See?' said Erik. 'This is the only acreage in LA where you can't even get rid of an empty lot. Nobody wants to build anything here. Actually it's not that bad. Wait till you see the section where we're going to have dinner. This stretch of Pico is what they *aspire* to.'

We crossed Crenshaw and a sign welcomed us to Country Club Park. None of the three components of the legend was apparent to us.

'Just goes to show,' said Erik, 'how the best intentions of urban planning can go awry.'

El Colmao was an unpretentious café that served good hearty Cuban food, plate-filling portions of pork and chicken, rice and beans. Rosanna and the Actress shamed us by speaking to the waitresses in fluent Spanish. Dimitri complimented the Actress on her recent role in Albert Brooks's *Defending Your Life*, a film that depicts the afterlife in terms that Dr Hubert Eaton might have found congenial. The Actress chose a chicken dish, though Rosanna recommended the breaded pork.

'I never eat *trafe*,' responded the Actress. She had been raised in New York but had spent long periods of her youth in Australia and Puerto Rico. Now it turned out she was Jewish as well.

'Talk of ethnic confusion,' Erik told me later. 'Make any remark about any ethnic group and you can be sure of offending her since she belongs to them all.'

Elliot became very excited when he heard that I was writing a book about Los Angeles. He told me he wanted to be in it. Not wishing to delay his gratification, I told him to write his name in my notebook.

'Capitals or cursive?' he asked.

'Your choice.' He took my pen and laboriously wrote his first name. He then wanted to know whether the book would be on sale by the morning, and I had to initiate him into the indolent ways of the publishing business.

We scoffed our food but wanted more. Dimitri proposed the Al Gelato ice cream parlour on Robertson just south of Wilshire. The armed guard in the car park had done his job; no windows had been broken, no radios stolen. We drove west and headed up Robertson.

At Al Gelato, the waitress tried to tempt us with various confections as well as ice cream. Dimitri was tempted but uncertain.

'It's real light,' she coaxed.

'Yes, but I'm not.'

The Actress was seated next to me.

'Are you still contagious?' she wanted to know.

'I doubt it.' This cold was on the wane.

'I really don't want to catch your cold,' she said, ostentatiously moving her chair away from me, asking Rosanna, who was seated on the other side of her, to move up so that she could put even greater distance between us. It is distinctly embarrassing when someone starts to make a visible and voluble slide away from you in a public place.

'I haven't got the plague,' I muttered.

'I know. But I have a heavy week coming up.'

'So do I,' I replied, not seeing why the activities of the Actress were automatically considered more valuable than my own. Dimitri, who was equally anxious not to catch my cold but had conveyed this to me with greater finesse, apparently upbraided her later for making a three-act drama out of my predicament. In mitigation, she had an important audition lined up for a few days later and wanted to be in top physical condition.

Dimitri and Erik were now engaging in mutual admiration on account of their thick piles of greying hair. As their contemporary, I pointed out that my hair was still pure and relatively unbesmirched by greys. Dimitri was dismissive: 'You just have prematurely black hair.'

There was competitive cat talk. I spoke of my cat Phylloxera's astonishing gifts, but Dimitri trumped me with tales of his ex-cat Puccini. In whimsical mood, Dimitri had taken to dressing up in African garb, complete with spear, and hunting the cat through the apartment. If he managed to catch Puccini, he would tie the cat's legs to a pole and carry it back to the bedroom in triumph. If I understood Dimitri correctly, this odd behaviour was part of a long-term plan to irritate his first wife. There was more to come. Puccini had a habit of racing around the flat late at night, trampling on the sleeping faces of Dimitri and his then wife and waking them up. So one night Dimitri successfully set a trap. The pinioned cat, already half berserk in the course of its nocturnal tantrum, shrieked with alarm and managed to free itself. In a wild dash for liberty, Puccini ran for the window and stunned himself. Dimitri, overcome with remorse, wrapped a bandage around Puccini's head, pinned sticks like crutches beneath his arms, and watched over him all night long. In the morning his wife appeared and found Dimitri still nursing the unconscious cat. 'I want a divorce,' she had said. 'You got it,' he'd replied.

28

WHIPLASH AND DING DONG

At Al Gelato, two tables had been occupied by some strangely dressed individuals, bearded men in white and pallid women of haughty demeanour, also in white and, like the men, turbaned. They were Sikhs, Dimitri had told me, who came from places like Ohio and all drove Mercedes. True enough, as we emerged from the ice-cream parlour, I saw parked outside an antique Mercedes with the licence plate YOGIJI.

This called for further investigation, and the next day I found the Sikh temple a few blocks south of the ice-cream parlour where the devotees of the cult had been indulging themselves. It stands close to the Coptic church, one of a small enclave of religious specialities just south of Pico. You enter the temple through curvacious doors of fine wood and brass, no expense spared. The marble floor was loosely carpeted and a Sikh in dark glasses lay on his back reading the newspapers. Others were standing about nearby. They were all white, which I found disconcerting, and the turbans worn by the women, which Dimitri had correctly likened to lobotomy bandages, were equally peculiar.

The sect, they told me, took root in the United States after Yogi Bhajan came from India in 1969 to give courses in yoga in Canada and in Los Angeles; his religious beliefs attracted thousands of converts in North America. Their religion is self-initiated and monotheistic; the emphasis is not on dogma but on personal experience and self-transformation. Drug-taking and extramarital sex are frowned upon, and there was disdain for the orgiastic hedonism of some other Indian-inspired sects. Womenfolk were tenderly regarded by the cult; they enjoy equal ritual status and are seen in some respects as more powerful and 'advanced' than the males. Their robes and wrap-around turbans secured with brooches were indeed a Western adaptation. 'We're worldly people but the robes offer the women a nunlike protection. We think of women as separate but equal.'

Worldly they undoubtedly were. For $35, the temple ran a Prosperity Course on 'the Siri Singh Sahib's teachings on how to become a prosperous person. . . . Prosperity is the right amount of money and resources to do what is truly meaningful in your life. Money invades our psyches and our emotions. It has more to do with our intimacy issues than sex or love. . . . Join Dr Khalsa in a contemporary and insightful workshop as he challenges you to take responsibility for your own prosperity by letting go of old beliefs and creating new ones about scarcity, abundance and self-worth.' It didn't sound far removed from Oral Roberts' Great Prophecy about your Finances.

I read a poster tacked up next to the temple entrance: 'Beloved Sikhs of the Guru: The Light of Light and Truth of Truths, our most exalted Sahib, Siri Guru Granth Sahib Ji Maharaj shall be escorted by sangat and police motorcade to the Baisakhi Darbar. . . .'

I had no idea what this was all about, but it was clearly an occasion not be missed, and a few days later I attended a kind of gathering of the clans on the top floor of the Scottish Rite Masonic Temple on Wilshire. The car park was full, except for spaces reserved for the master masons: they were marked Venerable Master, Wisemaster, Commander, and Master of Kadosh. I thought they should have provided an extra space for the Light of Light and Truth of Truths. Inside the hall a few hundred Sikhs were milling about, including some Indian ones. While the white offshoots were dressed in their pristine stockings and frock-coats, the genuine article from Indian stock came mostly in Western clothes, while their womenfolk wore saris. The white women looked exceedingly nunlike, since they wore no makeup and were pale of complexion.

At the far end of the main hall a broad painted backdrop depicted the Golden Temple at Amritsar. A golden canopy swayed in front of it, and beneath its draperies sat the guru, patiently swishing a fly whisk. Musicians, mostly on guitar and drums, sat alongside the canopy and sang lustily in English. At the entrance to this hall a young Indian was seated with a towel in his lap. After removing their shoes, the Sikhs would dip their feet into a shallow pool of water and this young man was charged with drying them. A boy stood nearby with a sign – 'Change for the Guru' – and some dollar bills were stuffed into his tunic. What surprised me about the gathering was its middle-class, middle-aged respectability. This was no dreamy-eyed bunch of addle-pated hippies, squandering their youth and their bodies on a sentimental pursuit of a purposefully ineffable wisdom. These people were making money.

Another room had been adapted as a bazaar, with stalls selling books and tapes, ritual daggers and turban fabric, exotic teas and wholesome oils. On a stall I found printed out the words of a particularly catchy chorus:

The year was 1969, across the sea he came
To find the ones of the Guru's court who slept in Maya's dream.
We were wakened from our dark night and led to the Guru's feet
By his humble servant Siri Singh Sahib Harbhajan Singh.

I whistled it all the way home.

There was a more congenial temple up in North Hollywood, in the directionless heart of the San Fernando Valley. This was the Wat Thai, a good facsimile of an Asian Thai temple which outclassed the Filipino-American Southern Baptist Church opposite. The Wat Thai compound embraces within its walls cells for the on-site monks, guest houses, a rose garden, and the temple itself beneath a flamboyant roof supported on gilded brackets. By the entrance sweet sickly aromatic wisps curl up from a pot filled with incense sticks. Within, a seated Buddha smiles on his dais, surrounded by incense, candles, and offerings of flowers and eggs.

My main motive for coming here was gastronomic, not religious. The Wat Thai also serves as a community centre, offering dance and language classes and courses on Buddhism. At weekends a food fair brings large crowds to the basement kitchens in the late morning. A few dollars buy you tokens to be exchanged for the foods of your choice. I decided to sample the stalls where the queues were longest, trusting the palate of the Thais more than my own. I began with a spicy soup with dismembered duck, wire-thin noodles, sprouts and herbs. There was a choice of noodles – I pointed at the thinnest – which were thrown into a boiling pot, whisked out and flung into a bowl; the meat and spices were added, and a pungent broth poured over the top. For my next course I had a kind of satay: marinated pork and chicken that had been skewered and grilled. I saw, but did not taste, other dishes such as poultry and curries and Thai pancakes prepared in a poached-egg pan with rice flour and coconut milk.

I carried my bowls and dishes to the picnic tables laid out behind the temple. Monks in orange robes emerged from their quarters to enter the temple or talk to visitors. There was only one other non-Thai there, and he sat there studying a mystical text. The elders jabbered in Thai, their children mostly in English, often with an exaggerated American drawl. A five-year-old was scurrying around on a new BMX mountain bike, yelling 'Jesus!' every time he slipped on the sandy ground. I finished the best Thai meal I was to encounter in Los Angeles and went on my way.

I came down the Hollywood Freeway, crossing the mountains, and left the freeway shortly before downtown, heading for Silver Lake. At the lights I idled behind a car with the plates QTPYKID. The lake is a reservoir and provides a focus for the socially varied district. On the heights, which are steep and crossed by winding roads, the small villas and modernist houses are comparable to those dotted over the Hollywood hills. Some of the houses are by Neutra and Schindler and proved worth seeking out. Tucked away in a cul-de-sac, Loma Vista Place, I found a touching tribute to Gaudi, a regular boxy house on which has been layered an irregular undulating façade, in front of which stood a wall with fragmented tiles of various colours and shapes embedded within it. (There's a swirling Gaudiesque design on a much grander scale on North Rodeo Drive in Beverly Hills, but I prefer the more obvious homage of this Silver Lake cottage.)

The flat sections of Silver Lake are very different, ethnically mixed and distinctly funky. Artists and musicians and students who ten years ago might have chosen to live in, say, Venice, but can no longer afford to do so, have chosen to live instead in Silver Lake, with its low rents, proximity to both downtown and Hollywood, and social unpredictability. A parked van was plastered with stickers that showed an admirable catholicity of opinion: 'I Brake For Auditions', 'Honk If You Are Elvis', 'No Grapes', and 'Gay Nazis For Christ'.

On Micheltorena Street, quite close to the freeway, I came across a charming little Russian Orthodox Cathedral, presided over by Bishop Tikhon. The church comes complete with gilt onion domes and wooden shutters, and I sat for a while in its shady gravelly forecourt. Tucked along Silver Lake Boulevard and Argent Place is the best concentration of houses by Richard Neutra in all Los Angeles. They share certain features, such as glass walls with thin roofs and decks of metal and wood, and strongly horizontal lines, but each house is shaped to suit its site.

Sunset Boulevard, at its eastern end, winds through Silver Lake. Just off the boulevard, on Hyperion, is Amok, a bookshop that specialises in outlandish publications, such as erotic comics, books on witchcraft, far leftwing politics, drugs, anarchism, and serial killings. Here you can buy the *Colour Atlas of Oral Cancers*, the *Lesbian S/M Safety Manual*, and hard-to-find periodicals such as *Fourth Dispatch* and *PHQ*, the Piercing Fans International Quarterly, full of advice on how to pierce your nipples and genitalia for ornamental purposes.

I would have thought the market for such publications was rather limited, but I clearly underestimated Silver Lake, which must be one of the self-mutilation capitals of the world. On an especially dingy stretch of Sunset Boulevard, once a week, a small disco is transformed into Club Fuck. Skip Arnold had recommended it as one of the city's livelier night spots, so very late one night I decided to pay a call. I always have the same problem when I'm off to a sado-masochistic club for the night: what to wear. I made do with a simple T-shirt and jeans. Dimitri had spoken mockingly of Beverly Hills' weight code, but I was more afraid of Silver Lake's youth code. I foresaw humiliation at the door as some body-building fanatic gave me the once-over and ruled me out.

Far from it. I was welcomed, paid my money, and had my hand stamped with the name of the club, which provoked a few questions over the following days, since the ink proved almost indelible. The disco was small, with a narrow stage and dance area, and then, in about the same amount of space, a bar and pool table. Behind the bar two video screens were showing ancient black-and-white bondage movies. The noise was deafening. I suppose it was music, but at a volume appropriately close to the pain threshold it was impossible to make out melody or harmony, and all my battered ears could pick up were the sounds of battle, with thumping percussion, shrieks, whistles, and hammerings.

My anxieties over my clothing were unwarranted, although most revellers had made a greater effort. Black leather was dominant, as it should be. Hair was considered superfluous. As well as shaven heads, there were very severe crewcuts which showed off nose- and ear-rings to greater advantage. Men and women dressed alike, and it was often hard, just glancing at a leather-clad ugly with no hair and a batch of tattoos slithering down its arms, to distinguish guys from gals. One girl wore a tight skirt with the word 'Fuck' neatly printed as a pattern. Peaked caps and studded wristbands like Rottweiler collars were standard accessories. Up on the stage a couple of go-go girls in skimpy black leather were singing and twirling animatedly, but the music drowned out the jangle of their navel rings. Between the two girls another lass was dancing happily inside a cage. Lipstick and mascara stayed unsmudged through all these exertions.

As the night wore on, the club became hotter and sweatier. This presumably was part of the pleasure, that thickness in the air, the sexual moisture, the sheen of sweat. Some of the men had removed their shirts, and another had removed his trousers, if he had been wearing any in the first place, to reveal a capacious cock-pouch, which I imagine was stuffed with Kleenex. There were happy hetero couples boogying on the dance floor, two men cuddling in a corner, and a large clutch of leather dykes. There was little going on that wouldn't have been acceptable at Crystal Cathedral until one skinny young man dressed only in jeans allowed himself to be handcuffed to the cage. He too had a navel ring, and his head was closely cropped, but his most striking feature was an immense symmetrical plant tattoo climbing grandly up his back. For the whipping he was about to receive he seemed truly thankful. The young man servicing him seemed to be generating more sweat than the recipient of the lash. Their little session continued for at least twenty minutes. In between whippings, the lasher would cuddle his friend from behind while coiling the thongs around his neck just to remind him who was in charge.

When I left, the men on the door wished me good night, and

hoped I'd had a good time, taken off my clothes and danced. I assured them I had. I drove home with a buzzing in my ears, a sure sign of serious damage to one of my senses, that lasted until I eventually fell asleep. Club Fuck, whipping apart, had been wholesome enough. If pretty young women wanted to imprint tattoos on their buttocks and thread metal through their nipples, well, that was fine with me, even if it did leave me erotically nonplussed. If this was the far edge of raunchiness on the Los Angeles club scene, then the morals police had little to worry about. The following week the club was assessed in a lengthy article in *LA Weekly*. Characterising the club, Craig Lee wrote: 'It's a club celebrating post-AIDS sexuality as body manipulation, set against a nonstop electro-techno/trance drone, a mutant version of post-punk S&M.' Now you know.

I didn't tell Karen where I'd spent that Saturday night. After all, we had a date to go shopping, and I didn't want to shock her with an account of primeval Silver Lake after dark. She was taking me to the Price Club, a wholesale supermarket named not in honour of its commendably low prices but after its founder, Mr Robert Price. Until recently only people shopping on behalf of organisations such as shops and restaurants could use the Price Club, but eligibility had been extended to include members of corporate bodies such as trade unions. These rules were apparently set up as a way to minimise credit problems.

To build up our energy levels before shopping, we stopped for lunch at Rally's drive-in in Inglewood. Karen had been singing its praises for weeks. I proposed that we lunch *al fresco* beneath one of the thoughtfully provided parasols. Karen looked doubtful because this part of Inglewood was a fairly rough area, but she gave in when I told her we would be able to keep a constant eye on the car. We went up to the counter.

'See? Short simple menu.' Karen was pointing at the few lines scrawled on the window. 'The fries are fabulous.'

We carried our food to our table, and I unwrapped the little bags. I had chosen a cheeseburger, which was passable, and a bag of fries that were speckled with – something.

'So what do you think of the fries?'

'A bit soggy.'

'Soggy! These are the crispiest fries in California!'

'Oh dear. They're tasty, I admit, despite their worrying pale orange colour. But what are these specks on them? Minced flies?'

'Seasoning. You obviously know nothing about what makes good fries.'

Karen looked away, disgusted. Other connoisseurs were beginning to throw glances at us, as though slightly embarrassed at being present during a lovers' tiff. I had to mend some fences. There is no more terrible falling out than a rift between two gourmets.

'They're getting crispier. Perhaps that first one was a freak fry. But what's this stuff inside them?'

'Potato.' She glowered.

The lunch – a CD of meat and a bag of matchsticks – didn't take long to complete, and we were soon on our way to the Club. It was, as I expected, a hangar surrounded by a parking lot. The prices were irresistibly low, but the minimum quantities were not. You had to commit yourself to twenty batteries rather than three, two pounds of Parmesan rather than a quarter, and so on. There was food and drink, but also pallets piled high with vacuum cleaners, tyres, electrical goods, garden furniture, compost. Computer disks were one third of the price I have to pay in London.

'Take them now,' urged Karen. 'You can always change your mind at the check-out counter.'

'No, I'll come back for them if I decide I want them.'

'You have amazing resistance. I have none. Squeegees!'

She bought a pack of torches. So did I, after I'd calculated that the batteries (included) would alone cost more than the entire contents, if purchased in my native land. Karen pounced on a six-pack of cotton briefs (male). So did I, which means that Mr X and I have at least one thing in common over the next year.

'Tampax. Close your eyes.'

I dithered over the two-pound bag of walnuts, but succumbed to the wild rice. Karen became excited over the baked goods.

'Bagel dogs! They're fabulous. And so are the Ding Dongs.'

Readers who are not famous restaurant reviewers may like to know that a Ding Dong is a 'chocolate' 'cake' with a 'creamy' filling. Karen was close to swooning. 'Hostess Ding Dongs. This is what I ate as a kid every day for breakfast.'

Our exhilaration faded at the check-out counter. I had come

along for the ride, and spent $80, but everything I bought was a bargain. All I had to do was lug it back to England.

At the check-out counter we stood behind two very scruffy Italian women, with bratty children. I spotted them again a few minutes later, when they overtook us in their Rolls-Royce. This must the first instance in recorded Californian history when two women were seen in a Rolls-Royce in baggy dungarees, scuffed nails, and unwashed hair. Karen was shocked.

I dropped her off at her house in Beverly Hills. Mr X hates visitors, but he allowed me to enter the hallway so we could sort out which goods belonged to whom. Mr X and I admired our new knickers.

'Karen, I have to run.'

'I know. Where are you off to this afternoon?'

'Gang patrol.'

'Oh my God. You've already done that. You're going back?'

'Have to. The first time was just to get acclimatised.'

'You're crazy. Call me. If you live.'

When I reached the Gang Services building on West Slauson, Ed Turley was mulling over which patrol I should go out with today. Once again I joined John Nettles, but his co-driver was someone I hadn't met before called David. David was no fun. He was sullenly aggressive towards me, and I could see that carrying passengers, especially white ones, wasn't going to make their task any easier. We hadn't even crossed beneath the Harbor Freeway before David was turning to me, unsmiling, and asking whether I wanted to put any questions to them. I had plenty of questions, but I preferred to pace them, to find a context. David was giving me limited permission to interview him. To be fair, on parting David told me that he had a cold, not that I'd noticed, and I suspect this was his way of apologising for his surliness towards me.

He gave me the usual defensive line on the media: 'You don't see anything on TV about good relations between blacks and Hispanics in this area. Only the killings and the bad news gets on TV.'

'So what's the good news?'

He told me about those who were trying to bring the warring factions together. Some of these intermediaries were ex-cons or former gang members who had acquired a more 'spiritual' view, men who had come to realise how destructive and purposeless all this gang activity was. David distinguished between mere gang members and gang-bangers, whom he seemed to regard as beyond the possibility of redemption. The new spirituality to which he referred was not, he told me, primarily religious, but more a sense of brotherhood, of revulsion at the increasing violence. John interrupted to tell me about the pastor of the church he attends, who organises marches to sing hymns outside the headquarters of notorious drug dealers.

In the Newton district, we stopped outside a ramshackle little house with iron grilles against the door and windows. John rapped on the door and asked for Juan. Juan was sixteen but looked younger. There was something unfinished about him. It wasn't just his weedy figure, his shrinking diffidence. It was as though he were an incomplete sentence, lacking a verb or a crucial noun. He didn't add up. I wouldn't have thought this shy awkward passive youth was obvious gang material, but he had been a member for three years. Perhaps Juan was feeling depressed. He had participated in a robbery of a store, but the owner had managed to raise the alarm, and the other gang members made a run for it. Juan was too dopey or confused to follow. He had been caught, tried, found guilty, and would be sentenced the following week. He had been given broad hints that he would not be jailed for this first offence, so Juan didn't have too much to fear from his next encounter with the judge.

We had stopped to see this very unthreatening young gang member not only so that I could meet him, but so that John could give him a pep talk. He began by reminding Juan that he had warned him that this would happen if he failed to extricate himself from the gang.

'Everything I told you was gonna happen has happened. Isn't that right?'

Juan, with a sag of the head, conceded that this was so.

'I'll come to the court and vouch for you at the hearing, as long as you tell me you're going to stay out of the Home Boys from now on.'

'You got to stand on your own,' added David, though poor Juan seemed barely capable of standing at all. 'You don't need twenty-five guys around you.'

John, looking on the bright side, suggested other ways, apart from robbery, in which he could bring in an income. He particularly recommended dog-breeding, which keeps you occupied and is a nice little earner. 'Rottweilers is good.'

As we were driving off, another gang patrol car pulled alongside and reported that there had been a drive-by shooting in the neighbourhood yesterday. This was noted. We drove past a Muslim school on Martin Luther King and Central. From the distance the black girls at play in their white headscarves looked like jumping tadpoles. David confirmed that Muslims stayed out of gangs.

'They ain't got time for this shit.'

We parked outside Jefferson High School. John greeted someone leaving the school yard, but the only response was a glare. A Latino man in white clothes, tossing a large bunch of keys in the palm of his hand, stood quietly on the corner watching the school entrance. John was clearly keeping an eye on him, and later told me he thought the man was armed, though he subsequently concluded that the man was probably waiting for his children to ensure their safe return home.

As we drove westward, away from the school, John started looking out for graffiti that, like a gangland newspaper, gave the latest news, including death threats against rivals. But just as he found what he was looking for, the radio reported a 'heavy situation' and 'a possible incident' back at Jefferson. John spun the wheel and we raced back towards the school, going carefully but speedily through red lights. He sliced along the streets behind the school, then turned into the playing-field area, bouncing along the grass to where about a hundred youths had formed a semicircle around two police cruisers.

Whatever was going on, we were not the first on the scene. One black had been arrested and sat handcuffed in the back of a cruiser; another boy, a Latino, was being arrested and not enjoying the experience. Neither was the white cop, who had his arm round the boy's throat and was dragging him towards the cruiser, while the other officer kept a firm eye on the crowd, which was expressing its displeasure. While this was going on, two more police cruisers arrived, along with another CYGS patrol and a car containing plain-clothes police.

'Back off!' the officer making the arrest yelled at the milling crowd. Superior force had brought the boy to his knees, and his head was pressing against the policeman's belly.

'What you fucking got? Eh? What you fucking got there?' screamed the cop, fright forcing his voice higher in pitch. A second policeman extracted a large screwdriver from the boy's pocket.

'Who's next? Who's next?' The policeman, who had by now managed to handcuff the Latino boy, turned belligerently to the jeering crowd and dared anyone to take him on. John later told me he thought this was a miscalculation – 'too cocky, too aggressive' – and I could see what he meant, but I also thought John was underestimating the cop's own terror. The policeman was afraid not only because the crowd might turn on him – though, given the number of policemen thronging the playing field by this time, this seemed unlikely – but, I suspect, because he had to be careful not to do anything that could possibly be construed as excessive force, especially with a hundred or more witnesses standing around.

The other CYGS patrol team told us that the black and Latino kids had gathered on the field simply to discuss the tension that had arisen between the two communities. This gathering had been spotted by the police who promptly misinterpreted it, believing that a violent confrontation was about to take place. There had been no fighting between factions, and nothing happening that justified an aggressive intervention.

'But,' said one of the patrol members, 'something *was* going to happen.'

As we drove off, David muttered, 'This is going to go on till somebody comes in to try and solve it.'

But who? David worried aloud that if relations between the races and with the police continued to deteriorate there could be another riot like the one that took place in 1965. 'There'll be another Watts.'

'Worse,' said John.

I asked John about their relations with the police. Patrol teams and officers had spoken cordially back on the playing field, but had not given the appearance of working together.

'We got to stay neutral, we can't let our feelings show. The police has got the authority, and if they're using it, there's nothing we can do. But the relationship between the police and the kids is definitely fucked.'

No sooner had our adrenalin levels returned to normal, than word came through of a possible shooting a few blocks away. Another high-speed journey through the ghetto, and we came to a halt on a corner where a few people were standing outside a shop. They reported that a Latino driver had collided with a car driven by a black – or vice versa – and a chase had developed. Some had heard shots; others were less sure. It all sounded very vague, and didn't seem to be a matter the patrol could deal with. We drove off.

'Strange how this race shit is beginning to hit our area,' said John.

A few minutes later we found a police cruiser parked by the kerb. The officers were making an arrest, and two kids had their hands behind their heads and were leaning against the car. They must have been clean, as the patrol easily persuaded the police to turn the kids over to another CYGS patrol that had just pulled up.

'I said we're gonna take these kids back,' said Sanchez, the leader of the other patrol. 'We know these kids.'

'That's cool,' said David. And we drove on.

John screeched to a halt alongside three twelve-year-old Hispanic girls in shorts. John rolled down the window and handed one of them his card, which seemed rather formal for the occasion. He was urging her and her friends to get in touch with him about a girls' baseball game he was organising. They didn't seem to find the suggestion enthralling, but said they might get in touch anyway. As we continued on our way, I asked John what that had been about.

'It's just to show them I love 'em, care about 'em. Those girls look cute, but they're so rough they'll jump on a guy so hard he don't know what's happening to him. And when that little girl and her big sister get into a fight, you gotta call the police to break it up.'

We drove back to the office along boulevards now becoming familiar to me. Before I contacted Ed Turley the map of South Central had been blank to me, as to countless Angelenos, a vast, uncharted sea of trouble, best avoided, best ignored. Now its networks, its personality, its shadings had begun to reveal themselves to me. Of course I had only skated across the surface of the many communities that live, often in fear and stress, in South Central, but my guides had done their best to present their turf as, above all else, a human knot, where tensions all had their causes and explanations, where desperate children were redeemable, where kindness and firmness could still challenge the free-market drug economy. John and the others wanted me to know that there was goodness as well as cynicism and brutality in the ghetto, and though I had seen little evidence of it apart from their own fanatical determination to reshape their community, I now saw the ghetto as more than a battlefield, more than the projected fearful fantasies of those whose colour and prosperity allow them to consign its existence to the realm of nightmare.

29

TOFU IN TOPANGA

Angelenos who make regular long journeys on the freeways, and that's most of them, devise strategies to pass the time: they learn Spanish from cassettes, they eat their breakfasts and sip hot coffee, they read the newspaper while coasting at 10 mph on the Long Beach northbound. I passed the time while crawling up the on-ramp by listening to the radio. That lusty conservative Rush Limbaugh provided the best entertainment simply by mocking the pieties of the day.

When militant vegetarians announced 'a great American meat-out', for one day in March, Limbaugh launched a counter-offensive. He had no objection to vegetarianism, he insisted; he just didn't want to be made to feel like a monster because he enjoys a slab of meat. My view entirely, so I was heartened when on the day of the 'meat-out' he organised a prime rib dinner to be served to his staff and some invited guests in the studio. During the course of his show he relayed live the sounds of clattering forks and china, and the grunts of gratified beef-chomping guests.

The proliferation of public holidays named after great dead Americans gave him a fresh target. He had a proposal of his own, and, moreover, the candidate was female, which he hoped would mollify the feminists who find his views objectionable. He urged Americans to celebrate the birthday of Mary Jo Kopechne, 'hon-ouring her courageous sacrifice whereby she ensured that there will never be a Teddy Kennedy presidency'. This was in deplor-able taste, and it kept me giggling for at least half a mile along the Ventura Freeway. When a caller referred to the iniquities of the male sex, Rush sighed sympathetically: 'Yes, you people out there know what men are like. We're neanderthals, we're wife beaters, child molesters, we're plunderers of ancient Indian lands. . . .'

Best of all were his updates on contentious social issues. There were 'homeless updates', not to mock those unfortunate enough to be roofless, but to pillory those who exploited their plight for, as he saw it, 'the furtherance of their own political agenda'. When I returned to London and found the likes of Jeremy Irons bedding down for one night with a bunch of the genuinely homeless and a few dozen television cameras, I longed for a Rush assault on celebrities whose well-publicised gestures do nothing to ease the plight of those they pretend to help. And there were 'condom updates', introduced with the theme song 'Would You Like to Ride My Beautiful Balloon', and bringing us the latest news on the efforts of school administrators in New York and elsewhere to distribute condoms to children without their parents' consent. The 'animal rights update' was introduced by Andy Williams singing 'Born Free', although the soundtrack had been tampered with by Limbaugh. Behind the mellow voice one could hear the sounds of automatic gunfire, shrieking cats, roaring elephants, and other animals in distress.

The outbursts of political reaction were less enjoyable, but no matter. Without Mr Limbaugh, the most dangerous man in America, on the car radio, riding the freeways would have been a far greater chore. One sunny morning I rode the Pacific Coast Highway on my way to Malibu. The highway's six-lane concrete sweep up the shore encourages speed, and this has to be the most terrifying road in the city. Northbound traffic streaming out of Los Angeles towards the beaches has to turn left across three lanes of southbound traffic to reach one of the shoreside parking areas. I was heading for the Getty Museum, which is perched on an escarpment above the highway. The entrance is easy to miss, and I made an inelegant screeching turn to the right just in time.

There has been much mockery of the fact that although admission to the museum is free, you are required to make a parking reservation. This stipulation does inhibit spontaneous visits, but it also ensures that the museum is rarely overcrowded and that local residents are not plagued all day long by parked cars blocking their driveways. Once you have stowed your car in the garage – and mine was nestled amorously alongside a convertible with the licence plate NOHUSBN – you walk up some steps that lead to the colonnades and garden planted above it. At the far end of the garden, which is divided by a long lick of a pool, a two-storey building houses the museum itself.

In 1754 the Swiss engineer Karl Weber produced a detailed floor plan of the excavated first-century Villa dei Papiri outside Herculaneum, which was used as a model for the layout of the Getty Museum. A vast amount of historical research and head-scratching went on to ensure that the reconstruction was as exact as possible. The justification for modelling a new structure on one that was almost 2000 years old was that the light of Southern Italy and Southern California were similar, and this was the ideal location, outside Italy itself, in which to attempt such a recon-struction. Furthermore, the Getty collection was particularly rich in classical antiquities, and it seemed appropriate to display them in a building in the same style. Anyway, Getty hated modernist architecture, and he was paying the bills.

There is something bizarre about the zeal with which not only the structures but the decorative schemes were so meticulously lifted from supposed Roman originals. The murals, the coffering, the marble floors, the busts, the fenestration, even the choice of plants were all deeply pondered. The atrium itself is modelled on a Herculaneum villa, while its central garden and colonnades are based on the House of the Faun in Pompeii.

What the visitor experiences, of course, is a new building, whereas all our other experiences of Roman villas are incomplete and filtered through the depredations of the centuries. The Getty Museum, white and clean in the Californian glare, sits and gleams. Its very meticulousness seems cold and lifeless. I longed for a chipped column, a noseless bust, a tumble of stone in a corner, weeds growing rebelliously through marble flags. For the designers of the Getty to have reproduced a dilapidated villa would, of course, have been an even greater absurdity, but it is impossible to walk through the peristyle gardens without finding it all out of kilter with the times, a pedantic fantasy.

Joan Didion put her finger on the oddity of the place in an essay she wrote in 1977. 'Ancient marbles', she wrote, 'were not always attractively faded and worn. Ancient marbles once appeared just as they appear here: as strident, opulent evidence of imperial power and acquisition. Ancient murals were not always bleached and mellowed and "tasteful". Ancient murals once looked as they do here: as if dreamed by a Mafia don. . . . The old world was once discomfitingly new. . . . The Getty tells us that we were never any better than we are and will never be any better than we were, and in so doing makes a profoundly unpopular political statement.' That's a sophisticated statement about the unease of sophisticates, and most visitors, who have no direct experience of Roman ruins, find the museum and its setting beautiful and enthralling. Nor do I imagine that Getty had any such programme in mind; the design reflected his imaginative conservatism. Having delivered his 'statement', Getty himself never took the trouble to visit his own museum, the mere act of possession being sufficient reward.

That said, the museum and its gardens are entrancing. The lushness of a well-watered California garden, the crisp Pacific air and light, the sheen of the pool's water, and the fine proportions of the structures, are very seductive. The Getty would be worth a visit even if it didn't house a remarkable artistic collection. The glory of the museum is its classical collection: the Roman mummy portraits and busts, the second-century Roman Mazarin Venus, a superb Late Classical Aphrodite, a terracotta group of a seated poet and sirens of the utmost naturalism, the Lansdowne Herakles, and caches of Roman and Etruscan jewellery.

All this is displayed on the ground floor where the various exhibition halls are linked, each leading out into the courtyard and garden. Everything is open and cool; outdoor and indoor become almost indistinguishable, a very Californian as well as a Roman experience. Light flows into the rooms; gardens and greenery are never distant. The upstairs rooms, where the paintings and drawings are displayed, are more conventional, as canvases need to be protected from the very light and air that are so becoming to marble and gold.

Whereas the other great collections of Los Angeles seem to have required every major artist to be represented by at least one painting, the Getty haul reflects a far more thoughtful approach to collecting. There are Rembrandts, of course, but there is also an exquisite still life by Bosschaert the Elder, a Gentile da Fabriano in gorgeous condition, a rare Masaccio, a marvellous portrait of Cosimo de Medici by Pontormo, two Joseph Wrights of rare quality, and some exceptional Impressionists. It is among the more modern works that the amazing purchasing power of the Getty Museum is most apparent. Van Gogh's *Irises* is a marvellous painting, but it cost the museum an unconscionable amount of money. Among the Renoirs and Cézannes are more unusual choices, such as a nightscape by Munch and a huge eccentric Ensor depicting Christ's Entry into Brussels.

Some of the upstairs rooms are reconstructed French salons of the eighteenth century. Often, in French furniture of this period, the workmanship is extraordinary, but the repertoire of shapes, the routine excesses of the ornament, the triumph of *objet* over utility, can become wearisome. But in this department too the Getty Museum has come up trumps, and most breathtaking of all is a small writing table with ivory and horn inlays that once belonged to Louis XIV. Nor do I recall seeing elsewhere Gobelin tapestries of the 1770s in such impeccable condition. There are hardly any ropes in front of the exhibits, no glass in front of the paintings. You are allowed to get close, a rare experience nowadays when museums, ever more conscious of security, virtually threaten electrocution if you try to peer at the detail in a Vermeer or the brushwork in a Redon.

When the museum was established, its endowment, and thus its purchasing power, was colossal, and there were fears that the curators' financial muscle would drive up prices, since the Getty could always outbid its rivals. What other museum would have, could have paid $35.2 million in 1990 for a Pontormo portrait? In recent years, only Japanese tycoons have been able to match its resources. Collectors of modern art can breathe more easily, as the terms of the endowment forbid the acquisition of works of art created after 1900.

There were other criticisms levelled at the Getty Museum. The curators, it was said, were reluctant to loan any of the collection, and no travelling exhibitions were sanctioned. It was partly to counter such criticisms that the administrators had to think up other ways to spend its vast income (and to retain its tax-exempt status). The organisation of this empire of the fine arts is quite complex. The central body, the Getty Trust, is armed with an endowment of $4.3 billion, spread among its seven divisions, of which the museum is only one. Others include the Getty Conservation Institute and the Getty Center for the History of Art and the Humanities. In 1990 the museum spent $140 million on what is euphemistically called 'collections development'.

Towards the end of the 1990s a 750-acre site in the Santa Monica Mountains should be ready to gather in one place all the outposts of the Getty empire. Even the contents of the museum, other than the classical antiquities, will be moved to the new site, which is being designed by Richard Meier. Until then the branches remain dispersed.

The Getty Center is concealed within the corporate blandness of a bank building in Santa Monica. Its function is to give academics the time of their lives. Each year a different theme is thought up, so that scholars invited to the Center can benefit from the knowledge of the other guests. The invited scholars are loaned flats and offices, and even their spouses are given office space so that they can keep themselves occupied. The scholars also have secretarial assistance, and can help themselves to ten hours of free research time each week from younger scholars. Every whim is catered for at this resort for academics: in the scholars' lounge, newspapers from their various countries of origin are ordered so they can keep up with the latest news from Taiwan or Serbia or Peru.

Since even this level of hospitality doesn't cost enough money, the Center also invites pre- and post-doctoral fellows, as well as visiting scholars who come to study here for much shorter periods. I asked the Center's assistant director, Dr Herbert Hymans, what was the purpose, in the electronic age, of bringing these scholars halfway across the world to Santa Monica. He suggested that the thematic basis of the invitations allowed a rare meeting of minds. It was not only art historians who were invited, but anthropologists and cultural historians and writers. Moreover, the Center was pursuing its ambition to assemble the best art-historical library in the world. It already contains 600,000 volumes and one million photographs in the study collection, in addition to its archival collections. I was not surprised to learn that Los Angeles already possesses the world's finest German Expressionist collection, although it is dispersed at present among various proprietors.

From the Getty Museum the coastal highway continues north along the curving coastline to the shopping malls that constitute, if anything does, the heart of the dispersed community of Malibu. Its social core is the Colony, a gated huddle of houses along the beach much favoured by the stars. These are some of the few stretches of coastline to which there is no public access, which is why it has become so attractive to the rich and famous. In the old days, twenty years ago or more, Malibu was a collection of beach huts. It's still not a resort, except for its residents; there are shopping malls now, but no attempt is made to dissuade visitors from leaving town at the end of the day. Although the beach houses of the Colony are relatively modest, the mansionisation and self-aggrandisement that afflict other wealthy suburbs of Los Angeles have come here too.

There are still unspoiled areas in Malibu, especially inland. A steep road, ablaze with azaleas, leads up to the Serra Retreat, a Franciscan foundation set against a backdrop of bare mountains, with wonderful views west to the ocean. Elsewhere, random developments blot the landscape. There are earthworks everywhere, and vulgar new palaces on hillsides and hilltops, raw in their isolation, with neither the intimacy of the Hollywood canyons nor the decorousness of Beverly Hills. New houses here make no attempt to blend into the landscape; instead they dominate it with screaming ostentation.

Many miles inland, along Malibu Canyon itself, is a palliative: a Hindu temple, festooned with carvings of the gods on its multiple roofs, but differing from Indian temples in its lack of colouring and in the gorgeousness of its setting, which seems far removed from the dust and grit and bustle found around most temples in India itself. Not only is an ancient religion celebrated here in Malibu, but just down the coast in another valley, Topanga Canyon, a relic of California's very own substitute for religion, New Age gobbledegook, is still tuned in to divine astral vibrations. Topanga is probably the last refuge of hippie culture in Southern California. The unregenerate long-haired, flower-power, keep-a-few-chickens, prefer-the-children-naked, bake-it-myself, jingle-jangle-mobile-making, pass-me-a-joint kind of hippie, still riding in a beaten-up but gaudily painted pickup truck, he's still here with his girlfriend, eking out a living with carpentry, odd jobs, construction work.

These remnants of the glorious easygoing dream world of the 1960s probably can't afford the Inn of the Seventh Ray, but this eccentric establishment fits perfectly into the pre-industrial environment of Topanga. The setting is blissful: a wooden house in a hollow near a creek, with candlelit tables laid with lilac cloths among trees strewn with fairy lights. Here you can eat no-cruelty foods to a chorus of very loud frog croaks and hope for a glimpse of a coyote taking a short cut across the creek.

The menu, however, is alarming. It offers a caution: 'To those who dare to pass these special gates: Sometimes the Inn is not just an Inn, or it may be just an Inn, or it may be your passport to somewhere else in time – an inner retreat experience – a special auric forcefield, and you may never be the same again.' The drivel continues: 'We at the Inn of the Seventh Ray believe in giving you the purest of nature's foods, energized as a gift from the sun with a dash of esoteric food knowledge, and ancient mystery school wisdom tossed in for your seasoning and pleasure. Or perhaps it just might raise your body's light vibration.'

And the food? Since dishes are listed in order of their esoteric vibrational value, expectations should not be pitched too high. Omritas melon is 'a well-kept Inn secret, direct from the violet Planet – nature's perfect vessel of transportation, an eggplant melon filled in with a balanced blend of olives, nuts, mushrooms, shallots, feta cheese and topped with our ruby ray tomato sauce' ($15.95). The New Age lasagna is 'an old favorite from an old Italian master chef' ($16.95), which isn't very enlightening. The worst of California cuisine is represented, surely, by the 'gourmet non-dairy seaweed pasta with shitake mushrooms, pea pods, tofu and red pepper laced with a ginger sauce'.

No preservatives, colourings, salt, or bleached flour are used in the kitchens, and the house wine is fermented from organically grown grapes. Instead of requesting diners not to smoke, the menu goes into a coy little song and dance: 'If you must smoke, you are very welcome to dine on the patio where the elemental beings of earth, air, fire and water can more easily do their purifying work. Bless you.' The menu closes with the following valediction: 'We want you to rest unhurried; partake of the Angelic Vibration of the violet ray, and to experience a timelessness of what can become the coming culture of a golden age.' I am too ill-tempered to dine at places where everyone is shimmering in an aura of beneficence (and high prices), but reports I've had from those who have done so claim that 'resting unhurried' is a necessity more than an option, since the service is incredibly slow.

It seems odd that amid the undisguised materialism of Los Angeles, the soggy embrace of the New Age quest for wholeness and niceness should still be so palpable. Perhaps devotees of Mammon and worldly success need some spiritual gloss so they can mouth the comforting formula, 'Of course, there's more to life than making money . . .' New Age waffle can give you the semblance of spirituality without the inconveniences of dogma and thought. 'Personal growth' is worshipped even though it is often no more than an anxious or complacent monitoring of a process that is in any event unavoidable. Relentless self-absorption can be disguised as coming to terms with the Inner Child, or other such garbage. New Age follies also allow urbanites to pretend that they are opening themselves to nature and wilderness, and a sentimentalised affection for Native Americans and their primitive but wholesome way of life puts you into a more acceptable relationship with some darker periods of American history.

New Age music is programmatic. You don't just make music, but, according to a review in the New Age journal *L.A. Resources*, you 'sculpt an atmosphere, build a sonic world and populate it with purifying energies'. Another review has to grapple with total blandness: 'Vaguely melodic yet still rather ambient, each track is designed to enhance whatever environment one is in through softly supportive electronic strains. Good for the office.'

The journal suggests countless ways in which readers and their money can soon be parted. You can spend $24 on 'serenity stones', 'unique, high energy crystals mined and imported from the caves of Madagascar, thought by many to be the last remnant of the lost land of Lemuria. . . . Serenity Stones embody the spirit of Lemuria, they can bring balance to your emotions while relaxing the body and relieving the stresses of modern living.' You can sign up for colon hydrotherapy with Bryan Moses, 'a Natural Health Practitioner with Herbology, Iridology, Scierology, and Food Combining'. Dr Carol Carbone, 'an ordained metaphysical minister . . . conducts past life regressions on a group and individual basis'. Allan Rosenthal offers 'a course in miracles' so that you can 'develop a loving relationship with your Inner Voice and psychic abilities'. A company called Transformation Tech offers a 'weekly small group workshop for exploring astral projection, lucid dreaming and altered states combining DAVID 1, our twenty station light and sound brainwave synchronizer with Monroe hemi-sync and other tapes'.

In West Hollywood I encountered Jim Watson's Metaphysical

ESP Center, where you can obtain psychic readings at two dollars per minute. Gift certificates are available. Watson is on to a good thing, since he also advertises to members of his networking group OASIS seminars on such subjects as 'Learn the Secrets of Creating a $1000 a Week Practice in the Intuitive Arts'.

The OASIS news sheet makes daring predictions, notably that a large earthquake will hit Orange County and the Palisades in the summer of 1991. (Southern California survived 1991 intact.) 'Card-astrologer extraordinaire' Joseph Jacobs offers his special prediction: '1991 will be much easier for relationships. Partnerships and cooperative efforts will be important.' His associate Rev. Karen L. Johnson is committed to the 'welling process' and offers energy healing ('a hand-on body approach energizing the body to the relaxation response, chakra balancing, counseling to dissolve energy blocks') as well as 'biorhythm character compatibilities'. Another flyer in Jim Watson's office brings to my attention China Kelly-Brogdon, who 'uses the technique of astral travel to locate missing people and objects' such as her colleagues' brains. Sheilaa [sic] Hite declares on her flyer: 'My work is Transformational, Empowering, & Healing. My commitment in this life is to assist and guide you into your rightful richness & remembrance of who you are.' Perhaps China can help her locate the English language.

None of this is new to Los Angeles. The primary reasons why people came out here in the first place was to improve their health or their fortunes, which made it a breeding ground for creative zaniness. Carey McWilliams, in *Southern California: An Island on the Land*, gives an account of the I AM cult of the 1930s, founded by Mr and Mrs Ballard: 'The deity of the cult, it seems, is the Ascended Master Saint Germain. While on a hiking trip near Mt Shasta in Northern California, Ballard relates that Saint Germain, appearing out of the void, tapped him on the shoulder and offered him a cup filled with "pure electronic essence". After drinking the essence and eating a tiny wafer of "concentrated energy", Ballard felt himself surrounded by "a White Flame which formed a circle about fifty feet in diameter". Enveloped in the flame, he and Saint Germain set forth on a trip around the world in the stratosphere, visiting "the buried cities of the Amazon, France, Egypt, Karnak, Luxor, the fabled Inca cities . . . and Yellowstone National Park".' The Ballards enlisted 350,000 fee-paying devotees, and marketed records, books, electronic toys, and 'New Age Cold Cream', all of which earned them $3 million, a tidy sum fifty years ago.

I had first met Erik in London in the early 1960s, where he and his family had moved after his blacklisted father had found it impossible to secure enough work in Hollywood. At that time I was dating a sweet, shy, and literally tight-lipped American girl. When Erik phoned to ask me how I was getting along with Miss Suzy, I explained the problem.

'Just a second.' I heard him yelling to his father, asking for his advice on my problem. Frank yelled back: 'Hold her nose!'

So I'd never forgotten Frank, but Frank had forgotten me. When I phoned him in Los Angeles, it hadn't occurred to me that, although my memories of Frank and his wife Lee were vivid, they had only the dimmest recollection of who I was. Youth is impressionable but middle age is rightly more selective. So it was all the more generous of them to pretend that they remembered me, and to invite me to dinner at their club. I went over to their house off Coldwater Canyon for a preliminary drink. Among the bottles behind the bar stood the Oscar Frank had won for best screenplay about twenty-five years ago. I did the hick thing and asked whether I could pick it up.

Frank explained that the party would also include Sheldon Leonard, the former television producer, who had often given him work despite the blacklisting. Sheldon, now in his eighties, had produced and directed highly successful shows such as *Mary Tyler Moore* and *Dick Van Dyke*. He was, I supose, the Aaron Spelling of his day, only with taste and wit and a smaller house.

'It was entirely different in those days,' explained Frank. 'Sheldon produced these major series, but there were only two or three people involved in each programme. Today a producer has a staff of at least five for each show. You have to have meetings and conferences and rewrites. Back in those days I would try out an idea for a show on Sheldon. If he liked it, he'd say, Fine, write it. Or he'd ask me to make certain changes and then go ahead. And that was it. But more recently I've found myself pitching ideas to twenty-two-year-old kids who don't know the first thing about TV comedy.'

We collected Sheldon from his house on Loma Vista. As we drove along Mulholland towards the club, Sheldon spotted an Oriental-style palace, newly built high on a ridge.

'Whose place is that?' he asked.

'I've no idea,' said Frank. 'I would guess the owners are Iranian or Middle Eastern.'

'Now what would you say it could cost' – long pause – 'to bomb the place?'

Frank was proud of the Mulholland Tennis Club, which he had helped to found. He was warmly greeted by the staff and we were ushered to a table by the window. The view is spectacular, as the club is one of the few places from which you can look down both on Los Angeles and the Valley. The actor Richard Dreyfuss was there with his family and came up to Sheldon to say hello. He reminded him that many years ago he had often worked for him. Sheldon didn't recall. To him, I suppose, Hollywood stars are a dime a dozen.

The conversation became less refined than the ambience. Frank told how he and two producers, finding themselves idle one month, had tried their hand at a pornographic movie.

'Usually a movie script is a hundred pages or more. My script for this one was twenty-nine pages – there wasn't that much talking. We didn't really know what we were doing, but the movie still made money. It played for months at the local adult theatres and was issued on cassette. The distribution guy took 50 per cent, and the three producers got the rest. We did okay, but the distribution guy really cleaned up.

'The shooting took twenty days, out in Agoura or somewhere in the Valley, and that's a long time for a porno movie. Two days into shooting, we lost our female lead. We were frantic. Then the director said his wife had agreed to play the part. I'd go on the set and find everybody walking around naked, including the crew. The lead actress would finish her big scene, get up, still naked, and walk over to me and ask for a cigarette.

'Once the movie was finished, there had to be a screening. Each of the three producers brought along his wife, and the lead actor brought along his sister, and the director, of course, brought along his wife. Then we all sat down and watched our new movie. I didn't realise it at the time, but what we were doing, if word had got out, could have had a bad effect on our careers. But we didn't think about that at the time.'

'Oh, I don't know,' said Sheldon. 'You could have turned it around. I can see the headline now: The Many Talents of Frank Tarloff.'

'Except acting in the movie.'

'I wouldn't have let him,' said Lee, 'though he'd have done a great job.'

'That's the nicest thing any wife could say.'

30

SLAUGHTERGATE

It was never easy to think of Los Angeles as an industrial city, and indeed 95 per cent of all businesses in the city employ fewer than fifty people. Yet the productivity of the region is astonishing. According to the report *LA 2000*, compared with the gross national products of other nations, Southern California's output – $290 billion worth of goods and services in 1987 – places the region eleventh among nations of the world, surpassing India, Switzerland and Australia.

The region's prosperity was based not only on Hollywood but on the aerospace industry, which had burgeoned during the Second World War. Within a few years employment at aerospace plants increased tenfold and when the war years ended the city had acquired a large and highly qualified workforce. The Cold War proved a godsend to those parts of the country, such as Southern California and South Carolina, with technologically sophisticated industries that could keep turning out costly products that would sustain the military superiority of the United States. Some 12 per cent of all workers in defence-related industries are based in Southern California, employed by Lockheed, McDonnell Douglas, Hughes, General Dynamics, Rockwell, and Northrop, as well as countless subcontractors.

The boom years, which continued well into the Reagan presidency, have clearly come to an end. Defence cutbacks are the order of the day, and the recession has made matters worse. Ironically, the economic success of Southern California has hurt the industries that spawned it, since employers are increasingly reluctant to pay the high wages to which Californian workers feel entitled. Now some of the industries are moving out. Lockheed has moved away to Georgia, and Burbank, which benefited from millions of dollars in tax revenues plus more millions from local subcontractors financially dependent on Lockheed's custom, will find itself much the poorer, as will the thousands of employees that must seek work elsewhere in a declining market. In 1990 Los Angeles lost about 17,000 jobs in aerospace industries. In the spring of 1991, a $72-billion contract for a new fighter plane was awarded to Lockheed rather than to Palmdale-based Northrop – another blow for Los Angeles. By February 1992 the unemployment rate in California had risen to over 8 per cent, and the economy was in a nose-dive.

The Jet Propulsion Laboratory at Altadena has strong links with the aerospace industry, but its survival is based on political rather than economic considerations, though of course it is simplistic to separate the two. Although administered by Caltech, the JPL, which is federally funded, is really part of NASA. Its director since January 1991, the former Caltech physics professor Edward Stone, finds that he spends much of his time exerting pressure on Washington politicians to ensure that his budget remains adequate. Since 1972 Professor Stone had been project scientist on the Voyager mission that travelled to Jupiter and Saturn, and it was the JPL that designed and operated these very complex unmanned space probes. The technical challenges are astonishing. Among other tasks, Voyager was to take a look at Saturn's moon Triton. To plot the most desirable course required accuracy to within one second in a craft that was by then some 3 billion miles away. The Voyager missions, having been launched in 1977 and having flown past Jupiter, Saturn, Uranus, and Neptune, are expected to remain out in interstellar space until well into the next century.

Stone is a thin ascetic-looking man, almost wilfully modest, with grey hair, grey complexion, grey suit. But if Ed Stone is far from flashy, he has other attributes of greater importance, including an ability to explain the purpose of space research. This is crucial, since public goodwill is essential to generate the political support that's necessary to keep such costly research going. The Galileo mission to Jupiter, launched in 1989, has been running into technical problems with its antenna which, if not solved, will greatly mar its capacity to transmit information, especially photographs, once it reaches the planet in 1995. The Voyager mission came to life for millions of people across the world when it succeeded in transmitting some marvellous colour photographs. They were lovely to look at, I said, but what was the real point of these missions?

'What Voyager and other such missions do is provide answers to specific questions, answers that may be generally applicable to broader questions, such as the nature of planetary atmospheres. They can help explain, for example, not only what the red spots on Jupiter are, but why they do what they do. The great red spot on Jupiter was first observed in 1979. It was a hurricane-like vortex. It took another ten years before scientists, applying the data we had, could produce theories about how the spot was formed, and how other spots were in fact subsidiary hurricanes that fed into it. We now know that jetstreams can contribute to spots, but why are there jetstreams in the first place? What determines them? And to answer questions like these we can develop models.'

Stone explained how the space probes had garnered practical information that helped to explain the formation and structure of the earth's atmosphere. He gave me a private tutorial on concepts that had long perplexed me, such as the heliopause. The scale and expense of the operations were astonishing, and I wondered whether as the technology develops, certain kinds of research would become less costly.

'The technology allows you to do more with your money. You can get more for your dollar. If that weren't the case, the costs would be prohibitive.' Nonetheless, less money is forthcoming from Congress, and the Freedom space station, its cost now estimated at $40 billion, has escaped cancellation only at the expense of the budgets of other space projects, which have been frozen.'

'What's next?'

'We're entering a new phase of exploration. We've done fly-bys. Now we'll be sending out long-term visitors that will go into orbit around planets, and put probes into their atmosphere. We'll be able to get a hundred times closer to the moons of Jupiter, and joint missions with the Europeans will do the same for Saturn. We'll be working on the radar mapping of the surfaces. The step beyond that is the actual exploration of those surfaces by robotic means, but I don't believe that will occur until the beginning of the next century.'

'You once described space research as an attempt to write an encyclopedia of the solar system. Of course somebody has to decide what is worthy of inclusion in an encyclopedia, but sidestepping that question for the moment, how complete is that encyclopedia now?'

'We have enormous knowledge and inventory, but what we don't yet have is a great deal of understanding and that will require many more volumes. But this decade is full of exciting developments that should add to that understanding. We're hoping to put into space an infra-red telescope facility – SIRTIF – which will be a thousand times more sensitive than facilities we now have on the earth. The same applies to X-ray astronomy. The goal of such astronomy will be to discover planets around other stars, and we need advanced optical systems to find them. With telescopes in space or on the surface of the moon, it seems quite probable that we will make those discoveries. I would guess we'll find other planets by the end of this century. Any planet we'll find is likely to be big, on the scale of Jupiter rather than Earth. But once you find a large planet, you can be virtually certain that there will be other, smaller planets closer to the star.'

Seated in the spacecraft, I was alarmed to discover that the pilots were novices and had little idea about how to keep their craft under control. We hurtled towards other spacecraft, narrowly avoiding a collision at the last second. Navigational errors brought us plunging into the heart of a city, weaving between skyscrapers and ducking beneath bridges. The craft shook and trembled with the violence of the flight, and there were the rushes and tightenings of acceleration and braking. Eventually the ordeal came to an end, and we stumbled out into the safety and relative placidity of the terminal.

This was not a sneak preview of a manned space mission, courtesy of Dr Stone, but the latest attraction at Disneyland: StarTours. Although I hated every minute, I had to admit that the simulation was brilliant. An hour earlier I'd joined the long queue waiting to board the spacecraft. We snaked through a kind of departure lounge; paging calls and departure announcements wafted from the loudspeakers. Lights flashed and robots grumbled. This hubbub served a dual purpose it established an atmosphere of excited anticipation and, equally important, it distracted the crowd during our hour-long shuffle towards the departure gates and the prospect of amazement. It's cleverly done, but there's no escaping the fact that in terms of entertainment it's no more riveting than an hour hanging about Gatwick waiting for a delayed flight.

It's a mistake to come to Disneyland, as I had done, with a notebook. I had first visited the theme park in 1979 with my cousin. We rode the rides, enjoyed the *frissons*, licked ice creams, and bought Minnie Mouse T-shirts, which I proudly wore to the editorial board meetings of the publishing house for which I was then working, a fad that probably contributed to my eventual dismissal. Now I was back with pen and pad, and scouring the park for copy I missed the fun of the place. Just one glimpse of that large sign over the entrance – 'The Happiest Place on Earth' – and my mood had instantly soured.

There may have been a time when intellectuals looked down their noses at Disneyland. Now the reverse is true, and the park's elaborate, inventive *mélange* of fakery and fantasy is much admired by cognoscenti. But to analyse Disneyland's subtleties – the slight miniaturisation of the buildings so as to increase our sense of domination, or the way Main Street is constructed in a trick of perspective, the street widening and trees growing in height so as to make the castle at the end appear larger and further away than it actually is – is to lose the spontaneity that marks the way in which most people, especially children, experience the place. But instead of marvelling at these strategies of construction, which are very successful since nobody notices them till they are pointed out, I found myself conscious of another kind of trickery, by which the quaint folksy façades on Main Street are fronts for supermarkets where Disney products are peddled with a kind of saturation merchandising.

The adroit management relieves visitors of all decisions other than those involving a choice among pleasures. Squads of smartly dressed parking attendants guide your car to a berth. An appeal for directions was met with an outpouring of helpful information and advice, even though there was an alarming tendency to talk about Mr Toad as though he were real. While everyone else was being the crowd, I was watching the crowd, remarking on the extraordinary number of monks and nuns until somebody pointed out that it was Catholic Schools Week, which also explained the huge numbers of copiously fertile families.

I kept away from the rides that exchange your brain for your stomach, and settled for the old favourites, such as Pirates of the Caribbean, with its nautical battle scenes and tableaux of debauched pirates making merry at the expense of their poor prisoners. The Jungle Cruise was marred by the constant patter of the guide, whose stupid puns – a baby elephant described as 'a little squirt' and a python 'that might get a crush on you' – irritated me beyond measure. The visual wit is considerable, especially in the shape of gorillas devouring the remnants of a ravaged camp, near which the wheels of an upside-down jeep are still spinning. The success of these rides is partly a function of the profusion of visual effects. There is too much to take in, as in a dream in which there are too many images and sensations to be processed but in which the impact remains powerful and memorable. At Disneyland no sooner have you reacted to a fright or a visual joke than another is looming up ahead. The enforced passivity of the visitor, who is guided and ferried and driven, increases his susceptibility.

By lunchtime the crowds were great and so was the noise. The twitter of excited children and the cries of harassed parents rose above a sostenuto of mechanical noise from the railways, roller-coasters, trams, and musical soundtracks. Crabby with hunger, children snivelled while their parents pondered which Disney hostelry to choose for their overpriced and mediocre lunch, since the management forbids the importation of food and drink into the park. Penalty: expulsion.

After lunch I queued for *Captain Eo*, a short 3D film starring the glittering Michael Jackson. The plot was incomprehensible to me, but I did grasp that the theme revolved around a confrontation between good and evil. My lack of comprehension didn't matter a jot, since the plot was secondary to the special effects, making the film a triumph of technique over intelligibility. Blurred 3D effects, to which my eyes never properly adjusted, only increased my curmudgeonly mood, especially since the whole show was simply an excuse for Jackson to strut his stuff, which he did with his usual taut excitement and military precision. As for his acting, that consisted solely of defiant stares. So I didn't enjoy it. But so what? Thousands did. The tremendous success of Disneyland provides its own answers to the strictures of the alienated.

My final visit was to the Haunted House, where a disembodied voice ushers us into a room without windows and doors. At this point my imagination took a definite wrong turn. While everyone else oohed and ahed as the room expanded in volume by the simple expedient of lowering the floor, I was reflecting on other airless chambers into which innocent crowds had been herded. Even though Walt Disney was a notorious anti-Semite – he had abundant opportunities to exercise his prejudices in Hollywood – to equate the Haunted House with a gas chamber was decidedly perverse. But there I was, and I knew it was time to go home. Anyone who comes to the empire of Goofy and Donald and finds echoes of extermination camps is clearly not in the mood for fun, fun, fun.

At the end of the Jungle Ride, the wise-cracking guide had remarked, as his script required, that we were now approaching the most dangerous part of our journey: returning to our cars and the California freeways. How right he was.

Since I was already in Orange County, I decided to visit another theme park, newly opened at Yorba Linda: the Nixon Library. The thirty-seventh president was born near here, and the Library adjoins his birthplace. Yorba Linda is a strange place: the local Orange Growers Association still exists, a reminder of the town's original economic base. Yorba Linda feels quite different from Los Angeles. With its sprawling malls, unexpected oil wells, and broad empty streets mapping the seemingly random housing developments, Yorba Linda is directionless. Like an amoeba, it flops and goes soft at the edges. The residents come from the planet Braindead. The women wear white, pink, or beige slacks; their hair is light and tightly curled, and they all look as though they had emerged from the hairdresser's just minutes before. In a local snack bar in the adjoining town of Placentia – or was it Placenta? – young men munching on pizza found the pastry and molten cheese instantly metabolised into Firestones of flesh that rolled and jived over their belts. They were wearing suits, but their ties were askew, their mouths foul.

The Library building, sprawling, low and bland, could easily pass for a clinic or insurance office. Its name is deceptive, since it contains no books, other than those by Nixon and his family and acolytes offered for sale in the gift shop among the frosted beverage glasses and T-shirts. The other presidential libraries were set up by the president's supporters but are administered by the federal government. The Nixon Library is the only one untainted by any federal support, since the government had a commendable reluctance to underwrite the glorification of a disgraced president. Perhaps this explains its modest scale. The only other presidential library I have visited, the Johnson Library in Austin, Texas, is megalomaniacal by comparison.

I feel a special closeness to Richard Nixon, as I lived in the United States during most of his presidency. I can think of no other elected politician for whom I felt then and feel now such unmitigated loathing. The cold-hearted Henry Kissinger comes close, but he wasn't elected to office, and Nixon was responsible for elevating Kissinger to his position of great power. The falseness and duplicity of Richard Nixon shocked me, frightened me. There were times in the early 1970s when an authoritarianism quite alien to the American political tradition was creeping up on the nation. Newspapers were harassed, student protesters killed on campuses, absurd but terrifying political plots hatched in the White House. The cynicism and brutality of the odious John D. Mitchell, Nixon's buddy and his attorney general, were exactly on a par with the stealthy hatred of individual expression you expect to find among secret-police bosses. I felt there was something evil, or at the very least malignant, about Nixon, and I still do, a feeling quite distinct from my lack of sympathy with right-wing policies.

Nixon, straining towards rehabilitation, is said to have mellowed with the years, becoming more statesmanlike with age and (forced) retirement, so perhaps a visit to the Library would soften my antipathy too. The visit begins with a movie. It only took one look at that shifty, grinning, insincere mask, and at those hands held high over the shoulders in a graceless, hungry victory gesture, for all the revulsion to come sweeping back. Of course the movie presents its subject in the most positive light, so I wasn't surprised when Nixon's failings were shown to have been, in fact, virtues. We were about to learn, declared the soundtrack, the story of a president who stood on the highest mountaintops and travelled through the deepest valleys. We are reminded that Nixon never gave up, and of 'his remarkable recovery, his astonishing renewal'. The Nixon of the 1990s, talking to camera, has more crumbly jowls and chins than the Nixon of old, but the slightly tremulous insecurity is still there, and the hair has been dyed a dark mousy colour no more convincing than the man to which it is attached. We are told the childhood stuff to establish the 'human' Nixon, and there's a tribute to the long-suffering Pat.

Nixon's notoriously opportunistic performance on the House Un-American Activities is attributed to his shock at the spread of communism in America and is depicted in terms of personal combat with Alger Hiss. Credit is claimed for the landing of a man on the moon. The Vietnam War, which Nixon prolonged while claiming to be ending it, is glossed over rapidly, as are the antiwar protests that dogged his presidency. Instead, the film narrates how Nixon brought Hanoi to the negotiating table (aided, it is not said, by a saturation of bombs, mines, and defoliants) and thus achieved peace with honour. The overtures to China, Nixon's one undoubted achievement, are dwelt upon at length. As for Watergate, Nixon knew nothing about the break-in and it was his aides who became involved in a cover-up. When threatened with impeachment, Nixon made his decision 'to put the interest of America first' – which isn't the way I recall it – and he resigned. You'd be forgiven for imagining that the near certainty of impeachment by Congress is an everyday hazard for American presidents. The film lingers on his maudlin farewell to the White House staff.

'He was in his deepest valley – but not for long.' No suggestion, of course, that the valley might have been a pit he had dug for himself. After his resignation he 'wrote bestseller after bestseller' and we are vouchsafed more glimpses of Nixon the family man. During his presidency he was often shown at the piano banging out 'Happy Birthday' – leading viewers to conclude it was the only tune he knew – and he's still at it, this time surrounded by grandchildren in frocks. The cameras just happen to be present every time these family gatherings take place. Nixon is now portrayed as a sage, mouthing platitudes: 'Never be discouraged by failures. . . . I can look back and say, the day has indeed been splendid.'

After half an hour, the captive audience is released to look at the exhibits, which are mostly documentary. A television of antique design replays the Chequers speech; alongside the set hundreds of supportive telegrams are spilling out from a mailbag. In another sentimental touch, a dozen or so letters from pre-teen kids supporting Nixon in 1960 are on display, but who cares what an eight-year-old thinks about the political debates of the day? There is a change of tone as we enter a beflagged hall filled with statues of world leaders with whom Nixon had been acquainted: Mao, Chou, Brezhnev, Khrushchev, Golda Meir, de

Gaulle, Adenauer. In showcases on the walls are dozens of the gifts bestowed on the incumbent of the presidency during official visits to Washington. An interactive screen allows visitors to learn about Nixon's relationship with each of the statues, and to read his current assessment of their standing. This is the major pitch of the Library: Nixon as world statesman.

The next halls expound Nixon's 'vision for peace in the world'. Space is given to China, rightly, and to Vietnam, where he 'charted a course which did not yield to the demands of a vocal, disruptive and sometimes violent minority'. You would never know that a substantial proportion of Americans were bitterly opposed to the war, and to Nixon's extension of that war into Cambodia in 1970: 'There were those behind the scenes whose aim was not vigorous dissent but violent destruction. . . . As the FBI reported, it appeared to be part of a nationwide terrorist offensive by radical student groups.' True enough, but only true of a minute proportion of antiwar activists. The Kent State killings are not omitted, but the script recalls how national guard patrolmen were 'pelted with rocks and chunks of concrete. Tragically, in the ensuing panic, shots rang out. 4 students lay dead.' This is not how I recall it. The mendacity of the Nixon years is clearly still with us. As for the My Lai massacre, 'antiwar critics tried to turn this isolated incident into a broad indictment of our presence in Vietnam'. The Nixon hagiographers become positively bad-tempered when dealing with the dreadful bombings of Hanoi in 1972: 'Antiwar critics were quick to denounce the President's actions. They screamed [sic] that he was widening the war, not ending it.'

Other halls catalogue Nixon's accomplishments in domestic policies. The credit goes entirely to Nixon. His cabinet apparently made no contribution whatsoever. John Mitchell's name is conspicuous by its absence, and there is hardly any mention of Secretary of State William Rogers, Secretary of Defence Melvin Laird, or Henry Kissinger. This is Nixon's library, and the spotlight is too tightly focused on him to leave room for his colleagues. By now one is itching to see how the packagers of the new Nixon will handle the Watergate scandal. When the Library was being planned, Nixon didn't want it handled at all, and his stubbornness delayed the completion of the Library. Any frankness shown in the Watergate displays has been achieved despite Nixon, not because of him. As the director of the Library conceded on a radio show I heard: 'You will find exhibitories [sic] that are inclusive of negative aspects of the presidency.' I hope that's clear.

First, a touch of contrition: 'Nixon himself said he made inexcusable misjudgments during Watergate. But what is equally clear is that his political opponents ruthlessly exploited those misjudgments as a way to further their own, purely political goals.' Exploiting the mistakes of the opposition is indeed a disgraceful thing for politicians to do, but they have always done it and Nixon himself was a master of the art. Each episode of the squalid affair and the prolonged cover-up is dealt with in some detail, but always defensively.

Finally, we reach the Presidential Forum, a rather grand name for a television set which offers Nixon's prerecorded replies to a series of questions visitors can put to him by punching an interactive screen. Although there were only two or three people in the hall, there was an eighteen-minute wait before another question could be put to the tape. I diligently sat through his responses to questions on baseball, his religious upbringing, his most memorable meal, his decision to resign. His biggest mistake in handling Watergate, as he recalls for us, was not to concentrate sufficiently on the issue, as he was too preoccupied with international issues at the time. This account, of course, is not borne out by the hundreds of pages of presidential transcripts, all of which I have read.

If my response was combative, so was the message delivered by the exhibits. Nixon's greatness would be self-evident, it tells us, had it not been for the mean-mindedness of his detractors. The Nixon Library is not, as it pretends to be, a record of a political era, so much as another set of moves in the long-term campaign to rehabilitate Richard Nixon. It is about as dispassionate as those now defunct Eastern European museums of Leninism and Communist achievement that nobody other than dragooned parties of schoolchildren ever went to. Sixteen years elapsed between Nixon's disgrace and the opening of the Library, since it took sixteen years for even his supporters' sense of shame to diminish sufficiently for funds to be raised. Now the former president is running again, not for office but for his place in the history books.

31

NIP AND TUCK

'If I came to you and said that I just wasn't happy about the way middle age was advancing, about the way I was looking these days, and wanted a few adjustments—'

'I wouldn't touch you. If you had bags under your eyes or drooping eyelids or a specific problem that you wanted seen to, then we could talk further. But the patient and the surgeon have to see eye to eye on what needs to be done. Every plastic surgeon knows it's a bad sign when a patient walks in with a file of photos. Our job is not to make you look like somebody else. A rule of thumb that's fairly reliable is that if the patient can articulate what he or she wants, it's probably okay.'

I had devised this little trap for Dr Tim Miller but he had refused to tumble into it. A well-known plastic surgeon who has tampered with some of the most glamorous bodies in Hollywood, he saw me in the consultation room of his offices in the UCLA Medical Center, an inner sanctum reached via a clutch of elegant long-legged secretaries. He was still wearing his green surgeon's tunic, a clear signal that our little chat would be no more than a brief interlude during a busy day with the scalpel.

Dr Miller didn't believe that there was any more cosmetic plastic surgery carried out in Los Angeles than in any other city of comparable size. Nor were most of his patients movie stars or the idle rich; instead they tended to be active professional people, and about three-quarters of them were women. I couldn't help thinking of these typical patients in terms of the description of the narrator's father in Bret Easton Ellis's dispiriting chronicle of

the gilded youth of Los Angeles, *Less Than Zero:* 'My father looks
pretty healthy if you don't look at him for too long. He's
completely tan and has had a hair transplant in Palm Springs,
two weeks ago, and he has pretty much a full head of blondish
hair. He also has had his face lifted.'

A face lift will cost you between $6000 and $12,000 and can be
repeated as often as you like, provided you remain healthy. Dr
Miller insisted that the only obstacle to the surgeon's art was not
age but poor health. Cosmetic plastic surgery, he insisted, was a
peculiarly demanding profession, because the surgeon is required
to improve on something that was already normal. The procedures he performs most frequently are eye lifts, face lifts, and
liposuction. 'Plastic surgery, if performed by someone qualified,
is a low-risk operation, even though it's a very complicated one.
Removing wrinkles can take five hours or more. After all, to
qualify as a plastic surgeon, you need to study for an additional
seven years after qualifying as a doctor.'

Liposuction, of which I had never heard before coming to
California, has had a bad press, but Dr Miller was indignant,
denying the claim that the fat cells removed by this vacuuming
procedure keep returning, requiring ever more operations.

'There are a finite number of fat cells. What liposuction does is
reduce fat in specific contour areas. It is not an operation for
obesity. What it can do is reduce fat in places such as the hips,
the chin, the outer thighs. Nor is silicone the disaster it's made
out to be. There's no data to link silicone implants with breast
cancer, and that's after two million implants performed
nationwide.'

I put to him that my objections to cosmetic surgery were not
on medical grounds, but because I like idiosyncrasies in people's
looks. I want my wife to look like my wife, not like Madonna or
Bo Derek. My own skin had its fair share of wrinkles and quirks,
spots and furrows, but I was quite happy with them, for without
them I would be even less physiognomically memorable than I
am. I suggested that people were seeking to align themselves
with some bland ideal.

'That may have been the case many years ago,' replied the
doctor, 'but the trend now is to be natural-looking. You used to
be able to walk into a room and recognise a face lift as a particular
doctor's work. I don't think you could do that any more. The
days when a face lift made you look as though you were in a

wind tunnel are probably over. If we can make our patients happier about themselves, then we're doing our job.'

It is certainly a widely held belief in Los Angeles that it's an excellent idea to submit to the knife in order to feel better about yourself, which suggests that levels of insecurity are alarmingly high. The same applies to major dentistry. The newspapers regularly advertise the services of local mouth furnishers. Clara Shapiro's dental office was offering 'specials': porcelain crowns reduced from 'regular' $450 to $250, and complete dentures from $500 to $250. 'Our staff', soothed the ad, 'is sensitive to your needs and determined to make your visit comfortable.' Alternatively, Greater California Dental Plan's SmileSaver offers you a complete programme and 'guarantees low, pre-set fees'.

Friends of mine who moved to Los Angeles ten years ago invited me to a party. They are the picture of health, as trim and vigorous as teenagers. I was startled by an outbreak of hugging among some of the women to celebrate the fact that two of them had just had the braces removed from their teeth after a lengthy procedure called, I believe, orthodonty. They explained to me that when we reach the advanced age of forty, our teeth start to get crooked – not a development I have noticed among my own pack of teeth – and the braces are supposed to haul them back into line. My elegant and very attractive hostess told me she was about to undergo orthodonty herself, even though her teeth looked perfect to me.

In a moment of candour I told her husband Jason that I thought they were all mad. He nodded sagely. 'Southern California is full of kooks – and those who treat them.'

He then introduced me to his acupuncturist, also a guest at the party. I've tried acupuncture myself for severe headaches and found the marginal improvement insufficient compensation for the sums I spent on the treatment. I asked Jason what he was being treated for.

'Attitude.'

The acupuncturist nodded contentedly: 'Sure, we can turn you up, turn you down, mellow you out.'

Jason's most serious ailment was his addiction to working out, which he did with the zeal of the true believer for up to two hours every lunchtime at his gym. He insisted that he felt much better, physically and mentally, since he started going to the gym regularly. I told him that I just didn't have the time, let alone the inclination, for such a regime. He was scornful, saying you could make time for anything if you're sufficiently committed to it. Jason's eyes took on an evangelical gleam when we talked about physical fitness, so I didn't dwell on the matter. If I were living permanently in Los Angeles, I too would be compelled to take some form of exercise. In my native land we have stairs, and the London streets are so clogged with cars that a bicycle is the only sensible means of transportation. None of this applies to Los Angeles, where the only unavoidable exercise consists of pushing a supermarket trolley once a week.

The fitness cult does claim victims, which is gratifying. I was visiting friends in Pasadena when their teenage son returned home after running in the Marathon. We saw his car grind up the driveway and come to a halt. The car door opened. Nothing moved. The boy was so stiff he couldn't move, and had to be helped out of the car. Around his neck swung the medal given to those who had completed the twenty-six mile course. His bare legs were tandoori-red, as was his face. He gradually extracted himself from the car, and, leaning heavily on the shoulders of his parents, he stumbled very slowly into the house.

Pandemonium. An orchestra tuning up, sound engineers arguing with each other, musicians grabbing a doughnut and coffee during a short break. I weaved through the crowd until I found Ralph Grierson, who had invited me to attend this recording session of David Newman's score for the animated film *Rover Dangerfield*. Ralph, a well-known pianist and composer, was one of a pool of about 500 musicians who participate regularly in these sessions. I felt quite at home on this occasion, since the composer was the son of Martha Newman, who had given me tea in Rustic Canyon, and Martha's daughter, whom I had also met, was playing the viola. David Newman waved the baton. It was not unusual for a composer to conduct his own film score. Music is the last component in the sequence of movie production, so the score is usually written in a hurry, which means that hired conductors rarely have enough time to learn the score properly. Composers who also conduct can make adjustments as they go along, as was happening right now.

Newman was leaning over the music stand and talking to the tuba player: 'Is this impossible to play?' – to which the answer was: 'Almost.'

'Okay. I'll fix it.' And he did.

While this was going on Ralph took the opportunity to practise a section he hadn't seen before. David had been working with such haste that some of the parts for that morning's session only arrived at the studio while the session was under way. Other musicians were perfecting the art of practising while balancing a copy of *Newsweek* on the knees.

Once he'd finished recording a passage, David ran into the booth to listen to the playback. Ralph and I followed. While it was being played, we could watch a rudimentary version of the animation sequence it was to accompany. Both composer and engineers have been aided by a new computer programme, Auricle, which allows them to time the music in relation to the animation with complete accuracy. After the recording is completed, it is blended into the sound track at the dubbing stage, along with dialogue and special effects. Composers usually hate this stage in the process, because their music is in competition with other elements of the movie.

David and the sound engineer okayed the recording, so we dashed back into the studio and resumed our places. David began tinkering again: 'I think the F sharp should be on the xyl, not the glock. Let's change that.'

Looking at the score as Ralph charged through it in response to David's fast-moving baton, I noticed that there were few dynamics notations.

'That's because the piano is recorded separately. If a passage sounds too soft or is drowned out by the brass, the engineer can just pull a switch and get the balance right.'

I asked Ralph how many takes were usually required.

'That depends on the budget as much as the competence of the musicians. You can cut costs in this business by using synthesizers rather than dozens of musicians, but then it takes much longer to record the score. So you don't gain anything. Speed is of the essence. There aren't many second chances in this business. Composers have to be able to shift gears and styles, and so do the musicians.'

It usually takes three to seven days to record a film score, but the next Spielberg film will require eighty three-hour sessions thanks to the vast budget he has at his disposal. A television show will take only three to six hours.

'Do you ever find that you're looking at music that's simply unplayable?'

'Occasionally, but you try not to let the composer know about it. You do a little editing on the spot. The cliché about this kind of work is that it's 80 per cent boredom, 20 per cent sheer terror. You never know when you're going to turn the page of the music and be hit by the terror.'

I drove back across the hills to Hollywood, and decided to lunch at the Formosa on Santa Monica near La Brea. I wasn't going there for gastronomic reasons but because the restaurant was a local legend now threatened with closure. It's just a box on a corner lot, but by Hollywood standards it's been there a long time. Lana Turner, Marilyn Monroe, Elvis Presley, and Lucille Ball were among the regular patrons. The walls and ceilings are painted either black or deep pepper-red, and plastered with hundreds of photographs of the stars of five decades. A shrine is devoted to a cult of Presley statuettes. My lunch wasn't particularly good, but the elderly waitresses were friendly old hens who seemed to have been here all their lives.

The Formosa was popular because it was next door to the former Goldwyn studios. Warner Brothers, the present owners of the studios, want to redevelop the site on which the single-storey Formosa stands by replacing it with a multi-storey car park. A vigorous campaign has been mounted to save the Formosa, and its defenders have won several stays of execution. I signed the petition. The last thing Los Angeles needs is another parking lot.

After lunch I drove west and called in at the Performing Arts Bookshop. The owner, Elliot Katt, is reputed to be a mine of information about the movies, so I sought his advice.

'Do you have any books that deal with the politics of the movie business?'

'All the books we have are on the shelves.'

This was an answer to a question I had not asked. Mr Katt, an anxious-looking man with a creased face and agitated hands, was riffling through papers on his desk. I tried again.

'I realise that, but I'm wondering if you could point me in the direction of books that will give me that kind of background.'

'That's way too wide for me. The books are on the shelves. Alphabetical.'

'But I can't check through every title! You must know the kind of thing I'm looking for. The structure of the business, how it works, books like Goldman's on the screen trade.'

'That's on writing. You say business and politics, and now you say writing. I can't help you.'

'I thought you were in the business of selling books. You must know how you arrange your stock better than I do!'

'I know what I can do.'

Thanks a lot, Elliot. I left empty-handed and drove on to the Academy, where I had a date with my landlady. As a member of both the Directors Guild and the Academy, she had access to free screenings. Nobody associated with the movie industry ever pays to go to a movie, and both guilds run an almost continuous programme of screenings, ostensibly so that members can be sure of seeing films that have been nominated for awards for which they will later have to cast their votes. The afternoon screenings at the Academy, where we went to scare ourselves stupid at *The Silence of the Lambs*, were especially popular with the geriatric set. As we made our way into the large and very comfortable auditorium, the trick was to greet the people you liked and discreetly avoid those you couldn't stand. After half a century working in the movie industry, both feuds and friendships went back a long way. The naming of the Academy is a deft attempt to confer respectability on the entertainment business, with Oscars substituting for honorary degrees. The elderly crowd stumbling towards the car park after the screening looked less like the scholars and footnoters of the industry than worshippers heading home for lunch after an excessively long synagogue service.

Watching cannibalism on screen certainly pricked my appetite for succulent meats. I had been invited to dinner by Carol and Case; she an academic social psychologist, he a semi-retired actor, both renowned deipnosophists. I had first met them at a dinner party given by my landlady which was briefly interrupted by the ringing of the door bell. A total stranger was on the step, asking her whether she could let him have any socks. She replied that she didn't have any men's socks, but pressed $5 into his palm and sent him on his way. None of the guests could recall a similar case of sock-begging.

I never tired of pressing those little buttons by the side of a gate and then waiting for that metal grille to swish geriatrically to one side, allowing me to drive in to the front yard. The conferral of the privilege of admission does wonders for self-esteem. Their house in the Hollywood hills was far from grand, but the garden was ravishing, packed with clivea and flowering peach that was shifting from a pink to a deeper red shade.

Other guests soon parked their cars alongside mine: my landlady purred in, then a screenwriter called Michael, and, making a belated appearance after a full day on the job, a British film writer who had come to Los Angeles to work on a television documentary on horror movies. The lamentable state of the movie industry was a major topic of discussion, and Michael, fresh from Tinseltown, told us that everybody at the studios was waiting for the axe to fall. In an industry in which the annals of poor judgment were thick and bulging, new records were being broken by Warner Brothers, which had initially backed *Home Alone*. Like most films, it had been costing more to make than the studio had wanted to spend, and when John Hughes requested an additional million dollars with which to complete the film, the executives said no. The cost-conscious executives thought they would win praise from their masters for their financial responsibility. Unfortunately for them, Hughes took the project to Fox, which completed it on his terms. The film went on to gross $600 million. The error of judgment was so colossal, according to Michael, that heads were bound to roll. 'Nobody gets a second chance after something like that,' he stated, in defiance of the evidence.

Michael's worries were justified. With stars just as Kevin Costner and Michael Douglas pulling in fees of $12 to $15 million per movie, it was becoming difficult to make commerical films such as *Hook* or *Bonfire of the Vanities* for under $50 million. The gambles had often paid off in the 1980s. In the 1990s the recession hit the movie industry. Box office receipts plummeted. No amount of hype could save *Bonfire* and many other films from financial disaster. All-powerful agents were sitting on packages that were no longer affordable. Salaries were being trimmed by a zero or two. There was no choice but to cut back, and the servants of the industry, the screenwriters and art directors, considered themselves lucky to be in work at all.

Michael's fears were no more than ominous rolls of thunder on the horizon. The pain wouldn't hit till later in 1991. For now we could relax with a round of Case's margaritas. On an earlier visit he had instructed me in the mysteries of the margarita. The classic version is a blend of tequila, lime juice, and Cointreau served on ice in a glass with a salted rim. Equally popular in Los Angeles, though rather looked down upon by some connoisseurs, was the blended margarita, in which all the ingredients are whisked up together, thus crushing the ice and creating a froth. This version gave the margarita the reassuring texture of a milk shake.

As he refilled our glasses, he produced a few of his vast store of stories about his fellow actors, of which the best, not surprisingly, was about Peter Ustinov. To celebrate the completed shooting of *Viva Max*, a party was held at the Alamo where much of the movie had been shot. An old man, bent double, was introduced to Ustinov as a descendant of the mercenary, Colonel Rose, who had escaped from the Alamo. 'Of course,' said Ustinov, 'the Yellow Rose of Texas.'

Case went off to supervise the barbecue, and returned with our main course, exquisitely cooked *mi-cuit* tuna with ginger. The conversation turned to a favourite topic, not only in Los Angeles but across the nation: litigation. Entire radio talk shows are sometimes devoted to the topic, with flabbergasted listeners phoning in with their horror stories. Case recounted one of his own.

Some friends had come to dinner. The party sat around the dining-room table, which is set on a dais eleven inches above the rest of the living room. One of the guests had leaned back on her chair, wobbled, toppled, and broken her hip. Case and Carol had been very upset by the accident and did all they could to make amends. The injured guest, although married to a very rich man, sued her hosts for $300,000. This was regarded as an attempt to clean up at the expense of the insurance company rather than as a wish to pauperise her friends.

But having sued, she and her husband then found a pretext for cutting Carol and Case socially, which upset my hosts more than the litigation, especially since their other friends felt required to take sides in the affair. Hours before the case came before the judge, the litigants were informed that their case was feeble, since they had often been visitors to the house and the existence of the platform was hardly a great surprise to them. So they settled out of court; and the insurance company paid up. For my hosts the only gratifying aspect of the affair was that the insurance company refused to pay the litigants' legal costs, which amounted to more than the settlement.

In another case, which had been doing the rounds of collectors, a teenage boy had been working out on a machine. He bent forward, the weights slipped, and the boy's organ of generation was flattened. The lad sued the manufacturers on the grounds that they should have known that a teenage boy might be dumb enough to misuse the apparatus. He lost.

'But that's not the end of it,' said Carol. 'The boy then sued the school for neglecting to watch over him to ensure he didn't behave stupidly. And this time he won. And there's been another case in which some kids broke into a house and trashed it. One of the burglars fell into the pool and drowned. His family sued the owners of the house and won. What all this means is that there is no longer any notion of an accident in this country. Or that something could be your own stupid fault. Moreover, people know that if they sue, on however flimsy a pretext, they stand a good chance of winning something. Juries are notoriously unwilling to give the benefit of the doubt to insurance companies, so most of these cases are settled out of court.'

Over coffee, Michael asked me if I had been to the Disney studios. I had, and we discussed the Team Disney building with the seven dwarves holding up the pediment. Somebody casually asked whether we could name the seven dwarves. We thought we could, but we couldn't. Between us, we eventually came up with six: Sneezy, Happy, Dopey, Grumpy, Sleepy and Doc. Then we were stuck.

'Beppy?' I offered.

'Of course not.'

'I know!' cried Case, eyes gleaming. 'Horny.'

'Nah,' said the film editor.

Case pulled the standard reference books from his shelves and we flipped through the pages. We got nowhere.

Michael tried the Seven Deadly Sins: 'Lusty, Slothy . . .'

I offered a new diversion, by asking my fellow guests to name all the Valkyries in ascending order of age. Not a popular move.

The conversation lost its sparkle. We talked of many things, but only one matter was on our minds. Suddenly Carol raised her hand. We froze.

'Bashful!'

'Yes, yes, yes!'

32

MELLOW AND OUT

In January 1979, I had flown into Los Angeles nonstop from the snows of Boston. Stepping from the plane, I'd felt the warmth of California pushing up from the expanse of tarmac. My winter coat was as appropriate as a bearskin in the tropics. I rented a car, flung the coat into the back seat, rolled down all the windows, found a trash music station on the radio, and drove straight to the secluded Bel Air Hotel. I sprawled. On my private patio I read the newspaper in the warm sunshine every morning, then strolled over to the pool for a swim and a light breakfast before beginning work. The hotel was uncrowded, and the only other amphibious guest at that hour was the talk-show host Dick Cavett, who was a novelty in the 1970s for displaying both wit and intelligence on network television. My work consisted of receiving the authors I had signed up for the publishing house at which I was an editor. Among the flowering shrubs, we sat and discussed projects, negotiated contracts, swapped jokes. It was, let me assure you, bliss.

Now, eleven years later, I decided to spend my final nights in Los Angeles back at the Bel Air Hotel. Despite the addition of a new wing, little had changed. The lobby was still easily mistaken for the manager's living room – no keys visible, just a simple counter at the far end, beyond the couches and armchairs and fireplace – and the swan lake and gardens, awash with splashy bougainvillea, tree ferns, sycamores, and palms, were as beautiful as ever. I strolled past small pink bungalows and plant-filled patios to my large, tranquil room.

The twelve acres occupied by the hotel were originally used as stables by the original developer of Bel Air, Alphonzo Bell. An oilman, Bell had had his eye on a hilly undeveloped 2000-acre tract to the west of Beverly Hills. He bought it, and by the 1920s its development was well under way. Beverly Hills is a district of splendid houses, but Bel Air, as it was intended to be, is filled with estates, some of them small, most of them large. From the top of Bel Air, along Stradella, you realise how high up you are, as you gaze down onto the deep green Stone Canyon reservoir with its backdrop of the snow-capped Sierras. Like Beverly Hills, Bel Air is an anthology of eclectic building styles, including Tudor Hysterical, Mausoleum, and International Party Deck. The greenery is everywhere, with ground cover, mostly deep purple gazania and ice plant, spilling over the walls and trees shading the twisting roads. Along Bellagio are some spectacularly beautiful Japanese gardens, but they are rarely open to the public.

The hotel was built in the late 1940s in unpretentious Spanish Colonial Revival style. Even after the new wing was added it remains small, with only about a hundred rooms and suites. The charm of the hotel is its respect for your privacy. The service is efficient but unobtrusive. Everything about the Bel Air urges relaxation. I wandered down to the pool in the late morning. Mr Cavett was no longer there and the decking was relatively crowded, yet it remained discreet, gentle, peaceful. Waiters in white jackets circulated, jotting down orders for poolside lunches, and friendly young women in shorts checked regularly to inquire whether I would care for some mineral water or fruit.

It was tempting to spend the whole day inert beneath my parasol, but I was going to a theatre matinée. Along La Cienega in West Hollywood a famous shop called Trashy Lingerie specialises in expensive lacy garments designed to be torn from the body with hot trembling hands. Next door is the 200-seater Serendipity Theatre, which usually puts children on the stage, but on this occasion was launching a play by Lisa-Maria Radano called *Brooklyn Laundry*. The show was the hottest ticket in town, but my extensive network of contacts among the rich and famous had procured me a ticket at cost. It was not the play that was drawing the crowds, but the cast. Glenn Close, portraying a middle-aged, abrasive, crop-haired Italian-American landlady who loses her virginity to an eccentric concert technician, was on the boards, joined by the delectable Laura Dern, who plays her niece, and by the television star Woody Harrelson, who plays the technician. To complete the line-up, the director was James L. Brooks.

One always wonders whether these stars of celluloid can really act. With the aid of camera angles, closeups, retakes, dubbing, and the snip of the editor's scissors, poor acting skills can be masked, if not concealed. On stage, it's just you and the audience. Dern and Harrelson were certainly adequate, if narrow in range, but Glenn Close, despite some overacting, did turn in a genuinely dramatic and enthralling performance. Since there's no money to be made in the theatre, it seemed remarkable that three stars who can earn colossal sums should give up a few weeks to add their lustre to a simple little play. Our applause, I expect, signalled our gratitude as well as our enjoyment.

Steve Milukan, the theatre editor of *LA Weekly*, had suggested to me that the modest theatrical revival in Los Angeles had complex roots: 'There's been a major change in the last decade. There's so much wealth in this city that a kind of cultural inferiority complex prompts many people to attend cultural events they wouldn't have dreamt of going to fifteen years ago. LA is essentially a movie town, but now people are beginning to feel they really ought to be attending other events too. So there's plenty of theatre in the city, but most of it is dross. There are very few working ensembles, so theatres have mostly become halls you can rent. It's tempting for actors with no other work to hire a theatre and put on a one-person confessional show, most of which are terribly self-indulgent. And let's face it, since theatre and movie actors are interchangeable, most actors regard theatre as something to do in between phoning your agent.'

A few weeks earlier I had sat blissfully through Peter Hall's superb production of *Così fan tutte* at the Los Angeles Opera. (When you phone up the Music Center to book tickets with a credit card, you are informed, with infuriating euphemism, that 'a convenience charge will be added to each order'.) The audience was surprisingly unpretentious. At the Met in New York, the salons are usually packed with opera queens and overdressed young matrons for whom operagoing is a social event with a tuneful background. Here in Los Angeles hardly anybody had dressed up – perhaps a blazer with some trousers that didn't quite match, or an ill-fitting silk dress – and only two men were wearing black ties. I had expected a deluge of the *nouveaux riches* but it did appear that the majority of those in the audience were there because they wanted to see the opera. They did shuffle about a bit, but there was a tremendous burst of applause after 'Come scoglio', rewarding Mozart for at last providing a full-blown aria in an opera dominated by exquisite ensembles.

After applauding Miss Close, I returned to the hotel to nibble on the excellent smoked salmon that the management had kindly placed in my room during my absence. I returned to the pool to read in the cooling air of early evening. I found myself seated near a rather heavy woman in a black dress. She was about thirty-five. She didn't look like a resident and when she started to talk to me, it was clear she wasn't. She lived in Studio City, she told me, and had recently split up with her boyfriend, so she had decided to come and spend a couple of hours at the Bel Air. In short, she was gate-crashing. That was fine with me, except that she wouldn't stop talking.

'I don't want to bother you, as I can see you're trying to read a book . . .' And then she'd bother me. Reading a book is a bizarre activity to most Angelenos, and she found it hard to conceive that I could prefer reading to answering her nosy questions. After an hour, she drove me away, and I returned to my patio, where I could turn a page without accounting for it to strangers.

Later in the evening I attended a party at the Mondrian Hotel to which I had been invited by the proprietor, Severin Ashkenazy. Many celebrities would be there, he assured me. Some suave gentlemen halted me at the door of the Café Mondrian. I had no written invitation, I had to tell them, but had been invited by Mr Ashkenazy. They let me through. Walking up to the hotel entrance, I had seen the limousines depositing their charges in the driveway. If the audience at the opera had been dressed as if they had been going to a friend's house for dinner, these guests were dressed as if they were expecting to receive an Academy Award. There were men with swept-back hair gathered into a ponytail, à la Steven Seagal, and an abundance of beautiful women, many in dresses that allowed the air to whistle through the cleavage. Some dresses were so tight you could have pressed flowers between fabric and flesh. Here, at last, I could see the end product: the purpose of those thousands of dollars spent on facials, manicures, pedicures, designer frocks, punitive diets,

Nautilus machines, nail jobs, orthodonty. They looked fabulous. Brittle, but fabulous.

Standing along the wall, halfway down the room, was Sylvester Stallone. Ashkenazy had not been joking. As celebrities go, Sly Stallone was a catch. I was impressed. Since I don't recall ever seeing one of his films, I couldn't think of a productive topic of conversation, so we breathed the same air but never spoke to each other.

I was thirsty. Wandering up to the bar at the far end, I asked for an orange juice. The barman poured.

'That'll be three dollars, sir.'

I made the exchange, and wondered what kind of party this was. Jewels dripping off the women, frocks costing thousands, Porsches and BMWs snoozing in the hotel garage – and I was being charged for an orange juice?

It was time for some investigative journalism. Two very glamorous women were seated on a banquette, and I approached them fearlessly. As is the custom in California, they greeted me affably.

'Excuse me,' I gabbled, 'but I've been invited to this party, and now I'm here, I realise I'm not sure why I'm here, and I'm hoping you can enlighten me.'

They couldn't.

'It's a private party.'

'Yes, I know that, but have you any idea why I have been invited by someone who is not the host to someone else's party?'

They had no idea.

'Well, who *is* the host? Who's giving this party?'

They had no idea.

'Are you from Los Angeles?' I said, sociably.

I'd asked that question because one of the women, dark and Italianate, had the trace of a foreign accent.

'We live here at the moment.'

'What do you do?'

'We're in the industry. Many of the people here are.'

'What aspect of the industry?'

The taller woman wore a stiff-fronted dress that precluded the need for a bra except when she leaned forward. She was leaning forward, reaching for her drink. She exchanged glances with her friend.

'Whatever pays best,' she offered.

Uh-oh.

'I'm an entertainer,' she added, hurriedly.

The penny dropped, but it was too dark for my blushes to show. Now I realised why this enticing pair looked like high-class hookers. They *were* high-class hookers. What's more, most of the women here looked like high-class hookers, though I am sure they were nothing of the sort. Fairly sure.

'Sly's here,' said the taller woman.

'Yes, I've seen him.'

'He is?' The Italianate woman became more alert.

'Yes, he's around the corner. He'll probably come over and join us.'

But why? The mystery deepened. They clearly didn't know anybody at the party either, yet were affecting acquaintance with Stallone, who, it soon became clear, was staying put.

I ran out of conversation, made my excuses, and left them. I approached a young man in glasses who, like me, was not dressed as a Steven Seagal lookalike.

'You look to me as though you're wondering what you're doing here. As am I.'

He admitted it, commended my perception. He turned out to be a screenwriter from New York on his way to a conference in New Zealand. An improbable story. This was not, he said, like parties he went to in New York. Even though he was more accustomed to showbiz gatherings than I was, he too was puzzled to find himself at a private party composed largely of strangers who have been invited by an unknown host who requires his guests to pay for their refreshments.

I decided to leave, succumbing to my social ineptitude. Here I was, surrounded by slebs and beautiful women, some of whom were for hire, and orange juice at only three dollars a shot, and I was bored. This was the most glamorous party I had ever been to, give or take the occasional bar mitzvah in North London, but I was too Hollywood-ignorant to understand what was going on.

I walked out of the lobby and turned the corner onto the street where I had parked the car. A man with a walkie-talkie stood nearby.

'Leaving already?' he asked me, though with no obvious reproach in his voice. I said I was.

'Mr Ashkenazy down yet?'

'I didn't see him.'

'Well, good night, sir.'

'Good night.'

As I walked to my car I wondered how he knew I had come from the party, and how he knew I had been invited by Ashkenazy. This was a seriously strange place. I had been in Los Angeles for three months and still had no idea how the place worked. To Hollywood folk, there was probably no mystery at all, but to me the whole evening had been steeped in unreality.

At least I was beginning to understand why someone like Julia Phillips could bare all and still seem utterly alien. She would have known what was going on at that party. She could have filled me in. But of course she wouldn't have spoken to me, so I would have been none the wiser. Having read her book, I could understand why Hollywood was so remote. Here was a highly intelligent woman who, after producing or co-producing or failing to produce a few movies in the early 1970s, had done nothing but consume unbelievable quantities of drugs until her recent decision to live for a few more years. Yet she still considered herself a player of sorts in the industry. However, as Richard Schickel observed in an article in GQ, 'The real penalty for failure here is being banished from the field, not allowed to play in the game anymore. There are, in fact, almost no retired movie people; all the old men I know sit in their big houses "developing" scripts they will never be involved with . . .' Which seemed to apply to this middle-aged woman too.

So after fifteen years or so of doing not very much, she had composed a self-indulgent and vicious vindication of her life. Her malice compelled her to publicise her ex-husband's new wife's obesity and to include a separate index entry for Jackie Collins's ankles. Most of those she had excoriated had made more of their lives than the burnt-out Phillips, but that didn't give her pause. 'At the risk of sounding pretentious,' she told a newspaper interviewer, 'my story is the iconographic, capitalist story of the second half of the twentieth century.'

Yet even today, wiser after the event, she still seems to believe that the most important things in life are designer labels and securing a good table at Mortons. Among my own Hollywood acquaintances there were a fair number of egotistical and wilful personalities. But there was also talent and generosity and wit. Nobody I had ever met in Los Angeles was remotely like Julia Phillips, for which relief much thanks. But clearly there is something iconic about her, and her values were not my values, and her world was not my world. And thoughtful Mr Ashkenazy's party – if indeed it was he, although absent, who was the host – was peopled with rich, glamorous, successful, not yet successful, corrupt, hard-working people with whom I had no connection.

I returned to the hotel and walked through the quiet paths and patios towards my room. Soft spotlights illuminated the gardens and made the petals glow, and everywhere I walked there was the soothing sound of water splashing in the courtyard fountains. The evening air was heady with the perfume of the flowers, and the only sounds were the crackle of cicadas and the purr of a passing car up Stone Canyon Road. This, for me, was the best of Los Angeles: the glorious climate, the transformation of desert into a vast garden, the harmony of flowers and stone. Riches and fame and power were not to be scorned, but they could never be enough.

There was of course no one image that captured the city. Manhattan could be encapsulated by the most amateurish snapshot of the Wall Street skyline, Boston by the warm-toned houses on Beacon Hill, Washington by any of its temples of government. The only icon of Los Angeles was the Hollywood sign, and even that had literally to spell out its message. Where other American cities soared, Los Angeles hunkered down and lolled on its back. The downtown skyscrapers and the high-rises of Century City were for most residents an irrelevance. I don't suppose any of my friends in Los Angeles had ever set foot in a downtown building. Los Angeles, by permitting its fragmentation into countless municipalities, had denied itself an urban identity, flawed and weakened its government and fostered a go-it-alone attitude which conferred individuality on communities while sacrificing the unity of the city as a whole. The contrast with a city such as Washington could hardly be greater, as the museum curator Howard Fox pointed out: 'In Washington, everyone from a senator down to a street cleaner has a sense of place, of fitting into a scheme of things. The whole city is organized around cores of power that reflect the nature of the city. But Los Angeles lacks a core. Instead it has many cores, none of which functions as a core.'

Yet it didn't matter. Los Angeles ignored all the assumptions we routinely make about cities, and got away with it. It was a city that until very recently denied itself a centre; even the downtown revival is solely commercial and cultural, for attempts to induce ordinary citizens to inhabit apartments downtown had led to frustration and flight. Not since the early years of this century had Los Angeles had a viable centre; so it simply bypassed the process of suburban dispersal that afflicted most other American cities. It had become the ideal grazer's city: begin the day with coffee in West Hollywood, shop in Beverly Hills, stroll along the beach at Venice, drive to Chinatown or Monterey Park for a *dim sum* lunch, take a long walk in Griffith Park, dine in Santa Monica. The swift recognition of the car as the primary means of transportation made distance of little account; even shopping on Wilshire was, from the 1930s, made as convenient as possible by the provision of large parking lots.

The price to be paid for this was the lack of communality. It could be seen not only in the political fragmentation of the city, its lack of urban identity, its willingness to be different things to different people, but in an impoverishment of human dealings. There was none of the rubbing of shoulders of New York or Tokyo; there was no obligation to confront your fellow human beings on a regular basis; there was no bustle, no street cries, no drama of the unexpected witnessing, no treasuring of an urban heritage one grew to know viscerally because it was part of one's daily experience. Instead, Los Angeles offered you ease and sunshine, and an often terrible blandness, in which all the activities of the day, going to work, shopping, dining, made identical demands on your energy and commitment. The immigrant communities retained a human vigour, the physical close-ness of crowded streets or markets. But the verdant suburbs, from the rolling estates of Palos Verdes and Bel Air to the uniformity of a Valley dormitory or an Inglewood street, shunned this human proximity. Communities went out of their way to isolate themselves from encounter, erecting gates and hiring guards to patrol the manicured streets with the same intensity one would expect in the most fearsome ghetto.

It was also a lazy city. Angelenos work, and many work very hard, but they do so to be better able to enjoy the pool, the jacuzzi, the beach, the hot springs, jaunts to the Sierras, weekend skiing trips, skating in Venice, going to the movies, tanning on the sundeck. Not everybody finds this way of life appealing, and it certainly isn't challenging. As the protagonist Alvy in Woody Allen's *Annie Hall* remarks on a visit to Los Angeles, 'When I get mellow, I ripen and rot.' Intellectual energy, outside the movie industry, is not prized, and the kind of intellectual exertion required by the movie business is narrow, especially since it mostly consists of inspired or catastrophic guesswork. Los Angeles encourages passivity. Clutchless cars propel themselves towards your destination with minimal effort on your part. There are few good bookshops because the screen, whether in the cinema or your own home, has won the day over the printed page. Buying newspapers is a minority pursuit.

Culture is less an offshoot of civic pride than an expression of personal vanity. Museums are permanent homes for personal collections. Small theatre companies are forms of self-promotion, usually directed at attracting the attention of the great gods of the movie business. Some museums, such as MOCA, and the opera company and symphony orchestra sometimes seem to exist more because it is felt that a city of this size can't be without such cultural institutions, which is not to deny their high standards. Ballet bores the Angelenos. In 1979 I had attended the premiere of a Glen Tetley ballet starring Baryshnikov and Makarova and found the Chandler auditorium half empty. In 1991 the Joffrey Ballet, a company that is highly prestigious but has never been able to pull in the crowds, was given notice by the Music Center where it had performed regularly for years.

Los Angeles writers, from James M. Cain and Raymond Chandler to Joseph Wambaugh and James Ellroy, have looked at the seamier side of the city, which serves as a backdrop to the age-old battle between order and chaos, honesty and corruption. More recent writers, John Gregory Dunne and, especially, Joan Didion, have taken a more thoughtful, almost poetic view of the city. Yet Los Angeles has spawned few writers; the overwhelming majority of writers in the city are there to be used, abused, and highly paid by the movie industry.

There had been a resurgence of the arts, especially among minority groups, in the 1970s, but it proved short-lived. The hundreds of once famous murals in East Los Angeles and elsewhere, which had begun as a genuine expression of folk art, were decaying, and radical contemporary arts organisations such as LACE were floundering. In large part this could be attributed to the Californian distrust of public funding. Just as schools were being starved of funds, so public arts organisations and projects were trying to struggle on with diminishing revenues. Rap music, this flow of rhythmic verbiage from the heart of the ghetto, was proving a more lasting cultural manifestation, and certainly some well-known rap artists, including the scabrous NWA (Niggers With Attitude), have emerged from the city. Rap music, in its authentic mode, reflects the tension, materialism, and murderousness of the ghetto in its justifiably aggrieved relation to the more prosperous society around it. But the adoption by rap musicians of a gangster persona makes their recordings morally ambiguous.

More decorous conversation persists in the salons of Hollywood and Brentwood, where some old leftwingers argue on, though nobody is listening. The prevailing political discourse deals with crime and the penalties for crime, with taxes, with immigrants. The left, with its penchant for social engineering and centralisation, flounders in a city that has no structure. Its energies are often directed beyond the water, to struggles in Latin America or Southern Africa, where money, which flows generously from these rich households of conscience, has more impact than fine words. As for the right, the passivity of the city matches them perfectly. They make no demands, and thus feel there is no need to contribute. Taxes should be kept low because only the poor benefit from the social services that are financed by taxes. It is a cramped vision of the world, a cheerful denial of communality and common cause, but in the well-run, prosperous, perpetually sunny Westside or Valley suburbs it seems a viable line to take.

Thus, on paper, Los Angeles was everything I despise. And yet I couldn't help enjoying the city, relishing the diversity that so many of its residents seemed to perceive as a threat. There was something horrific about its great Californian embrace, stretching for dozens of miles in all directions, and something heroic too in the transformation of semi-arid desert into a fertile garden. To live in a new tract on the edge of the sprawl would be for me a form of unendurable somnolence. But there were pockets, substantial pockets, of Los Angeles where urban camaraderie persists. I found it in the shops and cafés within walking distance of my house in West Hollywood, in Santa Monica and the other beach towns, along the more salubrious stretches of Sunset Boulevard, in the raffish street life of Silver Lake, in the coteries of Melrose, among the canals of Naples and the arches of Malaga Cove. I had found a community well entrenched in Rustic Canyon, and who knows how many other similar clusters are tucked into the valleys and canyons of the Santa Monica Mountains.

While the rich played tennis and polo and exulted in topography and climate, the new immigrants were straining mightily to establish themselves here. Their contribution to Los Angeles was, in a way, accidental. They do not come here to set themselves up as tourist attractions; their districts are not knowingly picturesque; their restaurants offer the food they enjoy, not what they think we will enjoy. Nonetheless the vitality of the city, its joyful fluidity, its open embrace, spring from the huge number of immigrants bringing different ideas, different cultures, different values – not superior, but different – to a city that has an almost boundless capacity for absorption. Almost – because the problems are beginning to overpower that capacity. A sizeable proportion of immigrants soon become dependent on the welfare system, which the state can no longer afford. In January 1992 Governor Pete Wilson, faced with a colossal budget deficit of $14.3 billion, was proposing savage cuts in welfare payments. The boom years were over with a vengeance.

While the rich insulate themselves on the higher ground, the poor spread out through the city as their means permit; while the rich lock themselves into luxuriously equipped cars for the endless freeway journeys, the poor throng the streets and markets. The division between rich and poor is codified in Los Angeles, aided by zoning restrictions and NIMBY fence-building. The enclosure of the rich entails the enclosure of the poor, with their greater lack of mobility and opportunity. To be poor in Los Angeles, especially if you are black, is to be confined, it must sometimes seem, to an open prison. While the white middle class feels almost obliged to employ private education, the black and Latino working class or underclass has no option but to use an increasingly inadequate public-school system. The two facts are related. Paradise and nightmare are two sides of the same coin, two facets of urban life that coexist starkly in this ultra-materialist city.

For Los Angeles is not unique in its more shameful aspects. All cities have their unsavoury features. Los Angeles also offers remedy, possibility. Its style is not for everybody. Berthold Brecht left seething, Woody Allen won't set foot in the city. Los Angeles is a blank cheque; there are no preconditions here. The very absence of control in the city makes it possible to negotiate the human and bureaucratic traffic as you see fit; you can change your style, your goals, your address, you can reinvent yourself and no one will think any the worse of you for doing it. The burden of the past is feather-light, and, as Carey McWilliams once observed, there are hardly any statues in Los Angeles. The city's vapidity, its sprawl, its rampant overdevelopment, its industrial decline, its smog, its indifference, its ignorance, its huddled enclaves of extreme wealth, all these blemishes fade behind the foreground of the city's expectations. The primary expectation, advancing as slowly and ponderously and inexorably as a steamroller, is that Los Angeles can hardly avoid becoming the great multi-ethnic city of the future, in which whites and Latinos in particular will have to live side by side, and in which countless other races and ethnic groups will pepper the stew and keep it fresh and spicy.

The entire city was an invention, created by far-sighted rogues who established its infrastructure – its rail links (later replaced by freeways), its harbours, its water supplies – and then invited the rest of America to join the party. Now, with that infrastructure in decay, with pollution sometimes reaching unbearable levels, with the prospect of droughts and earthquakes and all-destroying brush fires marring the earthly paradise, with a public sector in precipitous decline, Los Angeles needs to reinvent itself once more. The tremendous powers wielded by the city fathers in the early years of this century, those men who controlled the city's newspapers, real estate, railways, and other industries, are diffuse and defused; the political structures may not be sufficient to enact the necessary changes, whether they be new transportation systems, new emissions controls, or new housing policies, especially since there is no consensus as to what needs to be done to ensure that Los Angeles remains habitable. In Los Angeles you can find dullness if you seek dullness, but the future will be anything but dull. Chaotic maybe, unexpected possibly, but Los Angeles, the most fluid and open of great cities, will remain that way despite all the attempts to hide within it.

AFTERWORD

One spring morning in 1992 Los Angeles was its usual indolent, inchoate self. The next day it was a seething fireball, with some parts of the city ablaze with flames and hatred, and the remainder of the city crouched in terror lest that vengeful chaos should pass beyond the boundaries of the ghetto and invade the somnolence of the pool-speckled suburbs.

The violence, once the jury in the white suburb of Simi Valley had declared innocent the LAPD officers who had given Rodney King his salutory beating, was predictable. The verdict was not foreseeable, at least not by me, but once it was delivered, it was only a question of time before stupefaction gave place to rage. Hearing the news of the verdict, I could only sit back with a sigh and wait for the inevitable consequences. The wait was brief.

The rioting coincided with the hardcover publication of this book. I had not been sure, when writing the book, that it was wise to devote as much space as I did to the King beating and its political consequences, but in retrospect it was the right decision. The mantle of the expert fell temporarily on my shoulders. Invited to comment, I did my best to place the violence in some kind of context, while knowing all the time that pontifications from afar are no substitute for first-hand reportage.

The theorists of the city, of whom I was one, were in confusion. Those of us who had pondered Los Angeles as a city quite unlike any other were arranged in two broad camps: the optimists, among whom I tentatively counted myself, and the doomsayers. For the former Los Angeles was a brave experiment full of promise; it was easy to see why immigrants were drawn in their tens of thousands each year, and there were times when it was tempting to join their number. Sprawling Los Angeles was still an open city. Survival was hard anywhere, but in Los Angeles the enterprising, it seemed, had a fair chance of prospering.

For the pessimists, Los Angeles was a disaster waiting to happen. Far from being the grand multi-cultural experiment that the boosters and optimists never tired of hailing, Los Angeles was a Babel of mutually uncomprehending cultures. Blacks were not simply pitted against whites, they were equally at odds with Latinos and Koreans. The tangle of conflicts was awesomely complex. With no such thing as a city-wide identity, all loyalties were to locality or to tribal group. The Portuguese dockworker in San Pedro had little or nothing in common with the Bolivian carpenter in East Los Angeles or the screenwriter from New York now installed in a Burbank apartment. The dislocation was economic as well as tribal. The impoverished municipal services provided little more than a support network of last resort. No Angeleno who could afford private education would patronise the public schools. The inevitable consequence of this cultural mayhem, argued the pessimists, was a kind of civil warfare, as the privileged minority tried to keep a growing underclass at an ever greater distance. 'Gated communities' mushroomed, and threats of armed response against would-be intruders were more common than lampposts.

After the flames had died down the doomsayers seemed to have had the better of the argument. Those who felt betrayed by a system of justice that in effect aimed another blow at Rodney King while exonerating his tormentors rose up in rage. They took out their anger on the easiest targets, such as the businesses established within the ghetto by those who lived outside it. The sheer fury of the response was shocking even to those who had no difficulty understanding the response itself. When innocent passersby were dragged from vehicles and beaten as savagely as King himself fifteen months earlier, such violence surpassed an expression of wild indignation.

From afar, and I dare say from the centre of the storm too, it was impossible to distinguish between those whose rage had been sparked by the blatant injustice and those who realised that profits were to be made from mayhem. Torching a Korean store and looting its contents, grinning all the while, suggested criminality more than desperation and outrage. Liberal clichés were certainly inadequate to the complexity of the blazing ghetto. Images of righteous rage became muddied with vignettes of opportunistic theft and score-settling. Those condemned to a cycle of poverty in a city so conspicuously rich saw a chance to improve the balance, ever so slightly, in their own favour. The compassionate looked at the burning city and wrung their hands. Aghast conservatives made light of the causes of the rioting and pointed instead to the abundant excesses of violence and scoffed at those who sought deeper causes that could be transformed, by philosophical sleight of hand, into excuses.

The violence pushed at the boundaries of the ghetto and made lightning strikes into richer pastures. The arsonists came as far north as Hollywood Boulevard and within five blocks of the house in West Hollywood where I had lived. Telephoning my friends throughout the city, their response was measured by their distance from the flames. Some saw smoke, some saw nothing at all. Almost all stayed indoors and watched the immolation on television, just as I was doing thousands of miles away. Their sources of information were almost identical to mine, and London scarcely seemed further from South Central than Pasadena or Santa Monica. The riot, like all disasters, had become a media event, in which the disturbances could scarcely keep up with the army of those eager to comment on them. Who could say whether the screeching arrival of yet another television crew was prompting that extra brick through the window, that extra dash through broken plate glass to extract a handy kitchen appliance? Was the truce between the Bloods and Crips a genuine attempt to patch up their differences, or merely a consolidation of resources? Would it usher in an era of peace and harmony in the ghetto, or would it become an alliance aimed at maximising control over the sale and distribution of drugs? If the truce created a vacuum, smaller gangs were not slow to fill it.

The sprawl of the city had exaggerated the real damage. The destruction was bad enough, but not quite as bad as hurried observers had estimated. About nine hundred buildings had been torched, and an alarming proportion, about one-quarter, were Korean-owned. If what had occurred had been a riot of impulsive lawlessness, it had been remarkably focused. The arsonists and looters were right to suspect they could act with impunity. Few of the fifty-eight deaths, mostly murders, were likely to be pondered in court; anonymity would protect most of those who had torched the buildings. The principles of justice were driven into a cul-de-sac rich with ironies. Those who had looted and killed and burned were mostly black and Latino, and the men who had beaten up that white lorry driver while the television cameras whirred as definitively as George Holliday's camcorder were indeed brought to justice – which only high-lighted the very different treatment meted out to the LAPD officers in the King case. The correct application of justice simply drew attention to the preceding, and continuing, injustices. Although some of the most vicious rioters were arrested and charged, most were not. Justice for the victims of the riot was bound to be scant and piecemeal. There would be little justice for grieving relatives or for Koreans who had laboured round the clock for years and were now reduced to penury or for the many thousands who woke up to find their workplaces reduced to charred debris.

Fortunately the city was no longer dependent on the partial whims of Daryl Gates for the administration of its police services. Chief Gates, despite a ghastly threat to postpone his retirement, finally made his departure with typical ill grace by refusing to attend the swearing-in of his successor Willie Williams and by chucking more abuse at the politicians who had dared to criticise his performance both during and before the riots. Mayor Bradley got his own back by letting it be known that Chief Gates had brought Los Angeles to the 'brink of disaster', a judgment from which it is hard to dissent. The special commission headed by Warren Christopher, later to be President Clinton's Secretary of State, as well as a chunky Amnesty International report on LAPD abuses over the years merely put into writing what the over-whelming majority of the black and Latino community had known for decades. The acquitted officers who beat Rodney King were yet to appear in federal court on civil rights charges and were filling in the time between trials by appearing on television chat shows. Their former chief, Daryl Gates, would soon resur-face as a radio talk show host, thus rewarding bigotry with celebrity.

The political response had to be painstakingly balanced between recognition of the injustice that had prompted it and a reluctance to reward those who had resorted to violence. There was some indignation that districts where the violence had been at its most extreme would receive injections of funding and concern denied to equally deprived areas, such as most of the East Los Angeles *barrio*, that had remained calm. The federal government set up a task force and tossed some money into the city, although poverty was not the sole symptom that required treatment. Instead there was a potent cocktail of destitution, racism, drugs, inequality – you name it, every urban malaise of modern America contributed a rancid flavour to the brew. The problem was, of course, structural in the deepest and most intractable sense. Peter Ueberroth, who had made a financial and public-relations triumph out of the 1984 Olympics in Los Angeles, was brought in to wave his wand again by organising an agency called 'Rebuild LA'. Whether as a result of Ueberroth's lobbying or their own initiative, a few large corporations did boldly announce that they would be investing in districts such as South Central. Some retail chains with ghetto stores bravely showed more moral courage than commercial foresight by reopening their outlets within weeks. The mom-and-pop stores were slower to return, and most of them never would. By midsummer of 1992 a package worth about $200 million was announced for the city, which might be enough to regenerate this block of businesses or that housing development but was in overall terms a drop in the ocean. By the end of the year good intentions still seemed to outweigh positive achievements.

Nor was it realistic to look for much assistance from the public sector. The deficit in the state budget grew to $11 billion in 1992, and the usual legislative budget crisis led to payments to state employees being made in the form of IOUs. In such circumstances largesse towards riot-shattered central Los Angeles was not likely to be forthcoming. Throughout southern California the stagnation of the late 1980s continued, indeed worsened as defence contractors moved their operations to other states, so there seemed scant chance of internal regeneration through economic expansion. Even the police force would be heavily cut in numbers, which would give little comfort to the peaceable ghetto dwellers who huddled indoors and watched on television as their neighbours torched their way through the city. At the same time that police protection was likely to be reduced where it was most needed, there was no evidence that the gangs of

South Central and other run-down districts were any less ferociously armed than they had been before the riots began.

Bad news, in short. Yet it is by no means certain that the pessimism will be justified. It is a brutal truth that the city as a whole flourished for decades despite the gruesome conditions in which its underclass was living. Whether the current attempts to plaster over the cracks – an injection of federal funds, a reformed police department under a more sympathetic chief, an intensive dose of media attention, a truce between the largest gangs – will be sufficient to keep the ghetto calm is anybody's guess.

Cities, especially cities as diverse as Los Angeles, do not curl up and die. The tourists who understandably shunned the city will slowly return. The immense new convention centre close to downtown is said to be heavily booked for a year or more ahead. In the days immediately after the riot, men and women of good will from all over the city had driven to churches in South Central to deliver food and clothing and labour, and many months later prosperous Angelenos were still collecting money and goods for distribution to deprived fellow citizens. These were heartening signs, but perhaps not sufficient to stem the forces of violence and disruption that still threatened the city.

Los Angeles is not dependent on the fate of South Central for its survival. The riots had appalling consequences for its victims, human and economic, but the passage of time would heal many of the wounds inflicted during those few days. If the Crips and the Bloods returned to a state of warfare, if the Koreans transferred their businesses elsewhere, if impoverished families continued to have their lives blighted by drugs and violence, if the plans for regenerating parts of the inner city failed to live up to expectations – if, in other words, it was business as usual in the ghetto and the lessons politicians are so fond of deriving from disaster are not learned – well, frankly, it won't make a huge difference to the lives of those millions of Angelenos who had never set foot in the ghetto or the *barrio* before the riots and would not do so afterwards either. One could advance a cynical but plausible argument that the riots of 1992, instead of opening up the city in a love-fest of regeneration, would stiffen the barriers between the deprived districts and the prosperous ones. The rich or even the merely well off in Los Angeles may be slightly less well off after the recession, but the poor remain equally poor. Any narrowing of the gap has not improved the lives of those at the bottom of the heap.

In June 1993, the voters of Los Angeles, choosing a successor to Mayor Bradley, elected not the liberal Chinese-American local politician Michael Woo, but a very rich white lawyer, Richard Riordan, who had the backing of Ronald Reagan. Not for the first time, the blacks and minorities who comprise the majority of the city's population failed to cast a vote, leaving the decision to the increasingly anxious white middle classes, who picked the candidate most likely to protect their own interests. How successful Mayor Riordan will be in moderating – 'solving' is to ask too much – the city's dire fiscal and social problems, it is too early to say.

No one can be sure that the worst is over. Late in 1992 there were racial and gang-related incidents that brought hundreds of police to the scene for fear that the trouble might ignite a fresh round of rioting. New outbreaks did not occur, but the anxiety that they might have done had become constant. The eventual conviction in April 1993 of two of the officers involved in the King beating saved the city from a repetition of the previous year's riots. But in that same week reports that another black citizen – by chance, a friend of King's – had died after a similar chase and a lesser beating showed that the happy outcome of the new trial did not necessarily herald a new age of sweetness and light between police and policed.

'The violence is like earthquakes,' observed a friend. 'We know a major earthquake will occur but we don't know when. Similarly, despite the political changes of the past year the situation in the ghettoes hasn't really changed, and one of these days we can expect the worst. But just as people in California have learnt to live with the likelihood of earthquakes, so we're prepared to live with the prospect of riots.'

Urban warfare looks set to become part of the geopolitical landscape of southern California. Los Angeles, half blind, half fearful, will no doubt accommodate itself to that uncomfortable state of affairs.

Stephen Brook,
August 1993

INDEX

Actors Centers International, 236–7
aerospace industry, 24, 322–3
Alexander, John, 172–4
Allen, Woody, 352, 354
architects:
    Eames, Charles, 96
    Ellwood, Craig, 118, 211
    Gehry, Frank, 92–3, 94, 95,
        139, 170, 171, 196, 199–200,
        276
    Goodhue, Bertram, 215
    Greene & Greene, 63, 206–10
    Heineman, Arthur and Alfred,
        209
    Jerde Partnership, 53
    Johnson, Reginald, 205
    Kappe, Raymond, 15, 96
    Koenig, Pierre, 99
    Lautner, John, 97, 99
    Meier, Richard, 314
    Morphosis, 93, 94
    Moss, Eric Owen, 94, 95
    Neff, Wallace, 118, 209
    Neutra, Richard, 96, 298, 299
    Pelli, Cesar, 97
    Schindler, Rudolph, 95–7, 98,
        298
    Soriano, Raphael, 96
    Wright, Frank Lloyd, 16, 125,
        209
    Wright, Jr., Lloyd, 16, 199

architecture, 35–6, 37, 48–50,
    92–100, 107, 108, 118, 125,
    206–11
    Art Deco, 34, 35, 37, 39
    Churrigueresque, 39, 108, 215
    Craftsman, 95, 206, 209
    International Modern, 95,
        96–7, 98
    LA door, 49
    Queen Anne, 34–6
    Spanish Colonial Revival, 4,
        42, 95, 98, 124, 125, 145,
        198, 209, 215, 344
    Streamline Moderne, 50, 125,
        146
Arnold, Skip, 174–7, 299
Arundale, Scott, 156–9, 263
Ashkenazy, Severin, 152–5, 346–9,
    350

Bakewell, Danny, 254
Ballet, Joffrey, 352
Banham, Reyner, 96, 207
Bartelo, Robert de, 283–5
Beckman, Arnold O., 215
Berkeley, 135, 136, 228, 292
Beverly Hills, 4, 9, 13, 15, 27–8,
    34, 44–55, 60, 91, 92, 93, 94, 98,
    102, 113, 116, 118–9, 122, 129,
    141, 142, 143, 155, 183, 205, 229,
    233, 267, 299, 303, 315, 344, 351

Bedford Drive, 53
Beverly Drive, 50, 232
Canon Drive, 116
Civic Center, 50
Crescent Drive, 45, 46, 51, 118
Elden Way, 45–6
Loma Vista, 48, 319
Mapleton Drive, 119
Rodeo Drive, 50–1, 53, 298
Trousdale Estates, 48
See also schools, shops
Beverly Hills Gun Club, 283–5
Beverly Hot Springs, 250–2
bird-doggers, 3–4
Blessing of the Animals, 43
Boy Scouts of America, 266
Bradley, Tom, Mayor, 67–8, 71, 73,
  170, 226, 360, 363
Brecht, Berthold, 12, 354
Brooks, James L., 345
Brooks, Mel, 129, 158
Brown, Charles, 178
buildings:
    Avila Adobe, 42
    Barnsdall Park, 125
    Bell House, 99–100
    Beverly Center, 4, 97–8, 100
    Blacker House (Pasadena), 210
    Bradbury, 39
    Bullock's Wilshire, 35
    California Club, 37
    Carling House, 99
    Chemosphere House, 99
    Citadel Corporate Park, 57
    City Hall, 40
    Cordelia Culbertson House
      (Pasadena), 210
    Duncan-Irwin House
      (Pasadena), 209
    Eames House, 99
    Eastern, 39
    Ennis, 125
    Fitzgerald House, 107
    Gamble House (Pasadena),
      206, 207–8
    Garfield, 37
    Gehry House, 93
    Greenacre's estate, 48
    Greystone, 48, 119

Macy's, 79
Meade House, 95
Millard House (Pasadena), 209
Million-Dollar theatre, 39
Norton House, 196
Oviatt, 37
Pacific Design Center, 97, 120
Pelanconi House, 42
Pickfair estate, 48
Pico House, 43
Public Library, 37
Robinson House, 45–6
Schindler House, 96, 97
Security Pacific Bank, 34
Seventh Street Market Place,
  38
Spadena House, 49–50
Spelling House, 119
Team Disney, 160, 170, 342
Union Station, 41, 42
Wiltern, 35
Burum, Linda, 141
Bush, George, 181, 183, 268

California Cowgirls, 103–5
California Institute of Technology
  (Caltech), 213–23, 323
canyons:
    Beachwood, 5
    Benedict, 120
    Coldwater, 319
    Laurel, 99
    Malibu, 315
    Rustic, 11–19, 89, 99, 336, 354
    Stone, 120, 344, 350
    Topanga, 315–6
Cavett, Dick, 343, 344
Cedars-Sinai Hospital, 4, 94
cemeteries:
    Calvary, 145–6
    Forest Lawn, 145, 286–91
Cerullo, Morris and Theresa, 82–5
Christopher, Warren, 360
churches, 107, 259, 265–70, 304
    Coptic, 295
    Crystal Cathedral, 265–70, 300
    Russian Orthodox Cathedral,
      299
    St Vibiana Cathedral, 39–40

St Vincent de Paul, 108
Wayfarer's Chapel, 199
West Los Angeles Church of
    God in Christ, 105
    See also Cerullo, Schuller,
    Swaggert
Close, Glenn, 344–5, 346
clubs:
    At My Place, 91
    Club Fuck, 299–301
    Da Butt, 263–4
    Fleetwood's, 177–8
    Mulholland Tennis, 319, 320
    Sit and Spin, 63–5
    Tropicana, 270–2
Cohn, Sy, 3
conservation, 107–8
counties:
    Los Angeles, 8, 24–5, 53, 66,
        147, 150, 256
    Orange, 8, 24, 57–60, 75,
        265–6, 267, 268, 318, 328
    Riverside, 8, 24
    San Bernardino, 24
cuisine, 10
    California, 134–5, 136–7, 154
    Indian, 142
    Mexican, 141
    Thai, 297–8

Daniels, Michael, 141
Davis, Mike, 38, 261
Deni, Fred, 139–40
Dépardieu, Gérard, 190
Dern, Laura, 345
Didion, Joan, 311–2, 352
Dimitri, Richard, 129–33, 146,
    151–2, 156, 168, 189, 228–33,
    291–4, 295, 299
Disney, Walt, 328
Disneyland, 8, 57, 58, 325–8
dog names, 205
Doheny, Edward, 27, 48
Dreyfuss, Richard, 320
drought, 74–5, 76, 78, 248. *See also*
    water supply
drugs, 257, 261, 272, 281, 349

Eaton, Hubert, Dr., 287–91, 293
economy, 322–3, 354, 355
education, 149, 183–8, 259, 282,
    352–3
    private, 184–5, 354
    See also schools
Ellis, Bret Easton, 333–4
ethnic groups:
    Argentinian, 147, 149
    Armenian, 150, 226
    Asian, 82, 149, 150, 186, 225,
        226, 256, 264
    black, 105–7, 185, 186, 247,
        253–4, 256, 260, 262, 278,
        279, 281, 303, 307
    British, 88
    Bulgarian, 226
    Cambodian, 150, 255
    Canadian, 150
    Chinese, 41, 150
    Cuban, 146
    Filipino, 150
    Guatemalan, 146, 150
    Gypsy, 150
    Indian, 150
    Iranian, 143, 150, 188
    Israeli, 143
    Japanese, 41, 150, 254
    Jews, 10–11, 142–3, 145, 149,
        185
    Korean, 150, 193, 250–4
    Latino, 35, 36–7, 38, 39, 40,
        42–3, 82, 145, 146–50, 185,
        186, 187, 197, 225, 226, 247,
        254, 255, 256, 260, 262,
        274–5, 276, 278, 282, 303,
        304–6, 307, 355
    Mexican, 146, 149, 150
    Nicaraguan, 147
    Peruvian, 147
    Polish, 226
    Portuguese, 199
    Russian, 142–3, 150, 226
    Salvadoran, 147, 150
    Samoan, 150, 199
    Thai, 297–8
    Vietnamese, 150
    Yugoslav, 199

Fernandez, Perry, 195–6
Feynman, Richard, 213, 214
fitness, 335–6
    BodyTone, 53–5
    Sports Club LA, 111–6
Fox, Howard, 80, 151, 174, 350
freeways, 4, 5–6, 21, 25, 328
    Foothill, 69
    Harbor, 35, 36, 85, 105, 260,
        273, 303
    Hollywood, 36, 41, 298
    Long Beach, 273, 309
    Pasadena, 5, 60, 105, 204
    San Diego, 2–3, 105, 112, 263
    Santa Ana, 57
    Santa Monica, 5, 9, 105, 263
    Ventura, 6, 206, 310
Freund, Dan, 95

Gabor, Zsa Zsa, 1, 46, 47
Galanter, Ruth, 71
galleries, 89, 173–4
    Huntington Library, 62–3, 211
    See also museums
gangs, 186, 255–63, 280, 303–8,
    361–2
    colours, 256
    Community Youth Gang
        Services Project, 256–63, 303
    patrols, 259–63, 303–7
Garbo, Greta, 47
gardens:
    Huntington, 63
    Japanese (Bel Air), 344
    Murphy Sculpture, 110
Gates, Daryl, 70–3, 194, 228, 360
Getty, John Paul, 311, 312
Getty Center for the History of
    Art, 285, 313, 314
Glatzer, Richard, 63–5
Gold, Jonathan, 134, 135, 140
Goldman, William, 127, 339
Gordon, Larry, 156–7
Gowland, Peter and Alice, 14–15
Grierson, Ralph, 336–8
Guber, Peter, 127, 128
Gulf War, 20, 72, 73, 105, 179–82,
    196, 227, 268, 270

Hammer, Dr Armand, 48, 67, 80,
    290
Hancock, Ralph, 34, 185
Harrelson, Woody, 345
Hayes-Bautista, David, 147–9
Heit, Jay, 160–2, 163, 189
Hindu temple (Malibu), 315
Hobden, Ernie, 26–8, 48
Hollywood, 8, 50, 73, 85, 98,
    124–6, 142, 147, 255, 266, 270–2,
    298, 338, 353
    Boulevard, 124, 255, 270, 272
    hills, 7, 9, 97, 99, 298, 315, 340
    Mann's Chinese Theater, 126
Hollywood sign, 5, 170, 350
homelessness, 87–8, 310
Hood, Leroy, 221–3
Hope, Bob, 180–1
hotels:
    Bel Air, 343–4, 346, 350
    Beverly Hills, 47–8
    Mondrian, 152, 153, 346
    Westin Bonaventure, 36
    Westwood Holiday Inn, 103
human genome project, 221–3
Hunt, Myron, 61, 107
Huntington, Collis P., 61
Huntington, Henry, 61, 76, 81, 151
Huntington Library, 60–3
Hymans, Herbert, Dr., 314

immigrants, 150–1
    illegal, 149
Isham, Warren, 25–6
Isozaki, Arata, 170

Japanese investment, 38, 127, 129,
    130
Jet Propulsion Laboratory, 214,
    323–5

Katt, Elliot, 338–9
Kercheval, Ken, 51
Kimbell, Hal, 278, 281–2
King, Rodney, 69–73, 226, 228,
    357, 358–60
Kinney, Abbot, 192–3, 195, 196
Kissinger, Henry, 329, 331
Knott's Berry Farm, 57–9

Korean Federation, 252–4
Kramer, Matt, 87–8, 89, 91, 177–8

Lanzilli, Babetta, 286
Leonard, Sheldon, 319–21
Lipking, Larry, 206, 214–5
Lippincott, J. B., 76, 77
litigation, 341–2
Lombardo, Dana, 162–3
Los Angeles, history of, 23–5
Los Angeles Police Department
  (LAPD), 70–3, 118, 305–6
Los Angeles towns and districts:
  Alhambra, 7, 41
  Altadena, 69, 214, 323
  Angeleno Heights, 36, 95, 203
  Baldwin Hills, 186, 276
  Bel Air, 1, 9, 16, 98, 108, 117,
    118, 120, 122, 123, 185, 210,
    224, 255, 284, 344, 351
  Boyle Heights, 7, 141, 145,
    146, 148
  Brentwood, 12, 92, 142, 185,
    285, 353
  Buena Park, 57–60
  Bunker Hill, 36, 93, 170
  Burbank, 7, 9, 124, 129, 323
  Cabrillo Beach, 199–200
  Century City, 4, 9, 126, 350
  Cheviot Hills, 123
  Chinatown, 41, 253, 351
  Compton, 66, 255
  Crenshaw, 7, 105, 186, 276
  Culver City, 124, 126, 128, 142
  downtown, 5, 8, 36–41, 61,
    203, 298, 350
  East Hollywood, 125
  East Los Angeles, 146, 147,
    149, 247, 255, 352
  El Segundo, 192, 234, 235
  Fairfax, 11, 118, 142–3
  Glendale, 7, 66, 146, 287
  Hermosa Beach, 191, 192,
    197–8
  Huntington Park, 118, 146,
    186, 273, 274–5
  Inglewood, 276, 301–2, 351
  Koreatown, 35, 118, 145, 250
  Little Tokyo, 41, 171, 253

Long Beach, 61, 86, 146, 200
Malibu, 1, 87, 107, 191, 192,
  310, 314–5
Manhattan Beach, 192, 197–8
Marina del Rey, 91, 192
Monterey Park, 41, 351
Naples, 200–1, 354
Newton, 260, 304
North Hollywood, 297
Pacific Palisades, 11–19, 67, 86,
  89, 94, 102, 155, 218
Palos Verdes, 4, 86, 198–9, 351
Placentia, 328
Point Vicente, 199
Pueblo Historic District, 41,
  42–3
Rolling Hills, 7, 198–9
San Fernando, 21–4, 245–7
San Marino, 60–3, 151, 204,
  209, 210
San Pedro, 24, 86, 199
Sherman Oaks, 236, 238
Silver Lake, 7, 8, 99, 227,
  298–301, 353
Simi Valley, 357
South Pasadena, 204, 205,
  211–2
Studio City, 124, 236, 346
Tarzana, 236, 270
West Hollywood, 63, 65, 96,
  97–8, 124, 142, 177, 197,
  203, 263, 286, 317, 344, 351,
  353
Westwood, 34, 67, 92, 103,
  108, 124, 142, 182, 197, 243,
  247–8
Whitley Heights, 124–5
Yorba Linda, 328
See also Beverly Hills, canyons,
  Hollywood, Pasadena, Santa
  Monica, South Central,
  Venice, Watts

Mann, Thomas, 12, 46, 155, 285–6
'mansionisation', 120, 243
Manson, Charles, 18
Marder, Bruce, 139
margaritas, 340
markets, 38

Farmers, 10–11
Grand Central, 39, 52
McCarty, Michael, 135–9
McKee, Mickey, 11–18
McWilliams, Carey, 236, 318, 355
Mead, Carver, 215–20, 223
Meyerson, Harold, 68–9, 71–2, 185, 227
Miller, Tim, Dr., 333–5. *See also* plastic surgery
Milukan, Steven, 150, 151, 345
Mitchell, John D., 329, 331
Moscowitz, Jack, 186–8, 256, 278
Moross, Lev, 89
Mount Wilson, 5–6
movie industry, 126–33, 156–63, 189, 319–21, 336–8, 347, 349, 352
American Film Market, 89–91
Creative Artists Agency (CAA), 121
development, 158–9, 131–2, 157, 160, 168
executives, 128–9, 131–2, 157, 160, 168
market research, 162–3
producers, 156–60, 162, 243–7
screenings, 339
screenwriters, 129–33, 168, 243–4, 348
See also studios
mud-wrestling, 272
Mulholland, William, 77
museums, 174, 352
California Aerospace, 93
Fowler, 109
Getty, 154, 174, 310–13, 314
Hammer, 80–2, 154, 174, 211
LACMA (County Art Museum), 34, 75, 79–80, 151, 173
Museum of Contemporary Art (MOCA), 170, 352
Neon, 172–3, 174
Norton Simon, 154, 211
Temporary Contemporary, 93, 170–2
See also Huntington Library
music business, 238–42
rap, 353

nails, 30–1, 164, 252
NASA, 214, 323
Naumann, Bruce, 171
Nettles, John, 259–61, 278, 303–8
networking, 114
New Age, 86, 315–9
New York, 64, 80, 130, 135, 151–2, 154, 156, 171, 173–4, 175, 176, 239, 293, 350, 351
Newman, Alfred, 17
Newman, David, 336–8
Newman, Randy, 14, 17
newspapers and periodicals:
L.A. Resources, 317
LA Style, 226–7, 228
LA Weekly, 53, 68, 71, 72, 150, 151, 179, 183, 185, 226, 227–8, 301, 345
Los Angeles, 119, 226, 228
Los Angeles Times, 44, 68, 76, 105, 115, 118, 120, 134, 179, 182, 205, 226, 227
Nixon, Richard, 328–32
Watergate, 330, 331–2
Nixon Library, 328–32
Noguchi, Isamu, 41
Nolan, Mike, 7–9

Occidental Petroleum, 80, 81
Olmsted & Olmsted, 48, 198
open houses, 120–3
Opera, Los Angeles, 345–6
Oscars, 17, 113, 126, 163, 188–90, 319, 339
Owens Valley, 76–7, 78

parks:
Echo, 36
Exposition, 93
Griffith, 125, 205, 244–5, 351
MacArthur, 35, 50, 148
Rustic Canyon, 15
Will Rogers, 17, 101–3
Pasadena, 9, 47, 61, 95, 151, 191, 203–11, 224, 336
Arroyo Seco, 9, 205–7, 211
Art Center College of Design, 211
Green's Hotel, 204

Hillcrest Place, 210
Oak Knoll, 209–10
Prospect Boulevard, 209
St Andrew's Church, 204
South Oakland, 210
South Madison, 209, 210
See also buildings
Patti, Sandi, 268, 269
performance art, 174–7
Peters, Jon, 127, 128
Phillips, Julia, 161, 349–50
plastic surgery, 231–2, 333–5
politics, 68
    board of supervisors, 66, 68
    city council, 66, 71–2, 73
    police commission, 73
    See also Bradley, Gates, King,
        Riordan
pools, swimming, 248–50
postminimalism, 171
Prado, Toribio, 201
Proposition, 13, 17, 185
Puck, Wolfgang, 98, 135, 139
Pynchon, Thomas, 105

Rachlis, Kit, 227–8
radio stations, 56–7, 182–3
    Barbara De Angelis, 60, 168–9
    KFI, 7, 60
    KLOS, 111–2
    Limbaugh, Rush, 182–3,
        309–10
    Mark and Brian, 111–2, 144–5,
        202–3, 234–5, 273–4
    public radio, 44
Ragland, Martha Newman, 16–19,
    336
railways, 23–4
    Pacific Electric, 61
    Southern Pacific, 23, 61, 68
real estate, 116–123
'Rebuild LA', 361
restaurants and bars, 134–42
    Al Amir, 140
    Al Gelato, 293, 295
    California Pizza Kitchen, 98
    Carriage Trade, 100
    ChaChaCha, 201
    Chasen's, 4, 135, 137

Citrus, 140, 177
East India Grill Too, 142
El Cholo, 141
El Colmao, 291–3
Eureka, 135
Formosa, 338
Fox Inn, 91–2
Inn of the Seventh Ray, 315–6
Jimmy's, 52–3
Jody Maroni's Italian Sausage
    Kingdom, 196
Kate Mantilini, 94, 139
Larry Parker's Beverly Hills
    Diner, 229
Michael's, 135–8
Mortons, 349
Muse, 134
Paddington's, 28–32
Patina, 139, 177
Plum Tree, 166
Polo Lounge, 47
Rally's drive-in, 301–2
Rose Café, 193
Serenata, La, 141
Spago, 134, 135
See also cuisine
Riordan, Richard, 363
ritual slaughter, 143
Roberts, Oral, 265, 296
Rodia, Simon, 276–8
Rogers, Will, 102
Ruscha, Edward, 170–1

Sachs, Herman, 35
Salkin, Karen, 28–33, 163–7, 176,
    189, 198, 265, 301
San Fernando Mission, 21–3, 25
San Fernando Valley, 3, 6, 21–3,
    25, 76–7, 98, 164, 185, 234–8,
    266, 297, 320, 351, 353
San Gabriel Mission, 21
San Gabriel Mountains, 6, 9, 208
Santa Monica, 12, 24, 34, 66,
    86–93, 139, 143, 165, 185, 191,
    197, 314, 351, 353
    Adelaide Drive, 89
    Broadway, 89
    King's Head pub, 88
    Ocean Avenue, 86–7
    pier, 87

Third Street Promenade, 88, 89
Santa Monica Bay, 75–6, 87
Santa Monica Mountains, 3, 21, 87,
    197, 235, 314, 354
Schickel, Richard, 127, 349
Schoenberg, Arnold, 12, 46, 155,
    285–6
    Schoenberg Institute, 285–6
Schoenberg, Nuria, 286
schools:
    Bellagio, 224–6, 278
    Beverly Hills High, 52
    Markham Junior High, 262,
        278–82
    University High, 185–8, 256,
        278
Schuller, Robert, 82, 265–70
Scott, Willard, 19–20
Screen Actors Guild, 237, 238
Seagal, Steven, 73, 346, 348
security, 99–100, 125
Serra Retreat, 315
shops:
    Amok, 299
    Bharat Bazaar, 142
    Bristol Farms, 211–2
    Galleria (Sherman Oaks), 236
    Jim Watson's Metaphysical
        ESP Center, 317–8
    Juergensen's, 51
    Malaga Cove, 198, 199, 354
    Mrs Gooch's, 51–2
    Performing Arts bookshop,
        338–9
    Price Club, 166, 301–3
    Sharper Image, The, 51
    Sorcerer's Shop, 186
    Trashy Lingerie, 344
SigAlerts, 4
Sigmon, Loyd, 4
Sikhs, 295–7
Silverman, Mike, 116–8
Simon, Norton, 174
Skid Row, 37, 40
slow-growth movement, 66–7
smog, 6, 7, 355
Sony, 127, 129, 130, 133
South Central, 95, 108, 255, 256–7,
    263, 307

riots (1992), 357–63
Spelling, Aaron and Candy, 119
Splichal, Joachim, 139
sports:
    cricket, 101
    croquet, 13
    polo, 101–2, 354
    roller skating, 198
Stallone, Sylvester, 347, 348
Stansfield, Patrick, 238–42
Stein, Leonard, 285–6
Stone, Edward, 323–5
Stratton, Gilda, 237–8
Stravinsky, Igor, 46, 155
street murals, 86, 145, 194, 195,
    352
streets:
    Alvarado Terrace, 35–6, 98,
        108
    Bellagio, 344
    Beverly Boulevard, 97, 98, 100,
        142, 145, 250
    Broadway, 37, 38–9
    Central, 275, 305
    Chester Place, 98, 108
    Fairfax, 10–11, 25, 79, 142
    Figueroa, 38, 263
    Florence, 275
    Hoover, 35
    Ince, 94
    Kings Road, 96
    La Brea, 79, 142, 263, 338
    La Cienega, 29, 33, 75, 97, 344
    Main, 39–40
    Melrose, 25, 33, 89, 97, 173,
        201, 354
    Mulholland Drive, 77, 99, 319
    Olvera, 42, 43
    Olympic, 36–7, 38
    Pacific Boulevard, 274–5
    Pacific Coast Highway, 139,
        310, 314
    Pershing Square, 50
    Pico, 86, 263, 292, 295
    Robertson, 4, 293
    San Vincente, 88, 97
    Santa Monica Boulevard, 3, 4,
        44–5, 48, 112, 177, 286, 338
    Second, 39, 40–1

Silver Lake Boulevard, 299
Somma Way, 120
South Bonny Brae, 35–6
South Flower, 36
Sunset Boulevard, 8, 11, 17, 18, 48, 64, 73, 75, 79, 124, 272, 299, 353
Ventura Boulevard, 236
Vermont, 35, 82, 201
West Adams Boulevard, 107, 203, 285
West Slauson, 256, 259, 260–1, 303
Western, 270
Whittier Boulevard, 146
Wilshire, 4, 34, 35, 88, 103, 166, 263, 293, 296, 351
See also Beverly Hills, canyons, freeways, Hollywood, Santa Monica
studios, 126–9, 156–63, 236–8
Columbia, 127, 128, 129–33, 156
Disney, 128, 131, 132, 160–1, 342
Twentieth Century-Fox, 126, 156–7, 159, 340
Universal, 25, 127
Warner Brothers, 126–7, 128, 129, 237–8, 338, 340
Sutherland, John, 215
Swaggart, Jimmy, 82, 85, 166

tar pits, La Brea, 79
Tarloff, Erik, 228–33, 291–4, 319
Tarloff, Frank, 319–21
television, 131, 132
producers, 119, 319
public access, 30, 163–5, 176

termites, 236
theatre, 344–5
Thompson, Juliette, 224
Tuchman, Maurice, 173
Turley, Ed, 257–9, 260, 303, 307

Ueberroth, Peter, 361
University of California at Los Angeles (UCLA), 12, 92, 108–10, 147, 153, 184, 187, 201, 247
Chicano Studies Research Center, 147–9
Medical Center, 333
University of Southern California (USC), 108, 285–6
Ustinov, Peter, 340–1

Valley girls, 236
Venice, 26, 89, 175, 191, 192–7, 200, 201, 252, 298, 351
Vietnam War, 179, 181, 330, 331

Wat Thai, 297–8
water supply, 76–8, 126, 355. See also drought
Waters, Alice, 135
Watts, 5, 67, 175, 227, 255, 262–3, 275–82
riots (1965), 67, 105, 275, 306
Towers, 276–8
Webb, William, 243–7
Wild West Arts Club, 102–5
Williams, Fred, 281
Williams, Willie, 360
Wilson, Dennis, 18
Wilson, Pete, Governor, 109, 354
Winter, Robert, 49
Woo, Michael, 71, 72, 363
Writers Guild, 132, 243
Wyman, George, 39